Kalymnos
Rock Climbing Guidebook

Aris Theodoropoulos
2016 Revised Edition

Kalymnos Rock Climbing Guidebook by Aris Theodoropoulos

All uncredited photos and photo-topos by the author
Book design / Copywriting: Katie Roussou
Photo editing / Additional design: Nikos Krikelis
Proofreading: Sergios Soursos
Maps: TERRAIN

Copyright © Aris Theodoropoulos 2016

All rights reserved. This book or any portion thereof may not be reproduced or used in any manner whatsoever without the express written permission of the author except for the use of brief quotations in a book review. Some photo-topos in this book contain deliberate inaccuracies, included to protect the information contained herein against unauthorized copying/reproduction. These are minor and do not compromise the safety of the persons climbing.

Printed in Greece by Lyhnia S.A.
Second Printing, June 2016
ISBN: 978-618-5160-03-6
Published by: TERRAIN Maps
Karneadou 4, Athens 10675, Greece | terrainmaps.gr
Ordering information: Please contact the author | climb@climbkalymnos.com | climbkalymnos.com

On the cover: Liugong "Abond" Bang on "Tufa King Pumped" 7b+ (page 287).
Cover photo: Nikolaos Smalios

DISCLAIMER

Climbing poses some inherent risks, particularly if practiced without the necessary training and equipment. The information in this book is not meant to replace proper climbing training. The author and publisher accept no liability for any accidents or injuries occurring at any crag included in this book. Be sure that your equipment is well-maintained, and do not take risks beyond your level of experience, aptitude, training and comfort level. The safest approach for new climbers is to attend a full climbing course then join an experienced group of climbers. The route descriptions, grades, topos and other route information contained herein are only a guide. Readers are advised to take full responsibility for their safety and know their limits.
At the time of writing, access and climbing at all crags included in this edition was unrestricted. This is not guaranteed for the future and may change without notice.

Kalymnos goes digital

+App Guide inside

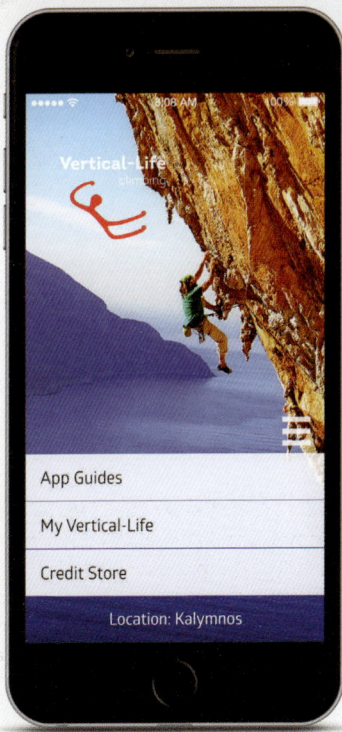

Vertical-Life brings **the best climbing guides** on your smartphone. Search, find, compare and mark your **spots** and the most beautiful **routes**. Compact and complete: Topos, route lists and all infos.

Kalymnos | Greece | Zillertal | Südtirol | Dolomites | Arco | San Vito | Amalfi | Lumignano | Erto | Oltrefinale… & many more to come

Vertical-Life climbing

Find the vertical-life app on

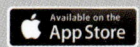

TABLE OF CONTENTS

- CRAG PLANNER ... 06
- INTRODUCTION ... 13
- KALYMNOS ... 14
- OUTDOORS ... 18
- CLIMBING ... 20

- **STYX** ... 26
  - Olive ... 27
  - Styx ... 28
  - François Guillot ... 31
  - Emporios Portal ... 32
- **KASTRI** ... 34
  - Kreissaal ... 35
  - Kastri ... 36
  - Sophie ... 38
- **PALACE** ... 40
  - Thalassa ... 42
  - Baby House ... 43
  - Palace ... 45
- **SIKATI CAVE** ... 46
- **THE BEACH** ... 52
- **SECRET GARDEN** ... 58
- **PALIONISOS** ... 66
  - Red Wall ... 67
  - Paradise Beach ... 69
  - Palionisos Bay ... 70
- **PROPHITIS ANDREAS** ... 72
  - Elephant Slide ... 74
  - Prophitis Andreas ... 76
- **SKALIA** ... 80
  - Skalia Pillar ... 82
  - Hote California ... 84
  - Skalia Balcony ... 85
  - Skalia Cave ... 86
- **GHOST KITCHEN** ... 88
- **CAVE** ... 96
- **GALATIANI** ... 102
  - Reservoir Dogs ... 106
  - Black Forest ... 107

- **NOUFARO** ... 108
  - Eagle Wall ... 110
  - Magic Wall ... 111
  - Nirvana ... 112
  - Upper Noufaro ... 112
  - Noufaro Main ... 114
- **BELGIAN CHOCOLATES** ... 116
  - Dalle à Patouche ... 118
  - Fotisi Wall ... 120
- **ARHI** ... 122
  - Chäpi ... 134
  - Balcony Helvetia ... 135
- **SEA BREEZE** ... 136
  - Far Left ... 138
  - Great Canyon ... 139
  - Pocket Wall ... 140
  - Sea Breeze ... 142
- **ARGINONTA** ... 146
- **ARGINONTA SKYLINE** ... 156
  - Haute Gorge ... 158
  - Kryptos ... 160
  - Ovoland ... 162
  - Little Verdon ... 164
  - Jägerwand ... 166
  - Piccalia ... 167
- **ARGINONTA VALLEY** ... 168
  - Arginonta Valley ... 168
  - Black Buddha ... 176
- **SUMMERTIME** ... 178
  - Local Freezer ... 180
  - Magoulias ... 182
  - Summertime ... 184
  - Nikoleta ... 186
  - Big Shadow ... 187
- **DOLPHIN BAY** ... 188
- **KASTELI** ... 192
- **NORTH CAPE** ... 198
  - Apollo ... 200
  - Peter ... 201
  - North Cape ... 202
- **SCHOOL** ... 206
- **ODYSSEY** ... 210

OCEAN DREAM	224
OLYMPIC WALL	228
ILIADA	232
Climber's Nest	234
Iliada	235
Emilio	240
Afghan Corridor	242
Muses	243
JURASSIC PARK	244
SPARTACUS	248
SPARTAN WALL	254
AFTERNOON	258
GRANDE GROTTA	262
PANORAMA	268
STANKILL	276
IVORY TOWER	278
KALYDNA	282
IANNIS	286
POETS	288
Coeur d'Armeos	290
Poets	292
White Shark	295
Zeus	296
Meltemi	299
GERAKIOS	300
Rainbow Wall	302
Upper Cave	303
Gerakios	305
Trois Ilots	306
OURANIA	312
Pyramid	313
Hump Piste	314
Mystery	315
Ourania	316
SYMPLEGADES	318
AUSTRIANS	326
MONASTERY	328
SAINT PHOTIS	330
View of Chapel	332
Chapel Wall	334
Icare	336
Spiders	340
PYTHARI	342
PSILI RIZA	344
DODONI	348
VATHY	350
E.T.	354
JE T'AIME	358
JULIAN	366
ROCKLAND	368

TELENDOS

THREE CAVES	372
NORTH FACE	376
ST CONSTANTINE	378
MILTIADIS	382
EROS	386
IROX	390
GLAROS	396
PESCATORE	398
The Magic Roundabout	399
Pescatore	400
LAMBDA	402
PRINCESS CANYON	406
CRYSTAL CAVE	410
SOUTH FACE	412
Wild Country	414
Eterna	414
Wings for Life	415
De Charybde en Cila	416
Crescendo	417
INSPIRATION	418

CRAG PLANNER • Part 1

No.	Crag	Page	Up to 5b+	5c to 6a+	6b to 7a	7a+ to 7c	7c+ and up	Approach
01	STYX	26	3	19	40	7	0	20 min
02	KASTRI	34	4	30	11	4	0	20 min
03	PALACE	40	4	14	17	8	0	5-10 min
04	SIKATI CAVE	46	2	3	5	12	10	30 min
05	THE BEACH	52	5	8	6	5	1	20 min
06	SECRET GARDEN	58	0	3	18	16	11	20 min
07	PALIONISOS	66	6	21	23	4	0	10 min
08	PROPHITIS ANDREAS	72	20	14	18	7	2	20 min
09	SKALIA	80	6	23	16	8	13	15-25 min
10	GHOST KITCHEN	88	2	18	33	8	1	20 min
11	CAVE	96	6	9	10	5	2	5 min
12	GALATIANI	102	8	6	16	9	5	30 min
13	NOUFARO	108	10	9	19	14	10	10-55 min
14	BELGIAN CHOCOLATES	116	6	21	19	4	0	15-20 min
15	ARHI	122	13	30	27	15	24	6-20 min
16	SEA BREEZE	136	23	33	38	5	0	5-8 min
17	ARGINONTA	146	18	21	31	9	1	5-10 min
18	ARGINONTA SKYLINE	156	15	29	34	5	1	10-75 min
19	ARGINONTA VALLEY	168	4	39	17	3	1	5-25 min
20	SUMMERTIME	178	10	13	16	18	12	3-45 min
21	DOLPHIN BAY	188	7	23	3	1	0	5-10 min
22	KASTELI	192	15	17	0	3	0	7-10 min

Exposure	Shade	Best Season	Busy?	Summary
S, SE	Until 11:00	Nov to April	-	A remote area with stunning views and mid-grade climbing on grey walls, but a bit sharp.
S	Until 12:00	Nov to April	👤	Climbing amidst the surroundings of an ancient castle. An orange vertical pocketed wall, and sharp slabs left and right.
S, SE	Until 11:30	Nov to April	👤	A photogenic rock arch and distinctive rock formations. Varied climbing, from slabby to slightly overhanging, on unusual features.
N	After 12:00	Autumn, Spring	👤👤	A massive hole in the ground and 3-D pumpy climbing on stalactites and tufas.
NE	Until 13:00	Year-round	👤	A crag just above a small beach, where climbing and swimming can be combined. Sharp grey slabs on the left, red overhanging rock on the right.
N	Until 18:00	Autumn to Spring	👤👤👤	Highly featured rock, stalactites, tufa mushrooms and sit-down rests at one of the best crags for summer climbing.
S	Until 10:00	Nov to April	👤	Three small warm crags with red and grey rock and fabulous views over the hamlet of Palionisos.
SW	Until 12:00	Autumn to Spring	👤👤	Well-bolted routes on an exceptional vertical grey wall. Ideal for grades from 6a to 7a. A very good new addition to the island's crags.
S	Until 12:00	Nov to April	👤	An impressive yellow pillar above Skalia Village with a few good but sharp routes, and a new cave to the right with very hard routes.
S, W	Until 16:00	Sept to May	👤👤👤	Mushroom stalactites in the middle and perfect slabs on the left and right for balancy and friction climbing.
SW	Until 13:30	Sept to May	👤	A small cave slotted with big pockets very close to the road. Vertical walls on each side with easier routes.
S	Until 13:00	Sept to May	👤	A large face plus a big cave with stalactites. Quality rock packed with tufas, stalactites and great routes. Two small sub-sectors with sharp slabs.
S	Until 13:00	Sept to May	-	An expansive sector with good grey slabs and walls, some technical multipitches, and a new very hard sub-sector.
SE	Until 11:00	Nov to May	👤👤	A smooth slab rising to 120m high. Great single pitches, but amazing two-pitch routes as well.
S	Until 14:00	Nov to May	👤👤👤	One of the most important crags. Hard steep routes in the middle, and grey curtains with easier routes on both sides.
SE	Until 10:30	Nov to May	👤👤	Several smaller crags with sharp yellow/black walls and steep grey slabs.
S, SW	Until 13:30	Year-round	👤👤👤	A series of red and grey rock faces overlooking Arginonta Village. One of the best crags for routes in the 5c-6b range.
S, E	Until 12:00	Autumn to Spring	-	Good quality grey walls and slabs plus a scary conglomerate sub-sector.
N	After 10:00	April to November	👤👤👤	Excellent slabs, walls with good holds and small bulges, even steep routes on red rock at a new shady venue perfect for hot-weather climbing.
NE	After 13:00	April to October	👤👤👤	Pleasant climbing on gentle slabs and vertical faces, steep cave climbing and more, all in afternoon shade and cool conditions.
S	Until 10:00	October to April	👤	A nice seaside crag in a pretty bay with a Calanques-like ambiance. White soapy rock in some parts.
N, W	Until 13:00	Year-round	👤👤	Several lower-grade routes and some vertical slabs overlooking the sea.

CRAG PLANNER • Part 2

No.	Crag	Page	Up to 5b+	5c to 6a+	6b to 7a	7a+ to 7c	7c+ and up	Approach
23	NORTH CAPE	198	16	25	15	9	4	5-12min
24	SCHOOL	206	11	9	3	0	0	20 min
25	ODYSSEY	210	13	11	23	26	19	8 min
26	OCEAN DREAM	224	3	7	6	4	4	35-40 min
27	OLYMPIC WALL	228	0	2	19	8	4	30 min
28	ILIADA	232	7	26	25	10	6	18-25
29	JURASSIC PARK	244	0	0	6	10	5	45-50 min
30	SPARTACUS	248	0	3	10	12	4	25 min
31	SPARTAN WALL	254	8	3	10	8	7	25 min
32	AFTERNOON	258	3	7	8	4	1	20 min
33	GRANDE GROTTA	262	1	2	5	7	7	20 min
34	PANORAMA	268	1	3	28	22	4	20-22 min
35	STANKILL	276	2	7	10	2	0	25 min
36	IVORY TOWER	278	1	4	8	6	5	25-30 min
37	KALYDNA	282	0	2	18	15	11	25-30 min
38	IANNIS	286	0	1	8	6	6	20 min
39	POETS	288	3	22	46	9	1	15 min
40	GERAKIOS	300	8	45	24	5	4	15-35 min
41	OURANIA	312	8	11	16	7	1	15-20 min
42	SYMPLEGADES	318	3	15	21	0	0	10-12 min
43	AUSTRIANS	326	0	1	3	5	1	15 min
44	MONASTERY	328	1	7	16	1	0	30 min

Exposure	Shade	Best Season	Busy?	Summary
S	Until 11:00	October to April	👤	Across the hillside from Odyssey, a long sharp wall with small interconnected caves.
S	After 12:00	October to April	👤	A training sector in an area of grey slabs rising to a height of 120 meters.
NW	Until 15:00	Year-round	👤👤👤	A major sector unfolding along 400m of interconnected caves and walls of the highest quality rock. Getting a bit polished by Kalymnos standards.
S	Until 12:00	October to April	-	A tall cliff in a mountainous landscape. Slabby climbing and some long multi-pitches.
S	Until 12:30	October to May	-	A huge, slightly overhanging wall above Odyssey, full of pockets, tufa pipes and stalactites.
S	Until 13:00	October to May	👤👤	To the right of Odyssey, the same high-quality rock with varied styles of climbing.
SW	Until 13:00	October to May	👤	A big crescent of pocketed rock with lots of holes and tufas. Rock and routes of very high quality.
N	Until 18:00	Year-round	👤👤👤	An impressive orange bowl of high-quality tufa streaked walls with smooth slabs on both sides. Getting polished by Kalymnos standards.
N	Until 14:30	Year-round	👤👤	A big face with some of the hardest technical wall climbs on Kalymnos. Some easy training slabs on the right.
NW	Until 16:00	Year-round	👤👤👤	A beautiful grey slab to the left of Grande Grotta. Routes from 4a to 7b+ and something for everyone.
SW	Until 14:30	Year-round	👤👤👤	The trademark of Kalymnos. An impressive cave with very steep three-dimensional routes on huge stalactites.
W	Until 13:00	Year-round	👤👤👤	A kingdom of tufas! The extension of Grande Grotta to the right, but with less steep routes.
W	Until 13:00	October to May	👤	To the right of Panorama, a narrow cleft in the rock and a good slab and wall.
W	Until 15:30	Year-round	👤	A pretty rock tower featuring technical wall climbs to the left of sector Kalydna.
W	Until 14:00	Year-round	👤👤	A giant yellow and red amphitheater. Gentle red slabs and walls with tufa blobs. Soapy when humid.
W	Until 15:00	Year-round	👤👤	A cave with tufas, a vertical grey wall to its left, and a steeper 40m wall to its right.
W	Until 13:00	Sept to May	👤👤	The closest sector to Masouri. Perfect vertical rock with a profusion of gouttes d'eau.
S	Until 12:30	Sept to May	👤👤	Several crags with diverse characters. The new sub-sector Trois Ilots is a 6a/6b heaven.
W	Until 16:00	Year-round	-	The huge cave of "Ourania" plus some yellow walls to its left. A short crag with easy grey slabs on the far left.
N, E, S	All day	Year-round	👤👤	Two rock walls facing each other with a small plateau in between. A heavily pocketed mid-grade paradise.
W	Until 16:00	Year-round	-	Short overhanging routes on mid-quality rock on a balcony over the sea.
S	Until 12:00	October to April	-	Good grey wall climbing in a sheltered crag above the sea.

CRAG PLANNER • Part 3

No.	Crag	Page	Up to 5b+	5c to 6a+	6b to 7a	7a+ to 7c	7c+ and up	Approach
45	SAINT PHOTIS	330	0	15	21	13	12	35 min
46	PYTHARI	342	2	4	3	1	0	60 min
47	PSILI RIZA	344	0	0	8	6	14	60 min
48	DODONI	348	0	3	5	6	0	10 min
49	VATHY	350	0	1	4	2	0	By boat
50	E.T.	354	0	3	16	3	4	20-30 min
51	JE T'AIME	358	19	13	11	3	2	3-10 min
52	JULIAN	366	11	4	0	0	0	8-10 min
53	ROCKLAND	368	3	8	13	8	0	25-30 min

TELENDOS

No.	Crag	Page	Up to 5b+	5c to 6a+	6b to 7a	7a+ to 7c	7c+ and up	Approach
54	THREE CAVES	372	1	7	12	6	3	30 min
55	NORTH FACE	376	0	0	2	0	0	45-50 min
56	ST CONSTANTINE	378	0	5	14	7	5	20-30 min
57	MILTIADIS	382	14	11	4	1	0	10-15 min
58	EROS	386	0	3	10	5	2	15 min
59	IROX	390	16	5	11	3	3	5 min
60	GLAROS	396	2	2	6	4	5	20 min
61	PESCATORE	398	1	9	16	4	6w	10 min
62	LAMBDA	402	11	12	15	3	0	25 min
63	PRINCESS CANYON	406	0	3	12	5	6	40 min
64	CRYSTAL CAVE	410	0	0	3	8	3	30 min
65	SOUTH FACE	412	0	2	2	3	4	40 min
66	INSPIRATION	418	0	3	3	5	1	50-60 min

Exposure	Shade	Best Season	Busy?	Summary
W	Until 14:30/all day at parts	Year-round	🚶	A good yellow wall and intensely overhanging cave in a peaceful setting overlooking the sea.
S	Until 11:30	October to April	-	A remote sector overlooking the wild bay of Pythari.
S	Until 13:00	Nov to April	-	Hard old-school vertical or slightly overhanging limestone walls
SW	Until 13:30	Sept to May	🚶	In a valley above Hora, some worthwhile routes on vertical rock
E, W	Until 13:00	Spring, Autumn, Summer	🚶	A narrow fjord with rock walls on both sides. A great introduction to Deep Water Solo.
NE, N	After 12:30	Spring, Autumn, Summer	-	Perfect vertical rock and 40m long routes overlooking the valley of Vathy. A small cave with tufas to the right.
SE, S	After 16:00	Year-round	-	Varied climbing on compact vertical or slightly overhanging walls of medium quality by Kalymnos standards.
SE	Until 10:00	October to April	-	Slab climbs and some squeezed routes along the Arginonta-Vathy road.
S	Until 12:00	October to May	-	A red and grey wall in a remote crag above the wild fjord of Pezonda.
E	After 13:00	Year-round	-	Superb routes on holes and small tufas inside the three caves overlooking Telendos village. Sharp routes on the grey walls outside.
N	After 9:00	March to Nov	-	An impressive north-facing crag rising up to 190m with two multi-pitches with an alpine feeling.
NE	After 14:00	Spring, Summer, Autumn	-	Three crags with very distinct characters. The surrounding terrain is wild and undeveloped.
NE	After 13:00	March to Nov	-	A crag in a pleasant setting on a well-featured, technical slab and wall. Sharp in places.
NE	After 12:00	March to Nov	🚶	A massive amphitheater over the sea. Smooth rock with vertical technical climbs alongside gym-like pumpy routes.
NE	After 14:00	March to Nov	🚶🚶	A popular sector with a diverse range of grades, from easy-angled climbing to massive overhangs.
N	Until 17:00	March to Nov	🚶	A small balcony suspended over the sea and diverse grades on smooth rock.
NW	Until 16:00	March to Nov	🚶🚶	A crag replete with large stalactites, tufa pipes, and an immaculate wall. Some nice long routes from 5c-6c on the left.
NW	Until 13:30	March to Nov	🚶🚶	First-class climbing on very long routes up to 50m on vertical or slightly overhanging rock.
S, N	All day at parts	Spring, Autumn	-	A very remote gorge with top-quality slabs and slightly overhanging, fully pocketed walls.
S	Until 10:00	Sept to May	-	A hardcore cave on Telendos for experienced climbers only, with a maze of huge stalactites.
S	Until 11:00	Sept to May	🚶	A massive face featuring some popular multi-pitches, plus "Crescendo", a wild cave full of stalactites.
S	Until 13:00	Spring, Autumn	-	An impressive and rugged crag with prominent features like a large arch, stalactites, and huge holes.

ACKNOWLEDGMENTS

I am very grateful to have a small team of hard-working, talented people helping with my guidebook projects.
I will try to express my gratitude with words, though words are not always enough.

Once again Katie, my partner in life, was multi-tasker extraordinaire. With her penchant for career changes, this time she added book design to her job descriptions; and the list keeps growing. Nikos Krikelis, my good friend and silent "MVP" partner, shared all of his design, photography, and web knowledge and never refused to help.
Nikolaos Smalios, my Kalymnian friend and photographer, contributed beautiful photos and invaluable help yet again from distant Australia, where he now lives, because his heart has never left Kalymnos. And John Koullias, the good doctor, photographer and human being, generously shared his photographs but also helped us through personal hardships while we worked on the book.

For the present edition I also owe very special thanks to the following people:

Claude, Christine and Yves Remy, who have fully adapted to the Greek character whilst continuing to put up wonderful new lines and sharing their photographs, quick corrections and constructive feedback. Sergios Soursos, for his uncanny ability to spot tiny discrepancies even on holiday time. George Kopalides, my friend and climbing partner, for helping with the unglamorous task of route maintenance on Kalymnos. Claude Idoux, for providing daily help at the field and for tirelessly finding and equipping elegant new lines. Simon Montmory, Hannes Webhofer, Luca Salsotto, and Bruno Fara, for also participating in the hard work of rebolting and for making time to do additional fieldwork as needed.
Sophia Lagoudi, for skillfully coordinating the advertising section under immense last-minute pressure.

Photographers Sam Bié, Rainer Eder, Elodie Saracco, Simon Carter, Jim Thornburg, Ola Brahammar,
Lee Cujes, David Munilla, Babis Giritziotis, and Damiano Levati, for all their wonderful photographs. And all the climbers who submitted their action shots, even though not all photos made it into the book—your generosity is much appreciated.

Peter Keller, Urs Odermatt, Falk Heinicke, Günter Hommel, Joachim Friedrich, Hans-Peter Hoidn, André Langenbach, Roger Runacher, Jürgen Rohrmann, Nicolas Szawrowski, Mauro Rossi and Pascal Etienne, for the various ways, big and small, in which they helped bring the 2015/2016 edition together. Terrain Editions, for supporting our projects time and time again. Carl and Ruth Dawson, our friends and neighbors, for always being available to help.

Chris Boukoros, a wonderful human being and talented photographer, whose life was cut tragically short in December of 2015. His generous smile and good heart will never be forgotten. His spirit will live on through the many beautiful photographs he contributed to this book.

Lastly, a very warm thanks to you, the thousands of climbers from all over the world who keep coming back to Kalymnos and supporting us by sending route comments and other feedback that helps us improve what we do.
Without you, this book could not have been made.

INTRODUCTION

Welcome to the revised and expanded 6th edition of the Kalymnos Guidebook! More than 15 years since rock climbing started on this little island, Kalymnos is still in the heart of the international climbing community as one of the best and safest sport climbing destinations in the world. In a country rocked by a long-term financial crisis, this is no small feat. Thanks to the steady influx and support of climbers, the lives of countless local families have dramatically improved. And in spite of the crisis, the quality of products and services available on the island has also improved significantly, and continues to do so.

This book was made from the bottom up. The majority of photos and photo-topos are new, and approximately 3,000 routes are included. Every page incorporates 17 years of inside experience with Kalymnos, hopefully helping to produce our best guidebook yet.

Is it sensible to make a 400+ page printed guidebook in our digital age? We often wondered. But after speaking with hundreds of climbers, we realized there were many others out there who love the printed page, the ability to re-live their climbing trip through well-thumbed pages, the *soul* that digital guides just don't have. A good topo is part guide, part memento. So we took the risk—but we are also practical, therefore each copy comes with a free guidebook app for tablets and smartphones created by *Vertical Life*. This will eliminate the need to download "new route" lists, and of course it can go with you whenever your guidebook stays home. Little extras, such as GPS coordinates for each crag, have also been added based on your feedback. Coordinates are in decimal degree format, so when you enter them into your GPS device, make sure it is set for the WGS84 datum and the decimal degree format.

Moreover, as the number of pages has increased, the text has simplified. Our webpage **climbkalymnos.com** is online for its 7th year to provide additional detailed information about all things Kalymnos. And since this guidebook goes to climbers from more than 45 countries, we have tried to make our writing simpler, more direct and easier to understand for every climber from every country.

For the season 2013-14, UIAA-certified stainless-steel bolts and carabiners for the lower-offs.

Last but not least, know that **by buying this guidebook you are giving back to Kalymnos climbing**. A significant percentage of the sales proceeds is used to buy bolts, anchors, and other hardware necessary for the voluntary rebolting of routes performed on the island over several years now. Even though 300 routes were rebolted in 2015/16 thanks to a large EU-funded maintenance project, many years usually pass with no organized rebolting. To fill this gap, a handful of dedicated volunteers, including myself, have made it their mission to keep Kalymnos safe. For this reason, since 2010 we have put aside approximately 5,000 euros every year from the proceeds of the guidebook to buy bolts and other necessary hardware. More information about rebolting can be found online at climbkalymnos.com.

So thank you for supporting Kalymnos climbing by buying this guidebook and not photocopying it, posting pages of the book online, or redistributing its content illegally in any other way.

Climb on!

Aris

The author during a voluntary rebolting project at Saint Photis.

Aris Theodoropoulos
June 2016

KALYMNOS

Population: 16,179 (2011 census) | **Capital:** Pothia
Area size: 134.5 km2 | **Highest elevation:** 700m
Time zone: GMT + 2 hrs | **Area code:** +30 22430

1 General information and a brief history of the island

Kalymnos belongs to the *Dodecanese Islands* in the Aegean Sea; it is located 183 nautical miles (339 km) southeast of Athens and 85 nautical miles (157 km) northwest of Rhodes, the capital of the region. Many smaller islands are nearby; most notably *Telendos*, (which was part of Kalymnos until it was separated by a devastating earthquake in 554 AD), *Pserimos*, and *Plati*. Kalymnos is the fifth largest amongst the Dodecanese Islands; the capital and main port of Kalymnos, **Pothia**, is a lively town built around the port and combines strict traditions with all the hustle and bustle of a modern town.

Sea sponges drying in the sun at Pothia, the capital and main port of Kalymnos. JOHN KOULLIAS

Kalymnos was once known as *Isola Umbrosa*, the "island of shade", but that is no longer the case. Today it is dotted with low vegetation, herbs (like thyme, oregano and sage) and small drought-resistant bushes. There are very few trees. The land is mountainous with a major rock escarpment all along the west coast. In the past, this harsh and dry land drove the locals to the sea for a living. The men of Kalymnos became sponge-divers, a traditional but dangerous occupation, in which they excelled to such an extent that their island became the most celebrated sponge trade center in the Mediterranean. The sponge trade began to decline in the 1980s, but to Greeks Kalymnos is still the "sponge divers' island", and the history of Kalymnos will forever be linked to that little creature, the sea sponge. Kalymnian sponges are still widely sold on the island.

2 Getting to Kalymnos and information about the Kos-Kalymnos ferry

The primary ways to get to Kalymnos are a) by plane via Kos island, just south of Kalymnos, or b) directly to Kalymnos by plane or ferry from Athens, the capital of Greece. The vast majority of climbers arrive via Kos island, since the international airport there accommodates charter and other international flights. The airport in Kalymnos is smaller, with a connection only to Athens.

• Via Kos island
This is the best way to get to Kalymnos if you are flying from a major city in Western Europe. It is probably also the cheapest way. There are direct flights between major European airports and Kos several months per year, including on most low-cost airlines. Once you land at Kos airport, take a local ferry to Kalymnos (30-50 minutes).

Here's what to do when you land in Kos:

a) From Kos airport, take a taxi to **Mastichari** port. Mastichari port is a small secondary port on Kos, from which the local ferries to Kalymnos depart. It is only 10 min by car from Kos airport.

b) From Mastichari port, catch the next ferry to Kalymnos. The local ferries between Kos and Kalymnos never stop (unless there is very bad weather). There are several crossings every day, 365 days per year.

c) When you get to Pothia (the main port in Kalymnos) there will be taxis waiting, or you can take the bus if it is not too late in the day. Ask somebody at the port to point you to the bus stop. Masouri, the main "climbing" village, is about 20 minutes away by car; longer by bus.

• Via Athens (airplane or ferry)
You can fly directly from Athens to Kalymnos. Depending on the season, there are between 1-3 flights from Athens to Kalymnos every day on the Greek airline Olympic Air. More details online at **olympicair.com**.

You can also take a ferry to Kalymnos from Piraeus, the main port of Athens. Ferries run year-round about 3 times per week, and take between 9-14 hours. More details online at **bluestarferries.com**.

Note: The sea connection between Kos and Kalymnos stops only when it is very windy (not often). When this happens it is best to wait, if possible, until sea travel is restored. If you cannot, there is a "pirate" boat making the crossing when all other boats stop. More details and Kos ferry timetables are online at **climbkalymnos.com**.

A distinctively Kalymnian moment of affection between grandfather, grandson and one of the family's baby goats.

3 Accommodation, transportation, and healthcare

You can find almost everything on Kalymnos (except trees!) and as climbing continues to develop, more and more basic amenities are now easily accessible.

ACCOMMODATION

Almost all types of accommodation are available on Kalymnos: very cheap rooms, nice clean rental studios/apartments, small family-owned hotels, and some "boutique" accommodation. (What Kalymnos does *not* have are large hotel complexes.) People agree that you get a very good value for money here compared to most other Greek islands. The majority of rental accommodations belong to the "studio" category; this typically means a room for two people with a private bathroom and small kitchen or kitchenette. July and August are the highest seasons, when there is also some non-climbing tourism, so prices can be slightly higher in summer months.

• **Is there a campsite on Kalymnos?**
No. There is no organized campsite on Kalymnos, and unregulated free camping is strictly prohibited.

• **Where do most climbers stay?**
Climbers actually stay in many parts of the island, because Kalymnos is a small island and therefore crags are never too far away. That said, the majority of climbers prefer the main "climbing" village, **Masouri**, and the two villages right next to it, **Myrties** and **Armeos**. These villages are on the beautiful west coast of Kalymnos, with the famous view of Telendos island and the sunset, where many of the major crags are gathered. Other points in favor of staying on the west coast are: a) you don't need a scooter, since you can also walk to mini-markets, restaurants and other shops; b) most other climbers hang out here, so you are sure to meet fellow climbers easily; c) you can walk to at least 3-4 different beaches, and d) you can easily walk to the jetty at Myrties and catch the boat to Telendos.

• **What if I don't want to stay in Masouri?**
You don't have to. There are other places to stay: try the quieter villages of **Arginonta**, **Skalia** and **Emporios** to the northwest (and also close to some major crags) or **Panormos**, **Kandouni**, **Linaria** and **Platis Gialos** to the south.

TIP: **Book accommodation in advance.**
We strongly suggest that you book your accommodation in advance if you are visiting between April and October. Otherwise you can ask around once you get there. If you are staying for an extended period of time, consider asking for a monthly rate, as many landlords are flexible.

TRANSPORTATION

From the Masouri area you can easily walk to many crags in 15-60 minutes, but scooters are especially popular. They are cheap, can take two passengers plus all their gear, and you can usually rent one with a simple driver's license. Or, you can rent a car, take the bus (infrequent), or rent a bicycle (increasingly popular).

TIP: **Helmets!**
Scooter rental places will provide helmets, or if they don't, wear your climbing helmet. Most Greeks don't wear helmets. Don't do as the Greeks do. Also, watch out for steep "blind" turns in the road; don't drive into them at high speed. (The rightward turn near Kasteli, by the big colorful house, is a good example.)

They're cute, but they'd be cuter with helmets.

KALYMNOS

HEALTHCARE

There is a hospital in Kalymnos, as well as several private doctors and labs. The **hospital** is on the outskirts of Pothia, on the outbound road from Pothia to Hora. Most doctors speak a reasonable amount of English. For **children**, there is a pediatrician on staff at the Kalymnos hospital and there are at least two pediatric practices in Pothia. Additionally, there are quite a few **pharmacies**. The one closest to the Masouri area is in Elies village, and the rest are in or around Pothia. If you need to find a pharmacy after closing hours, stop at *any* pharmacy and look on the door/window: the emergency rota will be listed. If it is only in Greek, pull a local over and use sign language by pointing to the notice. They will understand and help you.

4 Shops, services, and other useful amenities

Most basic amenities and services are found Pothia, the capital, but many essentials are now also available in the Masouri area. Here's a useful list; if you don't see what you are looking for below, check **climbkalymnos.com** for more.

• **Police**: You probably won't need it, but it is located on the main inbound road to Pothia, just before the taxi station. You can also call the universal emergency number (112) from any telephone free of charge.

• **Gas/petrol station**: There are many, but most are in Pothia and its outskirts. The closest one to the Masouri area is in Elies village (5-7 min drive).

• **ATM**: In the middle of Masouri, opposite *Oasis Hotel* and next to *Michalis and Cleo* jewelry store. If it doesn't work, the next closest one is in Elies village, opposite *Marinos* restaurant.

• **Drinking water**: You cannot drink tap water in Kalymnos. Your options are to buy bottled water or to fill your own bottles for free at the water machines all around Kalymnos. The water machines are large square structures marked with the word **TEMAK**. They are simple to operate. Place your bottle under the spout; press the green button to dispense water; press the red button to stop. Generally speaking, there is one water machine on the main road of each village. Bring a headlamp if you are refilling water bottles in the evening, as the machines are not always lit.

• **Mini markets and super markets**: The Masouri area is full of little shops where you can buy food, drinks, gifts, the guidebook etc, and there is a big supermarket in Elies.

• **Wi-Fi**: Almost everywhere. The vast majority of rental studios, hotels, cafes and restaurants offer free Wi-Fi.

• **Laundry**: There is a laundromat in Masouri, and many hotels or rentals may also provide laundry services for a small fee, so it doesn't hurt to ask.

5 Sightseeing, museums, daytrips and family activities

Kalymnos is a very family-oriented society, and there is no shortage of little kids everywhere. Kalymnians will go out of their way to accommodate families with kids. Nevertheless, you must know that there are no sidewalks anywhere, and the roads are narrow and busy, so be extra careful when walking with kids. Telendos is a good place to go with the kids, as there are no cars and the boat ride alone is exciting.

Fast friends: a Kalymnian boy and a Russian boy who just met.

SIGHTSEEING

There are castles on Kalymnos with considerable archaeological interest, as well as very interesting small museums. The Castle of Hora (11th century) near sector Dodoni was inhabited through the early 18th century. The Castle of Chrysocheria was built by the Order of the Knights of St. John in a prominent position between Hora and Pothia; in the area of the castle there is evidence of continuous human presence since the Neolithic era. Three stone-built windmills are nearby.

Other important archaeological sites are scattered throughout the island, such as the foundations of the ancient acropolis of Pothia; ancient and Paleochristian ruins in Vathy; and ruins of a fortified Byzantine settlement and a Paleochristian necropolis on the island of Telendos.

MUSEUMS
The island's museums include a very worthwhile Archaeological Museum in Pothia featuring prehistoric, classical and private collections, as well as the preserved interior of a 19th-century Kalymnian mansion. The Museum of Marine Finds in Vlychadia features assorted items found underwater or salvaged from sunken ships. The Sponge Diving Museum in Pothia is a poignant introduction to the island's centuries-old marine history and culture. The Kalymnian Home in Vothyni is a private folk art museum replicating a traditional local home. You will feel like you walked straight into a previous century, and talking with the friendly owner will give you a different perspective on what daily life on Kalymnos was like.

DAY TRIPS TO NEARBY ISLANDS
There is, of course, Telendos, but it's so close it hardly qualifies as a "day trip". Boats to Telendos leave every 30 minutes from the jetty at Myrties. Other islands to visit for a day are Leros, Kos, and Pserimos. Finally, excursion boats make daily trips to Bodrum in Turkey. Alternatively, you can hire a sailing boat with or without crew and set sail to all neighboring islands and the beautiful, but otherwise inaccessible, inlets along the NE coast.

6 Local products and culinary highlights

As one might expect, all the familiar Greek dishes can be found on Kalymnos (*souvlaki*, *mousaka* etc.). But be adventurous! Try something different! We are only too happy to talk about food, so here's a selection of less-ordinary Kalymnian dishes and very good local products.

• **Mermizeli**: The Kalymnos-style Greek salad. Each restaurant has its own version, but they all add dry rusk (crunchy bread) to to the usual suspects (tomato, cucumber, onion) plus extras like local goat cheese etc.

• **Mououri**: Greeks have a hard time pronouncing it, too; it's not just you. *Moo-oo-ri* does not come from a cow, as you might think; it is slow-baked goat stuffed with rice and cinnamon. It's the island's traditional Easter dish, but some restaurants make it at other times, too. If there are leftovers, they are cooked with scrambled egg the next day and re-christened *kavourmas*. If you have a stomach of steel, go for it.

• **Octopus "balls"**: a deep-fried croquette like a fishcake, but with octopus pieces in lieu of fish.

• **Goat cheese and yogurt**: Local cheese (from goat's, sheep's or cow's milk) or yogurt (sheep's or cow's milk) is definitely worth trying. The flavor is more pungent compared to commercial cheese/yogurt, but it's the real thing.

• **Eptazimo**: A slightly sweet, soft white bread with anise seed. People either love or hate anise; if you, like us, love it, this bread is great with coffee or at the crag.

• **Figs**: Fig trees grow like weeds in Kalymnos, and their fruit, the humble fig, is the tastiest you will find in Greece. Their season is short, unfortunately (late July/August). Pick them off the tree, or buy them if you can find them. Try them with eptazimo and goat cheese for a perfect meal.

Power snack from the fig tree down the road.

• **Thyme honey**: Kalymnian thyme honey is considered one of the best in Greece. It is widely available on the island and it really is incredible. Local herbs are also used to make skincare products, which are worth seeking out.

• **And lastly...the famous Kalymnian sea sponges**: Would you go to Italy and not try an espresso? Well, you can't go to Kalymnos and not buy a sea sponge!

OUTDOORS

1. How to poop at the crag without leaving anything behind

This is always the hardest section in the guidebook to write. It's no fun preaching to people about their toilet habits. But because not all climbers respect the crags as they do their own homes, we cannot skip this section. And we can't help but wonder: at your house, do you poo on the floor, stick toilet paper on top, then turn on the fan for some air? We didn't think so. Then why do this at the crag?

Many people think of toilet paper as eco-friendly trash. Well, it isn't. ("What do you mean? It comes from trees!") Toilet paper is not biodegradable, which makes it equal to any other piece of trash.

So when you have to answer nature's call at the crag, there is one basic rule: *Don't leave anything behind*.

To begin with, give yourself enough time to use the toilet *before* you hit the crags. Then, even if you enjoyed great success, always take a small bag with you to the crag for packing up used toilet paper in case nature calls again.

At the crag:

- Go far away from the cliffs and the path (at least 100m).

- Dig a deep enough hole using your hands or a stone.

- Squat over the hole and do your business.

- Pack used toilet paper in the bag you brought and take it with you. It is **not OK** to stick your toilet paper over your poo and top it off with a stone. You are not building a cairn here, people!

- Cover your hole up well with dirt and stones. Don't leave your poo exposed for others to step in (which is about as fun as it sounds).

2. Goat gates on the approach paths and goats at the crag

Goats are everywhere. Semi-wild goats hang out at most crags, as they have become accustomed to the presence of climbers, and smart as they are, they know that climbers equal food. No, they won't eat climbers, but they *will* eat all the snacks climbers bring to the crag. Goats have no shame: they will go straight to your backpack and snatch your food, even if it's wrapped. The only solution is to keep your backpack zipped up at all times. Also, if you go to Sikati Cave and find goats trapped inside, your first instinct will be to rescue them. (Been there, done that). It's not easy, but if you manage to catch and rescue a goat from the cave, be prepared for the outcome. As soon as the goat is out with your help, it will jump right back into the cave and make a beeline for your food.

"Aha! It must be that new guy the others mentioned. I'm off to raid his backpack."

Goat gates on the approach paths: You will often have to pass through barbed wire gates on the approach paths to the crags. These have been built by shepherds to control the movements of their animals. Please respect that, and leave each gate the way you found it: If it was open leave it open; if it was closed, don't forget to close it behind you.

3 Eco-friendly on Kalymnos: Little things can make a difference

Eco-friendly is not easy on Kalymnos. Take water bottles, for example. Tap water is not good for drinking or cooking, so the majority of people buy water in plastic bottles, and almost all restaurants offer bottled water only. There is no recycling on Kalymnos, so water bottles end up with the regular waste. And that's plastic from just one item; if you factor in plastic shopping bags, food packaging, and so on, that amounts to a huge amount of waste detrimental to the environment. But as we've always believed, any positive change is better than no change at all. If each of us changes just one small habit or behavior, all of us together can really make a positive change.

Little things you can do:

• Bring reusable shopping bags to the store

• Refill water bottles at the free water machines instead of buying new ones every time

• Use the mild, eco-friendly green olive oil soap for washing everything, including your rope

• Don't waste water; most Greek islands suffer from water shortages, including Kalymnos

• Support local products! They have traveled much shorter distances, are mostly seasonal, and they are very high-quality. Look for local yogurt, cheese, fruits and vegetables, honey, sea salt, soap and personal care products.

• And do we need to remind you that cigarette butts are litter, and cliffs are not ashtrays? Don't throw your cigarette butts on the ground or stick them in gouttes on the rock; pack them up and take them with you!

4 Other outdoor activities for active rest days

Beaches: If sunning yourself on the beach sounds like the perfect rest day, Kalymnos has got you covered: there are plenty of beaches, most with sun beds, for all tastes.
But if you are hoping for an active rest day, there are even more things to do: snorkeling, hiking, caving, scuba diving, horseback riding, herbal walks, to name a few.

Snorkeling and scuba diving: Kalymnos and Telendos are excellent for snorkeling and scuba diving. Basic, inexpensive masks, snorkels and fins are sold at tourist shops on the island. Watch out for sea urchins and passing boats (it's best not to stray too far from the coast). For scuba diving, there are instructors on the island offering professional instruction and certification.

Hiking: There are many wonderful hiking trails on Kalymnos, or you can try parts of the worthwhile *Kalymnos Trail*, a multi-day hiking trail linking mountain tops, remote beaches, archaeological sites, caves, lively villages, and ancient castles and towns via a continuous link along the best footpaths of the island. Both a hiking map of Kalymnos as well as *The Kalymnos Trail* are published by Terrain Edtions and sold everywhere on the island.

Now *that's* a rest day. SAM BIÉ

Caves: There are several caves with exceptional stalactite and stalagmite decorations in Kalymnos; prehistoric findings suggest that many of these caves were ancient ritual sites. Some of them worth special mention include Kefala Cave near Pothia; Daskalio Cave at Vathy; Skalia Cave at the village of Skalia; and the Cave of the Seven Virgins, in which according to local lore seven maidens disappeared trying to flee from the pirates.

CLIMBING

1. How it all started, a quick background, and past climbing events

The story is widely known by now: In 1996, the Italian climber Andrea di Bari visited Kalymnos for his summer holidays and literally stumbled upon cliff after cliff with huge climbing potential. He returned with some friends in 1997 to equip the first 43 sport routes, and the Kalymnos story started. Soon thereafter, this author collaborated with the local municipality to ensure a series of measures were in place for the proper development and promotion of climbing on Kalymnos.

A series of climbing events followed starting in 2000, and the first Kalymnos Guidebook was published that same year. Eight climbing festivals were organized in the period between 2000-2014, the turning point being 2006 with the Petzl RocTrip, which brought the biggest names in climbing, at the time, to this little island. Most recently, The North Face sponsored three consecutive climbing events. You can read more about Kalymnos climbing festivals online at **climbkalymnos.com**.

Nina Caprez during the 2014 TNF festival. PERIKLIS RIPIS

2. Climbing character, seasons, route grades and descriptions

The rock of Kalymnos is **limestone** of the very best quality. It is a little sharp in places, but free of choss (i.e. rotten, loose rock). There is nothing monotonous about climbing on Kalymnos: there is a great variety of rock, with slabs, delicate walls, pumpy routes with pockets and stalactites or tufas on overhanging rock and roofs. In some respects the rock resembles that of Thailand, only a little sharper.

Many visitors have described the equipping of routes on Kalymnos as "the gold standard of sport climbing." Grades range from F4a to F9a, although there are quite a few project routes which are expected to exceed 9a. Many have an athletic, steep and challenging character and are equipped in a sensible, friendly manner using stainless steel bolts. The rock on Kalymnos seems to come in three varieties:

• **Extremely overhanging** with blobs, tufas and stalactites, which, even when tilted 20 degrees past vertical, can still check in at a "mere" 7a!

• **Slightly overhanging or vertical**, smooth white and orange walls with pockets and smaller tufa features.

• **Grey slabs** with sharp rock full of water pockets (*gouttes*) with little iron knobs cemented into the matrix.

The best of the routes can combine all three types of rock in one pitch. Of equal importance is that the limestone is showing little sign of polish, in contrast to the rock at some other well-known climbing areas of Europe. This situation will be slow to change given the particularly rough surface of the rock. Most routes are about 30m long on average, but there are several longer routes around 3-5 pitches, and a lot more potential for great new routes at all levels.

SEASONS

Kalymnos is known for its dry climate and year-round climbing is definitely possible. Still, some periods (spring and autumn) are better than others.

Autumn: The ideal climbing period for Kalymnos. The weather is generally good, with a comfortable temperature, so you can climb all day. It doesn't typically rain in Kalymnos during September and October, and mid-October to mid- or late-November is usually perfect. It's no accident that October is the peak of the climbing season.

Winter: Beautiful, sunny, clear days are frequent in Kalymnos during winter, and many stunning crags, mostly between Arginonta and Emporios, are perfect for winter. A handful of restaurants and rental studios do stay open year-round in the Masouri area, so you can still find places to eat and sleep, but your choices will be more limited. The serenity you will enjoy in return is priceless.

Spring: Almost as good as autumn for climbing. The sea is too cold to swim in and the chances of rain are higher, but generally speaking, the rock on Kalymnos dries fast. Note, though, that If the previous winter has been rainy the tufa may be seeping, and stalactites sometimes drip during the spring and are more inclined to break, as they are softer. However, you can climb inside the caves even when it rains, but **do not climb in the caves during a thunderstorm**.

Climbing on wet rock in the lightning. Don't do it.

Never climb in a cave during a thunderstorm!
Here, an electrical storm over Telendos. OLA BRAHAMMAR

Summer: Not people's first choice, but summer climbing is usually perfectly possible. The obvious rule to follow is: *only climb in the shade*. Shady crags are usually refreshed by a cool breeze and oftentimes you may need long sleeves to belay on summer mornings.

ROUTE GRADES + DESCRIPTIONS

Sport routes on Kalymnos are graded according to the French grading system. Great efforts have been made toward consistent grading, but since routes on Kalymnos are being put up by climbers from all over the world, and a few of these routes have not yet seen their second ascent, some may need re-grading. In the route descriptions, we try to give you a feel for most routes without giving away specific beta that will spoil your onsight. If you disagree with a certain grade or description, you can post your feedback on **climbkalymnos.com**'s online route database.

What do the stars mean?

?	Incomplete or unconfirmed route details
0★	Thumbs down
1★	Good, worth trying
2★	Very good
3★	Excellent
♪	Outstanding! Includes older and newer routes

3 Standard gear: How many quickdraws? What rope length?

QUICKDRAWS (QDs): 15 QDs is the standard gear for Kalymnos. Always check the length of your route and use this as a general guide:

- Routes up to **20-25m**: 10-12 QDs
- Routes from **25-35m**: 15 QDs
- Routes from **35-40m**: 20 QDs
- In most cases, in routes needing **more than 15 QDs** it will be mentioned in the route description (i.e. "18 QDs").

That is the **minimum** amount of QDs required to climb safely. Beyond that, we strongly suggest you bring along 30-40 QDs. There are some monster routes on Kalymnos requiring 24-28 QDs, and furthermore, if you leave your QDs in on a project to try later, you will still need 12-15 extra QDs to use on a different route in the meantime.

For climbing routes on stalactites, bring medium-to-long quickdraw slings. For the monster routes at Grande Grotta and Sikati Cave you will also need 5-6 long slings to reduce rope-drag, directing your rope around tufas and stalactites.

ROPE: 70m is the minimum standard single rope length for Kalymnos (9-10,5mm diameter). However, many remarkable long routes (40-45m) have been opened all over Kalymnos in the past few years. We would recommend investing in a long rope before you travel to Kalymnos. A rope length of 80m will do nicely for most new monster routes or extension pitches. Remember always to check the length of the route before starting to climb.

CLIMBING

4. Partner check, cleaning tick marks, and stripping very steep single pitches

Most climbing accidents in Kalymnos can be prevented by always doing a partner check. The illustration and descriptions below are courtesy of PETZL. Don't skip them!

During a partner check, the climber and the belayer must check each of 4 key areas to ensure climber safety. **Do this before starting each climb.**

- **Belay system setup**: Check that the rope is installed in the right direction in your belay device; the carabiner is connected to the right place on the harness; and the carabiner is locked.

- **Harness**: Check that the harness waistbelt is above the hips, and that the harness is adjusted to fit snugly.

- **Tie-in knot**: Check that you are tied in to the right place on the harness; that the knot is proper; that the knot is completed and tightened.

- **Rope**: Make sure a knot is tied in the end of the rope. Failure to tie a knot is *the most common cause of climbing accidents on Kalymnos* (which are 100% preventable!)

REMOVE YOUR TICK MARKS AND CHALK

This isn't a safety issue, of course, but it's the right thing to do. Please remove your tick marks and chalk from holds after you are finished with a route! No need to spoil the next climber's attempt or to deface the cliffs with all the white marks.

STRIPPING VERY STEEP SINGLE PITCHES

When you remove the quickdraws from an overhanging route, do not unclip from the 1st bolt as you lower back down. Keep yourself clipped in through the quickdraw in the 1st bolt until you reach the ground. If you don't, there's a chance of a big swing which, with the rope stretch, can easily lead to hitting the ground at speed. Keep in mind that on almost all the routes in Kalymnos the first bolt is placed close to the ground (2-3m), so you can strip the quickdraw by re-climbing the first few metres after you've untied. Alternatively, re-clip the third bolt on the way down, then lower down to strip the bottom two, before re-climbing to the remaining quickdraw to take the swing at a safe height.

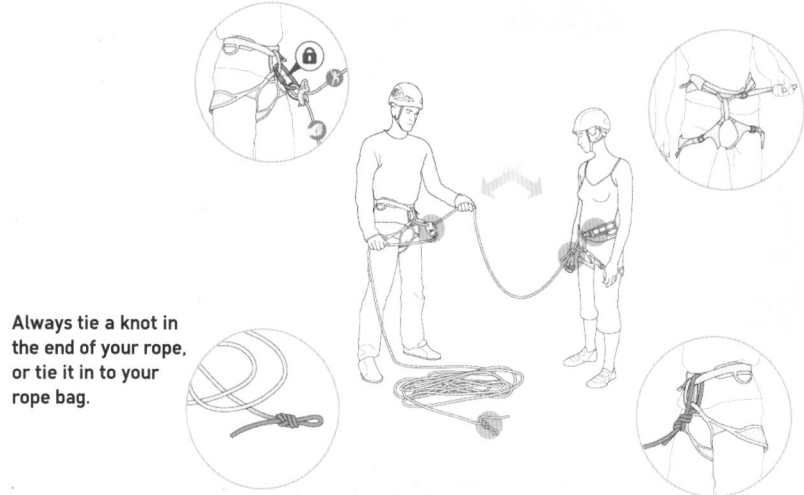

Always tie a knot in the end of your rope, or tie it in to your rope bag.

PETZL.COM

5 Lowering, top-roping, and keeping the anchors of Kalymnos safe

After tens of thousands of ascents, permanent carabiners at the anchors of popular routes are showing clear signs of use. Most climbers clip their rope directly through the carabiners at anchors, but they may not know that this damages the carabiner metal and decreases its lifespan.

How can you help keep the anchors of Kalymnos safe?
It's very simple. Do not lower directly off the anchor's carabiner, but **place one of your quickdraws or carabiners in addition to the permanent carabiner to lower from**. Use the permanent carabiners at the anchor only after your last go, when you are ready to strip the route.

Top-roping: When top-roping, don't simply clip the rope through the single permanent carabiner at the anchor. **As a back-up, also add a runner/quickdraw**. Make sure the gates of the carabiners are opposed to each other so they don't accidentally open or, better still, add one quickdraw with a locking carabiner. To avoid wear and tear on the carabiner, do not top-rope from it directly. You should place a short quickdraw or screwgate carabiner on the bolt of the anchor (see photo) as well as clipping your rope through the fixed lower-off carabiner. When you are finished with the route the last climber in your party removes the quickdraw and lowers from the permanent carabiner.

6 Guidelines for equipping new routes on Kalymnos

Everybody's goal is for the climbing on Kalymnos to be as safe as possible, so that climbers can concentrate on the technical difficulty of the routes without worrying about being injured or risking their life. To this effect, we have proposed a set of detailed equipping guidelines for equippers who would like to put up new routes on Kalymnos.

In brief, the most essential guidelines are:

a) Use only EU-certified 316L stainless-steel bolts (10-12mm) or EU-certified titanium bolts. Please do not use homemade bolts.

b) Use only proper 2-bolt lower-offs:

2 bolts + chain + stainless steel clippable carabiner

or

V-type with 2 bolts + chain + 2 stainless steel carabiners

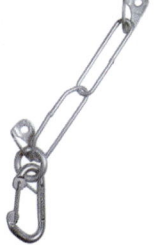

c) Clean the cliffs very thoroughly of loose rock.

d) Follow the "Kalymnos-style" bolting philosophy.

e) Notify the local climbing community about your plans before putting up routes. Let us know at Climb Kalymnos about your equipping experience and the new route(s) you are planning, and notify the Kalymnos Rescue Service about the hardware you plan to use to ensure it is appropriate and safe for the particular environment of Kalymnos.

The full set of equipping guidelines can be found online at **climbkalymnos.com/climbing**

CLIMBING

7 The Kalymnos Rescue Team and Emergency Numbers

An excellent mountain rescue team, the Kalymnos Rescue Service, was formed in Kalymnos in 2014. The team is staffed by volunteers and relies on donations from climbers to continue offering its very important services.
The volunteers staffing the Rescue Service have been profesionally trained to rescue an injured person from crags and approach paths, with or without the use of ropes, and to provide first aid.

The Rescue Service relies on donations to keep operating. To support them, visit **www.kalymnosrescueteam.org**

In the image above, the Kalymnos Rescue Service rescues two climbers in 2014 after they tried to abseil down the 80m rappel at Grande Grotta. Their rope was much shorter, and the couple got stuck hanging in the void of the cave. The rescue operation took several hours and it was dark by the time the climbers were lowered to the ground.

8 What to do in case of an accident

Do not try to move the injured climber. Call one of the Emergency Numbers and be ready to answer the following questions.

• **Who?** Name of injured climber and a telephone number where you can be contacted.

• **What?** Type of injury, how many people were hurt, how serious is the injury? Be as accurate as possible.

• **Where?** Name of crag, sub-sector, and route.

• **When?** Time of the accident.

EMERGENCY NUMBERS

Hospital: (+30) 22430 22166, 22430 23025

Police: (+30) 22430 22100

Universal Emergency Number: 112

In the image below, the Rescue Team transports a climber with a leg injury from the hard-to-approach sector Eros, in Telendos, in July 2015. The climber is expected to make a full recovery and be back on the rocks soon.

Always tie a knot in the end of your rope, no matter how long your rope is or how short the route is. Help prevent the most common climbing accidents on Kalymnos!

9 Grade conversion table

FRA	UIAA	USA	AUS	FRA	UIAA	USA	AUS
3a	III-	5.4	9	7a	VIII	5.11d	23
3b	III	5.5	11	7a+	VIII/VIII+	5.12a	24
3c	III+	5.6	12	7b	VIII+	5.12b	25
4a	IV-	5.6/7	13	7b+	IX-	5.12c	26
4b	IV	5.7	14	7c	IX	5.12d	27
4c	IV+	5.8	15	7c+	IX/IX+	5.13a	28
5a	V-/V	5.7/8	15/16	8a	IX+	5.13b	29
5b	V/V+	5.9	16	8a+	X-	5.13.c	30
5c	V+/VI	5.10a	17	8b	X	5.13d	31
6a	VI+	5.10a/b	18	8b+	X+	5.14a	32
6a+	VII-	5.10b	19/20	8c	XI-	5.14b	33
6b	VII	510.c	20	8c+	XI	5.14c	34
6b+	VII+	5.10d	21	9a	XI+	5.14d	35
6c	VII+/VIII-	5.11a	21/22	9a+	XII-	5.15a	36
6c+	VIII-	5.11b/c	22	9b	XII	5.15b	37
				9b+	XII+	5.15c	38

SAM BIÉ

01 STYX

26

37.049491
26.930720

GRADE RANGE	up to 5b+	5c to 6a+	6b to 7a	7a+ to 7c	7c+ and up
No. OF ROUTES	3	19	40	7	0

Labels on photo: OLIVE, FRANÇOIS GUILLOT, KREISSAAL, KASTRI, STYX MAIN, EMPORIOS PORTAL, SOPHIE, Emporios Village

Sector Styx is an enormous rocky crescent overlooking picturesque **Emporios**, the village at the end of the coastal road. This is the quietest, most peaceful part of the island. **Styx** has four sub-sectors: **Olive**, **Styx**, **François Guillot**, and **Emporios Portal**.

Climbing: On good but sharp grey walls. Several good mid-grade routes and relaxing surroundings.

Conditions: Warm and protected from the north wind. Best for cold days.

Kids: The approach is not easy, but there are some suitable areas near the cliffs.

Approach: From Masouri, drive to Emporios. Before the beach, turn right. You will see a large gate; park there (37.049491, 26.930720). Go through the gate and make sure you close it again. Walk about 100m until you see a concrete wall. Follow the uphill trail on the right with red marks. **Walking time**: 20 min.

MAX NANAO

Olive is situated above an abandoned animal pen with ancient olive trees.

Climbing: On the grey wall left of the cave. Some sharp but interesting routes. A big part of the cave with narrow tufa pipes is still undeveloped.

Conditions: Hot. Perfect for climbing on cold winter days.

Shade: Until 11.00. **Exposure**: SE

Approach: See left page. Then, when you reach sub-sector François Guillot, traverse left for 200m. Open the gate of the old pen, go through and close it again.
Walking time: 25 min.

1 Charly's Cat — 1★ 6a+ 25m
Needle climbing, runout finish. Same anchor as "Olive Tree". *C Brendel, 2013*

2 Olive Tree — 2★ 6a 25m
Another grey wall at the grade. *J Friedrich/G Hommel, 2009*

3 Meckerfritze — 1★ 6b 25m
Wall climb on sharp holds. *J Rohrmann, 2013*

4 SFH — 1★ 6b+ 26m
Interesting climb with small tufa at the end. Needs traffic. *J Rohrmann, 2013*

5 Kalite — 2★ 6c+ 32m
Quality climbing on sharp rock with the crux midway up the small roof. *L Salsotto, M Quaglia, A Langenbach, 2013*

6 Aquila — 2★ 6c 33m
Interesting climbing on holes. *L Salsotto, M Quaglia, A Langenbach, 2013*

7 Babele — 2★ 6c+ 34m
A sharp, fingery climb. *L Salsotto, M Quaglia, A Langenbach, 2013*

8 Oil — 2★ 7a+ 20m
Go up an excellent steep arête. *J Friedrich, G Hommel, 2009*

9 Crazy Dream — 1★ 5a 13m
A non-typical crumbly chimney. *J Friedrich, G Hommel, 2009*

10 Fix — 2★ 7b 18m
J Friedrich, G Hommel, 2015

11 Stamina — 2★ 6c 25m
Interesting, pocketed red rock. *G Hommel, J Friedrich, 2010*

OLIVE

01 STYX

MAIN

37.049491
26.930120

Styx Main is a long stretch of pocketed grey wall or slightly overhanging red rock. There are some long, more demanding climbs in the middle. **Styx Main** features two small sub-sectors: **Troll**, a short vertical wall with good mid-grade routes, and **Moirae**, a little cave to the right, with only three routes on good, unusual red rock.

Climbing: On vertical or slightly off-vertical grey slabs.

Shade: Until 11:00 (left) or 12:30 (right). **Exposure**: S

Approach: As on page 26. When you reach the cliff, traverse left for 100m. **Walking time**: 20-25 min.

1 Tönerner Krug 3★ 6a 22m
A photogenic edge on some jugs and flakes. *2008*

2 String Secret 2★ 6b 20m
Technical bridging on the obvious red corner.
B Girardin, C + Y Remy, 2009

3 Killbit 2★ 6c 20m
Athletic moves on jugs and a tufa. Shares second half with "String Secret". *B Girardin, C + Y Remy, 2009*

4 Praline 3★ 6b+ 15m
Excellent red rock, spaced red pockets and slots.
B + C Arnold, 2006

5 Zugabe 3★ 6b 15m
Interesting climbing on good holds. *B + C Arnold, 2006*

6 Golden Top 1★ 6a+ 22m
The wall with good holds. *B Girardin, C + Y Remy, 2009*

7 Litlost 1★ 6b 25m
Wall and overhang (with holds!); sharp rock.
B Girardin, C + Y Remy, 2009

8 Paulina 1★ 6c 20m
Wall, overhang, 2-mono crux and sharp rock. *2007*

9 Lene 1★ 6b 25m
Wall climbing on small holds.
C Heinicke, A + C Riemer, 2009

10 Johanna 1★ 6a 20m
More wall climbing. *2008*

11 Stachet Schwein 0★ 6a+ 20m
An uninspiring wall and slab. *2008*

12 Bunker 2★ 6a+ 25m
The wall, slab + juggy overhang. *B Girardin, C+Y Remy, 2009*

22 Innuendo 2★ 6c 25m
Wall and overhang with small tufas. *G Buchs, P Gobet, 2005*

23 Waiting for the Spring 2★ 6b 22m
The wall and overhang. *G Buchs, P Gobet, 2005*

24 Leningrad Cowboys go America 2★ 6b 22m
More wall climbing. *G Buchs, P Gobet, 2005*

25 For Kids 3★ 4a 20m
A very well-bolted mini-pillar. *2006*

26 Hades 1★ 6c 20m
A nice tufa start. *J Friedrich, G Hommel, 2009*

27 Medea 2★ 7b 15m
A bouldery start on tufa blobs then a tricky move. Don't touch the huge suspicious block above the anchor. *2007*

13 The Deal 3★ 6b+ 31m
Slab, wall, and small overhang. *B Girardin, C + Y Remy, 2009*

14 Team no Werk 2★ 6c 31m
Wall with sharp holds. Same lower-off as "The Deal". *B Girardin, C + Y Remy, 2009*

15 Nissim 3★ 6b+ 25m
Wall and overhang; gain the ledge at the bottom from the left. *B Girardin, C + Y Remy, 2009*

16 Nissim Ext. 2★ 6c 33m
Steep, well-bolted wall. *B Girardin, C + Y Remy, 2009*

17 Boleskine House 1★ 6b+ 28m
The wall with good holds. *B Girardin, C + Y Remy, 2009*

18 Boleskine House Ext 3★ 7a 36m
A sustained extension on an overhang and tufas. *B Girardin, C + Y Remy, 2009*

19 Zolotas 2★ 6b 28m
A nice but sharp wall climb. *B Girardin, C+Y Remy, 2009*

20 Zolotas Ext. 2★ 7a 36m
Steep climbing, good holds. *B Girardin, C+Y Remy, 2009*

21 Silbermond 1★ 6c 25m
Sharp with an athletic 2nd half. *F Heinicke, A Riemer, 2008*

Tiia Porri on the superb "Portokali Taxidi" 6c (next page).

01 STYX

MAIN (RIGHT)
FRANÇOIS GUILLOT

37.049491
26.930720

28 Kapilotracté — 2★ 6c+ 15m
Athletic moves lead to a fingery crux.
B Girardin, C + Y Remy, 2007

29 Dragoner — 3★ 6b 18m
Steep, pocketed, sustained. 2nd/3rd bolt are high. 2006

30 Pablo-Luca — 2★ 6a 18m
Wall with horizontal breaks; same anchor as "Dragoner".
B Girardin, C + Y Remy, 2007

31 Troll — 1★ 6a+ 15m
Not as good as you'd expect; just a grey, sharp wall. 2006

32 Portokali Taxidi — ♪ 6c 15m
Superb, sustained climbing on alluring orange rock.
B Girardin, C + Y Remy, 2007

33 Otavi — 2★ 6b 22m
A nice wall with some good but sharp holds. 2006

34 Poco Loco — 1★ 6a+ 15m
Wall climbing, sharp holds. B Girardin, C + Y Remy, 2007

35 Harmonie — 1★ 5c 18m
Spaced bolts at the start; good 2nd half on big jugs. 2007

36 Klotho (Do You Remember?) — 2★ 5c+ 18m
A fine grey and red wall leads to some broken rocks. 2007

37 Lachesis (Sixpack) — 3★ 5c 20m
A gentle, red, and fully-pocketed wall. 2007

38 Atropos (Keep on Smiling) — 2★ 6a 18m
The smooth red/black slab; go right on the final ramp. 2007

MAIN (RIGHT)

François Guillot is a sub-sector by Claude & Yves Remy. It was named to honor the mustachioed Frenchman who first put up routes at *Verdon*. Monsieur Guillot has been a longtime Kalymnos regular.

Climbing: Technical, on sharp grey or red rock, vertical or slightly overhanging walls, and a nice corner and chimney. Protected from the wind, so ideal for winter climbing.

☁ **Shade**: Until 12:30. **Exposure**: S

Approach: As on page 26. **Walking time**: 20 min.

1 Ziegenstall 2★ 7c 64m
A short multi-pitch (7a 12m, 7b 22m, 7c 20m). A stellar 1st pitch on small tufas leads to sharp grey rock. *2005*

2 Antonella 1★ 7b 40m
A hard crux at the overhang then wall. *C + Y Remy, 2006*

3 Coloria 1★ 6c 30m
Interesting lower part, then sharp wall. *C + Y Remy, 2002*

4 I Love Kalymnos 2★ 6b 30m
Varied wall with pockets and slots. *C + Y Remy, 2002*

5 Guillot Corner 3★ 5c+ 31m
A classic, excellent technical corner. *C + Y Remy, 2002*

6 Guillot Corner Ext 3★ 5c+ 50m
Also possible as one long, 50m pitch. *C + Y Remy, 2002*

7 Music of Rock 2★ 6b+ 25m
A technical wall with some tufas. *C+Y Remy, 2002*

8 Tiny Tina 3★ 6b+ 25m
Hard start, then slab and wall. *C + Y Remy, 2006*

9 Loutraki 2★ 6c+ 25m
A fingery wall leads to better red rock. *C + Y Remy, 2002*

10 Ivan is Grand 3★ 7a+ 25m
Tufa intro, a sharp then great blank wall. *C + Y Remy, 2006*

11 Warm Bier 2★ 7a+ 25m
A very thin red corner followed by a grey wall. *2006*

12 Select 1★ 6c 30m
A thin, sharp wall. *C + Y Remy, 2002*

13 Andros 1★ 6a 30m
Absorbing, if you like chimneys. If not... *C + Y Remy, 2002*

FRANÇOIS GUILLOT

01 STYX — EMPORIOS PORTAL

37.049491
26.930720

Emporios Portal. features a distinctive elongated cave. The quality of rock inside the cave is not good, but the limestone on the sides of the cave and the cliffs around it is of excellent quality.

Climbing: Technical, on unusual rock formations inside the cave and on its edge. Athletic on the short-but-steep red wall on the right.

Shade: Until 12:30. **Exposure**: S

Approach: As on page 26. When you reach the cliffs, traverse uphill and to the right for about 5 minutes.

Walking time: 25 min.

1. **Circus** — 2★ 7a+ 35m
   The rock inside this cave looks really broken, but surprise! It's...good. 17 QD. *C+Y Remy, 2011*

2. **Ingo** — 2★ 6b 25m
   A wall climb inside the cave. *C+Y Remy, 2011*

3. **No Exit** — 2★ 6a+ 45m
   Spectacular end in the grand dome, 15 QD. *C+Y Remy, 2011*

4. **Metro** — 2★ 6a+ 47m
   Wall inside the cave, with an out-of-this-world finale. 17 QD. *C+Y Remy, 2011*

5. **Olivenbaum** — 2★ 6b+ 25m
   A well-bolted route, but some loose rock at the start. *2009*

6. **Olivenbaum Ext.** — 3★ 6c+ 50m
   An impressive extension; can be climbed as one pitch with an 80m rope. *2009*

7. **Schnappi** — 2★ 5b 30m
   Interesting slab and corner. *F+C Heinicke, A+C Riemer 2009*

8. **Stadtaffe (Town Monkey)** — 2★ 7a 30m
   A steep pocketed wall leads to easier terrain.
   F + C Heinicke, A + C Riemer, 2009

EMPORIOS PORTAL

The new updated edition of **TERRAIN** map of Kalymnos, ideal supplement to this climbing guide

- All climbing crags, with their approaches
- Walking trails with distance indication
- Town plans of Masouri and Pothia
- The complete road network of the island
- All inhabited areas
- All sights (castles, monasteries, churches, archaeological sites, thermal springs etc)
- All beaches
- Printed in 100% waterproof and rip-proof Polyart material
- 100% field research, GIS cartography (WGS 84)

www.terrainmaps.gr

02 KASTRI

37.047559
26.934601

GRADE RANGE	up to 5b+	5c to 6a+	6b to 7a	7a+ to 7c	7c+ and up
No. OF ROUTES	4	30	11	4	0

A large limestone semicircle, sector Kastri comprises three sub-sectors: **Kreissaal**, **Kastri**, and **Sophie**. The crag is directly above the first houses of Emporios village. A special feature here is that the main crag is in the area around an ancient castle of the Hellenistic period. Sadly, until recently the hillside was used to house animal pens, with detrimental effects. Now the area has been enclosed to protect it. This ancient site is peaceful and charismatic; it is well worth the hike up to the small tower, whether or not you are a climber.

Please be respectful when visiting and climbing near this important archeological site.

Conditions: Sunny and warm. Ideal for climbing in winter, early spring and late autumn. Dries quickly after rainfall.

Kids: So-so. The last part of the path is hard, but there is some open terrain for playing near the ancient walls.

Approach: Drive towards Emporios village. Park at the left-hand turn just before reaching the village (37.047559, 26.934601). Go up a short dirt road and follow the red marks on the right side of the gully to the steeper hillside and an ancient wall. Scramble up the slippery last bit to the small castle.
Walking time: 20 min.

Nikolaos Smalios

KREISSAAL

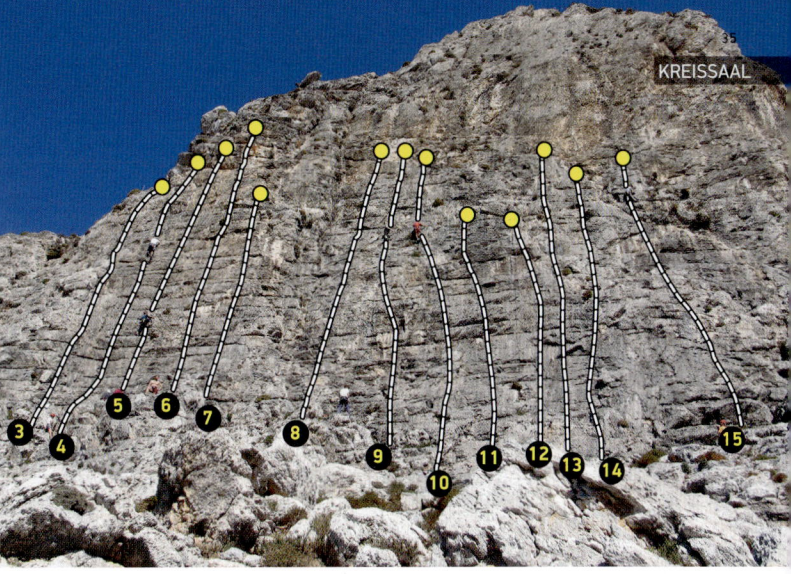

Kreissaal is above a slab of very sharp grey rock with horizontal ledges. It is protected from the wind and good for cold sunny days.

Climbing: Balancy on highly featured rock with sharp edges. Not recommended for inexperienced climbers; the rock is very sharp, so take care when climbing above a bolt. The first two routes are on a smaller face 30m to the left. (Another 5 min further left is sector **Styx**).

☁ **Shade:** Until 10.30. **Exposure:** S

Approach: As on left page, then continue left to the grey slabs further left of the big cave. **Walking time:** 20 min

1 In the Mood for Love 2★ 6b 18m
The neat pillar. *G Buchs, P Gobet, 2005*

2 Little Leo 2★ 5c 18m
A well-bolted wall with good holds. *G Buchs, P Gobet, 2005*

3 Lea 2★ 5a 27m
Long, sustained, good for the grade. *G Buchs, P Gobet, 2005*

4 Ovulation 2★ 5c 30m
Great *gouttes d'eau* and ledges. *M Schmed+Team, 1999*

5 Climax 2★ 6a 30m
Hard at the end, as you'd expect. *M Schmed+Team, 1999*

6 Embryo 2★ 6a 30m
A crucial reach for the lower-off. *M Schmed+Team, 1999*

7 Tamangur 1★ 5c+ 20m
On the crest of the buttress. *G Buchs, P Gobet, 2005*

8 Supernanny Ingrid 2★ 5c 30m
Nicely sustained with sharp holds. *G Buchs, P Gobet, 2005*

9 Bossa Nova 2★ 5c+ 30m
Again, beautifully sustained. *G Buchs, P Gobet, 2005*

10 Para Ti Ursula 2★ 5c+ 34m
Hard/reachy at the small overhang. *G Buchs, P Gobet, 2005*

11 Dzodzet Connection 2★ 5c+ 25m
Sharp rock, but nice climbing! *B Girardin, C+Y Remy, 2005/6*

12 Liloh 1★ 6a 20m
A powerful move at the small roof. *G Buchs, P Gobet, 2005*

13 Gastlosenlis 2★ 5c 35m
Mostly easy and steady. *B Girardin, C+Y Remy, 2005/6*

14 Jassou Stefanie 2★ 5c 25m
More pleasant as you go up. *G Buchs, P Gobet, 2005*

15 For Sue 1★ 5c+ 28m
Some good climbing; one hard move. *G Buchs, P Gobet, 2005*

02 KASTRI

KASTRI MAIN

37.047559
26.934601

The main section of sector **Kastri** is at the same level as **Kreissaal** but a bit further right (east) above a sheep pen. The ancient castle (*Kastri*) still standing there dates to the late 4th century BC. With its sturdy walls, *Kastri* was a safe retreat for the people of Emporios; there is also an ancient cistern and the heart-shaped limestone base of an olive press. To respect this ancient site, **no route names are written on the rock**.

Climbing: On slightly overhanging rock with big pockets behind the castle. On the right, long routes around two major corner features. Good for routes from 6a-7a+.

Shade: Until 12:00. Routes #4-#10 come into the shade again after 17:00. **Exposure:** S

Approach: As on page 34, until you reach the cliff. Then, enter the animal pen under the ancient wall and follow the carved steps to the castle tower.

Walking time: 20 min.

1 Kazonis 3★ 6a+ 15m
A bolted hand-crack to a roof. (*Kazonis* was a Kalymnian resistance fighter who soloed many of the cliffs during WWII; he was eventually shot.) C + S Luebben, 2004

2 Cook 1★ 5b+ 30m
Low-angle slab with big steps. J Friedrich, G Hommel, 2008

3 Cook Ext 2★ 5c+ 45m
The steeper extension. J Friedrich, G Hommel, 2008

4 Red Rooster 1★ 6a 25m
The slab and wall. J Friedrich, G Hommel, 2008

5 Fata 2★ 6a 25m
Slab then wall to a steep finale. B Girardin, C+Y Remy, 2007

6 Bibou 3★ 6a+ 25m
Well-bolted and thoroughly enjoyable as it steepens. B Girardin, C + Y Remy, 2007

7 Enchanted Castle 3★ 6b 25m
Steep, unusual climbing with big holes. C + S Luebben, 2004

8 Principessa Giulia ♪ 6c+ 25m
Superb, steep pocket-pulling with well-spaced pockets and slopers. A classic. C + S Luebben, 2004

DETAIL ON RIGHT PAGE

DETAIL 2-11

DETAIL 12-21

9 **Majestic** ♪ 7a+ 40m
Fantastic moves between good pockets and slopers on a leaning wall and overhang, starting where conglomerate meets limestone. *B Girardin, C + Y Remy, 2007*

10 **Tower Staircase** 1★ 5a 15m
Natural staircase up some dubious rock. *C+S Luebben, 2004*

11 **Dragon's Lair** 1★ 6c 22m
Sharp pockets and a steep finale. *C + S Luebben, 2004*

12 **Dark Corner** 1★ 6b 25m
The arête starts with a hard bulge.
J Friedrich, G Hommel, 2009

13 **Wasp** 2★ 5b 20m
Natural line, easy cracks. *J Friedrich, G Hommel, 2012*

14 **Game Over** 2★ 6b+ 40m
Athletic climbing up a steep wall with big holds. 17 QD.
F Heinicke, C + A Riemer, 2008

15 **X-Over** 3★ 6a+ 40m
The crag's obvious line. 17QD. *B Girardin, C + Y Remy, 2007*

16 **Haramiss** 2★ 6a+ 30m
Technical and well-protected. *B Girardin, C + Y Remy, 2007*

17 **Haramiss Ext.** 3★ 6c+ 55m
Great bridging and a tricky finale over the top bulge. Well-protected, 20 QD. *B Girardin, C + Y Remy, 2007*

18 **Side Cut** 3★ 6a+ 35m
A thin crack on perfect rock and an exposed pillar; well-protected. *B Girardin, C + Y Remy, 2007*

19 **Side Cut Ext.** 3★ 6c 45m
A demanding, well-bolted little overhang; 18 QD.
B Girardin, C + Y Remy, 2007

20 **Gotti** 3★ 7a 30m
Steep and fun, but pumpy and crazy. Lower-off up and to the right of the big bird's nest. *B + C Arnold, 2007*

21 **Borni** 2★ 7b+ 25m
An overhanging wall with a steep exit. *B + C Arnold, 2007*

02 KASTRI
37.047559
26.934601

SOPHIE

Sophie, a bit higher and further right from **Kastri**, is a grey/red wall with a distinctive corner/crack. Most routes are very sharp and their quality is far below Kalymnos standards. However, 2-3 good routes are worth the visit.

Climbing: Slab climbing on sharp, rough holds.

Shade: Until 11:00 **Exposure:** S

Approach: See page 34. After you reach the sheep pen, continue uphill and to the right following the blue marks for 5 minutes.

Walking time: 25 min.

1 Fahrenheit   2★   6a+ 20m
The interesting corner. *S Holzel, T Jaenichen, 2007*

2 Sigrid   0★   5c 20m
A sharp, unclean grey wall. *H Mothes, S Kerber, 2007*

3 Wolli   0★   5c+ 20m
A sharp thin crack and steep finish. *T + S Jaenichen, 2007*

4 Rasp   1★   6a+ 17m
A sharp wall climb. *J Friedrich, G Hommel, 2008*

5 Dario   1★   6c 20m
A sharp, pocketed wall. *V Serra di Migni, E Jimenez, 2006*

6 Bee   2★   6a 25m
A bouldery start leads to an excellent, juggy orange/white headwall. *J Friedrich, G Hommel, 2008*

7 Dolce Eugenia   2★   6a 25m
Varied, with an interesting ramp and final wall. *V Serra di Migni, E Jimenez, 2006*

8 Alessandro   2★   6a 30m
A classic corner climb; use the final flakes with care. *V Serra di Migni, E Jimenez, 2006*

9 Sophie   2★   6a+ 15m
A compact slab with good moves. *V Serra di Migni, 2004*

10 Fatolitis   0★   7b 25m
Very sharp crux; needs cleaning. *V Serra di Migni, 2005*

11 Maria Grazia   1★   6b 20m
Interesting traverse on a vertical wall. *V Serra di Migni, 2006*

12 Betty Bop   0★   6b+ 32m
A very sharp, intimidating wall. *V Serra di Migni, 2005*

Michel Scheirs on "Majestic" 7a+ (page 37), a route true to its name.

03 PALACE

37.043561
26.947709

GRADE RANGE	up to 5b+	5c to 6a+	6b to 7a	7a+ to 7c	7c+ and up
No. OF ROUTES	4	14	17	8	0

Simon Montmory on "Martina" 7b+ (page 43). CHRIS BOUKOROS

Palace is a long strip of cliffs which extends to include three sub-sectors: **Thalassa**, **Baby House**, and **Palace**, a distinctive rock arch that has been widely featured in climbing photographs.

Climbing: On everything from grey slabs to slightly overhanging climbing on unusual features.

Conditions: Very warm. Protected from the north wind, therefore ideal for climbing on cold winter days or on cloudy days.

Shade: Until 10:00-11:30. **Exposure:** SW

Kids: Very good. The approach is very short and easy, and there are several flat areas around.

Approach: From Masouri, drive towards Emporios. After Skalia village, turn right towards Palionisos. About 200m further is a rough dirt road. Park near it on the main road (37.043561, 26.947709). Walk up the dirt road for 100m until you see a big gate for the goats. Open the gate on the right, pass through, and close it again. Slightly further, the dirt road splits. **Palace** is to the right; **Baby House** and **Thalassa** straight ahead.

Walking time: 5-7 min.

PALACE
BABY HOUSE
THALASSA
PALACE SUB-SECTORS

Dani Belisha climbs "The Roof is on Fire" 7a (page 45).
NIKOLAOS SMALIOS

42

03 PALACE
37.043561
26.947709

THALASSA
BABY HOUSE (LEFT)

Thalassa has sharp grey/red rock with potential for more routes. The sun comes early, so cold days are best.

Climbing: Mostly face, on vertical-to-slightly overhanging red and grey walls.

Shade: Until 10:00 and in late afternoon.

Exposure: SE

Approach: As on previous page. Traverse past Palace and Baby House to the fence. Go through a gate 10m lower, then up along the fence. **Walking time:** 10 min

1 Zestama 2★ 5a 15m
The flake, sharp in parts. L Piguet, 2003

2 Perdica 2★ 6a+ 15m
A compact wall. L Piguet, 2003

3 Hi Goat 1★ 6c 18m
A good start then a sharp wall. J Friedrich, G Hommel, 2006

4 Thalassa 3★ 6c+ 30m
A good wall, but hard to onsight. L Piguet, 2003

5 Old Men 1★ 6b+ 18m
A natural corner with a runout, prickly finale.
J Friedrich, G Hommel, 2006

6 Aroma 2★ 7a 32m
Chimney and wall climb; the first part is 5a. L Piguet, 2003

7 Dysi 3★ 6a 25m
Technical with good holds and pumpy finish. L Piguet, 2003

8 Anatoli 2★ 6a 25m
Hard moves low down; bolts a bit spaced. L Piguet, 2003

9 Aramis 2★ 7a 20m
Compact wall, interesting finale. F Heinicke, A Riemer, 2005

10 Anemos 3★ 5c+ 22m
A good corner; not as easy at it looks! L Piguet, 2003

11 Universum 2★ 7b+ 23m
Wall, fine rib, overhang, wall. F Heinicke, A Riemer, 2010

THALASSA

Baby House is an attractive crag offering interesting climbing on red rock with big pockets.

Climbing: Mostly athletic routes on overhanging red rock. The routes on grey rock have some sharp holds. Additionally, there are two beautiful but painful cracks (rare on limestone), and a nice route along a big flake.

Shade: Until 11:30. **Exposure:** S

Approach: As on page 40. Then, with Palace on your right, continue along a level path for 50m.

Walking time: 5-6 min

1 Kartoffelacrep   1★   5b 10m
Beyond the fence, a short sharp line on conglomerate rock. 2009

2 Lampen Laden   1★   6a 12m
The well-bolted rib, bulge and slab. 2009

3 Leda   3★   7a 20m
A beautiful, athletic route.
H Bartu, A Odermatt, U Neu, A Neiger, 2001

4 Saia   3★   6b+ 20m
Unusual moves on good pockets. Try to bridge, especially near the top. M Zanolla, S Moro, 1999

5 Zocchi   3★   7b 25m
A fingery wall with crimpy finish. S Moro, B Zwerger, 2006

6 Ifaistos   1★   7a 25m
A distinctive but sharp line up the pillar. C + Y Remy, 2003

7 Totta   3★   7a+ 20m
Excellent, with a demanding and tricky final bulge.
M Zanolla, S Moro, 1999

8 Martina   3★   7b+ 20m
A pocketed red wall with long reaches and elegant moves.
M Zanolla, S Moro, 1999

9 Silvia (Melis)   1★   6b 25m
A "painful" crack, rare for Kalymnos. M Zanolla, S Moro 1999

10 Hello Baby YOYO   3★   5c+ 30m
Nice climbing up an impressive flake to a stunning finale!
M Schmed + Team, 2000

11 Misplaced Childhood   2★   7a 25m
Morpho and reachy with a lack of footholds.
P Stadie, S Rumpf, 2003

BABY HOUSE (LEFT)

03 PALACE

BABY HOUSE (MAIN) PALACE

37.043561
26.947709

12 Gickelhahn — 1★ 7a 12m
The wall, fingery and sharp. *M Creutz, 2004*

13 Stine — 1★ 6c 12m
A sharp, vertical slab. *M Creutz, 2004*

14 Hilde — 1★ 7a+ 12m
Fingery climbing on sharp grey rock. *F Heinicke, A Riemer, 2005*

15 Frieda — 1★ 6a 12m
Five meters are 6a; the finish is very easy. *M Creutz, 2004*

16 Estia — 3★ 6a 22m
An interesting corner leads to a steep wall with good holds. *C + Y Remy, 2003*

17 Dimitra — 3★ 6b 25m
Awkward start, then goes steeply right. *C + Y Remy, 2003*

18 Hermes — 1★ 7a 22m
A technical mid-section but poor finish. *C + Y Remy, 2003*

19 Pikata — 2★ 5c+ 18m
The compact wall with good holds. *C + Y Remy, 2003*

20 Phermos — 2★ 6a+ 18m
Interesting climbing up a small pillar. *C + Y Remy, 2003*

21 Andrea — 1★ 6a 6m
A bolted boulder problem. *J Mendez, D Kouros, 2001*

22 Axel — 1★ 6a+ 6m
A bit harder but similar to *Andrea*. *J Mendez, D Kouros, 2001*

BABY HOUSE (MAIN)

PALACE

Palace is a relatively small area with rock of average quality rock, but incredible—and widely photographed—rock formations. The first Kalymnos Guidebook (2000) featured the rock arch of **Palace** on its cover.

Climbing: On mostly overhanging rock with some tufa blobs and huecos.

Shade: Until 11:30. **Exposure:** S

1 Thermos 2★ 4c 15m
Easy, but don't go onto the ridge. Bad rock. *C+Y Remy, 2003*

2 Room 13 1★ 7b 18m
Expo start and hard exit at the roof. *M Schmed +Team, 1999*

3 Hammer 2★ 7b+ 18m
F + J Friedrich, 2015

4 The Roof is on Fire 2★ 7a 18m
Goes right at the overhang. Some hard clips; easier with quickdraws in place. *S Piskurek, M Wiesenforth, 1999*

5 Ballroom 2★ 5c 18m
A nice airy route, but hard to clip the anchor! *M Schmed+Team, 1999*

6 Mia's Place 3★ 6a+ 25m
Classic but greasy! Can you bridge? *M Schmed + Team, 1999*

7 King Suite 2★ 7a+ 25m
Bouldery start, then pocket-pulling. *M Schmed + Team 1999*

8 Balcony 3★ 6c 25m
A super technical crux low down. *M Schmed + Team, 1999*

9 Graue Hirsche 1★ 5a 20m
A grey slab 50m up and to the right of Balcony. *J Friedrich, G Hommel, 2006*

10 Green Boys 2★ 6b 30m
Interesting wall climbing. *J Friedrich, G Hommel, 2006*

JEAN-PIERRE TAUVRON

04 SIKATI CAVE

37.050397
26.952091

GRADE RANGE	up to 5b+	5c to 6a+	6b to 7a	7a+ to 7c	7c+ and up
No. OF ROUTES	2	3	5	12	10

THE BEACH

Sikati is a giant hole in the ground; a massive cave on the northeast side of Kalymnos with no roof, 50-60m in diameter, and up to 70m deep. With walls full of tufas and stalactites, the steep, overhanging limestone inside the cave is otherworldly, with mega-long routes and trademark Kalymnos "3D" climbing. The only drawback of **Sikati** is that, once inside, your only contact with the outside world is the sky above. You can't see the sea, and the air inside the cave can feel stuffy and claustrophobic. On a hot day, after climbing you can cool off at the gorgeous little beach below.

Climbing: In a three-dimensional forest of stalactites. The rock is extremely overhanging, which makes the climbing dynamic and pumpy. However, there is also a grey wall on the west-facing side of the cave with potential for new routes from 5c-6c.

Gear: A rope at least 80m long, especially for the extensions, and very long quickdraws to reduce rope drag.

Conditions: There is shade all day, but avoid **Sikati** on humid, still days. It can be unbearably hot. It is best to climb here on clear days with a northerly breeze.

Shade: Almost all day. East-facing routes (from "Por una Sociedad..." to "Kontrato") get sun early in the morning until 12:00. The easier routes (from "BMW" to "Abrazos") get some sun in the afternoon. **Exposure:** N

Kids: The approach is quite long, but if you bring the kids here and lower them into the cave with a rope, there are several flat areas. As always, make sure the kids are **far away from the climbers; never near or below them.**

Approach: From Masouri, drive to Skalia village. Turn right onto the uphill road to Palionisos. Drive to the top of the hill. From the col, continue downhill for another 300m to the first big 180° turn. Park there (37.050397, 26.952091). Go through the gate in the wire fence and traverse down and to the left. Continue traversing after the fence ends, until you reach two distinct boulders and an old ruin on the col. Go through one more gate after the ruin, and follow a path with red marks until the cave. Go down into the cave using the fixed rope.

Walking time: 30 min.

(Alternatively, if you are a large group you can have a boat take you to Sikati. Ask at Melitsahas, the jetty where you take the boats to Telendos, the day before. **Time:** 30-35 min on the boat + 8 min to walk.)

A note about goats: Goats come down to the cave because well-intentioned climbers feed them. Then, the goats get trapped inside the cave. No matter how many times climbers rescue them, the goats go straight back down to the cave. Rescue attempts are usually futile.

SIKATI CAVE

CAUTION: Never stand immediately under the routes. Stalactites can break when you climb.

When belaying, keep into the base of the crag with your back against the wall. It's safer and much more comfortable.

Adam Ondra flashes "Jaws" 8c (page 49) in 2009.
NIKOLAOS SMALIOS

04 SIKATI CAVE

37.050397
26.952091

ENTRANCE AREA
JAWS AREA

1 **BMW** — 2★ 6b 15m
A good orange wall climb.
A Theodoropoulos, A Kokkinos, N Iatropoulos, 2005

2 **B69** — 1★ 5b+ 15m
A distinctive slab.
A Theodoropoulos, A Kokkinos, N Iatropoulos, 2005

3 **Exit** — 2★ 4a 15m
The cave's entrance/exit, with a fixed rope. *2005*

4 **Abrazis** — 3★ 5c+ 20m
A well-bolted pocketed wall.
PETZL Team 2006: L Triay, G Fanguin, A Catzeflis

5 **Adini** — 3★ 5c 25m
The corner. Trad, not equipped yet. *2004*

6 **Abrazos** — 1★ 6c+ 20m
PETZL Team 2006

7 **El Choco Loco** — 2★ 6b+ 20m
Easy-looking but not obvious, pumpy climbing.
PETZL Team 2006

8 **El Chupodromo** — 2★ 6c+ 25m
Crimpy start, then a technical big tufa. *PETZL Team 2006*

9 **Les Pirates de Sikati** — 3★ 7a+ 30m
Well-bolted slabby climbing up the black streak.
PETZL Team 2004: L Triay, G Fanguin, A Cherbonnier, R Cabessut

ENTRANCE AREA

JAWS AREA

10 Les Pirates de Sikati Plus 3★ 8a 45m
Direct extension of "Les Pirates...". PETZL Team 2006

11 Des Dents de La Mer 3★ 7c 40m
Rightward extension of "Les Pirates...". 8b+ 55m if you use this as a finish for "Jaws". PETZL Team 2006

12 Jaws ♪ 8c 50m
The men's "ultimate route" in 2006's Roctrip. It has several cruxes: a bouldery lower section, a long hard move under the main roof, and a steep headwall with tufa blobs. Flashed by Adam Ondra in 2009. PETZL Team 2006

13 Mort aux Chèvres 3★ 7a+ 30m
A stellar, technical, pumpy tufa climb. PETZL Team 2006

14 Mort aux Chèvres Ext 3★ 8a+ 60m
The roof full of stalactites. PETZL Team 2006

15 Morgan 3★ 7b+ 25m
Very steep. An endurance tufa route. PETZL Team 2004

16 Adam 3★ 7c 32m
The short extension of "Morgan" is an awesome tufa orgy with a great finale. PETZL Team 2004

17 Morgan Adam est une Andalouse 3★ 8a 75m
The triple extension is a trip through the entire cave in a planet of tufas! To avoid rope drag: use a 2nd rope for the final pitch and leave the 1st rope clipped. PETZL Team 2004

18 Por Una Sociedad con Mujeres Satisfechas
  3★ 7c+ 30m
An amazing traverse through tufas then some hard moves and easier finale. Needs good conditions, as the rock is a bit brittle and dirty. PETZL Team 2004

19 Por Una Sociedad con ... Ext 1 ♪ 8b 60m
A super-overhanging climb that goes on forever through surreal tufas and stalactites. Routes 18/19 were the women's "ultimate route" in 2006's Roctrip. PETZL Team 2006

20 Por Una Sociedad con ... Ext 2 3★ 8b+ 75m
The full length of the line up to the top. Rope drag problems; better to use a 2nd rope for the final pitch. PETZL Team 2006

21 Les Arts du Vide ♪ 8b 40m
Crazy tufa action (a big single colonette) with a roofy crux. Onsighted by Dave Graham in 2006. PETZL Team 2006

04 SIKATI CAVE

50
37.050397
26.952091

RIGHT

22 Lolita — 3★ 7a 25m
A gem tufa-blob climb (but spaced bolts). *PETZL Team 2004*

23 Super Lolita — 3★ 7c+ 45m
A stellar route! Excellent rests but also a struggle against rope drag and a crimpy, pumpy finale. *PETZL Team 2004*

24 Kalyrock.com — 2★ 7c 70m
Multi-pitch (7a 26m, 7b+ 22m, 7c 22m). Enjoy the whole cave through overhangs and stalactites. Not possible in one pitch. *2006*

25 Little Bulbos — 3★ 7c+ 33m
Starts with strange moves then big pockets almost all the way. *PETZL Team 2006*

26 Armata Sikati — 3★ 7b 35m
Tufa blobs, pockets and organ pipes throughout. It doesn't get any better than this. **Attention**: Dangerous swing when you strip the quickdraws. Stay clipped into the first bolt and remove it from the ground. *PETZL Team 2006*

27 Armata Sikati Ext — 3★ 7b+ 50m
Still exceptional, but more complex. **Attention**: Dangerous swing when you strip the quickdraws. Stay clipped into the first bolt and remove it from the ground. *PETZL Team 2006*

28 Laurent...y'a Quelqe'un — 3★ 7c 38m
A mega-classic, with tufa and stalactite-riding and reachy cruxes. *PETZL Team 2004*

29 Où Est L'Équipe — 3★ 7b 25m
Very good climbing up the juggy tufa columns with a bouldery finale. *PETZL Team 2004*

30 Dropzone — 3★ 6c 25m
Technical start then nice tufa to a steep crux section on big jugs; cool exit on tufa blobs. *M Dettling, S Raab, 2012*

31 Happy Boyfriend — 2★ 6a+ 20m
Start on jugs, then move through the steep flowstone wall with pockets and slopers. *M Dettling, S Raab, 2012*

32 Body Buldeuse — 3★ 7b+ 20m
Wall climb with steep finish on big jugs. *PETZL Team 2006*

33 Kontrato — 2★ 7a+ 20m
The overhang with big jugs, but slippery and pumpy. *A Theodoropoulos, A Kokkinos, N Iatropoulos, 2005*

ARMATA AREA

Ruben Firnenburg on "Mort aux Chèvres Ext" 8a+ (page 49).
VISUALIMPACT.CH/RAINER EDER

05 THE BEACH

37.051539
26.957169

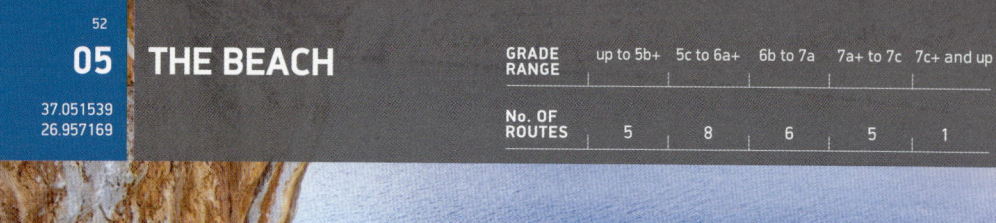

GRADE RANGE	up to 5b+	5c to 6a+	6b to 7a	7a+ to 7c	7c+ and up
No. OF ROUTES	5	8	6	5	1

Simon Montmory loves the jugs on "Elizabeth" 7a+ (page 54).
CHRIS BOUKOROS

The Beach is the only crag in Kalymnos next to a beach, hence the name. To be exact, it is to the right and slightly above a small, pretty beach on the island's north coast. It is ideal for swimming, snorkeling, and family picnics.

Climbing: On pleasant but rather sharp grey slabs on the left. On the right, athletic climbing on better, gently overhanging red, white and orange rock.

Conditions: Good for climbing on breezy summer afternoons.

Shade: After 13:00 and for the rest of the day.

Exposure: NE

Kids: Very good. Bring hats; the path is in the sun.

Approach: From Masouri, drive to Skalia village. Turn right onto the uphill road to Palionisos. Drive to the top of the hill and over the col at the top. Drive all the way down until you reach the lower col, which is at the last distinct right-hand turn in the road. Park off to the side of the bend (37.051539, 26.957169), and follow the clear path NW to the sea (Sikati Gulf). First, you will come to a big beach and a chapel to its right. (This unfortunate beach faces north, so it is full of trash washed ashore.) Continue walking to the left, along the beach, and about 5 min later you will come to a smaller, more sheltered beach. The crag sits just past some small stone structures built during WW2. **Walking time**: 20 min

See also: Crag Panorama on page 46.

1. 3 Generations 3★ 6a+ 18m
50m left of the main wall, behind the ruins. Juggy and overhanging. *T + S Jekel, M Hensel, 2014*

2. Pieks 1★ 6a 18m
Very sharp and not very special; trends left to the belay. *T + S Jekel, M Hensel, 2014*

3. Starfish 2★ 5a 22m
J Friedrich, G Hommel, 2013

4. Sailor 2★ 6a 23m
J Friedrich, G Hommel, 2013

5. Goat Memorial 2★ 5b 25m
The left-hand edge of the main wall. *T + S Jekel, 2011*

6. Sea Urchin 1★ 6a 20m
U + J Friedrich, G Hommel, A Lehmann, 2013

Eleni Basbanelou on "Rocco Family" 6c+ (page 54).
CHRIS BOUKOROS

FAR LEFT

ROUTES 7-21

05 THE BEACH — MAIN

54
37.051539
26.957169

7 Family Business — 2★ 5b 25m
A compact slab full of big pockets. *T + S Jekel, 2011*

8 Suite — 2★ 5c 30m
A good slab with some big holds, but hard to clip the belay. *Z Tibia, 2009*

9 Piero + Angela — 2★ 6a 30m
A fingery and technical slab. *Z Tibia, 2009*

10 Ciuccia Bau — 2★ 6b 30m
Technical wall climbing. *Z Tibia, 2009*

11 One Year — 2★ 6c+ 25m
Interesting bulging wall with a tricky sequence. *Z Tibia, 2009*

12 Rocco Family — 1★ 6c+ 24m
Some fingery climbing and a stiff red headwall. Tricky last move. *Z Tibia, 2009*

13 Apollo's Miracle — 3★ 7b+ 25m
A powerful subterranean start leads to an excellent huecoed red and white wall. *Z Tibia, 2010*

14 Elizabeth — 3★ 7b 25m
A stunning technical line on great rock. *Z Tibia, 2009*

15 Four Years — 3★ 7c+ 20m
A smooth overhang with *huecos* and some sharp broccoli holds. *2011*

16 Material Man — 3★ 7a+ 18m
A good slab leads to a tufa and tough bouldery finale. *Z Tibia, 2010*

17 Where Are My Bolts? — 2★ 6b+ 18m
A red wall with bouldery moves. *2012*

18 Levante — 2★ 6b 20m
A technical red wall with small holds. *2012*

19 Bronchitos — 1★ 6a 18m
Tricky, with some small holes and sharp crimps. Bolts are badly positioned in the middle section. *2013*

20 Sweet Remy — 1★ 5a 15m
A short, sharp slab climb. *2013*

21 Blue Lagoon — 2★ 5b 25m
Fine cracks, a left low-angle intersection and wall. *F + C Heinicke, A Riemer, I + S Heberstreit, 2012*

MAIN

Sofia Paraskevopoulou on 'Material Man' 7a+. CHRIS BOUKOROS

05 THE BEACH
FAR RIGHT

37.051539
26.957169

The **Far Right** wall is about 50 meters to the right of "Blue Lagoon", down a slope, behind a huge boulder.

Climbing: Technical and dynamic on tufa flakes, cracks and other unusual features on a small orange cliff with impressive features on flowstone. Only four routes are here at the moment, all excellent.

Shade: After 13:00. **Exposure**: NE

1 Tomboy 3★ 6c 25m
Brilliant flowstone with pockets, slots + mini-flakes. *2013*

2 Karpouzi ♪ 5c+ 20m
Amazing flowstone holds next to a large mountain-style flake. *2013*

3 Octopus Crack ♪ 7b+ 35m
A slightly overhanging crack system, unique for Kalymnos. You don't have to jam; it's all laybacking, bridging, and other fun octopus-style moves. *H Webhofer, E Ovchinnikova, 2014*

4 Flying Fish 3★ 7a+ 20m
Great overhanging moves over two roofs, some big jugs, and long reaches. *H Webhofer, 2014*

Ziwi Richter on the superb "Karpouzi" 5c+. Z. RICHTER ARCHIVE

FAR RIGHT

CRAG PANORAMA
Ghost Kitchen to Arginonta

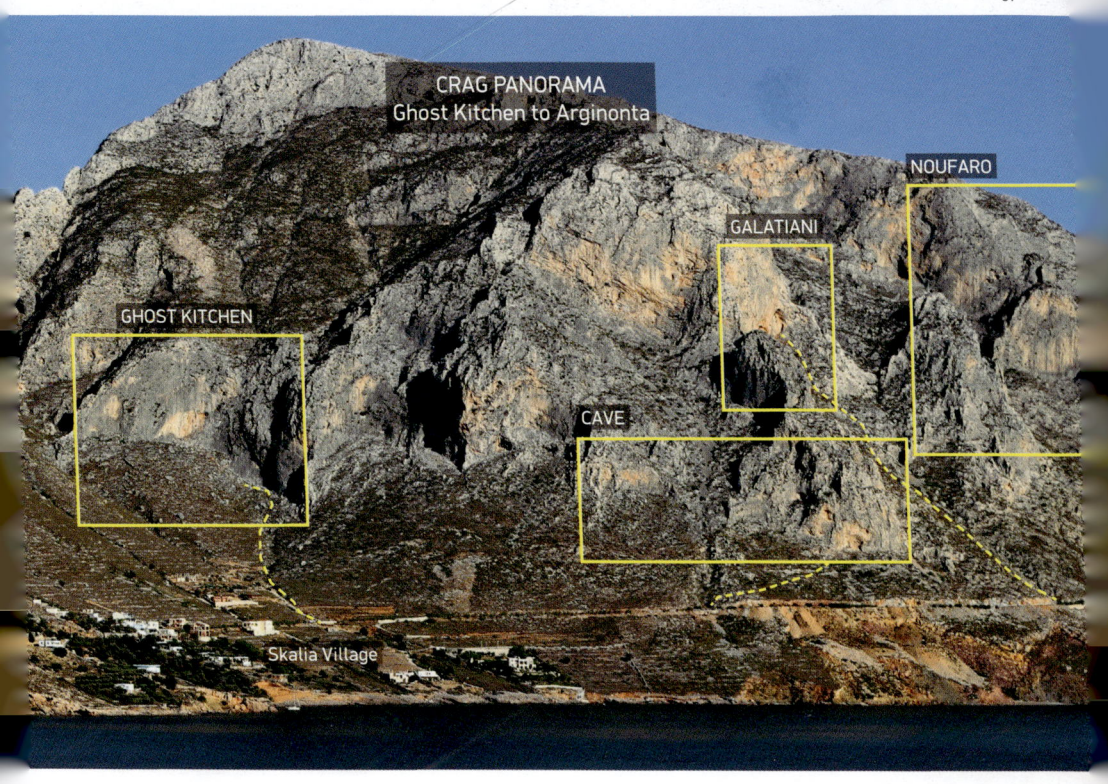

06 SECRET GARDEN

37.051531
26.957100

GRADE RANGE	up to 5b+	5c to 6a+	6b to 7a	7a+ to 7c	7c+ and up
No. OF ROUTES	0	3	18	16	11

The no-longer-secret Secret Garden is in a remote area on the north coast of the island; it is very close to the sea and it overlooks Leros Island as well as the smaller islets Pitta, Kalolimnos and Imia and, further back, the west coast of Turkey. **Secret Garden** is an important recent addition to Kalymnos climbing and it has already become one of the island's major crags—in fact, it could easily be called "Famous Garden"! It's a cross between sectors Odyssey and Ghost Kitchen, with stalactites growing out of the slightly overhanging red cliff face like wings and branches. And your day at **Secret Garden** doesn't have to end when you are done with climbing: head down to the beach at Palionisos (only 3 minutes by scooter) for a snack, drink, or a swim in the calmest, most beautiful emerald green waters on the island.

Climbing: Exceptional, with a variety of tufa jugs and single pipes and plenty of opportunities for knee bars and sit-down rests. Routes are very well-bolted and encouraging for onsight attempts. The existing routes have already been climbed quite a bit, so they are relatively free of sharp/loose bits. Still, don't stand, lay, or sleep (often done) below a person climbing. Pieces can still break off. Helmets are always a good idea.

Highly featured rock, tufa jugs, and plenty of sit-down rests. Route: "Frapogalo" 6c (page 63). SAM BIÉ

Conditions: Very cool. Ideal for climbing on hot days.

Shade: All day in fall and winter. Until about 18:00 in spring and summer. **Exposure**: N

Kids: Good, with a smooth path and flat terrain under the cliffs. That said, make sure the kids are **far from the climbers; never near or below them.** There are better spots for kids on the west side of the crag.

Approach: As for sectors **The Beach** and **Palionisos**, drive to Skalia village and turn right onto the road over the col to Palionisos. Drive past the parking spot for Sikati and continue down the winding road. Park where the paved road intersects a short dirt road on the left leading to a small clearing (37.051531, 26.957100). It's the same as for "The Beach". Walk down the dirt road to the clearing and continue NE to the col. The path is clearly visible and marked with cairns and blue paint. Go over the col, then down and rightwards into a small ravine. Don't worry if you can't see the cliffs yet. Keep following the blue paint around the hill and to the right. Once you go around the small escarpment on your right, the cliff reveals itself down to the right. **Walking time**: 20 min.

Left: Argryro Papathanasiou on "Savina" 7c+ (page 62). Chillin' on the ground directly below a climber is a terrible idea, Stalactites can break at any time. JOHN KOULLIAS

Below: The sun comes to the cliffs very late in the day. In the background Kalolimnos islet, and further back the Turkish coast.

06 SECRET GARDEN
LEFT

60
37.051531
26.957100

1 Parthenon 2★ 5c 25m
Delicate grey wall climbing, demanding for the grade.
A Theodoropoulos, L Salsotto, 2013

2 Pantremenos 3★ 5c 25m
A hard balancy start, then an easier juggy slab.
L Salsotto, A Theodoropoulos, 2013

3 Roofianos 2★ 6b 18m
A short roof. Look for big hidden holds and watch out for some loose rock. A Theodoropoulos, L Salsotto, 2013

4 Kalolimnos 3★ 6b 20m
A tricky intro then a technical steep groove.
A Theodoropoulos, L Salsotto, 2013

5 Nissos Pita 2★ 6b+ 25m
Good warm up with a strange start and an intense crux at mid-height. A Theodoropoulos, L Salsotto, 2013

6 Achinos 2★ 6a+ 25m
Technical and sustained wall climbing up small holds.
A Theodoropoulos, 2013

7 Ricci di Mare 2★ 6b+ 28m
Take care with the small juggy tufa, then go on to a couple of technical moves. L Salsotto, A Langenbach, 2012

8 Tzivaeri 2★ 7b 25m
A bouldery, bulgy start *and* finish.
A Theodoropoulos, G Kopalides, 2015

9 Baglamas — 3★ 7a+ 20m
A steep tufa start leads to a technical wall.
A Theodoropoulos, 2013

10 Sam Suffit — 2★ 7a 20m
A pocketed wall with some reachy moves and a crimpy finale. *C Idoux, 2010*

11 Markoutsi — 2★ 7b 25m
The wicked boulder problem with a thin pinch leads to a technical wall. *A Theodoropoulos, 2011*

12 Magioros — 3★ 6c+ 25m
A technical climb up a wall full of pockets and hidden holds. *A Theodoropoulos 2011*

13 Remetzo — 3★ 6c 20m
Steep and juggy with a reachy and technical second part. *A Theodoropoulos, G Kopalides, 2011*

14 Bratsera — 3★ 6c 20m
Very steep but with big holds. Think laterally at the distinct crux; it may help. *A Theodoropoulos, G Kopalides, 2011*

15 Margarita — 3★ 6c 20m
A steep tufa start leads to a corner, then again to a steep finale. *A Theodoropoulos, G Kopalides, 2011*

Left: Climbing late on a mellow spring day, one of the few times the sun briefly warms the cliffs at Secret Garden.

06 SECRET GARDEN
MIDDLE

37.051531
26.957100

16 Dirlanda   3★ 7b+ 25m
A gem! The steep and bouldery start on big tufas is followed by a technical wall. *S Montmory, A Theodoropoulos, 2010*

17 Syrtaki Lessons   3★ 7c+ 25m
A single-tufa testpiece, a good mix of power and technique. *A Theodoropoulos, S Montmory, 2010*

18 Savina   3★ 7c+ 25m
A wandering line through tufa territory, with a bouldery connection. *A Theodoropoulos, 2010*

19 Chien Jaune   3★ 7b+ 35m
A steep challenge with power moves up to the hole (fantastic kneebar). Then sustained and reachy climbing. *C Idoux, L Salsotto, 2010*

20 Full Job   3★ 8a 30m
Some pleasant tufa action leads to a testing bouldery wall at mid-height. *G Kopalides, 2015*

21 Half Job   2★ 7b 30m
Get high onto the tufa then make hard moves left. Mid-section almost common with "Pomponidoux". *L Halsey, 2011*

22 Pomponidoux   3★ 7a+ 30m
A leftward line of blobs leads easily to the 'bridge-tastic' tufa groove and a moment or two of excitement. The headwall is nice though easier. *F Poncet (Pompon), C Idoux, 2010*

23 Route 69   3★ 7b+ 30m
The lower wall of blobs leads to a wild, slappy sequence and a well-deserved rest. Don't underestimate the thin, off-balance finale. *F Poncet, C Idoux, 2010*

Kevin Huser taking "Syrtaki Lessons" (7c+).
VISUALIMPACT.CH/RAINER EDER

24 Melodrama   3★   **7a 25m**
Juggy tufa blobs lead to a demanding single-tufa finish, with a couple of hard clips. *A Theodoropoulos, 2011*

25 Frapogalo   3★   **6c 25m**
Steep on wild tufas and blobs. If you get to the large tufa, the rest is never hard. *A Theodoropoulos, S Montmory, 2010*

26 Ballos   2★   **7a 25m**
Dance, as the name suggests, on this tufa blob party! *A Theodoropoulos, S Montmory, 2010*

27 Adolflahaut   2★   **7a+ 25m**
One more route with jug-pulling on tufas, which gets trickier towards the top. *F Andolfatto, A Langenbach, C Idoux, 2010*

28 Ikariotikos   3★   **7a+ 25m**
Jug pulling on tufa blobs, but then? Tricky corner or thin tufa blade? It can go both ways. *A Theodoropoulos, 2011*

29 Ricounet   3★   **6c+ 25m**
Crazy action on the huge parallel tufa wings and curtain. Choices to confuse at the very top! *C Idoux, 2009*

30 Crisis   3★   **7a 25m**
Insanely technical, on the right of the big tufa blade. *A Theodoropoulos, 2011*

31 Princesse Marine   3★   **7c+ 25m**
A steady lower wall then a bouldery crux reaching (and leaving) the cracked overlap. *F Poncet, C Idoux, 2010*

32 L'Insoutenable Légèreté de L'Etre   2★   **7b+ 25m**
An intense middle section with tufa pinches. *F Musso, C Idoux, 2010*

06 SECRET GARDEN RIGHT

64
37.051531
26.957100

33 Tricky Katie   3★   7a+ 22m
An easy tufa intro leads to a slopery and balancy slab, which in turn leads to a tricky brown bulging wall.
A Theodoropoulos, 2013

34 Apocalypse   2★   7a 20m
A technical, bridgy and slabby climb with reachy pockets, crimps and smearing for the feet. *A Theodoropoulos, 2011*

35 The Floodgates Part 1   2★   6c+ 18m
A super-technical rightward traverse on a slab is followed by a smooth groove with nice flakes.
N Gresham, 2011

36 The Floodgates   3★   8a 40m
A steep and sustained climb with a devious finale.
N Gresham, 2011

Andrea Kümin on the powerful "Silence of the Abyss" 8a+.
RAINER EDER/VISUALIMPACT.CH

37 Stigma   3★   7b 20m
A crimpy crux leaving the tufa blobs to get established on the black streak. *A Theodoropoulos, N Hadjis 2011*

38 Khaos (Stigma Ext)   3★   8b+ 40m
A powerful and very steep line. FA: Alex Megos, 2013. *G Kopalides, A Theodoropoulos, 2013*

39 Bourré Mais Pas Pleine   3★   7b+ 35m
This route has it all: a baffling intro wall, slab, single black tufa, evil roof and final corner. *C Idoux, 2010*

40 The Silence of the Abyss   3★   8a+ 38m
A very technical slabby start for the first part; steep, powerful climbing on tufa features and pockets on the second part. *G Kopalides, A Theodoropoulos 2013*

41 Abyssos   3★   8b+ 38m
1st part is on the immaculate convex slab on tiny holds; shares 2nd part with "The Silence of the Abyss". FA: Alex Megos 2013. *G Kopalides, A Theodoropoulos 2013*

42 Puffa Puffa Puffa   2★   7b+ 30m
A short tufa entrance leads to a non-obvious compact wall, a resting slab and a powerful tufa finale. *R Russell, 2011*

43 Dogma   3★   7c+ 30m
A technical spartan wall with monos. Use the final thin tufa with care! *A Theodoropoulos, 2013*

44 Narcissus   3★   8a 30m
A stalactite, a challenging crimpy slab and a powerful finish. *A Theodoropoulos, 2013*

45 Kaly Diva   3★   7c 30m
A short "slopey" crux then steep endurance climbing on good pockets and tufa material. *A Theodoropoulos, 2013*

46 Play Buzuki   3★   8a 30m
Excellent, varied climbing on tufas and wall leads to a "shocking" final boulder problem. *A Theodoropoulos, 2013*

47 Mayumba   3★   7a 25m
A tricky entrance on the big tufa followed by an interesting pocketed wall. *C Idoux, L Salsotto, A Theodoropoulos 2010*

48 Mayumba Ext   1★   7c 30m
Sharp rock and bouldery moves. *C Idoux, L Salsotto 2010*

49 Hyper   2★   6c 12m
Short and powerful with good jugs. *L Salsotto, 2013*

50 Ymer   2★   6b+ 12m
A tough start, then tufas and good jugs all the way (if you can discover them). *A Theodoropoulos, 2011*

51 Extra Secret   2★   6c+ 15m
Short again and full of pockets, but not in the right order! *L Salsotto, 2013*

07 PALIONISOS

37.051531
26.957100

GRADE RANGE	up to 5b+	5c to 6a+	6b to 7a	7a+ to 7c	7c+ and up
No. OF ROUTES	6	21	23	4	0

Palionisos is a small hamlet with just a few houses around a gorgeous narrow bay on the island's northeast coast. A tarmac road goes almost all the way there, with only the last few meters down to the beach being a dirt road.

Climbing: The area features three small sunny crags with approximately 50 routes, most in the easy and mid-grades (from about 4 to 7b).

Conditions: All three sub-sectors are in the sun all day, so they are best for winter or cloudy days.

Kids: Good. Short paths and some suitable areas.

Approach: Palionisos is approximately 30 min by scooter from Masouri. Drive from Masouri going north to Skalia village. As Skalia ends, turn off sharply right onto an uphill winding road. Go up to the col and down to the other side. Check each crag's detailed approach.

Sabrina Bull on the bright red "Flipper" 7a (page 68). TOM ECKERT

The green/blue water, clean beach, and a handful of good *tavernas* make this a perfect after-climbing spot. NIKOLAOS SMALIOS

Palionisos Red Wall is a bright orange/red wall standing alone near the road (you can't miss it!). It was the first crag to be bolted in the Palionisos area.

Climbing: Technical wall climbing (mostly from 6a to 7a+) on mid-quality rock with sharp holds; some routes are on better red rock.

Shade: Until 10:00. **Exposure**: S

Approach: After the top col on the road to Palionisos, drive down the winding road to the lower col, before the last distinct right-hand turn to Palionisos. Park as for sectors The Beach and Secret Garden (37.051531, 26.957100). There is a small square structure with an antenna on the right, and on the left, a short dirt road leading to a small clearing. Walk down to the clearing, then traverse rightwards (SE) on a nearly flat path marked with cairns. **Walking time**: 12 min.

1 Laius   2★   6a+ 20m
The red/white wall with nice sidepulls + underclings. Spaced bolts above mid-height. *J Stringfellow, D Vose, 2012*

2 Max   2★   6c 28m
The white wall with small holds and good sidepulls. *K Batetzko, J Rohrmann, 2011*

3 Jocasta   3★   7a+ 30m
Athletic climb on steep red and white rock. *A Grondowski, J Stringfellow, D Vose, 2012*

4 Etsi kai Etsi   2★   6b 25m
The wall and some big pockets. #4, #5: *C + Y Remy, 2010*

5 Isos   2★   6c 25m
Interesting red/white wall, but a loose block left of the end.

6 Oedipus   1★   6b+ 30m
A demanding, steep finale. *J Stringfellow, D Vose, 2012*

7 Paola   1★   6b 30m
Sharp rock and bouldery moves. *C Idoux, L Salsotto 2010*

8 Ratgnagna   3★   6a+ 30m
Nice sustained climbing with a fingery section. *L Salsotto, C Idoux, 2010*

9 Louise Attack   2★   6b 30m
Pleasant, with a crimpy bulge. *C Idoux, N Gatti, 2013*

10 Hiro   2★   6b 30m
Engaging crack climb, but with a couple of spaced bolts. *L Salsotto, C Idoux, 2010*

07 PALIONISOS

37.051531
26.957100

PALIONISOS RED WALL
PARADISE BEACH

PALIONISOS RED WALL (RIGHT)

11 Tom Pouce — 2★ 6a+ 30m
Sharp wall with a couple of big sidepulls.
L Salsotto, C Idoux, 2010

12 Meister Proper — 2★ 6a+ 30m
A pleasant warm-up with an interesting finale.
L Salsotto, C Idoux, 2010

13 Angis Singing — 2★ 6b+ 26m
The wall with a pumpy finish. *J Rohrmann, 2011*

14 Ma Tante Daye — 3★ 6c 30m
An amazing climb on the smooth red rock; some spaced bolting on the first half, though. *L Salsotto, C Idoux, 2010*

15 Brad Spit — 2★ 7a+ 30m
One tricky section, hard to read, as it looks like it overlaps with the next climb. (It doesn't.) 3rd bolt is too high; danger for a ground fall. *L Salsotto, C Idoux, 2010*

16 Rhâ Ma Dent — 3★ 6c+ 30m
Nice climbing, though sharp at the end.
L Salsotto, C Idoux, 2010

17 Flipper — 3★ 7a 30m
An absorbing climb with two consecutive short crux sections, but with a good rest in-between.
L Salsotto, C Idoux, 2010

18 Os Court — 3★ 7a+ 30m
Some loose rock at the start, but impressive climbing all the way. Easier grade if you go from the right.
L Salsotto, C Idoux, 2010

19 Scorpion — 3★ 6c 30m
An unusual corner climb. *L Salsotto, C Idoux, 2010*

20 Kali Tyhi — 2★ 6c 30m
Fingery climbing on the compact wall. *C + Y Remy, 2010*

21 Come un Cane Senza Balle — 2★ 7a 30m
A thin wall climb, sharp in places.
L Salsotto, C Idoux, 2010

22 Kalo Mou — 1★ 6b+ 30m
The wall with conglomerate rock and some small pockets. *C + Y Remy, 2010*

Paradise Beach is a small brown/grey wall with 15 routes around 6a on relatively sharp rock, but a really good view over the bay.

Climbing: Pleasant, technical wall climbing.

☁ **Shade**: Until 10:00. **Exposure**: S

Approach: After the top col on the road to Palionisos, drive down the winding road all the way until it ends. Then, turn left onto the dirt road. Before the beach, turn left following the signs to *Taverna Ilias*. Park at the taverna's parking area at the end of the road (37.042419, 26.972539). Walk to the left along a well-trodden smooth goat path, then up to the cliffs through steeper terrain for the last 50m or so. **Walking time**: 10 min.

1 Pool — 2★ 5b 22m
Slab, short ledge and wall. *J Friedrich, 2014*

2 Canoe — 2★ 6a 25m
Wall with big holds, then a slab and two small bulges.
J Friedrich, 2014

3 Evagelia — 2★ 6a 20m
Slabby wall with a tricky finish to the right.
H Weninger, D Kaiser, 2013

4 Elena — 2★ 6a+ 20m
Grey wall with finish on compact red rock.
H Weninger, D Kaiser, 2013

5 Startschuss — 2★ 5c 20m
A nice weaving line.
F Seidenschwarz, H Weninger, A Hafner, 2013

6 Hanetti — 2★ 6a 20m
A pleasant route with a slab, bulge, and tricky finish.
J + H Weninger, 2014

7 Schwarte — 2★ 6a 20m
A wonderful slabby wall. *J + H Weninger, 2014*

8 Sharp — 1★ 6b 20m
Sharp holds; not easy to onsight. *J + H Weninger, 2014*

9 Hope — 2★ 6a 30m
A steady climb on brown pocketed rock, and a steep blocky-rock finale with big holds. *T Hoch, S Mühlbacher, 2013*

10 Ilias — 2★ 6b+ 27m
A steep brown wall with good holds and slots when needed. *T Hoch, S Mühlbacher, 2013*

11 Sorry — 2★ 6a+ 25m
A slabby climb on grey and brown rock.
H Weninger, D Kaiser, 2013

12 Kalidonis — 2★ 6a 25m
A grey slab with a harder, blocky finale.
J + U Friedrich, 2012

13 Pockets — 2★ 6a+ 25m
An easy grey slab leads to a pocketed red groove.
H Weninger, D Kaiser, 2013

14 Nikolas — 1★ 6a 23m
A grey slab with a ledge in the middle.
J Friedrich, G Hommel, 2011

15 Bay — 2★ 6a 20m
Slabby with a short, vertical finish.
J Friedrich, G Hommel, 2011

PARADISE BEACH

07 PALIONISOS

PALIONISOS BAY

37.051531
26.957100

Palionisos Bay is a red wall with big holes and a roof on the left, and quality grey slabs on the right. Here, too, the views over the sparkling bay are phenomenal.

Climbing: Varied, with some absorbing easy climbs from 5 to 6a/6a+ and a few interesting, well-featured routes from 6b+ to 7b.

Shade: Until 10:00. **Exposure**: S

Approach: As for Paradise Beach, turn left before the beach following the signs to *Taverna Ilias*. Park at the taverna's parking area at the end of the road (37.042419, 26.972539). From there, continue to the right along a fence following the blue dots. Then, scramble up the hill to the obvious crag with the orange roof. **Walking time**: 10 min.

See also: Crag Panorama on page 66.

Christine-Julia Remy on the wonderful "Iltis" 6a+. CLAUDE REMY

1. Sun 2★ 6a 25m
A grey pillar full of *gouttes*. J Friedrich G Hommel 2014

2. Jug Parade 3★ 5b 30m
Big holes and jugs; very unusual features for the grade.
C Schmidt, A Hafner + Drilling Gang, 2011

3. Teardrop 2★ 6c 30m
A compact technical wall, not easy to onsight.
T Hoch + Drilling Gang, 2011

4. Matze Alive 3★ 6c+ 21m
An easy start, then a bulge with good holds and a compact wall with blobs. A + J Rohrmann, 2011

5. Wiesel 3★ 6b+ 25m
Varied; one short hard passage. J Friedrich, G Hommel, 2011

6. Iltis ♪ 6a+ 25m
A natural line between the holes, with delicate climbing on various features. H Weninger, A Hafner, C Schmidt, 2010

7. Iltis Ext 1★ 7a 30m
Bridging at the roof, but a hard finale on scary rock. B + C Arnold, Drilling Gang (A Hafner H Weninger C Schmidt 2010

8. Baden Mit und Ohne 2★ 7a 30m
Broccoli wall with blobs, a final tufa, and bulge. Un-friendly bolting, though. B + C Arnold, Drilling Gang, 2010

9. Novembersonne 3★ 7b 30m
A fingery slab and final bulge. Needs traffic to clean the crumbly cauliflower rock. B + C Arnold, Drilling Gang, 2010

10. 67 3★ 6b+ 30m
Go straight at the black tufa holds and bridge to get into the corner. Routes 10-16: H Weninger, A Hafner, C Schmidt, 2010

11. Fingerpull 2★ 6a+ 30m
What the name says, at the top.

12. British Pubbull 2★ 5c+ 30m
Steepens above the hole. Pull your rope carefully so it doesn't get stuck.

13. No Spirit, No Station 2★ 5c 30m
A fingery wall climb; hardens as you go.

14. Corax 3★ 5b 30m
An easy route on good rock, but with spaced bolts.

15. Colchicum Autumnale 3★ 5a 30m
One delicate technical move.

16. TakTakTak 3★ 4b 30m
A nice easy climb.

17. Rocco 2★ 4c 25m
The juggy slab. A Hedgecock, 2013

PALIONISOS BAY

08 PROPHITIS ANDREAS

37.043448
26.952927

GRADE RANGE	up to 5b+	5c to 6a+	6b to 7a	7a+ to 7c	7c+ and up
No. OF ROUTES	20	14	18	7	2

Sabrina Bull on "Prophet Andreas" 7a (page 76), one of the sector's highlights. TOM ECKERT

Prophitis Andreas, a recent addition to Kalymnos climbing, is a large area filled with numerous long lines, very solid rock, ample variety in climbing styles, and a stunning location (at the top of the road leading to Palionisos) which gives it a bird's eye view of the sea, the islet of Calavros and a less "commonplace" view of Telendos from the north. **Prophitis Andreas** is already a big crag, but there is potential for more lines. A smaller sub-sector, **Elephant Slide**, features short routes on low-angle grey rock and lower grades.

Climbing: Varied, with some fantastic compact slabs up to 30-40m high in the middle of the crag. Routes are well-bolted and "user-friendly", though still somewhat sharp, but they are sure to improve over time.

Attention: For maximum enjoyment, bring an 80m rope and 21 QDs. (It is still possible to climb several routes with a 70m rope and 16 QDs, though.)

Don't forget the knot at the end of your rope!

Conditions: Warm. Best in the spring, fall and winter, as the cliffs stay rather dry even after heavy rain. Summer climbing is possible early in the morning on days with a soft northerly breeze. Not good on very windy days.

Shade: Until 12:00. **Exposure**: SW

Kids: Good. The approach is fairly easy and the terrain beneath the cliffs is relatively safe.

See also: Crag Panorama on page 81.

Approach: From Masouri, drive towards Emporios. Pass Skalia village, then turn right towards Palionisos. At the top of the road there is a chapel. Across the road from the chapel, on your right-hand side, there is a sign to the crag and a parking area. Park there (37.04348, 26.952927). To go to **Prophitis Andreas**, walk eastwards following the good trail marked in red. It passes to the left of the distinctive ridge overlooking Palionisos and the island of Leros then it goes up to the col, where an incredible southwesterly view of Telendos unfolds. To go to **Elephant Slide**, follow a goat path at the level of the parking area to a big hidden olive tree (400m), then walk up to the cliff.

Walking time: 15 min (Elephant Slide), 20 min (Prophitis Andreas).

Bettina Cantamessa on "Damocles is Watching You" 6a+ (page 77). LUCA SALSOTTO

08 PROPHITIS ANDREAS
ELEPHANT SLIDE

37.043448
26.952927

Elephant Slide is a newer sub-sector (2013/14) near the col on the road to Palionisos. The routes are not very long and the rock is not top-quality, but both the approach and the route grades are easy. Routes need further cleaning, so extra attention and helmets are recommended.

Climbing: On low-angle slabs and walls indicated for new climbers. All routes were equipped by Joachim Friedrich and Günter Hommel, unless otherwise noted.

Shade: In the morning and until about 12:00 noon, but the sun is never too far from the rock, so it may feel quite warm (though there is also a breeze most of the time).

Exposure: W, NE

Approach: See previous page. **Walking time**: 15 min.

Kalamies Beach, just before Emporios, is a popular place for climbers to chill out after climbing at crags around Skalia village.

ELEPHANT SLIDE

1 Herd — 0★ 4c 18m
Watch out for loose rock. *2014*

2 Ottifant — 1★ 5b 19m
2014

3 Dumbo — 2★ 5a 17m
Not so bad! *D Hommel, J Friedrich, 2014*

4 Elephant Slide — 2★ 4a 23m
An easy low-angle arête and groove; great value for the grade. *2013*

5 Mamut — 2★ 4c 23m
2013

6 Jumbo — 2★ 5a 15m
2013

7 Trunk — 2★ 5b 13m
A steady slab. *2013*

8 Safari — 1★ 5b 13m
A harder finish. *2013*

9 Thick Skin — 1★ 5a 14m
Gets harder at the top. *2013*

10 Dryness — 2★ 4c 15m
Pleasant and steady. *2013*

11 Stubborn — 2★ 4c 21m
Good holds all the way. *2013*

12 Wedel Ear — 1★ 6b 20m
A bouldery start, then easy. *2013*

13 Hip — 2★ 6a 20m
Again, harder at the beginning. *2013*

14 Backside — 1★ 5c 22m
An interesting bulge at the middle section, but needs more cleaning. *2013*

15 Tail — 1★ 5a 17m
Poor rock at some places. *2013*

16 Trumpet — 2★ 5a 20m
Good pockets until a short, steep finish. *2013*

17 Push Tooth — 2★ 4c 20m
A leaning slab leads to a steeper section with good pockets. *2013*

18 Ivory — 2★ 4a 21m
A steady low-angle slab. *2013*

19 Bumpkin — 2★ 5a 17m
Nice finale. *2014*

08 PROPHITIS ANDREAS
FAR LEFT
LEFT

37.043448
26.952927

FAR LEFT

The main cliff of **Prophitis Andreas** features a lot of variety in climbing styles and grades, though slab climbs are its forte.

☁ **Shade:** Until 12:00. **Exposure:** SW

Approach: See page 73. **Walking time:** 20 min.

1 No Credit   1★   5b 18m
A Langenbach, 2013

2 Cepasidur   2★   6b+ 18m
A Langenbach, 2013

3 Pax Alsaciana   1★   7b+ 15m
A steep and bouldery route on agressive rock.
A Langenbach, 2013

4 Kalidonis   ?★   ?? 18m
A Langenbach, 2013

5 Capogiro   ?★   ?? 20m
A Langenbach, L Salsotto, 2012

6 Gruviera   1★   7c+ 25m
A bouldery start then powerful climbing. *L Salsotto, 2012*

7 To Taksidi   1★   7c 20m
Painful pockets! *L Salsotto, 2012*

8 Torcicollo   1★   7c+ 27m
A steep start and sustained to the end. *L Salsotto, 2012*

9 Nemo Propheta in Patria   1★   7b 30m
Some painful holds to start, and many "razor blade" flakes in the upper slab. *L Salsotto, 2012*

10 Senza Sosta   1★   7b+ 30m
Like its neighbor, a powerful start but smaller pockets. *L Salsotto, 2012*

11 Calliopi   2★   7a+ 30m
A bouldery start, absorbing upper part. *L Salsotto, 2013*

12 Helleni   2★   7a+ 30m
The lower part is a little bit sharp and hard to read. Then, excellent technical climbing on water-worn rock with many small holds. *A Langenbach, 2012*

13 Prophet Andreas   ♪   7a 32m
Technical, well-protected face climbing on wonderful rock.
A Langenbach, 2012

14 Le Talent   3★   6c+ 38m
Vertical slab climbing with a crux that is harder for short climbers. *L Salsotto, 2012*

15 Pame Roger   3★   6b+ 28m
A steep slab and then you can choose: a dihedral or the left face on edges. Superb climbing. *R Runacher, 2012*

16 Pame Roger Ext   2★   6c 38m
Steady and sustained; will keep you on your toes! *L Salsotto 2012*

17 Pame Hilti   2★   7a 30m
Better than it looks, and quite different than other routes around it. *A Langenbach, R Runacher, 2013*

18 Bonjour Vieillesse   2★   6b+ 25m
Delicate at the middle, then pleasant and sustained. *L Salsotto, A Langenbach, 2012*

19 Damocles is Watching You   3★   6a+ 37m
Excellent face climbing on the best grey rock. *B Fara 2012*

20 L'Armée du Prophète   3★   6b 25m
The 1st pitch is on perfect grey rock. *B Fara, 2012*

21 L'Armée du Prophète Ext   2★   6b+ 37m
L Salsotto, 2012

22 Thavmasia   3★   5c+ 25m
A wonderful warm-up and friendly bolting. *B Fara, 2012*

23 The Lords   3★   6a+ 37m
A long slab full of hidden holds. 16 QD. *C Idoux, 2013*

24 Cima Piccola   3★   6a 37m
Pleasant slab climbing. *C Idoux, 2013*

25 Le Retour du Stratège   2★   6a 37m
Pleasant and varied with a nice bulge. *B Fara, 2013*

26 Tyche   3★   6a+ 37m
A steep start on good holds and an airy finish! *B Fara, 2013*

27 Philotimia   3★   6b 25m
A jug parade; a steep athletic start, then easier. *B Fara 2013*

28 Rien Dans la Tête   3★   7a 20m
A hard, bulging start, then easier. *L Salsotto, A Langenbach, 2013*

08 PROPHITIS ANDREAS
MIDDLE RIGHT

37.043448
26.952927

Andre Langenbach on wonderful "Thavmasia" 5c+ (page 77).
LUCA SALSOTTO

Federico Rollari on "Prophet Andreas" 7a (page 76).
UNKNOWN PHOTOGRAPHER

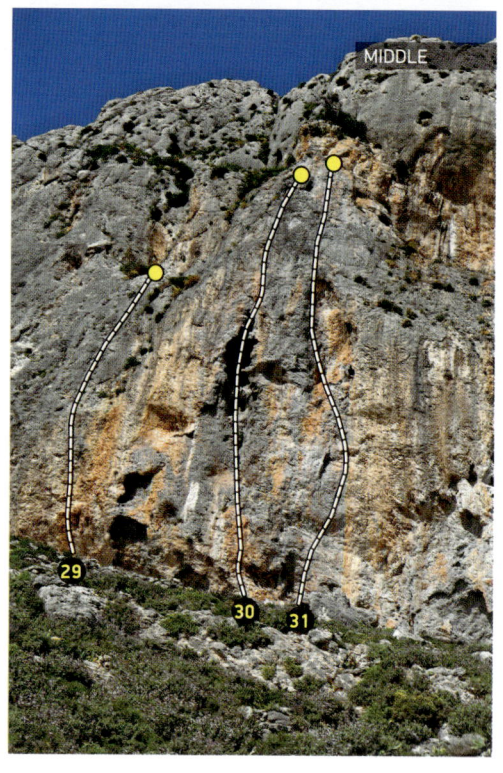

MIDDLE

29 Tsopanakos   2★   7a+ 30m
Again, a bouldery bulging start, then easier wall climbing to the lower-off. *A Langenbach, R Runacher, 2012*

30 Éphémère Éternité   2★   6c 36m
A chimney. Strange features and a great headwall.; 21 QD. Caution when removing the QD in the chimney. *B Fara, 2013*

31 Le Combat des Chefs   3★   7a 40m
A sustained 1st part then an amazing red wall. *C Idoux, 2013*

32 Alzheimer   3★   6b 38m
17 QD. *B Fara, R Guerin, 2016*

33 Libertad   3★   6a+ 38m
18 QD. *B Fara, 2015*

34 Save the Forest   2★   6b 38m
A slightly bulging wall with good holds followed by a pleasant slab. *L Salsotto, 2012*

35 Just Bolted   1★   6a+ 37m
Enjoyable climbing with a slab finish that makes you think. Easy sections not very densely bolted. *L Salsotto, 2012*

36 Pour Notre Ami Christian   1★   5c+ 35m
Some loose rock. Caution! *L Salsotto, A Langenbach, 2012*

37 Entre Nous   3★   5b+ 35m
B Fara, R Guerin, 2016

38 No Extension   2★   5b 35m
Varied climbing. 15 QD. *B Fara, 2014*

39 Serial Driller   3★   5c+ 35m
Pleasant, well-bolted climbing. *B Fara, 2014*

40 Lavraki   2★   5c+ 35m
B Fara, 2014

41 Y a de la Pomme   2★   6a+ 30m
The 1st part is nothing special, but then there is a nice corner with sharp rock. *A Langenbach, 2013*

42 Y a Autre Chose Roger   3★   6c 28m
An attractive red corner with an athletic start, then technical climbing and an intricate finale. Very dense bolting. *R Runacher, 2014*

43 Roger de L'Ill   3★   6c+
Multi-pitch (6c+ 35m, 6b+ 40m, 5c+ 25m). Climb the entire height of this face. To return, follow the red marks on the left. *R Runacher, L Salsotto, 2013*

09 SKALIA

80
37.040406
26.953834

GRADE RANGE	up to 5b+	5c to 6a+	6b to 7a	7a+ to 7c	7c+ and up
No. OF ROUTES	6	23	16	8	13

Skalia is a large area of cliffs overlooking Skalia village, with views of the sea and Telendos from an unusual angle, and sub-sectors **Skalia Pillar**, **Hotel California**, **Skalia Balcony**, and **Skalia Cave**.

Climbing: Varied. Everything from low-angle walls to steep overhangs, depending on the sector.

Conditions: Warm. Best for winter climbing or on cloudy days year-round. Protected from the north wind, but exposed to the rain. **Exposure**: S

Shade: Mostly in the morning. Check each subsector.

Kids: Relatively good.

Approach: Drive from Masouri going north to **Skalia** village. As Skalia ends, turn off sharply right onto an uphill winding road. About 1km further, on the left U-turn, there's a big gate and fencing. Park (37.040406, 26.953834). Pass the gate, and traverse to an olive tree. After the tree, go down and to the right; you will find a small gate to pass through the fence. Then, follow a slightly uphill (but poorly marked) path to Skalia Pillar, then the other sectors **Walking time**: 15-25 min.

Alternate approach: If there are lots of baby goats running around, shepherds may keep the gate shut. In that case, drive to Skalia village. Just before the village, there is a colorful house up to the right (approx. 50m past the Ghost Kitchen marker). Park (37.034481, 26.957254). Walk up the concrete road on the side of the house for 50m. Turn left, then right after the fence. The steep path goes up between two old olive trees following cairns. At the foot of the cliff, go left.
Walking time: 20 min.

PROPHITIS ANDREAS

SKALIA PILLAR

SKALIA BALCONY

HOTEL CALIFORNIA

SKALIA CAVE

SKALIA SUB-SECTORS

Skalia Cave was the competition crag during the 2013 TNF Festival. JOHN KOULLIAS

09 SKALIA

SKALIA PILLAR

37.040406
26.953834

Skalia Pillar is an impressive yellow pillar with some good routes and patches of sharp rock.

Climbing: On walls of varying angles.

Shade: Until 12:00 **Exposure:** S

Approach: See previous page.

Walking time: 15 min.

1 Koutouzis 2★ 6a+ 25m
The wall + corners. Named after a famous local artist. C + Y Remy, 2010

2 Koutouzis Ext 2★ 7a+ 35m
A bit exposed; same anchor as "Fakir". C + Y Remy, 2010

3 Fakir Plaisir 2★ 6c 35m
What a great name! And yes, it is sharp. C + Y Remy, 2010

4 Razor Edge 2★ 6b 33m
Fingery with razor-like holds. Who needs route descriptions with names like these? C + Ch + Y Remy, 2003/4

5 Sea, Sun + Pain 1★ 7b+ 33m
The wall has a hard start. C + Chr + Y Remy, 2003/4

6 Stone Dead for Ever 2★ 7b+ 35m
A fingery orange wall leads to a compact grey slab. C + Y Remy, 2010

7 The Orange Grove 3★ 7a+ 30m
An interesting fingery climb. J + H De Montjoye, 2003

8 Kaly Magic ♪ 7a 36m
Great climbing on a steep and compact orange wall. C + Y Remy, 2010

9 Kaly Minogue 3★ 6c 35m
A fingery slab and final bulge. Needs traffic to clean the crumbly cauliflower rock. C + Chr + Y Remy, 2003/4

10 Kaly Dream 3★ 6c 33m
A wall with sharp holds, but still interesting climbing with expo bolting. C + Chr + Y Remy, 2003/4

11 Kalytaly 2★ 6c 35m
More wall climbing. C Idoux, L Salsotto, 2009

12 Captain Koymantaros 2★ 6c 33m
A sustained wall climb. C + Ch + Y Remy, 2003/4

13 The Snow Must Go On 2★ 6b 35m
The pocketed wall, tricky near the top. C + Y Remy, 2010

14 Zymoto 2★ 6b 32m
A slab, wall, overhang and pockets. C + Chr + Y Remy, G Hatzismalis, 2010

SKALIA PILLAR

15 Big Merci — 2★ 6b 32m
A pocketed wall with lots of rest points and good onsight potential. C + Chr + Y Remy, 2003/4

16 Fegafjyva — 2★ 6a+ 25m
The wall and some good pockets. C + Y Remy, 2010

17 Fegafjyva Ext — 2★ 6c 30m
Small pockets and a short crux. C + Y Remy, 2010

18 Tealhamas — 2★ 6a 30m
A pleasantly sustained wall climb. C + Chr + Y Remy, 2003/4

19 Mamas Reporter — 2★ 5c 30m
Varied slab climbing, but watch out for the huge loose flake. C + Chr + Y Remy, 2003/4

20 Eat the Rich — 2★ 6a+ 22m
A demanding headwall; easier from the right. B Girardin, C + Y Remy, 2008

21 7c+ — 2★ 5c+ 22m
Steep wall, good holds, and a fingery crux. B Girardin, C + Y Remy, 2008

22 Tandori Love — 2★ 6a+ 20m
The wall with some "spicy" conglomerate. C + Y Remy, 2010

23 Callas — 1★ 6a+ 20m
More wall climbing. C + Y Remy, 2010

24 Video Clip — 2★ 5c+ 20m
A one-move wonder. C + Y Remy, 2003/4

25 Run Around Spits — 1★ 5c+ 20m
The corner, then an interesting conglomerate exit. C + Y Remy, 2010

26 Egeo TV — 2★ 5c 20m
A steep juggy start leads to a delicate traverse on the slab. C + Chr + Y Remy, 2003/4

09 SKALIA

84

37.040406
26.953834

HOTEL CALIFORNIA
SKALIA BALCONY

Hotel California is a short cliff made up of compact grey slabs. Most routes were bolted in 2010 but are still likely to improve with some traffic.

Climbing: Slabby climbing, not always homogeneous.

Conditions: Warm. Good for winter or cloudy days.

Shade: Until 11:00 (left) or 12:00 (right). **Exposure**: S

Kids: So-so. There are a few decent areas at the base of the routes.

Approach: From Masouri, drive to Skalia village. Just before the village, there is a colorful house up to the right (approx. 50m past the Ghost Kitchen marker). Park (37.034481, 26.957254). Walk up the concrete road on the side of the house for 50m. Turn left and again right after the fence. The steep path goes up between two old olive trees following cairns. At the foot of the cliff, go left. **Walking time**: 20 min.

Alternatively, go to Skalia Pillar until you pass the fence. Past the distinctive gully, follow the cairns to traverse the hill. Pass Skalia Pillar and another small gully, and follow the cairns up to the crag (25 min).

1 Eagle — 2★ 5b 24m
J Friedrich, G Hommel, 2013

2 Noserl — 2★ 5a 25m
Needs traffic; not bad, though. S + T Jekel, 2011

3 Morro — 2★ 5b 25m
Starts poorly but improves as you go. S + T Jekel, 2011

4 Spooky — 0★ 4c 22m
Needs cleaning. S + T Jekel, R Blaser, M Blattmann, 2010

5 Jim — 2★ 5c 22m
Nice rock up a clean pillar.
S+T Jekel, R Blaser, M Blattmann 2010

6 Stately Pleasure Dome — 1★ 5c 22m
Nice; stay to the left. S+T Jekel, R Blaser, M Blattmann 2010

7 Love and Haight — 1★ 6a+ 22m
A tricky start (some bolts stick a long way out) then easier.
S+ T Jekel, R Blaser, M Blattmann, 2010

8 Quarter Dome — 1★ 5b 25m
S + T Jekel, R Blaser, M Blattmann, 2010

9 Tuolumne Knobs — 1★ 5a 25m
S + T Jekel, R Blaser, M Blattmann, 2010

10 Les Blablas — 1★ 6a 20m
#10, #11: S + T Jekel, R Blaser, M Blattmann, 2010

11 Moitié-Moitié — 1★ 5c+ 20m

Skalia Balcony is a vertical grey wall with long routes rising over a natural balcony with sweeping views.

Climbing: Well-cleaned, very long mid-grade routes (6a-6c+) on generally good grey limestone, though there are short sections of crumbly conglomerate on some routes. All routes are by Claude Idoux, 2012/13.

Conditions: Warm. Good on sunny winter days or on cloudy days year-round.

Kids: No. The balcony is narrow.

Shade: Until 11:00. **Exposure**: SE

Approach: As for Hotel California (left page). At the foot of the cliff, go further left. **Walking time**: 22 min.

Alternatively, from sector Ghost Kitchen traverse left for 10 min. (Total walking time: 30 min.)

1 L'Abri-Côtine — 3★ 6c+ 40m
A long, thin wall. 20 QD.

2 La P'tite Arvine — 3★ 6c 40m
Good slab climbing. 18 QD.

3 La Moussa Kaka — 2★ 6c+ 40m
A fine slab but with a crumbly mid-section. 18 QD.

4 La Fêta Pipi — 2★ 6b 34m
Compelling and homogeneous.

5 Double Salchow — 2★ 6c 40m
Long and interesting. 16 QD.

6 1512 — 2★ 6a 30m
A pocketed wall with a steep finale.

7 Haute Pierre — 2★ 6a+ 34m
Similar to its neighbors.

8 Gelleretlli — 2★ 6a 24m
Nice steady climbing; no real crux, but far from monotonous.

9 Singha — 2★ 6a 30m
Long and pleasant, with two short bulges.

10 Chang — 2★ 6a 26m
Starts steeply, then becomes easier.

11 Leo — 2★ 6a 26m
Pleasant, with good holds on the two short bulges.

12 Kô-Tao — 2★ 6a 25m
Good climbing on the slab and orange groove further up.

13 Lune de Miel — 2★ 6b+ 38m
A good pocketed wall leads to an interesting traverse. Use 20 long QD to avoid rope drag.

09 SKALIA
SKALIA CAVE

37.040406
26.953834

Skalia Cave was established as the *PRO Competition* crag for the 2013 festival by The North Face. It is a pretty, featured semi-circle, with sections of both excellent rock and bad, crumbly rock. Only the sections of good rock have been bolted, though the bolting is often not "Kalymnos-style". For the record, the 2013 competition winners were Alexander Megos and Caroline Ciavaldini.

Climbing: Athletic, cruxy and bouldery. These hard overhanging testpiece routes were bolted by TNF athletes Jacopo Larcher, Hansjörg Auer, Iker Pou and Siebe Van Hee.

Conditions: Good for spring and autumn climbing.

Shade: In the morning on the right (until 13:00); in late afternoon on the left. **Exposure**: S, W

Kids: Not good. There are scrambling bits along the path and the terrain beneath the cliffs is steep.

Approach: As for Hotel California (previous page). Go up the steep path between the two old olive trees, and follow the cairns all the way up. **Walking time**: 20 min.

Alternatively, from sector Ghost Kitchen (page 88) traverse left for 10 min. (Total walking time: 30 min.)

1 The Fridge — 1★ 7b+ 18m
2013

2 The Oven — 1★ 7b+ 18m
2013

3 Sweet Balls — 3★ 8b 40m
Beautiful endurance climb with a crimpy mid-section. Women's competition route in 2013, but unclimbed. *2013*

4 Indar Gorri — 2★ 7c+ 40m
A hard section over the lip of the roof and single tufa. *2013*

5 Shoot — 2★ 7c 12m
Bouldery; sharp holds, but compelling nevertheless. *2013*

6 Don't Call Me Greasy — 3★ 8b 12m
A bouldery start, a nice toehook, then a big jump. *2013*

7 Don't Cry 'Til it's Over — 2★ 7c+ 14m
A short bouldery wall. *2013*

8 The Hesitaters — 2★ 7c+ 25m
A wall with a nice finish on well-spaced jugs. *2013*

9 Klesha — 3★ 8c+ 35m
FA Alexander Megos, Oct 2013. *2013*

10 Match Point — 3★ 8b 33m
A hard one-finger pocket at mid-height. *2013*

11 The Alchemist — 2★ 7b+ 33m
A very powerful bouldery move, then very sustained. *2013*

12 Do First, Talk Later — 2★ 7b+ 33m
2013

SKALIA CAVE

Ruben Firnenburg is on "Skin on my Left" 8a.
RAINER EDER/VISUALIMPACT.CH

13 Skin On my Left 2★ 8a 40m
2013

14 The Unexpected Journey 2★ 8a 38m
A hard wall with a steep tufa finale. 2013

15 Don't Touch My Balls 2★ 8b 35m
2013

16 KFC 2★ 7c+ 35m
2013

17 Le Jeu des Perles de Verre 2★ 7c+ 35m
2013

18 Banana Party ♪ 8a+ 35m
Being a competition route, it gets harder and harder. 2013

10 GHOST KITCHEN

37.033891
26.957804

GRADE RANGE	up to 5b+	5c to 6a+	6b to 7a	7a+ to 7c	7c+ and up
No. OF ROUTES	2	18	33	8	1

Ghost Kitchen is a major crag. With a dominant, massive roofed dome full of stalactites growing outwards like the limbs of a limestone tree, this is a hugely popular sector. On both sides of the roof are medium-difficulty walls, while the pleasant grey slabs on the lower right offer splendid technical and friction climbing. So far there is only one multi-pitch route, "Rigani", using the full height of the cliff to go all the way up.

Climbing: On slightly overhanging tufa-madness routes, immaculate vertical walls, and delicate slabs, all of exquisite quality and aesthetic value. The only drawback at this crag is the absence of hard routes (above 7b+), though there is still potential for new harder routes and challenging extensions to existing lines.

An unknown climber climbs "Remember Wadi Rum" 6c (page 93). GORDON JENKIN

LEFT WALL

5c

MAIN WALL

6c

5c+

RIGHT SLAB

LOWER RIGHT WALL

23

Conditions: Good for year-round climbing. Protected from the north wind.

Shade: Until 13:30-16:00 depending on the route.

Exposure: S, W

Kids: OK, with a good approach and some suitable areas.

Approach: From Masouri, drive towards Emporios. Approx. 2.3km km past Arginonta village (100m before Skalia village), there is a white marker reading *Seaside Kitchen**. Park there (37.033891, 26.957804) and walk up the concrete road for 100m. Then, follow the path and the red marks. **Walking time**: 20 min.

See also: Crag Panorama on page 57.

*Kaspar Ochsner, who bolted the first route here in 1999, named the crag **Ghost Kitchen**. Shortly after, from a free translation of the name into Greek by this writer, the crag's name was re-translated to English on the municipal marker as "Seaside Kitchen", causing much confusion. The proper name, of course, is **Ghost Kitchen** and shall be changed if new crag markers are installed in the future.

Little David is fearless on "Absent Friends" 6a (page 91).

10 GHOST KITCHEN
LEFT WALL

37.033891
26.957804

Left Wall is a fully-pocketed wall offering some very good technical climbing on top-quality rock.

Climbing: Technical wall climbing with grades between 5c-7a.

Shade: Until 13:30. **Exposure:** SW

Approach: As on previous page, then walk to the left of the crag. **Walking time:** 20 min.

1 Hour of Ghosts   2★ 6a 25m
The slab with a stiff headwall. *J Friedrich, G Hommel, 2006*

2 Exotic Ambeli   3★ 6a 25m
A leaning slab full of pockets. *C Idoux, 2010*

3 Route 66   3★ 6a+ 25m
A good, pocketed wall. *C Idoux, 2010*

4 Pirates of Kalymnos   3★ 6b+ 25m
A steep start leads to a very technical upper part. *C Idoux, 2010*

5 N7   3★ 7a 26m
Classic old-school grey wall climbing: steep, sustained, and interesting throughout. *C Idoux, 2010*

6 Haunted Castle   1★ 7a+ 26m
A very good wall then a small sharp bulge. *J Friedrich, G Hommel, 2006*

7 Le Type de la Taverne   1★ 6c 20m
Not homogeneous; one bouldery move. *C Idoux, 2010*

8 Le Type de la Taverne Ext   2★ 7a 35m
Technical and fingery. *C Idoux, 2010*

9 Le Mythe de la Caverne   2★ 6c+ 30m
A tricky sequence of pockets over the bulge. *J-N + I Bourgeois, 2009*

10 Resista   3★ 6c 35m
A superb red/grey wall. A committing route, despite incredible pockets and great moves. *B Girardin, C + Y Remy, 2006*

11 Globus 3★ 6c+ 35m
Excellent balancy moves on a red huecoed wall; a technical crux, then fun, steep pockets. *B Girardin, C + Y Remy, 2006*

12 Joy in the Garden 3★ 6a+ 25m
A beautiful, classic slab and wall climb. Very well-bolted. *H Bartu, A Odermatt, U Neu, A Neiger, 2001*

13 Absent Friends 2★ 6a 25m
A good warm-up. Climb the wall keeping left of the upper corner. *D Musgrove, K Morgan, D Campbell, 2007*

14 Sea Side 3★ 5c 25m
Another good warm-up full of pockets. *C Idoux, 2011*

15 Weissmatten 3★ 5c 25m
Again, a pocket parade; harder if you go straight up. *C Idoux, 2011*

16 5 Ans Après 2★ 5c 25m
Good rock; short but worthwhile. *J-N Bourgeois, 2014*

17 Bali Balo 2★ 5b+ 18m
A squeezed line. *J-N Bourgeois, 2014*

18 Taverna Psirri 3★ 6b 27m
A steep, compact slab with a conglomerate section at the top. You can trust it. *C Idoux, 2008*

19 Pic Pic 3★ 6b 30m
A delicate wall climb; thin, sustained and beautiful. *C Idoux, 2008*

20 Baldwin 2★ 6b 30m
A good wall with some fingery moves but sharp holds. *F Heinicke, C + A Riemer, 2008*

21 Olympiakos for Elias 3★ 6b+ 33m
A well-bolted long pitch with no easy sections. *B Fara, R Guerin, 2008*

22 Rombo di Tuono 2★ 7a 37m
Technique and balance up the steep wall. *L Salsotto, P Bertotto, 2014*

23 Rigani 2★ 6c 90m
Multi-pitch (5c+, 6c, 5c) and rather run-out. The 1st pitch is a steady diagonal traverse to the right. *G Albert, 2001*

24 Thribi 2★ 6c 20m
Single tufa then wall with not-obvious holds. *G Albert, 2001*

No holds? No problem! Just do as Kirsten Hollander does on "Parasitos" 6a+ (page 94) and yank the next person's quickdraw. SCOTT HOLLANDER

10 GHOST KITCHEN
MAIN WALL

37.033891
26.957804

Aris Theodoropoulos tries "Ghost Rider" 7b+. SAM BIÉ

The **Main Wall** of **Ghost Kitchen** is also its main attraction: a giant bowl of magic 3-D tufa mushrooms for thoroughly enjoyable full-body contact climbing.

Climbing: On outstanding tufas up a gently overhanging wall. Most grades are between 6c-7a, plus a few 7b-7b+.

Shade: Until 13:30. **Exposure:** S

Approach: See page 89. **Walking time:** 20 min.

1 Talon 1★ 6a 15m
Up the white slab. *B Girardin, C + Y Remy, 2006*

2 Achilles 1★ 5c+ 15m
A sharp slab with a delicate, exposed finale.
H Bartu, A Odermatt, U Neu, A Neiger, 2001

3 Achilles Ext 3★ 7a+ 35m
Swarm up the tufa jugs to a very technical transition onto the final wall. Hard for the short and rope drag problems.
B Girardin, C + Y Remy, 2006

4 Durgol 3★ 7b 35m
The wall and overhang with a pumpy, demanding finish.
B Girardin, C + Y Remy, 2006

5 Sisyphus Junior 3★ 7a+ 25m
A super wall with small tufas and very technical moves. Hard for the grade.
H Bartu, A Odermatt, U Neu, A Neiger, 2001

6 Sisyphus Junior Ext 2★ 7b 30m
A powerful bulge on small pockets. Not easy to onsight.
K + R Ochsner, F Meier, 1999

7 Ghost Rider 3★ 7b+ 40m
A single tufa leads to tufa wings and a demanding, thin final wall. *A Theodoropoulos, S Montmory, 2010*

MAIN WALL

8 Totenhansel   3★   6c+ 25m
Very sustained tufa pinching on the first half; then, easier with good rests on stalactites. Superb.
K + R Ochsner, F Meier, 1999

9 Remember Wadi Rum   3★   6c 25m
Fun to straddle the single tufa, but easier if you think laterally. *H Bartu, A Odermatt, U Neu, A Neiger, 2001*

10 Dafni   3★   6c+ 30m
Full-body contact climbing on huge tufa mushrooms.
G Albert, O Didon, L Catsoyannis, P Pezzini, 2001

11 Dafni Ext   2★   8c? 37m
A hard extension. Open project. *N Gresham, 2010*

12 Fantasma   3★   7b+ 30m
Pumpy tufas, a fingery crux and a reachy final clip.
A Theodoropoulos, S Montmory, 2010

13 Elia   2★   7b 30m
A very bouldery crux on a sloper and thin holds. If successful, enjoy the fabulous tufas all the way to the chain.
G Albert, O Didon, L Catsoyannis, P Pezzini, 2001

14 Thimari   3★   7a 30m
Up a crack between tufas to more tufas, then jugs. Go for the onsight! *G Albert, O Didon, L Catsoyannis, P Pezzini 2001*

15 Ioli   3★   7a 30m
Tufa climbing with underclings and pockets. The final overhang is like the cherry on top. *B Girardin, C + Y Remy, 2006*

16 Axium   3★   6c+ 30m
Otherworldly Kalymnos-style tufa mushrooms. Strip the QDs by top-roping the route, otherwise you risk breaking the tufa saddle. *B Girardin, C + Y Remy, 2006*

17 Delta   2★   6a+ 25m
The slab with tufa blobs at the entrance of the cave. A distinct crux (sandbag!) *B Girardin, C + Y Remy, 2006*

18 Kalyminette   2★   6c 40m
The slabby lower wall rises to a tremendous finale. Take care with the rock and the bolting in the lower half.
C + Y Remy, 2010

10 GHOST KITCHEN

94
37.033891
26.957804

RIGHT SLAB
LOWER RIGHT WALL

The **Right Slab** offers excellent technical climbing between 5a-6b+ on very compact rock.

Climbing: Good footwork and smearing are necessary.

Shade: Until 16:00. **Exposure:** W

Approach: As on page 89. Then, aim for the slabs to the right of the main cliff. **Walking time:** 16 min.

1 Tchao Regina — 2★ 6b 36m
A grey slab leads to a technical wall on soft tufa material. *B Fara, R Guerin, 2011*

2 Au Revoir — 0★ 6a 35m
A runout pillar with sharp holds, trad feeling, and some big suspicious blocks. *A Vizeli, R Hammann, 2009*

3 Casimir — 1★ 5a 20m
A leaning slab climb. *N Szawrowski, 2012*

4 Myrthe — 2★ 6a 22m
More good slab climbing. *J + F + U Friedrich, 2004*

5 Parasitos — 3★ 6a+ 18m
Friendly bolting on a technical friction slab. *P Muller, A Bader, 2003*

6 Zyklop — 3★ 6a+ 25m
An archetypal slab, but stiff for the grade. *HP Bartens, K Hildenbrand, 1999*

7 Persephone — 3★ 6b 28m
A good slab with delicate moves at the bulge. *P Muller, A Bader, 2003*

8 Lothar — 3★ 6b+ 25m
In memory of Lothar Hanl. Some bolts are poorly positioned. *J Friedrich, G Hommel, 2005*

9 Serena — 3★ 6b+ 25m
An easy slab then a pocketed overhang with tufas. Short + sweet on good holds. *B Girardin, C + Y Remy, 2006*

10 2046 — 3★ 6c+ 20m
An unusual technical exercise; brilliant wall climbing. *U Rutsch, G Buchs, 2006*

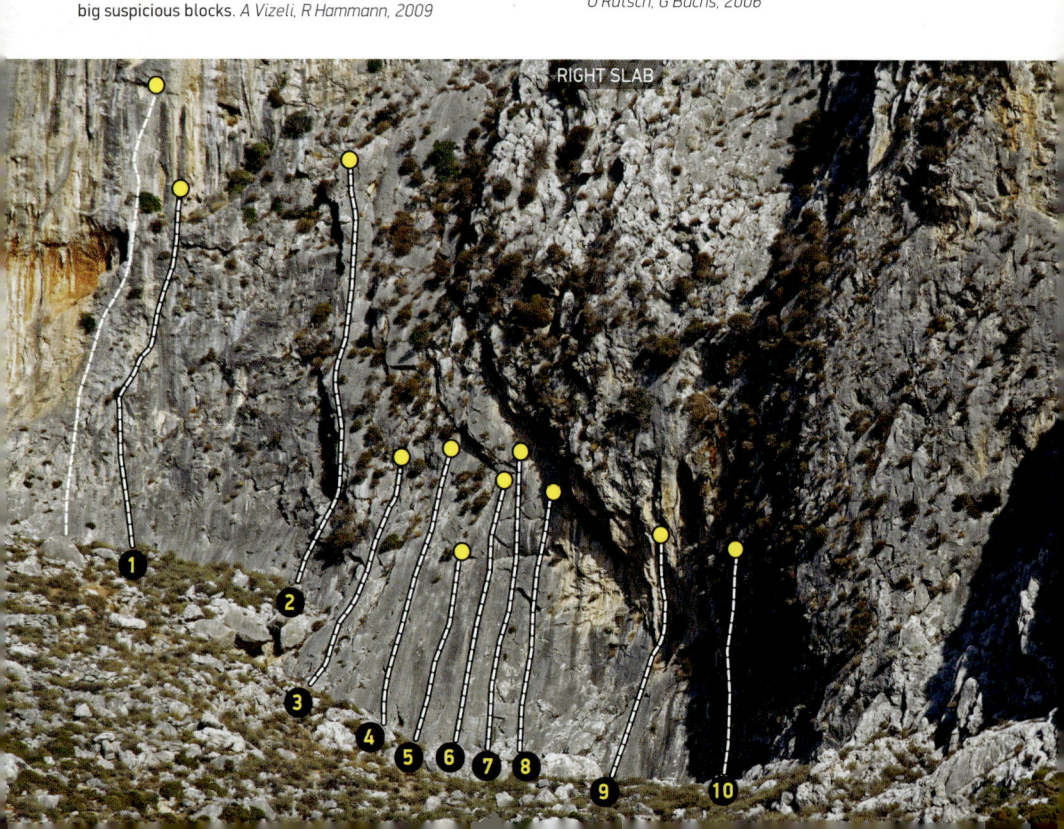

RIGHT SLAB

LOWER RIGHT WALL

The **Lower Right Wall** used to be full of vegetation, but it has now been cleaned to add some long mountain-style routes from 6a-7a.

Climbing: Technical and generally well-bolted, but it sometimes feels exposed.

☁ **Shade:** Until 16:00. **Exposure:** W

Approach: As on page 89. The first wall on the right as you go up the path. **Walking time:** 15 min.

1 Tahar ta Gueule   2★   7a 35m
Unusual style on this thought-provoking wall.
L Salsotto, C Idoux, 2011

2 Hara Kiri   2★   6c+ 40m
Homogeneous, but a bit expo. L Salsotto, C Idoux, 2011

3 7 à c   2★   6c+ 35m
A steep start then a technical wall. L Salsotto, C Idoux, 2011

4 A.C. D'Essais   3★   6c 35m
A thin, tough mid-section and sustained finale.
Not very encouraging bolting. C Idoux, 2011

5 Pourquoi Paniquer?   3★   6c+ 40m
Sustained climbing with small pockets up a hectic wall; but, don't panic! C Idoux, 2011

6 L'Ange et le Bac   2★   6c 40m
A tricky wall leads to a pleasant slab with a "spicy" finish.
C Idoux, 2011

7 Zyva   3★   6b 40m
A compact slab with good but spaced pockets. C Idoux, 2011

8 Oh My Gosh!   3★   6a+ 37m
Escalating difficulties, spaced bolts and balancy moves just before the anchor. C Idoux, 2011

9 Sacray's/Price   2★   6a 32m
Compact slab climbing; discouraging bolting. C Idoux, 2011

10 Witch   1★   6a+ 33m
A pleasant slab climb. J Friedrich, G Hommel, 2012

11 CAVE

37.031134
26.957429

GRADE RANGE	up to 5b+	5c to 6a+	6b to 7a	7a+ to 7c	7c+ and up
No. OF ROUTES	6	9	10	5	2

NIKOLAOS SMALIOS

Sector Cave, a distinctive small cave slotted with big pockets, features vertical walls with easier routes on each side. Furthermore, it is very close to the road, so it is a perfect choice if you don't feel like walking!

On the left side of the main cave is the entrance to **Underworld**, a deep and interesting cave pictured above and decorated with stalactites, with an iron gate across its entrance. Two ladders lead down into the deeper recesses of the cave.

ATTENTION: If you want to go down into **Underworld**, make sure you are not alone. There must be at least two people with two headlamps at all times.

Climbing: Hard sport climbing; overhanging routes on tufa blobs and big pockets in the steep main area. Interesting, though sharp, grey slabs on the right.

Conditions: Warm and protected from the north wind, but not from the rain. Climbing the central hard routes on humid days is not recommended.

Shade: Until 14:00 inside the cave. A bit earlier outside the cave.

Exposure: S

Kids: The approach is short and easy. The area around the cliffs is OK but not the best. Don't allow kids to play below the grey rock on the right, as loose rock may fall.

Approach: From Masouri, drive towards Arginonta and then continue towards Emporios. Park 2 km past Arginonta village, and 300m after the white marker to sector Galatiani. (37.031134, 26.957429). There is another white marker here for sector Cave on a gentle turn over a small bridge. Follow the cairns up a good path to the cave. **Walking time:** 8 min.

See also: Crag Panorama on page 57.

CAVE SUB-SECTORS

FAR LEFT WALL

UPPER CAVE

MAIN CAVE

Underworld Entrance

FAR LEFT WALL

The **Far Left Wall** is a short, sharp vertical wall.

Climbing: On a vertical or slightly overhanging wall with small holds.

Shade: Until 12:30. **Exposure:** S

Approach: Walk up to the crag, then continue left without an established path for another 7-8 minutes.
Walking time: 15 min.

1 Rifugio Bozano   2★   7b+ 20m
Hard and painful! *L Salsotto, M Quaglia, 2013*

2 BOH (Unfinished)   ?★   ?   20m
L Salsotto, M Quaglia, 2013

3 Buon Giorno   3★   6c 20m
Nice climbing on small tufas and sharp water pockets.
L Salsotto, M Quaglia, 2013

11 CAVE
UPPER CAVE

98
37.031134
26.957429

Upper Cave is a low vertical wall above a small natural balcony.

Climbing: Mostly vertical wall climbing.

Shade: Until 12:30. **Exposure:** S

Approach: Walk up to the crag (previous page) then continue left following the marks for another 4 minutes. A bit of scrambling is required.
Walking time: 12 min.

1 Playground 1★ 6b 16m
J Friedrich, G Hommel, 2010

2 Slide 1★ 4a 21m
J Friedrich, G Hommel, 2010

3 Zicke 1★ 6b+ 18m
The technical wall with a hard start and bulging finish.
G Hommel., J + F Friedrich, 2005

4 Olympics 776 BC 2★ 6b 18m
A good pocketed wall with a challenging move at the top. S + J Welich, 2004

5 Olympics 2004 3★ 7a+ 20m
An amazing wall climb with a tricky, technical finale.
S + J Welich, 2004

6 Red Monkey 2★ 7a 15m
A reachy start leads to climbing on pumpy, sharp pockets. G Hommel, J + F Friedrich, 2005

7 White Snake 2★ 6a+ 15m
Move left on the slab, be careful! A cruxy mid-section.
S + J Welich, 2004

8 White Mouse 1★ 6a+ 18m
S + J Welich, 2004

9 Grey Chilli 1★ 5c+ 18m
The wall with spaced but good pockets. S + J Welich, 2004

10 Thyme Honey 1★ 5c 18m
Rather inconsistent. Uneventful climbing if you stay right, but very hard if you go straight up. S + J Welich, 2004

Christine Remy on the pocketed wall of "Olympics 776 BC" 6b. CLAUDE REMY

11 CAVE
MAIN CAVE

100
37.031134
26.957429

Main Cave features hard sport climbing in the middle and some easier, sharp slabs on the right.

Climbing: On overhanging terrain with tufa blobs and big pockets, and on sharp grey slabs.

Shade: Until 14:00 or a bit sooner. **Exposure:** S

1 Sam 2★ 6c 25m
The wall with a steep and juggy finale. The bolts are a bit spaced at the start. *B Girardin, C + Y Remy, 2007*

2 Legolas 2★ 5c 18m
Skin-biting, persistent, and feels much longer than it actually is. *S + J Welich, 2004*

3 Aragorn 2★ 5b 22m
A corner, flake and crimpy wall.
A Hedgecock, D Selwyn, M Reed, 2013

4 Pony Luz 2★ 4b 15m
From the left it is 4b; from the right of the bolts, following the pillar, it is 5b. *S + J Welich, 2004*

5 84 3★ 5b+ 25m
A well-protected steep juggy wall, impressive for the grade. Marcel Remy did the FA when he was 84 years old, hence the name. *B Girardin, C + Y Remy, 2007*

6 Dios 2★ 6b+ 25m
A technical wall climb, not very typical for Kalymnos.
B Girardin, C + Y Remy, 2007

7 Saroman 2★ 7a+ 25m
A strenuous, bouldery start. *S + J Welich, 2004*

8 Eirini 1★ 7c+ 25m
With a bouldery crux at the exit over the lip. *1998*

9 Anthi 3★ 7c 20m
Huge holes and a looooong reach.
1998

10 Florianopoulos   3★   7c+ 20m
This excellent tufa line is powerful but does not rely on pinch-power alone. The angle eases at mid-height, but still. *F Hass, 2001*

11 Sascha on the Road   3★   7b 20m
Lean across onto the tufa and go on to a "wobbly" moment. Polished and stiff for the grade. *F Hass, 2001*

12 Golden Eye   2★   5c 18m
An easy slab and a tricky wall lead into the cave.
J Friedrich, G Hommel, 2010

13 Zizanie   3★   6b+ 33m
Good holds following the red, white and blue hangers.
C Idoux, 2013

14 Orea   3★   6b 25m
A steep slab leading to a demanding sequence.
H Weninger + Friends, 2002

15 Titine   3★   6b 35m
A nice technical corner. *B Girardin, C + Y Remy, 2007*

16 Mathitis   1★   5b 22m
Start on the block. Your first piece of protection is an hourglass hole in the rock, and the finale is tricky, too.
H Weninger + Friends, 2002

17 Sto Kalo   1★   5b 18m
Pleasant scrambling. *H Weninger + Friends, 2002*

18 Cat Walk   2★   6a+ 18m
A delicate groove with pleasant technical moves.
G Hommel, J Friedrich, 2010

19 Phidias   1★   5c 18m
A fill-in slab with good holds all the way. *L Thielmann, 2001*

20 Sleepwalker   1★   6a 25m
A tricky bulge at the start. Loose feeling.
J Friedrich, G Hommel, 2010

12 GALATIANI

37.028176
26.958038

GRADE RANGE	up to 5b+	5c to 6a+	6b to 7a	7a+ to 7c	7c+ and up
No. OF ROUTES	8	6	16	9	5

Galatiani is a massive rock face high above the road, with a substantial cave to its right. It is still under-appreciated (probably because of the long path) but it has the potential to become one of the island's most important crags. The excellent rock is packed with features, amazing routes, and more room for single- and multi-pitch lines. Two smaller sub-sectors, **Black Forest** and the brand-new **Reservoir Dogs**, are to the lower right and left, respectively.

Climbing: On top-quality tufas and stalactites.

Conditions: Warm. Protected from the north wind and the rain. Good for winter.

Kids: No. The approach is long and there is always the risk of stalactites breaking.

Shade: Until 12:30-13:00. **Exposure**: S

Approach: From Masouri, drive towards Emporios. Approx. 1.7km past Arginonta village, park on a distinctive turn over a bridge with a white marker for sectors Galatiani and Black Forest (37.028176, 26.958038). Walk steeply uphill on the left side of the streambed, following the waymarks. **Walking time**: 30 min.

See also: Crag Panorama on page 57.

Jean-Philippe Brisson on "Gegoune" 7c (page 105). E. SARACCO

① **Bella**   2★   4b+ 25m
K + R + M Ochsner, 2003

② **Veros**   2★   4a 20m
K + R + M Ochsner, 2003

③ **Sunrider**   2★   6b+ 33m
Long and sharp; quite tricky. *K + R + M Ochsner, 2003*

④ **Crispy**   3★   6c+ 35m
Wall climbing. *B Girardin, C + Y Remy, 2006*

⑤ **Lustzapfen**   2★   7a 30m
Will improve with more traffic. *K + R + M Ochsner, 2003*

⑥ **Wendenexpress**   3★   7a 135m
Multi-pitch (6c+ 35m, 7a 30m, 6a 20m, 6c 30m, 6a 20m). 6b+ obligatory. 2x50m ropes recommended. Abseil from the same route with 5 rappels; possible with a single 80m rope too. A demanding route with an alpine feel; bolting is not Kalymnos-style. *K Ochsner, F Meier, D Croth, 2002*

⑦ **Grip**   3★   7b 35m
An excellent, varied route with pockets and tufas. *B Girardin, C + Y Remy, 2006*

LEFT

12 GALATIANI
CALCITE CAVE

104
37.028176
26.958038

François Legrand on "Calcite Star" 7b.

Aris Theodoropoulos on "Calcite Star Plus" 7b+. N. SMALIOS

Calcite Cave is a fantastic cave on the right.

Climbing: Comparable to the Grande Grotta. On the left, 3D climbing on substantially overhanging routes and massive stalactites. On the right, less overhanging terrain and easier routes, mostly on tufa pipes.

Shade: Until 13:00. **Exposure:** S

8 Focus 2★ 7c 35m
Harder after a tufa broke. *K Ochsner, F Meier, D Croth, 2002*

9 K44 3★ 7a 22m
Quality tufa-covered red rock leads to a reachy crux. Persevere and be devious. *K + R + M Ochsner, 2003*

10 Nymfi 3★ 7b 30m
Amazing moves at the start, then big tufas and one hard move. *B Girardin, C + Y Remy, 2006*

11 Feuerdorn 3★ 7a+ 22m
A cool line with a sustained vertical start then harder climbing through the roof with tufas. *K + R + M Ochsner, 2003*

12 Sueur D'Hommes 3★ 8a 40m
The extension of "Feuerdorn", with phenomenal tufas.
Routes #12-#16: L Triay, G Fanguin, A Catzeflis, 2006

13 Debout Les Morts   3★ 7c+ 40m
Seriously good cave climbing.

14 Zero Chichon   3★ 7c+ 40m
Even more excellent steep stuff; well worth the walk.

15 Zero Chichon Ext   3★ 8a 50m
The extension is possible in one pitch.

16 Gegoune   3★ 7c 40m
Slap up the colonettes to gain the left-leaning ramp (no feet, all hands). Then head for the huge distant tufa. Superb!

17 Calcite Star   3★ 7b 27m
From the "Gegoune" ramp make a very hard stretch, then race up while you still can. *K Ochsner, F Meier, D Croth, 2002*

18 Calcite Star Plus   3★ 7b+ 40m
From tufa system to tufa system, the extension is a major expedition. *K + R + M Ochsner, 2003*

19 Kroterih   3★ 7b 28m
Nice single-tufa climbing. *K Ochsner, F Meier, D Croth, 2002.*

20 La Perceuse A Dede   2★ 7a 30m
Starts with "Kroterih", but too squeezed. Spoils the neighboring route as well. *Aubel, Saunier, 2012*

21 Rognol   3★ 7a 30m
A technical tufa groove leads to a pumpy finale.
Routes #21-#26: B Girardin, C + Y Remy, 2006

22 Latex   2★ 7a+ 30m
The overhanging wall.

23 Vagina   2★ 6c 30m
A fingery wall then a chimney/hole which often dribbles.

24 Anal+   2★ 6b+ 25m
A technical wall with a greasy second half. Pop up the chimney.

25 B2   3★ 6a+ 25m
A technical slab with some nice moves on a steeper finale.

26 Stanouch   2★ 5b 20m
The pleasant pillar.

27 Metaxa   3★ 8b 20m
L Triay, G Fanguin, A Catzeflis, 2006

28 Sounet   2★ 5a 20m
The slab with big holds. *B Girardin, C + Y Remy, 2006*

CALCITE CAVE

12 GALATIANI

RESERVOIR DOGS
BLACK FOREST

37.028176
26.958038

Reservoir Dogs is a small but noteworthy new sub-sector with room for many new routes. It was equipped by Jean Noël Bourgeois in August 2015.

Climbing: A low-angle grey slab to the left and a steeper slab and wall to the right. At the time of writing, loose blocks were reported above the left routes. Check **climbkalymnos.com** for updates before you climb.

Shade: Until 11:00. **Exposure:** S

1. **Mister White** 2★ 5c 20m
   2015
2. **Mister Brown** 2★ 6a 20m
   2015
3. **Mister Black** 2★ 6b 27m
   2015
4. **Mister Pink** 2★ 6b 25m
   2015
5. **Mister Pink Ext** 2★ 7a 35m
   2015

Climber on "K44" 7a (page 104). NIKOLAOS SMALIOS

RESERVOIR DOGS

Black Forest is a relatively small, quiet crag featuring a low-angle grey slab (left) and a sharp grey/red wall (right) with some prickly holds.

Climbing: A bit sharp, but still interesting and technical.

Kids: Not good. The approach is hard and the terrain beneath the cliffs is steep.

Shade: Until 10:00. **Exposure:** S

Approach: From Masouri, drive towards Emporios. Approximately 1.7km past Arginonta village, park on a distinctive turn over a bridge with a white marker for sectors Galatiani and Black Forest (37.028176, 26.958038). Walk up the right side of the gully following red marks. **Walking time:** 15 min.

1. **Game** — 3★ 4c 32m
   J Friedrich, G Hommel, 2012

2. **Play** — 3★ 5a 30m
   J Friedrich, G Hommel, 2013

3. **Dilldabbe** — 3★ 5c+ 25m
   A steady slab with gouttes d'eau on great rock. *F Henssler, G Tiefzer, C Heinrichs, U Kreiss, 2002*

4. **Für Betta** — 3★ 6a 25m
   Not just another grey slab; a great one. *L + B Salsotto, 2011*

5. **Eiruhr** — 3★ 5b+ 23m
   Good sharp holds + flakes. *Routes #5-#11: F Henssler, G Tiefzer, C Heinrichs, U Kreiss, 2002*

6. **Wunderfitz** — 3★ 6a 25m
   Easy for the grade, with big holds where it steepens.

7. **Schneckle...mach dir nid ins hem** — 2★ 6c+ 27m
   Athletic and steep final part on juggy tufa material.

8. **D'Luft Isch Dusse** — 2★ 6c+ 28m
   The wall, sharp in places.

9. **Bragele** — 1★ 6b+ 18m
   Compact slab with a hard headwall.

10. **Schofsackel** — 2★ 7a 32m
    The grey and orange wall.

11. **S'Mauselchen** — 0★ 6c 26m
    A sharp wall, and the crux is not well-protected.

BLACK FOREST

13 NOUFARO

37.024526
26.961287

GRADE RANGE	up to 5b+	5c to 6a+	6b to 7a	7a+ to 7c	7c+ and up
No. OF ROUTES	10	9	19	14	10

Alex Megos did all the first ascents of the hardest routes at Noufaro. Here, he is on "Le 7a de Myriam" 8b+ (page 113).
SIMON MONTMORY

Noufaro is a crag where many new routes have been added since the last guidebook was published in 2010. The crag keeps expanding upwards to include new sub-sectors, namely (from top left) **Eagle Wall**, **Magic Wall**, **Nirvana**, **Upper Noufaro**, **Noufaro Slab**, **Noufaro Main** and **Noufaro Right**.

Climbing: Almost everything, from adventurous long multi-pitch routes to really hard sport climbing (a "Megos playground!") as well as easier—but still very good—walls and slabs.

Conditions: Warm and protected from the north wind, so good for climbing on cooler or cloudy days. Exposed to the rain.

Shade: Until 13:00 at all sub-sectors. **Exposure:** S

Kids: The areas below **Noufaro Slab** and **Noufaro Main** are fairly suitable for kids, and the approach path is easy. Sub-sector **Nirvana** is *not* good for kids.

Approach: From Masouri, drive towards Emporios. Approximately 1.1 km past Arginonta village, you will see a white marker to sector Noufaro (37.024526, 26.961287). Follow the red marks slightly uphill and to the right until you arrive at **Noufaro Main**, by the route "Viavai". From there, go right for **Noufaro Right**, or left for **Noufaro Slab** and **Upper Noufaro**.

Walking time: 10 min (**Noufaro Main**), 15 min (**Upper Noufaro**), 40 min (**Magic Wall**), 45 min (**Nirvana**), 55 min (**Eagle Wall**).

Note: You can take a "shortcut" of sorts to **Upper Noufaro**, **Nirvana**, **Magic Wall** and **Eagle Wall**.
Walk uphill from the road to the solitary tree pictured on the right page. From there, walk carefully along the base of the cliffs to each sub-sector.

See also: Crag Panorama on page 57.

109

NOUFARO SUB-SECTORS

EAGLE WALL
MAGIC WALL
NIRVANA
UPPER NOUFARO
DALLE à PATOUCHE
NOUFARO MAIN
Solitary tree
NOUFARO SLAB
NOUFARO RIGHT

Members of the Swiss national team craning their necks. From left to right, Vladek, Obed, Miro, Beni, and their coach Peter "Beautiful Young" Keller. RAINER EDER/VISUALIMPACT.CH

13 NOUFARO

EAGLE WALL
MAGIC WALL

37.024526
26.961287

Eagle Wall is a new sub-sector featuring two long multi-pitch routes. The character of these routes is quite adventurous, even though they are equipped with bolts.

Climbing: Mostly on grey rock of good quality.

Approach: See previous page. **Walking time**: 55 min.

Return: After you top out, walk right along the ridge (look for the cairns) making a big U-turn until you end up above Magic Wall. Then, continue down an easier path to the base of the climb. **Walking time**: 20 min.

❶ Eagle Hotel 2★ 7a 140m
Multi-pitch (6b+ 35m, 7a 25m, 6c 20m, 6c 20m, 7a 20m, 6c 15m). Six pitches; 6c obligatory. Beautiful, elegant and demanding! A serious line without dense bolting. Impressive climbing in a variety of styles on the high-quality orange rock. Vertical and slightly overhanging in places. To enjoy this route to the maximum it is recommended that you have the grades 6c-7a under control. Cruxes are well-protected and could be aided if necessary, but otherwise you really have to climb between the bolts.
B Schneider, H Webhofer, 2013

❷ Free Bird 2★ 7b 160m
Multi-pitch (6a+ 25m, 6b+ 20m, 7b (6b/A0) 30m, 6a+ 20m, 6b 25m, 6a 35m). Six pitches; 6b+ obligatory. Fantastic wall climbing on grey rock of good quality. Quite well-bolted all the way. The 3rd pitch is a hard, consistent technical vertical wall with a small roof, but bolts are close all the way so it can be aided (6b/A0... 15 bolts). Experience in alpine climbing/multi pitch climbing is necessary.
H Webhofer, 2013

Magic Wall is somewhat different from the usual Kalymnos style; it can be compared to sector Kalydna. There are three multi-pitches here leading to the top, as well as some unfinished projects.

Climbing: Technical and thin, on a vertical wall with just a few overhanging sections and sharp rock.

Approach: See page 108. **Walking time**: 40 min.

1 Lyttos   2★ 6b+ 25m
The wall with pockets. *B Girardin, C + Y Remy, 2006*

2 Skevos   3★ 6c+ 28m
The wall, this time with small pockets.
B Girardin, C + Y Remy, 2006

3 Great Albert   3★ 6c 25m
More small pockets. *B Girardin, C + Y Remy, 2006*

4 Great Albert Ext   2★ 7a+ 35m
Continues with wall climbing. *B Girardin, C + Y Remy, 2006*

5 Black Beauty   ♪ 7a 33m
Quality wall climbing; sustained and very technical finish left of the black tufa. *B Girardin, C + Y Remy, 2006*

6 Grua   3★ 7a 90m
Multi-pitch (7a 30m, 7a 30m, 6b 30m). Climb the wall followed by two more pitches on walls and overhangs.
B Girardin, C + Y Remy, 2006

7 Rammstein   3★ 7b+ 93m
Multi-pitch (7a+ 33m, 7b+30m, 6c 30m). The first wall is followed by two more pitches on walls and overhangs.
B Girardin, C + Y Remy, 2006

8 Vouros   3★ 7b+ 90m
Multi-pitch (6c 30m, 7b+ 30m, 6c 30m). Climb the wall, followed by two more pitches on walls and overhangs.
B Girardin, C + Y Remy, 2006

9 Greek Wedding   2★ 6a 25m
The slab and wall. *B Girardin, C + Y Remy, 2006*

10 Tony   2★ 5b+ 25m
Easier slab climbing. *B Girardin, C + Y Remy, 2006*

13 NOUFARO

37.024526
26.961287

NIRVANA
UPPER NOUFARO

Nirvana is a high quality, technical grey wall. All routes were bolted by Hannes Webhofer in 2014.

Climbing: Vertical or off-vertical wall climbing requiring excellent footwork. The two longer climbs are exactly 40m from the belay ledge. Clip yourself in and belay from there. **Always make a knot in the end of your rope.**

Kids: No. Belay ledge.

Approach: See page 108. Fixed rope for final 5m to the belay ledge. **Walking time**: 45 min.

1 Greek Stallion — 3★ 6b 30m
A good intro/warmup. Technical and needs good footwork.

2 Private Dancer — 3★ 7a 30m
Several moves on finger pockets, then an interesting upper part with a long move to a "blind" pocket.

3 Nirvana — ♪ 6c 40m
Verdon-style with water pockets and fantastic moves. A complex crux with friction, smooth sidepulls and pockets.

4 Siberian Husky — 3★ 7a 40m
Long moves, good pockets, foot friction. Quite a journey!

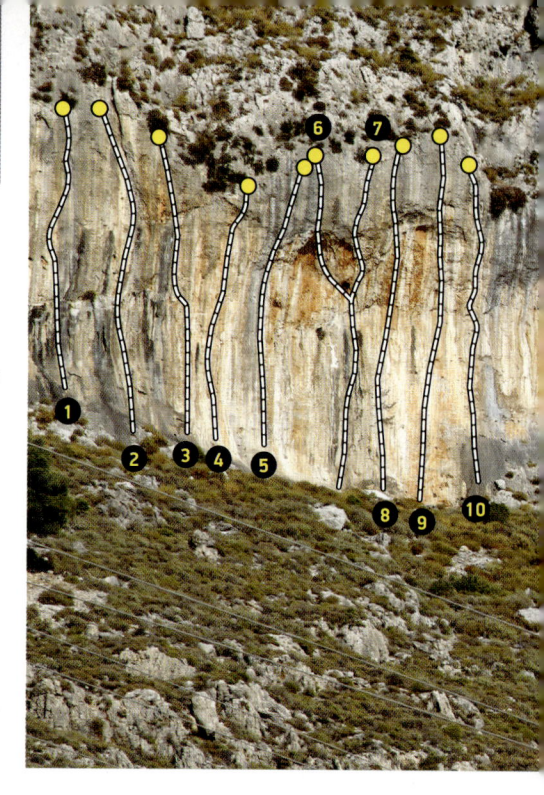

Upper Noufaro is a wavy expanse of ultra-compact red/grey rock, plus a long grey slab to the right. Unusual, intense short routes on tufas and small pockets, and impressive long wall climbs with the occasional tufa.

Climbing: Hardcore on small holds and features, plus some technical wall climbs on the right. Alex Megos did the first ascents of the hard routes in 2013-14.

Approach: See page 108. **Walking time**: 15 min.

1 Good Grip — 2★ 7c 15m
S Montmory, J Kraus, 2013

2 Schwert — 2★ 7b+ 18m
Very sharp and crumbly; can use traffic. *B + C Arnold, 2011*

3 Bolting Addiction — 3★ 7c 18m
Nice, with a short boulder. *S Montmory, A Megos, 2013*

4 Develop As You Are — 3★ 8a+ 20m
The higher up the harder! *J Kraus, 2013*

UPPER NOUFARO

5 Stay As You Are — 3★ 8c 20m
Our friend Simon says "you must do it bim bam boom".
J Kraus, A Megos, 2013

6 Team Gawafes — 3★ 8b 20m
A little boulder. J Kraus, 2012

7 Fibula — 2★ 8b 20m
A hard boulder section after a fragile tufa. M De Vogel, 2013

8 Feel the Cold — 3★ 8c+ 20m
"No time to read a book on the route!" S Montmory, 2013

9 Le 7a de Myriam — 3★ 8b+ 20m
Simon underestimated the grade just a bit. Quelle surprise!
S Montmory 2013

10 Amédé the Stuikerspin — 3★ 7c 20m
Beauty with two difficult parts. M De Vogel, 2013

11 Schild — 2★ 7c 35m
A thin, crimpy wall. B + C Arnold, 2011

12 Myself Not a Fish — ♪ 8a 25m
Wall, crimps + a "swordfish tufa". S Montmory, L Bonin, 2012

13 Myself Not a Fish Ext — 3★ 8a+ 30m
A short boulder section. S Montmory, L Bonin, 2012

14 Opal — ♪ 8b+ 30m
A major line. S Montmory, L Bonin, 2012

15 Harnisch — ♪ 6c+ 35m
Quirky + varied; odd moves, but lots of fun.
B + C Arnold, 2011

16 Mira — 2★ 7b 25m
Steep start + technical slab. L Salsotto, A Langenbach, 2012

17 Kathrin Island — 2★ 6c+ 20m
A slab with an awkward, thin crux. H Gargitter Group, 2002

18 Big Back — 2★ 5c 15m
A tricky finale. H Gargitter Group, 2002

19 Revue — 3★ 6a+ 30m
A sustained, technical slab. J Friedrich, G Hommel, 2010

20 Glaros Bar — 2★ 6a+ 30m
A more demanding second act. J Friedrich, G Hommel, 2011

21 Fis — 2★ 5c 30m
A good, long climb. J Friedrich, G Hommel, 2011

22 Fes — 1★ 5b 27m
Vegetated rock. J Friedrich, G Hommel, 2011

13 NOUFARO

37.024526
26.961287

NOUFARO SLAB
NOUFARO MAIN, NOUFARO RIGHT

Noufaro Slab features excellent slabs for beginners.

Climbing: On easy slabs, plus more technical, vertical lines on the right.

Approach: See page 108. **Walking time**: 10 min.

1 Quarte 1★ 4c 16m
A short fill-in route. J Friedrich, G Hommel, 2010

2 Quinte 2★ 5a 16m
A very short crux. J Friedrich, G Hommel, 2010

3 Samba 3★ 5a 25m
Easy, but take care near the end! T Scmih + Zuricl, 1999

4 Blues 3★ 5a 23m
Good for beginners, though the holds are sparse on the steep section. T Scmih + Zuricl, 1999

5 Polka 3★ 5a 23m
Beginners' route. H + J Weninger, A Hafner, C Schmidt, 2008

6 Boogie 3★ 5b 25m
A bit stiffer than its neighbors. T Scmih + Zuricl, 1999

7 Jive 3★ 5b+ 23m
A good slab. Easier from the left. T Scmih + Zuricl, 1999

8 Sirtaki 2★ 5b 25m
Keep your weight on the feet and you will find the holds. H + J Weninger, A Hafner, C Schmidt, 2008

9 Cha Cha 2★ 6b 25m
Technical and tricky at the final bulges. Don't go too high on the traverse. T Scmih + Zuricl, 1999

10 Rumba 2★ 6a+ 25m
Good holds but trickier upper section. T Scmih + Zuricl, 1999

11 Reigen 2★ 6b+ 25m
Unusual climbing, with a harder mid-section by the brown tufa. H + J Weninger, A Hafner, C Schmidt, 2008

Noufaro Main is a beautiful, compact red and grey wall.

Climbing: Mostly vertical, technical wall climbs.

Approach: See page 108. **Walking time**: 10 min.

1 Bolero 2★ 6a+ 32m
A slabby wall with steep finish. J Friedrich, G Hommel, 2010

2 Viavai 3★ 6a+ 32m
A diagonal line on good holds. L Salsotto, P Bertotto, 2014

NOUFARO SLAB

3	**Buona La Prima**	2★ 6c+ 20m

Bouldery start then gouttes. *L Salsotto, P Bertotto 2014*

4	**Naoshi**	3★ 7b 25m

A hard start then thin climbing. *L Salsotto, P Bertotto 2014*

5	**Ho Perso la Bussola**	2★ 7a+ 28m

A powerful move on a small finger-pinch. Caution when clipping the 3rd bolt. *L Salsotto, P Bertotto, 2014*

6	**Gecko's Team**	3★ 7a+ 23m

A nice tufa start + 1 hard move. *L Salsotto, P Bertotto 2014*

7	**Garbulli**	3★ 7a+ 23m

Bouldery and continuously interesting.
L Salsotto, P Bertotto, 2014

8	**Ericstotle**	1★ 6a+ 15m

Use the huge suspicious-looking block on the right with caution. *E Sorenson, J Martin, 2005*

9	**Spice**	3★ 6b+ 25m

Needs some traffic, but amazing well-featured rock.
J Friedrich, G Hommel, 2010

10	**Twist**	2★ 7c 15m

Short and powerful with an intense sequence at the final bulge. *B Arnold, M Creutz, 2003*

11	**Themelio**	2★ 8a? 18m

Steep with small tufas. *C Tzioufetas, V Batsios, Y Telis, 2014*

Noufaro Right: Vertical, well-featured red/grey rock.

Climbing: Technical wall climbing.

Approach: See page 108. **Walking time**: 10 min.

1	**Tango**	0★ 6c 22m

Very sharp and some loose rock. *T Scmih + Zuricl, 1999*

2	**Rock 'n Roll**	2★ 6c 25m

A well-bolted natural crack line. *F Heinicke, A Riemer 2005*

3	**Mambo**	2★ 6b+ 25m

Easier than it looks; compact + gentle. *Scmih + Zuricl, 1999*

4	**Salsa**	1★ 6c+ 20m

Sharp and stiff for the grade. *T Scmih + Zuricl, 1999*

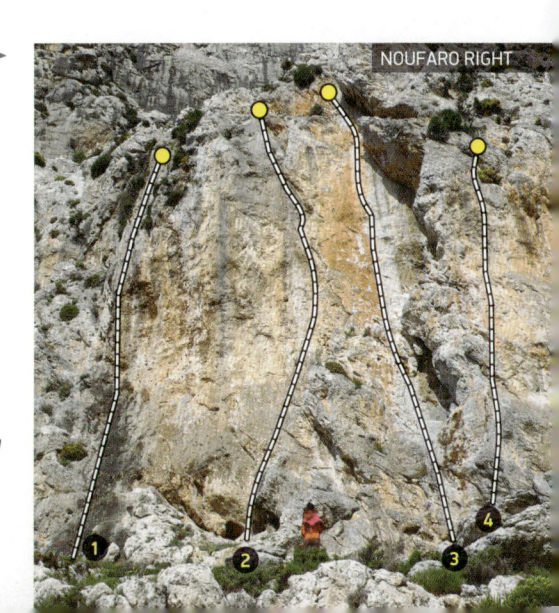

14 BELGIAN CHOCOLATES

37.020072
26.964530

GRADE RANGE	up to 5b+	5c to 6a+	6b to 7a	7a+ to 7c	7c+ and up
No. OF ROUTES	6	21	19	4	0

Belgian Chocolates, a nice smooth slab rising up to a height of 120m, is just a bit further left of sector Arhi, one of the island's classics. Besides the single-pitch routes, several fabulous multi-pitch routes can be found here. On the left side of the crag is a massive slab, **Dalle à Patouche**, where several steep, dynamic routes were recently added. On the right is **Fotisi Wall** for more airy, delicate slab climbing.

Climbing: On immaculate grey limestone of the best quality, full of water pockets and chickenheads. This is some of the finest slabby face climbing on Kalymnos.

Eugenia Odermatt trying "Dodo" 6a+ (page 121).

BELGIAN CHOCOLATES SUB-SECTORS

DALLE à PATOUCHE
FOTISI WALL
ARHI
NOUFARO RIGHT

Conditions: Warm. Good for climbing when it is cool or cloudy; perfect on sunny winter days.

Shade: Until 11:00.

Exposure: SE

Kids: So-so. Just OK on the right of the sector (Fotisi Wall), though not very practical. Not good for kids on the left (Dalle à Patouche).

Approach: From Masouri, drive to Arginonta. Pass the last houses and park on the right-hand side of the road after some new stone houses (37.020072, 26.964530). Follow the path, and when it splits, follow the left branch. Traverse along the base of the routes at sector Arhi, and then go up briefly until you come to **Fotisi Wall**, the first sub-sector.

Walking time: 15-18 min.

See also: Crag Panorama on page 57.

A stylishly cool Urs Odermatt on "Syriza" 5b at sector Arhi's Far Left Wall, adjacent to Belgian Chocolates (page 125).

14 BELGIAN CHOCOLATES
DALLE à PATOUCHE

118
37.020072
26.964530

Dalle à Patouche offers some great slab climbing and many multi-pitch routes (mostly 2-3 pitches). The solid limestone is reminiscent of the pretty grey slabs of Verdon. It is worth climbing at **Dalle à Patouche** just for the second pitches; full of *gouttes*, each and every one deserves a musical note! Most routes here are graded between 6a-6b, with some also in the 6c-7c range.

Climbing: Excellent face climbing on easy-angled walls; some steep athletic climbing to the left.

ATTENTION: As a multi-pitch sector, it is very important to bring your helmet. Also, an **80m** rope is necessary.

Shade: Until 11:00. **Exposure:** SE

Approach: See previous page. Then, just before you reach the huge boulder below Fotisi Wall, stop going up along the base of the rock, and traverse left instead (behind the boulder). **Walking time:** 20 min.

1 Utah — 2★ 7a 30m
Hard start up an overhanging crack, then an easier slab.
L Salsotto, C Idoux, 2011

2 Pietro — 3★ 7c+ 35m
Overhanging start with a hard exit to the headwall.
L Salsotto, C Idoux, 2011

3 Grazie alla Vita — 3★ 7c+ 33m
Nice mix of overhangs + fine slabs. *L Salsotto, C Idoux 2011*

4 Megalo Skilo — 3★ 7c 30m
A steep start on good holes, then the crux on the upper column. *L Salsotto, C Idoux, 2011*

5 Privi di Spirito — ?★ ?? 20m
L Salsotto, 2011

6 Spaghetti Connection — ?★ ?? 20m
L Salsotto, 2011

7 Punti di Vista — ?★ ?? 25m
L Salsotto, 2011

8 Myticon — 2★ 7b 20m
L Salsotto, C Idoux, 2011

9 Pitaman — 2★ 6b+ 20m
L Salsotto, C Idoux, 2011

10 Grignotte — 3★ 6a+ 47m
2 pitches (6a+ 27m, 5c+ 20m). Shares the 1st pitch with "Madeleine" and "Marie-Laure". *C Idoux, 2008*

11 Madeleine — 3★ 6a+ 59m
2 pitches (6a+ 27m, 6a 32m). Shares the first pitch with "Grignotte" and "Marie-Laure". *C Idoux, 2008*

12 Marie-Laure — 2★ 6b 57m
2 pitches (6a+ 27m, 6b 30m). Technical wall climbing.
C Idoux, 2008

13 Loulou — 3★ 6a+ 40m
A good wall with fingery moves. 18 QD. *C Idoux, 2008*

14 Le Glod — 3★ 6b 65m
3 pitches (6a+ 27m, 6b 20m, 6b 18m).
C Idoux, L Salsotto, 2009

15 Mika — 3★ 6b 65m
2 pitches (6a+ 27m, 6b 38m). *C Idoux, 2008*

16 Plouf — ♪ 6b 65m
2 pitches (6b 27m, 6a+ 38m). The 2nd pitch is superb!
C Idoux, 2008

17 Stone Diver — 3★ 6a+ 62m
2 pitches (5c+ 27m, 6a+ 35m). Starts with a delicate move on the slab, then becomes quite intensive. *C Idoux, 2008*

18 Patouch — 2★ 6b 62m
2 pitches (6a+ 30m, 6b 32m). *C Idoux, 2008*

19 Jump — 2★ 6b 65m
3 pitches (6b 20m, 6b 20m, 6b 25m). *C Idoux, 2008*

20 Milka — 2★ 5b 17m
A good route for beginners. The bolts are easily reachable, though there is a hard move at the top of the groove.
C Riemer (7 yrs old), A Riemer, 2005

21 Bevers Bolts — 0★ 7b 113m
5 pitches (5a 18m, 7b 20m, 6a+ 25m, 6b 25m, 6a 25m). Not homogeneous at all. *J Jooren, Sepperoels, Vincente, 2004*

22 Red Spot — 2★ 5c 18m
A grey slab with an interesting middle section.
J Jooren, Sepperoels, Vincente, 2002

23 Strange Tree — 2★ 5c 18m
Again, a good slab. *J Jooren, Sepperoels, Vincente, 2002*

24 Strange Tree Ext — 2★ 7b 35m
L Salsotto, C Idoux, 2011

25 Rock Shrimps — 2★ 6a+ 17m
Delicate with some hidden holds.
J Jooren, Sepperoels, Vincente, 2002

26 Rock Shrimps Ext   2★ 7a 35m
L Salsotto, C Idoux, 2011

27 Sharp Things   2★ 5c 15m
The right-hand line, varied and interesting.
J Jooren, Sepperoels, Vincente, 2002

28 Sharp Things Ext   2★ 7a 32m
L Salsotto, C Idoux, 2011

29 Colibri   3★ 6b+ 25m
Excellent climbing. C Idoux, 2011

30 5 à 7   2★ 7a 30m
3 pitches (7a 30m, 6c 25m, 6b 30m). C Idoux, 2009

14 BELGIAN CHOCOLATES

FOTISI WALL

120
37.020072
26.964530

At **Fotisi Wall** you will find some of the best smooth, compact grey limestone on Kalymnos.

Climbing: Thin and technical on immaculate low-angle walls and slabs. Best for winter and cold days.

Shade: Until 11:00. **Exposure:** SE

Approach: See page 117. **Walking time:** 15-18 min.

1 La Puffetta 2★ 6a+ 30m
Hard start up an overhanging crack, then an easier slab.
C Idoux, 2009

2 Il Grande Puffo 2★ 6c+ 30m
C Idoux, 2009

3 Le Coq 2★ 6c 30m
Very good climbing on the photogenic pillar. C Idoux 2008

4 La Mouette 3★ 6c 30m
Stiff for the grade, with an expo crux, and hard to onsight.
C Idoux, 2008

5 Sweety 2★ 6c 32m
A short thin crux near the end. *C Idoux, 2011*

6 Nicole 3★ 6a 30m
A testing start leads to an enjoyable wall. *H-P Bartens, K Hildenbrand, 2001. Extended by C Idoux, L Salsotto, 2008*

7 Gali-Gali 2★ 6a+ 35m
C Idoux 2011

8 Dix Corde 3★ 6b 35m
Nice and balancy, but spaced bolts. *C Idoux, 2011*

9 Thia Fotisi 3★ 6a+ 32m
Excellent technical climbing up a compact slab.
T Michaelides, A Theodoropoulos, 2000. Extended by C Idoux, L Salsotto, 2008

10 Goatfather 3★ 6a+ 30m
A squeezed line, but absorbing climbing.
H + J Weninger, 2014

11 Dodo 3★ 6a+ 28m
A great slabby route requiring good balance. You can trust the small flake at the top. *U Hofler, S Flugge, 2000*

12 C.A.P. 3★ 6c 30m
Compact steep slab with a definitive technical crux.
C Idoux, 2015

13 Ewa 3★ 6b 26m
Continuously delicate slab climbing, with one hard clip.
U Hofler, S Flugge, 2000

14 Faron 3★ 5c 27m
The brown slab is tricky, but the holds get better higher up. *T + S Jekel, 2007*

15 Jolli 3★ 5b+ 27m
Steady slab climbing. A flake and a tufa add interest.
J Friedrich, G Hommel, 2005

16 Sunny Mousse 3★ 5b+ 30m
A demanding slab after the small roof. Not easy to onsight. *T + S Jekel, 2007*

17 Cahin-Caha 3★ 5c 20m
Pleasant climbing on flakes, a bulge and a compact slab.
C Idoux, 2016

18 Bling-Bling 3★ 6a 25m
A compact slabby wall with good holds but not very easy feet. *C Idoux, 2016*

19 Tic-Tac 3★ 5c 28m
A fine grey slab with big holds. *C Idoux, 2016*

Local climbing guide Tania Matsuka enjoys the fabulous 2nd pitch of "Mika" 6b (page 118). HEINZ ZAK

20 Tchin-Tchin 3★ 6b 30m
A reachy bulge then a compact slab. *C Idoux, 2016*

21 Couci-Couça 3★ 5c+ 28m
A nice slab with a short bulge. *C Idoux, 2016*

22 Fric-Frac 3★ 5c+ 28m
A juggy voyage on black and grey rock with two short bulges. *C Idoux, 2016*

23 Sponge Diver 3★ 5c 27m
Starts easy, then small holds on the black slab and a sustained section. *A Hafner, C Schmidt, 2008*

24 CU at the Wall 2★ 5b 27m
Good climbing, good holds. *A Hafner, C Schmidt, 2008*

25 Gocce 2★ 5b 27m
One more nice slab climb. A tricky move if you go direct at the bulge. *T + S Jekel, 2007*

26 Plaisir 3★ 4c 30m
Shares the last bolt and anchor with "Gocce". The mid-section is really nice and the last meters harden.
T + S Jekel, 2007

15 ARHI

37.020072
26.964530

GRADE RANGE	up to 5b+	5c to 6a+	6b to 7a	7a+ to 7c	7c+ and up
No. OF ROUTES	13	30	27	15	24

Sergios "S" Soursos breezes through "Orione" 6a (page 132).

The Greek meaning of the word *arhi* (ar-HEE) is *beginning*. And indeed, this was the beginning of the Kalymnos story in 1997. Andrea Di Bari and his friends equipped their first routes here when they first discovered the Kalymnos cliffs, and all these years later, sector **Arhi** still ranks as one of the most important crags on the island.

Climbing: Everything from absurdly overhanging lines up to 9a on yellow-red rock with stalactites and elongated slots, to easy slabs from 4c, to an abundance of fantastic routes in the 6th grade.

Conditions: Warm and protected from the north wind, so it is perfect for winter climbing. The interior of the cave is protected from the rain.

Not recommended for very hot days, humid or windless days. **Exposure:** S

Shade: Until 10:30 (left) or 14:00 (middle).

Kids: So-so. The approach is short, but the terrain can be steep and goats sometimes walk along the ledges above.

Approach: From Masouri, drive to Arginonta. Pass the last houses and park on the right-hand side of the road after some new stone houses (37.020072, 26.964530) Follow the clear path up towards the main cave, then go either right or left along the base of the cliff.
Walking time: 6-8 min.

See also: Crag Panorama on page 57 and 156.

ARHI SUB-SECTORS

15 ARHI
FAR LEFT WALL

37.020072
26.964530

The **Far Left Wall** of Arhi teems with quality wall climbs, many of which go all the way up to 40m.

Climbing: On top-quality, solid grey limestone full of *gouttes d'eau*. Delicate face climbing at its best.

☁ Shade: Until 10:30. **Exposure:** SE

Approach: As on page 122, then traverse to the far left side. **Walking time:** 12 min.

ATTENTION: Routes are long! Always tie a knot at the end of your rope.

Bring at least 16-18 QDs and an 80m rope.

1 Minimum   1★   5a 28m
A new slab climb. Needs some traffic. *H Weninger, 2015*

2 Syriza   3★   5b 40m
Long and impressive for the grade. 17 QD. *B Fara, 2015*

3 Etsi   3★   6a 40m
A wall climb with jugs appearing as needed. *C Idoux, 2009*

4 Ki Etsi   3★   6b 30m
An amazing compact slab. *C Idoux, 2009*

5 Axe   3★   6b 36m
The steep wall; 16 QD, 70m rope. *B Girardin, C+Y Remy 2007*

6 Komak   3★   6a+ 36m
Steep; one of the best in the grade. 16QD, 70m rope. *B Girardin, C + Y Remy, 2007*

7 Kalyneus   2★   6a+ 38m
A good, technical corner + nice headwall. *C Idoux, 2009*

8 Apoplus   3★   6a 25m
Slab climbing with the potential for some bridging. *1999*

9 Tsopanakos   3★   6a+ 25m
A slab climb with small holds. *B Girardin, C + Y Remy, 2007*

10 Dell Mabul   3★   6a 25m
Great slabby climbing with a small tufa bulge. *1999*

11 Dell Mabul Ext   3★   6a+ 38m
A wall worth climbing. 16 QD, 80m rope. *C Idoux, 2009*

12 Kalymero   2★   6a 38m
Excellent climbing up a tufa slab. *C Idoux, 2009*

13 Adonis   3★   6a+ 30m
An encouragingly-bolted line with really nice climbing on small holds. *C Idoux, 2009*

14 Adonis Ext   2★   6b 40m
A bulge with small holds. 18 QD, 80m rope just enough. *C Idoux, L Salsotto, 2009*

15 Green Line   2★   6b 42m
A squeezed line with green hangers. Uses some holds from neighboring routes, but climbing is really good. *C Idoux 2015*

16 4 U   2★   6c 40m
Another really good line. 16 QD. *C Idoux, 2009*

17 Le Bras du Guide   3★   6b+ 38m
Pocket heaven and a short bulging wall. 16 QD. *C Idoux, 2009*

18 Masouri   3★   6b 38m
An excellent technical corner. 16 QD. *C Idoux, 2009*

19 Nixou   2★   6a+ 35m
An easy slab, then a steeper, balancy wall. *C Idoux, 2009*

20 Les Pénibles   2★   6a 35m
Easy climbing save for a tricky bulge. *C Idoux, 2009*

21 Small Fish   2★   6b 28m
A fingery wall with a tricky start and spaced bolts. *J Friedrich, G Hommel, 2005*

22 Monolith   3★   6b 33m
Varied climbing with a challenging small bulge and technical upper slab. *F + X Heinicke, A Riemer, R Donath, 2005*

23 Black Snake   2★   6b 25m
Spaced bolts, especially at the start. Reachy and tricky for the grade. *J Friedrich, G Hommel, 2005*

24 Simba + Zabur   3★   6a+ 33m
A sustained diagonal line with a lot of excellent climbing. *C Idoux, 2011*

25 Stanislas   3★   6a+ 30m
Continuously absorbing climbing rightwards. *B Girardin, C+Y Remy 2007*

26 Killian   2★   6b 30m
A distinct tufa crux followed by a nic wall. *B Girardin, C + Y Remy, 2007*

You talkin' to me?

15 ARHI
MAIN (LEFT WALL)

37.020072
26.964530

Katelyn El Fuge Merrett on "The Underclings" 7a.
ELODIE SARACCO

Left Wall features some of the island's first easy slab routes, plus many stellar extension pitches added later.

Climbing: Vertical or slightly slabby; long extensions on tufa material; blank walls with unusual underclings.

Shade: Until 11:00. **Exposure:** SE

Approach: As on page 122, then traverse to the far left. **Walking time:** 8 min.

1 Harry Parterre 3★ 6c+ 40m
Steep, with an increasingly harder final wall and good tufa pipes. Spaced bolts; 18 QD. *B Girardin, C + Y Remy, 2007*

2 Phobos 2★ 6c 25m
A stiff crux up a tufa with slopery sidepulls leads to a pleasant slab. *B + R Ferrante, 2000*

3 Deimos 2★ 6a+ 25m
An engaging wall climb right of the flowstone with some delicate moves at mid-height. *B + R Ferrante, 2000*

4 Deimos Ext 3★ 7a+ 45m
A tempting single-tufa climb.
C Idoux, S Montmory, A Theodoropoulos, 2011

5 Pares 3★ 6a 28m
Excellent climbing. Look for holds on top of the tufas. *1999*

6 Mars Attack 3★ 7b+ 45m
"Pares" extension. A technical start, tufas, and smeary slab section higher up. *S Montmory, C Dawson, 2014*

7 Scacco 2★ 5c 25m
A fun slab with some tufa blobs. *A Di Bari Team, 1997*

8 Europa 3★ 6a 30m
An amazing 2nd part on the black tufa slab with blue bolts. *C Idoux, 2014*

9 Argonauti 2★ 5b+ 25m
Nice moves up the slab. *A Di Bari Team, 1997*

10 Argonauti Ext 2★ 6a 28m
Crumbly rock but good climbing on side-holds. *C Idoux, 2014*

11 Teseo 2★ 5b+ 25m
An easy slab; hardens near the top. *A Di Bari Team, 1997*

12 Pegaso — 2★ 5b 25m
Another good slabby route. *A Di Bari Team, 1997*

13 Chrysaor — 2★ 5c+ 25m
A squeezed line, but nice slab climbing. *C Idoux, 2015*

14 Centauro — 2★ 5c+ 25m
Easy at first, then delicate and reachy. *A Di Bari Team, 1997*

15 Ercole — 2★ 6a 22m
A direct line that hardens at the final yellow wall. Hard to clip the chain. *A Di Bari Team, 1997*

16 Kotopoula (Ercole Ext) — 3★ 7c+ 40m
Compelling moves on unusual rock for Kalymnos. *S Montmory, 2011*

17 Ziwi — 2★ 6a 25m
Slightly different, on yellowish rock. *M Schmed, 2007*

18 Diskolo (Ziwi Ext Left) — 3★ 8a 40m
A unique pitch. Almost entirely underclings without rest, so use your feet well or you will be pumped in no time. *S Montmory, 2011*

19 Efkolo (Ziwi Ext Right) — 3★ 7b+ 37m
Reachy, bouldery moves on compact rock. *S Montmory, 2011*

20 The Underclings — 3★ 7a 40m
What the name says! Beautiful and good for improving your technique. *S Montmory, 2011*

21 Galopoula — 3★ 6c 30m
Quality rock with some small tufas. *S Montmory, 2011*

22 Galopoula Ext — 3★ 7c 40m
A provocative sequence. *S Montmory, 2011*

23 Megala Kotopoula — 2★ 7c 30m
Some interesting bouldery moves. *S Montmory, 2011*

24 Megala Kotopoula Ext 1 — ?★ 8? 40m
Slopery edges, crimps, dynamic moves. *S Montmory, 2011*

25 Megala Kotopoula Ext 2 — ?★ ?? 60m
S Montmory, 2011

15 ARHI
MAIN (TROULOS LEFT)

128
37.020072
26.964530

Troulos, which means "dome" in Greek, is the beautiful orange cave in the middle of Arhi. Some of the hardest routes and projects on the island are housed within the vast central arch. Chris Sharma, Adam Ondra and Alex Megos have all stopped by. The routes on the right of **Troulos** are very popular, as they are full of tufa columns at a relatively reasonable angle, but it can feel cramped when busy.

Climbing: Steep, athletic tufa climbing.

Shade: Until 14:00.

Approach: As on page 122.

Alex Megos flies up "J.F.O." 8c+

---

26 Orgasme Minéral   3★ 7b+ 25m
A strange, height-dependent rightward traverse on tufa blobs. Easier for the tall. *R Cabessut, 2004*

27 Little Yosemite   3★ 8b+ 40m
After the 1st part of "Orgasme", go straight above the chain and follow the Yosemite-like crack. Two boulder problems. *S Montmory, 2011*

28 Orgasme Minéral Ext   3★ 7c+ 50m
A spooky continuation up big holes and small tufas. 80m rope. Top-rope to remove quickdraws. *R Cabessut 2004*

29 Call Me Baby   3★ 6a+ 20m
A fine climb with big holds and tufas. *S Montmory, 2014*

30 Call Me Baby Ext   3★ 8b+ 30m
Really bouldery, with astonishing moves on good rock. FA by Alex Megos, 2014. *S Montmory, 2014*

31 Youpi L' École Est Finie   3★ 8c 25m
Very steep climbing on small holds. FA by Alex Megos 2014. *S Montmory, 2014*

32 J.F.O.   3★ 8c+ 30m
A massive roof at a 50° angle with a testpiece boulder problem. FA by Alex Megos, 2013. *S Montmory, 2011*

33 Kalymnostrobe   3★ 8a 35m
Brilliant and reachy with two distinct boulder problems. *Routes #33-37 L Triay, G Fanguin, A Cherbonnier, 2004*

34 Kalymnostrobe Ext   3★ 8b 55m
The long, exposed, and unforgiving wall with beautiful tufa pipes. Onsighted by Adam Ondra in 2009. 80m rope.

35 Takopoulos   3★ 8a 40m
Work high up the groove to a wild span across the abyss. Then things get really exciting. 80m rope.

36 Los Rocos di Cantalos   2★ 7c 25m
Feels short, but with a very disheartening crux.

37 Los Rocos di Cantalos Ext   3★ 8a+ 50m
The very impressive central line of the Troulos cave has an exposed feeling. 80m rope.

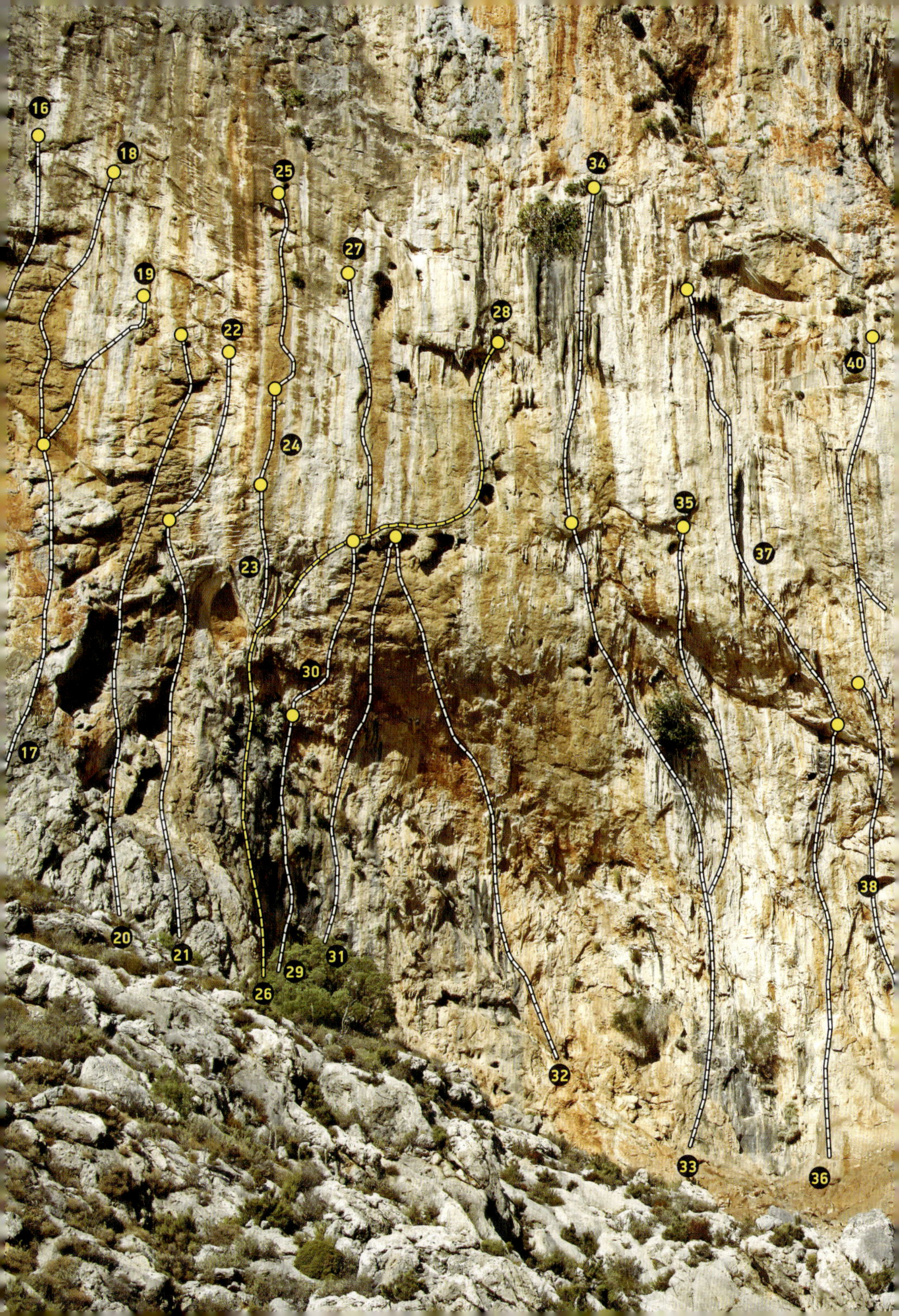
16
18
25
34
27
19
28
22
40
24
35
23
37
30
17
38
20
21
31
29
26
32
33
36

15 ARHI

MAIN (TROULOS RIGHT)

37.020072
26.964530

38 Bijou Caché   3★   8c 25m
An obvious natural line. A very hard boulder problem makes all the grade. FA Alex Megos, 2014. *S Montmory, 2014*

39 Giorgio de la Jungle   2★   7c 20m
Absorbingly tricky moves. A bit scary because of the spaced bolts... *L Triay, G Fanguin, A Cherbonnier, 2004*

40 Giorgio de la Jungle Ext   3★   9? 45m
Open project; 80m rope.
L Triay, G Fanguin, A Cherbonnier, 2004

41 Sharma Variation   3★   9? 50m
Chris Sharma equipped a high link from "Mammifere Vibes Ext" to the "Giorgio" extension. The finale looks mega by anyone's standard. *C Sharma, 2006*

42 Mammifere Vibes   3★   8a+ 25m
An intense bouldery traverse.
L Triay, G Fanguin, A Cherbonnier, 2004

43 Mammifere Vibes Ext   3★   9a? 40m
A stunning route attempted by Sylvain Millet in 2005 and Chris Sharma in 2006. 80m rope.
L Triay, G Fanguin, A Cherbonnier, 2004

44 Ne Pas Toucher à ma Bite   3★   8a+ 30m
Start up "Eros" but then continue left via an overhanging traverse on tufas and sloping holes. Two crux sections plus a dyno. Polished by Kalymnos standards.
L Triay, G Fanguin, A Cherbonnier, 2004

45 Ne Pas Toucher à ma Bite Ext   ♪   9? 42m
A "King Line" with a mad dyno. *S Montmory, 2011*

46 Eros   3★   7b+ 20m
An island classic. Easy climbing to a bouldery crux sequence, then some large tufas and impressively steep terrain. *T Michaelides, A Theodoropoulos, 2002*

47 Angelika   3★   8a 25m
Superb and continuously challenging steep climbing up tufas, pockets and some crimps before the final tufa.
A Theodoropoulos, 2005

48 Kastor   3★   7a 15m
A short route with steep moves connecting tufa blobs, a long reach and a hard final clip. It is easier than it looks, but still. *T Michaelides, A Theodoropoulos, 2000*

49 Super Kastoras   3★   8a+ 35m
A hard extension with a bouldery move after the first anchor, then an impressive roof. Save energy for the final moves on a hard red wall. *A Theodoropoulos, 2005*

50 Polydeykes   3★   7a+ 18m
A stiff pull up small tufas, then a very technical corner formed by the huge tufa. Experienced technical climbers may find it easy for the grade, but a sandbag for everybody else. *T Michaelides, A Theodoropoulos, 2000*

51 Il Pittore   3★   6b+ 18m
Steep tufa-pulling with just one very thin stopper crux move. *A Di Bari Team, 1997*

52 Barbara   3★   7a+ 35m
The first part, athletic and sustained, follows tufas up to the roof, with some nice and some not-so-easy moves. The second part after the roof is completely different: technical, vertical climbing on micro-holds. *A Theodoropoulos, 2005*

53 Thetis   3★   6b+ 18m
A very impressive route up the corner formed by the huge stalactite. The better you can bridge, the easier. Many opportunities for no-hands rests. *A Di Bari Team, 1997*

54 Poseidon   3★   6c 27m
A bouldery tufa start, then bridging on the huge tufa to a delicate finish up a sustained slab. *A Di Bari Team, 1997*

55 Mofeta   3★   6c+ 27m
A good route up the slopery black flowstone with a power crux *and* a technical crux. Easier for the tall. *M Skafar, 2001*

Natasa Manou climbs "Polydeykes" 7a+.

15 ARHI
MAIN (RIGHT WALL)

37.020072
26.964530

Right Wall features some of the most popular face climbs on Kalymnos. Good routes for beginners can be found to the far right.

Climbing: On vertical or slightly slabby walls; mostly face climbing.

Shade: Until 12:00. **Exposure:** S

Approach: As on page 122, then right.

Walking time: 8 min.

56 Nereidi 2★ 6a+ 25m
Stiff for the grade, but an excellent slab with small holds. *A Di Bari Team, 1997*

57 Icaro 2★ 6c 25m
Nice moves on subtle holds and slopers up the brown streak. *A Di Bari Team, 1997*

58 Triaina 2★ 6b 25m
A straightforward, delicate climb on small holds right of the flowstone. *T Michaelides, A Theodoropoulos, 2002*

59 Orione 3★ 6a 25m
A pleasant slab leading to a tricky small overlap. A bit polished but very densely-bolted. *A Di Bari Team, 1997*

60 Dedalo 3★ 6a+ 25m
Hard at the finale, where it steepens. *A Di Bari Team, 1997*

61 Medusa 3★ 6a+ 27m
An excellent route, again with a tricky finale.
A Di Bari Team, 1997

62 Perseo 3★ 6a+ 25m
Very easy climbing until some hard crimpy moves before the lower-off. *A Di Bari Team, 1997*

63 Kalymnian Cheese 2★ 7a 150m
Multi-pitch (6a+ 50m, 6b+ 50m, 7a 45m). A serious route, in part on loose rock, linking the three distinctive caves. Climb "Perseo"; after the first belay continue to a vegetated slab (spaced bolts); the superb 2nd pitch goes through the caves, the 3rd is steep and powerful. Especially impressive is the narrow rock bridge near the 1st cave. **Gear**: One 60m rope + one 50m or 60m for the abseil. **Helmets are strongly recommended**. Do not climb when there are other climbers below. **Experienced climbers only**. See also photo-topo on next page. *T Michaelides, A Theodoropoulos, 2000*

64 Minotauro 3★ 5c 18m
Enjoyable climbing with good sidepulls. *A Di Bari Team 1997*

65 Hey Birdy Namnam 1★ 6c+ 30m
Somewhat inconsistent, with a hard bouldery start followed by a more pleasant, easier slab. *D Stratigos, 2005*

66 Carlo Non Farlo 3★ 5b 20m
Steady, delicate slab climbing. *A Di Bari Team, 1997*

67 Optasia 3★ 5b 20m
Fun slab climbing; one of the best in this style. *1999*

68 Arianna 3★ 5a+ 20m
Nice moves up a gentle, steady slab. *A Di Bari Team, 1997*

69 Cerbero 3★ 5b 20m
More good, delicate slab climbing. *A Di Bari Team, 1997*

70 Arhaggelos 2★ 5a 18m
Starts easy, then there is a reachy move at mid-height. *D Stathakos, A Papadimitropoulou, 2000*

71 Caronte 2★ 4c+ 16m
Easy but satisfying slab climbing. *A Di Bari Team, 1997*

72 Pinipon 2★ 4c 16m
An easy climb, but tricky for the grade. *A Di Bari Team, 1997*

73 Aristos 2★ 5b 18m
Some sharp holds; not as slabby as it looks. *A Mantoglou, 2000*

74 Alba 1★ 6a 20m
A stiff bouldery start then an easy but sharp slab. *2000*

15 ARHI
CHÄPI
BALCONY HELVETIA

37.020072
26.964530

Chäpi is another beautiful, airy and exposed terrace above sector Arhi. Its pretty tufa pipes are visually very tempting even down to the road as you approach.

Climbing: On a steep, compact wall with tufas.

ATTENTION: Be very careful not to dislodge any loose rocks when you approach or climb. They may hurt climbers down below at Arhi.

Shade: Until 12:00. **Exposure:** S

Approach: Walk up to Balcony Helvetia and traverse via a fixed rope. **Walking time:** 20 min.

Sub-sector **Chäpi** is dedicated to **Kaspar Ochsner**, the 48-year old Swiss guide who perished in 2007 during a solo winter climbing trip in the *Engelhorner*. He was well-known for making many hard/expo routes in the Bernese Alps, particularly in *Wenden*, *Engelhörner* tand *Fitz Roy*.
Chäpi was also one of the active early route setters on Kalymnos.

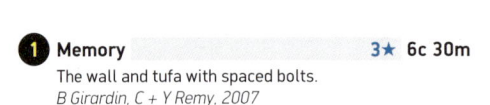

1 Memory 3★ 6c 30m
The wall and tufa with spaced bolts.
B Girardin, C + Y Remy, 2007

2 Chäpi 3★ 7c 40m
A route up the huge, impressive tufa. 24 QD.
B Girardin, C + Y Remy, 2007

3 Milo 2★ 7a 25m
The wall and overhang. *B Girardin, C + Y Remy, 2007*

4 French Kiss 2★ 7a 32m
The slab and wall left of "Swiss Kiss", then a shared lower-off. *B Girardin, C + Y Remy, 2007*

Balcony Helvetia is a stunning, natural narrow balcony overlooking the sea, with a great exposed feel. It is a hard zone of very high-quality rock full of red overhangs, roofs. holes and stalactites.

Climbing: Athletic and excellent on dramatic tufa-covered rock.

Shade: Until 12:00. **Exposure:** SE

Approach: Walk uphill to sector Arhi. Go to the routes on the far right. Walk past "Alba", and continue to the end of the cliff. Go up and around the cliff for another 5-6 minutes of walking/scrambling. **Walking time:** 15 min.

5 Swiss Kiss 3★ 7a+ 28m
A spectacular climb with queasy exposure. Handle the stalactite with care.
Routes #5-#10: K Ochsner, F Meier, Zerro, 1999/2000

6 Gruene Feigen 3★ 7c+ 28m
Steep pocket- and tufa-pulling.

7 Mr Souvlaki 3★ 7c 30m
A perfect tufa system, wonderfully technical + sustained.

8 Chnosis Zange 3★ 7c+ 30m
Great climbing on tufa-covered rock and the hard, bulging headwall.

9 M40 3★ 7b 30m
A long weaving pitch through some impressively steep and intimidating ground. Mostly good holds, but sustained climbing and some hard moves.

10 Fracaso 0★ ?? 30m
Bad rock. Do not climb it.

11 Patsamama 3★ 8b? 30m
Still a project. A stunning tufa leads to a hard open corner.
A Mavromatis, C Daniil, 2006

12 The End of Mythos 3★ 6c 20m
Intoxicating climbing on flakes and tufa lumps. A perfect warm-up for this sector. *J Seidel, 2005*

BALCONY HELVETIA

16 SEA BREEZE

37.017997
26.966431

GRADE RANGE	up to 5b+	5c to 6a+	6b to 7a	7a+ to 7c	7c+ and up
No. OF ROUTES	23	33	38	5	0

From its stunning vantage point overlooking Arginonta Bay, sector **Sea Breeze** includes several sub-sectors with trademark yellow/dark grey walls and steeply inclined grey slabs.

Climbing: Mostly face climbing; very pleasant.

ATTENTION: Many routes are 40m long. If your rope is 60m or 70m, you will have to re-thread at intermediate belays.

An 80m rope is highly recommended.

Kids: Good, with a short approach and several flat areas near the cliffs.

Conditions: Sunny. Best for climbing in winter or on cloudy days.

Shade: Until 10:00-12:00. Check description for each sub-sector.

Exposure: S

Approach: From Masouri, drive to Arginonta. Pass the last houses of the village and park approx. 150m further. There is a white marker reading "Sea Breeze" and "Grey Zone" (37.017997, 26.966431). Go up and to the right or left depending on which sub-sector you are climbing at. See overall plan on the right page.

Walking time: 5-7 min.

Blindly following the leader can often lead to precipitous situations!
PAUL HINTERWIMMER

SEA BREEZE SUB-SECTORS

FAR LEFT

GREAT CANYON

POCKET WALL

MAIN

Arginonta Village

Arginonta is a quiet little village in a small valley leading to a narrow bay with blue/green water. It is always a good alternative to the much busier stretch along the main road in Masouri. The beach is never crowded and there are no sunbeds or bars playing loud music.

The cliffs around **Arginonta** have developed quite a bit over the last five years, with a choice between several very high-quality crags: **Sea Breeze**, **Arginonta**, **Arhi**, **Summertime** and **Arginonta Skyline**, to name a few. And even though the Arginonta area is best for climbing in winter, if you wake up early enough in the summer you will see many other climbers enjoying the fantastic red/grey cliffs before hitting the beach and the quiet seafront *tavernas* afterwards.

See also: Crag Panorama on page 57 and 156.

SAM BIÉ

16 SEA BREEZE

138
37.017997
26.966431

FAR LEFT
GREAT CANYON

The **Far Left** face has only two routes, but there is still potential for routes on slabs and low-angle walls.

Shade: After 18:00. **Exposure:** SE

Approach: Follow the stone cairns above the stone houses. **Walking time:** 4 min.

1 Tropfen 2★ 5a 25m
J Friedrich, G Hommel, 2013

2 Regensburg 2★ 5c 150m
Multi-pitch (5b 30m, 3a 20m, walk 5min, 5a 25m, 5b 25m, 5c 30m, 4b 20m). A newer training multi-pitch on the nice slabs above the newly-built stone houses after Arginonta village. P1: Steep slab with good holds. P2: Scramble into the gully. P3: Walk for 5 min, first to the right, then uphill. P4: Nice and compact low-angle slab. P5: A big flake and steep slab. P6: Steep slab with a delicate passage. P7: Low-angle rock. Watch for any loose rock. **Return:** Abseil down the route. Alternatively, walk 15 min more (left then uphill) to Haute Gorge sector and climb some routes there, too.
P Hinterwimmer, A Theodoropoulos, C Idoux, 2013

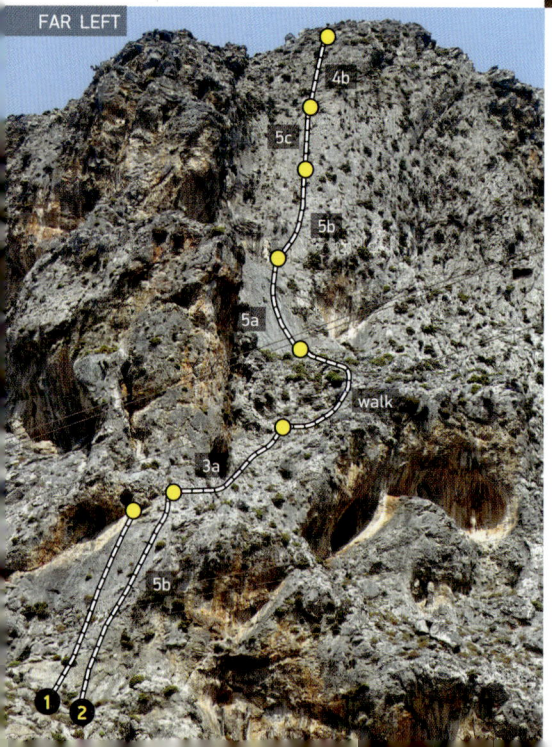

Yves Remy on "Tzatziki kai Sokolata" 7b. CLAUDE REMY

FAR LEFT

"Project of the Heart"

In June 2013, a Mr. Paul Hinterwimmer emailed us. We did not know each other. He introduced himself as a 76-year old man from Regensburg, a small town in Germany. He had fallen in love with Kalymnos, he said, like so many climbers do. On a long shot, he wrote to share his dream with us: to equip a route here, an easy multi-pitch, any line we suggested. He had never put up a route before, but was willing to do whatever we asked to fulfill his wish; for him, he said, this was a "project of the heart". We could not refuse. This is how "Regensburg" was created and how we came to be friends with Paul, an old-fashioned gentleman in the true sense of the word, who honored his promise by visiting Kalymnos repeatedly and spending long hours on the ropes, helping to clean and equip, to the best of his abilities and despite his advanced age. One day as Paul cleaned the rock, he found this heart-shaped stone and brought it to us as a keepsake.

Great Canyon was bolted by the Remy Brothers in 2011.

Climbing: On high quality slabs and walls, and a small steep cave to the right side.

Shade: Until 13:00 (but routes in the cave have shade almost all day). **Exposure:** SW

Approach: Follow the gorge to the canyon entrance.

1. **Melomakaronas** 2★ 6c 35m
A slab, ledge and wall with small tufas and overhang.

2. **Mystic Land** 2★ 7a 35m
Goes left at the ledge. There is only one crux move.

3. **Plastic Surgery Disaster** 2★ 7b 32m
Starts with "Mystic" then goes right at the ledge.

4. **Art in the Air** 2★ 7a 34m
A slab, ledge and wall.

5. **Vromikos** 2★ 6c 33m
A slab, ledge and wall.

6. **Boulderhoelle** 2★ 6b+ 33m
A slab, ledge and wall.

7. **Hazouli** 2★ 6b 32m
A slab, ledge and wall.

8. **Hazouli Ext** 1★ 6c 38m
A short extension on a crimpy, sharp wall and friction slab.

9. **Me Ponai** 2★ 6c 32m
A slab, ledge then wall on the right of the cave. Learn some Greek before this climb, the equippers say.

10. **Rock Out** 2★ 6c 20m
Wall to the roof.

11. **Loubis's Angels** 2★ 6b 20m
Another wall to the roof; always good holds.

12. **Brave a New World** 3★ 5c+ 30m
After a slab and short wall/crux, a long traverse between two overhangs. Impressive and well-protected. 16 QD.

13. **Divine Comedie** 2★ 7a 20m
A short roof with very good holds.

14. **Sex Pistols** 2★ 7a 15m
A short overhang. Very good holds, not rotten like Johhny.

15. **Tzatziki kai Sokolata** 3★ 7b 15m
A short, powerful overhang with "killer" holds.

16. **Beta Lambda** 1★ 7b+ 15m
Overhanging, with a desperate short and sharp crux.

GREAT CANYON

16 SEA BREEZE
POCKET WALL

37.017997
26.966431

Pocket Wall is a grey/red wall with good pockets, and a shorter, steep and compact grey slab on the right ("Grey Zone"). Routes are squeezed a bit too closely, but there is a good choice of grades.

Climbing: Thin and technical wall and slab climbing on small holds. Some impressively long pitches.

☁ **Shade**: Until 12:00. **Exposure**: S

1 Fasolada — 2★ 5c 12m
Steady slab to a short bulge, then left. Easy bridging, very well-bolted and soft for the grade. *C + Y Remy, 2011*

2 In Dubio — 1★ 6a 18m
Inconsistent. Easy, then stiff, then easy again. A 3-bolt variation of #3 with a bulgy crux. *C + Y Remy, 2011*

3 Falakro — 2★ 5b+ 18m
Avoid the overhang, which involves 6a moves, by going to the right. *C + Y Remy, 2011*

4 Stars on Stage — 2★ 6a 25m
Surprisingly exposed; lovely moves on the steep red slab. *C + Y Remy, 2010*

5 Cacoyannis — 3★ 6b+ 35m
Brilliant steep finish up the groove. 18 QD. *C + Y Remy, 2010*

6 Comicland — 3★ 5a 16m
A well-bolted slab and a friendly red bulge. *C+Y Remy, 2010*

7 Mercouri — 2★ 6c 30m
"Comicland" extension: wall + overhang. *C + Y Remy, 2010*

8 Kazantzakis — 2★ 7a 30m
Pumpy climbing and a tricky crux section. *C+Y Remy, 2010*

9 2F@ — 1★ 5a 15m
An easy grey slab; big holds where it steepens. *The Drilling Gang (H Weninger, A Hafner, S Muehlbacher, C Schmidt, 2008)*

10 Swedish Blonde — 2★ 5a 12m
Easy-going route, friendly bolting. *A Hedgecock, 2012*

11 Rand Problem — 3★ 6b 28m
Some hard moves up the steep wall. *The Drilling Gang, 2008*

12 Climbing, the 2nd Best Feeling — 2★ 6a 25m
Technical with small holds and a short shared section with the next route. *The Drilling Gang, 2008*

13 Slalom — 3★ 6a 25m
Slightly meandering, technical climbing on often small but positive holds. *The Drilling Gang, 2008*

14 Newcomer — 3★ 5c 25m
Pleasant and sustained. *The Drilling Gang 2008*

15 Rockcleaner — 2★ 5b+ 25m
Nice climbing on good pockets. *The Drilling Gang, 2008*

16 Strats for Heroes — 2★ 5c 20m
The slab and pockets. Harder near the top. *C + Y Remy, 2010*

17 Strats for Heroes Ext — 2★ 6b+ 30m
The wall and overhang. *C+Y Remy, 2010*

18 Saphirniac — 2★ 6c 38m
Wall with unusual, impressive climbing at the end. Lower-off above the roof. *C + Y Remy, 2011*

19 Charopalévi — 2★ 6a+ 20m
The wall and pockets. *C+Y Remy, 2010*

20 Charopalévi Ext — 3★ 6c 40m
A stiff bulge and great finale. *C + Y Remy, 2010*

21 Best Connections   3★   6a+ 20m
Juggy, with tricky moves on the red wall. *C + Y Remy, 2010*

22 Best Connections Ext   3★   6c 40m
A pocketed wall with cracks and overhang. *C + Y Remy, 2010*

23 Voutimata   3★   6c+ 40m
The wall, pockets, cracks and overhang. *C + Y Remy, 2010*

24 No Laugh, No Fall   1★   7a+ 40m
A steep and very, very sharp wall. *C + Y Remy, 2010*

25 Rockcreeper   1★   7a 30m
A sharp, cruxy start. *B + C Arnold, The Drilling Gang, 2008*

26 Felsentaube (Rockdove)   1★   7a+ 30m
A bouldery start with a traverse to the right. Steep at the rock dove's nest. *B + C Arnold, The Drilling Gang, 2008*

27 Christian's Groove   1★   6a+ 18m
A bouldery route. *M Crook, A Newton, 2005*

28 Berliner Kindl   2★   6a 18m
A hard start, then a slab. *S Piskurek, M Wiesenfarth, 1999*

29 Arginonta Beach   2★   5c 18m
A thin, fingery slab which gets harder with height. *S Piskurek, M Wiesenfarth, 1999*

30 Fakir   1★   6b 18m
A delicate compact slab. Friction and thin moves. *S Piskurek, M Wiesenfarth, 1999*

31 Chicken Hawk   1★   6a 18m
More thin and slabby climbing. *M Crook, A Newton, 2005*

32 Graue Zone   1★   6b+ 18m
Tricky at the small bulge. *S Piskurek, M Wiesenfarth, 1999*

33 Kill the Cock   2★   6a+ 18m
Classic slab climbing on thin pockets and small edges. *S Piskurek, M Wiesenfarth, 1999*

34 Utopia   2★   6a 20m
Slab and wall with good pockets. Good, tricky moves at the top of the grey rib. *C + Y Remy, 2011*

35 Utopia Ext   3★   6b+ 36m
Compact wall with hidden holds. Go for the onsight! *C + Y Remy, 2011*

16 SEA BREEZE
MAIN (LEFT)

37.017997
26.966431

Sea Breeze Main includes an easy pillar, a featured grey/orange vertical wall, and a low-angle slab.

Climbing: Mostly face climbing on good holds, chickenheads, gouttes, and some very long pitches.

Shade: Until 10:30. **Exposure**: S

1 Shark Teeth 0★ 5b+ 25m
Good name for it; very sharp rock. *A Hafner, C Schmidt, 2010*

2 Leonie's Smile 1★ 5c+ 25m
Not so easy to read. *T Hoch, S Mühlbacher, 2010*

3 Noah's Arche 2★ 5c 25m
Find the undercling and the grade is OK.
T Hoch, S Mühlbacher, C Schmidt, 2010

4 Chero Poli 3★ 5b 23m
A short traverse at the bulge. *C Schmidt, A Hafner, 2003*

5 Karlomanos 1★ 5a 26m
Use the flaky groove to the right of #4.
C Schmidt, A Hafner, 2006

6 Drosia 2★ 5a 25m
A beginner's delight with a testing finale.
C Schmidt, A Hafner, 2003

7 Glaros 3★ 4c+ 30m
A long, quality route for the grade. *C Schmidt, A Hafner 2003*

8 Colissimo 2★ 5a 30m
A good, easy warm-up. *B Fara, R Guerin, 2014*

9 Early Riser 1★ 4b 12m
A short one up the leaning pillar of doom. *A Hedgecock 2010*

The formidable Marcel Remy, climbing 'Stars on Stage' 6a (page 140) in 2010, at 88 years of age. CLAUDE REMY

10 Rhizarthrose 2★ **5b 30m**
A wall with good holds, but rope drag problems plus two suspicious blocks at the 4th bolt. Keep to the left and don't touch them. *B Fara, R Guerin, 2012*

11 Windjammer 3★ **6a+ 30m**
Satisfying and consistently interesting, with thin moves and good holds. *F Heinicke, A Riemer, 2010*

12 Zoe 3★ **6b 30m**
A steep wall which then eases off. *B Fara, R Guerin, 2011*

13 Rico 2★ **5c 30m**
Hidden holds to a small bulge and left. *B Fara R Guerin 2006*

14 Fountagio 1★ **6a 20m**
A squeezed line with a sneaky 2nd part.
H Weninger, S McDonnell, J Weninger, 2014

15 National Day 3★ **5b+ 26m**
Varied with a steep but juggy finale. *B Fara, R Guerin, 2012*

16 Babis 3★ **6a 24m**
A hard start on a bulge with big holds, then easier.
B Fara, R Guerin, 2012

17 Psarokatastasi 3★ **5c+ 24m**
Again, a steep start then eases off. *B Fara, R Guerin, 2012*

18 P'tit Loulous 3★ **6b 35m**
Long and enjoyable, with some small bulges. *C Idoux, 2013*

19 Chute de Pierre et de Paul 3★ **6c 40m**
An exciting, devious intro leads to a series of interesting passages. *C Idoux, 2013*

20 Prisunic 3★ **6c 40m**
Stiff start at the hole, then good wall climbing. *C Idoux 2013*

21 Sharky 2★ **7a 15m**
Starts with a sharp boulder problem. *H + J Weninger, 2007*

16 SEA BREEZE
MAIN (RIGHT)

144
37.017997
26.966431

Gilles Bourgoin on the route "Sintro" 6a+
PATRICK MARICHEZ

1 Aeras — 2★ 6b+ 15m
A hard but stunning finale. *H Weninger + Friends, 2002*

2 Sintro — 2★ 6a+ 20m
Wall climbing on very featured rock and a sloping but easy finale. *H + J Weninger, P + B Zerb, 2001*

3 Tir ô Pigeons — 2★ 6b+ 36m
Challenging 1st half on tufa material. Suspicious looking block on the left of the finale. *C Idoux, V Lebret, 2011*

4 Tire Toit — 3★ 6b 37m
Varied, with two tricky sections. It is usually wet and vegetated in early spring. *C Idoux, 2011*

5 Ate — 2★ 5c 20m
A steep groove but with good holds all the way.
H + J Weninger, P + B Zerb, 2001

6 Seeigel — 3★ 6b 37m
The extension pitch up a sharp but interesting headwall.
F + X Heinicke, A Riemer, R Donath, 2005

7 Tire Doigts — 3★ 6b 37m
A tricky but pleasant grey wall. Don't follow the bolts too closely; left or right may be easier. *C Idoux, 2011*

8 Sea Breeze — 3★ 6b 37m
A tricky first bulge leads to a continuously interesting headwall. A 70m rope is OK. *H Weninger + friends, 2002*

9 Tire Bouchon — 2★ 6a 37m
A stiff start up the soft white rock; the last two bolts are shared with "Piranha". *C Idoux, 2011*

10 Piranha — 3★ 5c+ 20m
A delicate climb up the flowstone. *H Weninger+Friends 2002*

11 Piranha Ext — 3★ 6a 37m
Starts hard, then a bit run-out to a glorious finale. A 70m rope is just enough. *H Weninger + Friends, 2002*

12 Piranha Ext Right — 2★ 6a+ 40m
Sustained face climbing; hard to read. *C Idoux, 2012*

13 Selene — 3★ 5b 20m
Pleasant slab climbing in a sea of chickenheads.
H + J Weninger, P + B Zerb, 2001

14 Selene Ext — 2★ 6b 40m
Several bulges with good but hidden holds. *C Idoux, 2012*

15 Hellas — 3★ 4c 20m
A good beginner's wall. *H + J Weninger, P + B Zerb, 2001*

16 Hellas Ext 2★ 6b+ 40m
A tricky start leads to a couple more short cruxes. Excellent climbing. *C Idoux, 2012*

17 Bleuet 2★ 6a+ 30m
A squeezed line with blue bolts up a crumbly, bulging upper wall. *C Idoux, 2014*

18 Thalassopouli 3★ 5c 28m
Goes straight up on small holds. *C Schmidt, A Hafner, 2006*

19 Hera 3★ 5c+ 28m
Strange start, then good scrambling. *P Stadie, S Rumpf 2003*

20 EOS 2★ 6a 25m
Steady climbing if you manage to find the best holds. *H + J Weninger, P + B Zerb, 2001*

21 Sea Parc 2★ 5b 25m
A pleasant slab. *A Hafner, C Schmidt, 2008*

22 Charika Poli 2★ 5b 25m
Steady, with friendly bolting. *A Hafner, C Schmidt, 2006*

23 Fat Boys Arête 2★ 4c 25m
A natural line following the right arête; gaining the lower-off is a bit more difficult. *A Hafner, C Schmidt, 2008*

24 Fiona 1★ 3c 20m
Attention: the 2nd bolt is in a loose rock. *A Hedgecock, 2012*

25 Beginnings 1★ 3c 20m
A better line than "Fiona". *A Hedgecock, 2012*

17 ARGINONTA

146
37.014301
26.972157

GRADE RANGE	up to 5b+	5c to 6a+	6b to 7a	7a+ to 7c	7c+ and up
No. OF ROUTES	18	21	31	9	1

At first glance, **Arginonta** does not look very impressive—but this long strip of red and grey rock offers outstanding climbing and many gems, especially in the 5c-6b range.

Climbing: Very varied on excellent quality limestone, with multiple styles often found in a single route.

Conditions: Warm and protected from the north wind. Dries quickly after rainfall. Best for cold or cloudy days.

Shade: Until 11:30 (right) or 13:30 (middle, left).

Exposure: S, SW

Kids: So-so. The approach needs care, and the terrain beneath the cliffs is not very level.

Approach: From Masouri, drive to Arginonta. Pass the church and immediately after turn right onto the road to Vathy. Park approx. 600m further (37.014301, 26.972157). There is a large cairn on the left and some fixed metal rungs like steps. Go up and follow the path right, then back up left. **Walking time:** 5-8 min.

See also: Crag Panorama on page 156.

Rock Round is a newer sub-sector on the left side of the crag. It features good quality red/grey rock and fairly good potential for additional new routes.

Climbing: On grey/red rock. Somewhat inconsistent, lacking routes in the mid-grades.

Shade: Until 12:30. **Exposure:** S

1 Joy   1★ 5a 16m
G Hommel, J Friedrich, 2011

2 Toy   1★ 5a 15m
G Hommel, J Friedrich, 2011

3 Rock Round   2★ 6c 25m
G Hommel, J Friedrich, 2011

4 Puzzle   2★ 7b 26m
Finishes nicely up the orange wall.
G Hommel, J Friedrich, 2011

5 Study   1★ 7a 22m
Inconsistent, with a boulder problem.
G Hommel, J Friedrich, 2011

6 Organ   1★ 5b 27m
G Hommel, J Friedrich, 2011

7 Gaga   1★ 6a 25m
G Hommel, J Friedrich, 2011

ROCK ROUND

17 ARGINONTA

148
37.014301
26.972157

HOLIDAY

Sub-sector **Holiday** is a small vertical grey wall with some worthwhile wall climbs plus some cracks and flakes.

Climbing: Mostly on a typical grey wall.

Shade: Until 12:00. **Exposure:** S

8 Donkey   1★ 6b+ 24m
50m left of "Bolt Obsession". *G Hommel, J Friedrich, 2011*

9 Bolt Obsession   2★ 4c 20m
Slab, flakes, cracks and a wall with a hard finish.
C + Y Remy, 2011

10 BB   2★ 5a 20m
A tricky start, then easy. Dedicated to Bernard Bolliger.
C + Y Remy, 2011

11 Takis   2★ 4a 16m
Rare: the easy climb is the most beautiful! *C + Y Remy 2011*

12 Rebecca   2★ 4c 20m
A Hedgecock, 2011

13 No Blabla, Do It!   2★ 4b 14m
Slab, corner, holds and pleasant moves. *C + Y Remy, 2011*

14 Mammut Step   2★ 4c 14m
Big steps and big holds. *C + Y Remy, 2011*

15 Studio Fatolitis   1★ 6a 20m
J Rohrmann, 2013

16 Blitz   1★ 5c+ 20m
Wall, crack and bulge. *J Rohrmann, 2009*

17 Donner   1★ 5c 18m
Past a hole then up the slab and flake crack.
J Rohrmann, 2009

18 Sturm   1★ 5c 17m
The groove and bulge. *J Rohrmann, 2008*

19 Ilona   1★ 5a 17m
The rib on the right, past a suspicious flake. *M Rauer, 2008*

20 Flying Doctor   2★ 5c+ 20m
Up the corner groove. *A Hedgecock, D Selwyn, 2013*

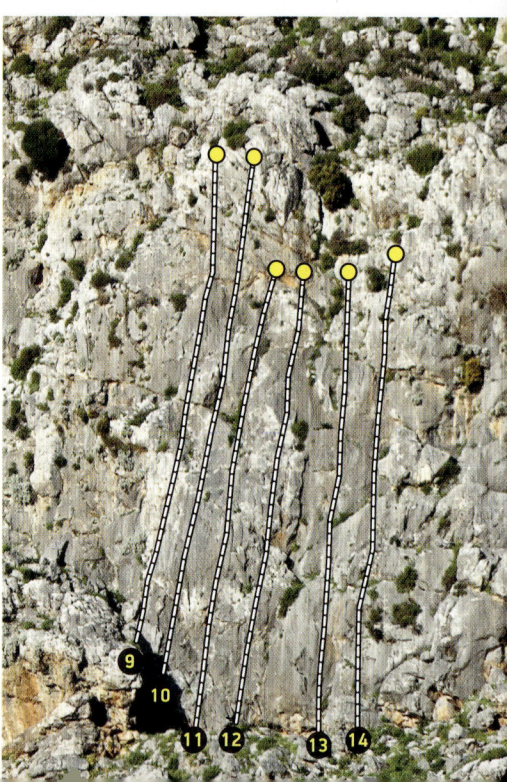

149

17 ARGINONTA
AMPHITHEATRE

37.014301
26.972157

Amphitheatre is the hardest sub-sector of **Arginonta**. A former animal pen, this rock amphitheatre offers high-quality overhanging red rock with some impressive stalactites. It also stays in the shade the longest.

Climbing: Athletic and dynamic on overhangs, holes and some stalactites.

Shade: Until 13:30. **Exposure:** S

21 Xaveri   2★   7b 22m
Same start as "Electra", then branches off to the left. Great climbing on a tufa/flowstone formation with some sharp crimps; athletic but also technical. *M Dettling, 2011*

22 Electra   2★   7a 18m
Good climbing on pockets, tufas, smooth holds + a hard bouldery move. *"New route clinic": L Triay, G Fanguin, A Theodoropoulos + 10 participating climbers, 2004*

Claude Remy on his route "Koubinos" 6b. CHRISTINE REMY

23 Pandora   3★   7c+ 25m
Steep and powerful climbing. *C Dawson, 2012*

24 Lysistrati   3★   7a+ 30m
Excitingly steep in and out of large holes. Absorbing moves over the lip and up the headwall. *"New route clinic": L Triay, G Fanguin, A Theodoropoulos + 10 participating climbers, 2004*

25 Oresteia   2★   6c+ 20m
A stiff but interesting wall with continuous difficulty. *L Triay, G Fanguin, A Theodoropoulos + 10 participating climbers, "new route clinic" 2004*

26 Sexy   1★   5c+ 25m
A squeezed line, similar to #27. *J Rohrmann, M Rauer, 2008*

27 Hot Shot   2★   5c+ 25m
A steep brown friction slab, sustained and crinkly. *J Friedrich, G Hommel, 2006*

28 Blood Sport   1★   6a 25m
An easy scramble leads to some good wall climbing at half-height, very close to "Hot Shot". *J Rohrmann, M Rauer, 2008*

29 NAB/FAW   2★   6c 33m
An easy start, then pleasant wall climbing to a devious athletic bulge. *C + Chr Remy, 2014*

30 God is Lemmy   3★   6a 25m
An easy first part leads to a red wall with wonderful, varied climbing. *C + Chr Remy, 2014*

31 Papagalos   2★   6b 25m
A bit harder than its neighbor. Save your energy until the very last move. *C + Chr Remy, 2014*

32 64 You   1★   6b 25m
Starts left of the small cave; a wall with hard finish. *F Heinicke, X Heinicke, C Heinicke, A Riemer, 2013*

33 Schniedel   1★   6c 25m
A direct start of "64" crossing the roof of the cave. *F Heinicke, A Riemer, 2014*

34 Bouboulina   3★   6b 25m
The pocketed wall. *C + Y Remy, 2010*

35 Koubinos   2★   6b 25m
Technical, full of hidden holds. *C + Y Remy, 2010*

36 Aristocrats   1★   7a 25m
A squeezed start; for the first short wall you may have to share some holds of "Kubinos" with your left hand. *C + Chr Remy, 2014*

17 ARGINONTA

INFRARED WALL

152
37.014301
26.972157

Infrared Wall rises to 30m high and we sometimes like to call it "the 6b wall". Some of the best 6bs on the island are here, but all routes are in fact excellent, with a variety and quality that may surprise you. The bright red wall is full of hidden holds and pleasant surprises.

Climbing: Wonderful and varied on a slightly overhanging red wall, steeper on the right, with tufa pipes as well.

Shade: Until 13:30. **Exposure:** S

37 No Mercy 2★ 6b+ 25m
The harder, steeper left finish. *A Theodoropoulos, 2010*

38 Merci 2★ 6b+ 25m
A pumpy but worthwhile start at the right edge of the cave needs foresight to avoid a cul-de-sac. *H Weninger, 2007*

39 Pornokini 3★ 6a 28m
A classic, varied route. The steep bits have good holds. *B Girardin, C +Y Remy, 2007*

40 Test Under Stress 1★ 6c 30m
A very well-protected overhang. *C + Y Remy, 2011*

41 Kosmas 3★ 6b 30m
A pocketed, steep wall. Good holds keep coming, don't give up! *C + Y Remy, 2010*

42 Free Style 3★ 6a+ 28m
A juggy, delightful wall, all the way up to the top section. *B Girardin, C + Y Remy, 2007*

43 Wild Sex 3★ 6b 25m
Wild but "safe" sex, with flowing climbing up a well-protected pocketed wall. *B Girardin, C + Y Remy, 2007*

44 Bôrhok 3★ 6b 25m
A well-protected, sustained juggy wall. *B Girardin, C + Y Remy, 2009*

45 Cap Arvithis 3★ 6b 25m
The wall with a tricky bulge in the upper half. *B Girardin, C + Y Remy, 2007*

46 Barba Yorghos 3★ 6c+ 25m
A great climb with escalating difficulty up a technical wall to a tufa roof. Easier if you are tall. *C Remy, 2008*

47 Anna-Maria 3★ 6c 25m
Pumpy tufa jugs; not easy to find the moves! *B Girardin, C + Y Remy, 2007*

48 Katergo 2★ 7b 25m
After a pleasant start, the upper half follows a nice tufa. *C Remy, 2008*

49 Motörhead 3★ 7b 25m
A bouldery start then athletic tufa climbing. *C Remy, 2008*

50 No Sleep 'til Hammersmith 3★ 7a+ 25m
Dedicated to the best (say the equippers) live album of Motörhead. Fans will love the macho start, but go easy on the hollow flake higher up. *B Girardin, C + Y Remy, 2007*

51 Romance of Stone 3★ 6c+ 25m
Overhang with tufas and big holds. Finish on a wall. *C + Y Remy, 2011*

52 Sex in the City 2★ 7a 25m
Starts with a bouldery crux, then hard, fingery moves. *F Heinicke, A Riemer, 2008*

53 Papou 2★ 5c+ 20m
The brown overhanging edge of the wall with a steep and technical slab. Stiff at the end. *B Girardin, C + Y Remy, 2007*

Christine Remy on the challenging "Anna-Maria" 6c.
CLAUDE REMY

17 ARGINONTA

154
37.014301
26.972157

KATHARINA
FIRE WALL

Katharina and **Fire Wall** comprise a small, gentle grey slab next to a fiery red wall full of pockets and holes.

Climbing: Well-bolted, easy routes at **Katharina**. Technical climbing on slightly overhanging rock at **Fire Wall**.

Shade: Until 11:30 at **Katharina**; 12:00 at **Fire Wall**.

Exposure: S

54 For Sue and Steve — 1★ 5a 18m
Needs problem-solving uncommon for the grade. Pleasantly sustained. Routes #54-#56: J + S Jekel, R Mayer, N Preining, D Bolius, C Kerner, G Linder, V Wallner, 2005

55 Missing Link — 1★ 4c 18m
Attention: Don't touch a big loose block between #55-#56.

56 Shark Bite — 1★ 5c+ 20m
Strange at the bulge; inconsistent.

57 Stock Fish — 2★ 5b 20m
A good slab, nice for warming up. T + S Jekel, 2004

58 Clean — 3★ 5c 20m
A technical, delicate start. H Weninger, 2005

59 Katharina — 2★ 5a 20m
Sustained, but spaced bolts for the grade. T + S Jekel, 2004

60 Victoria — 2★ 5a 20m
Another beginners' slab, though tricky. T + S Jekel, 2004

61 Tufa Slab — 2★ 5b+ 20m
Unusual slab climbing on slippery tufa rock. T+S Jekel, 2004

62 Mike's Rescue — 2★ 5a 22m
Varied climbing and interesting finale. T + S Jekel, 2004

63 Loukoumades — 2★ 5c+ 25m
Interesting, surprising, sharp. Routes #63, #64: T+S Jekel R Mayer N Preining D Bolius C Kerner G Linder V Wallner 2005

64 Adonibert — 2★ 6a 25m
An easy slab, then steep, reachy moves.

65 Asche zu Asche — 2★ 6a+ 25m
Brown and red tufa via a hole. B Girardin, C + Y Remy, 2007

66 Kel Karma — 3★ 6b+ 20m
A non-stop challenge with rests in-between. C+Y Remy 2010

67 Avri — 3★ 6b 15m
Cool moves between good holds on an excellent red wall. Pumpy but well-bolted. B Girardin, C + Y Remy, 2009

68 Kolhinet Kafhouille — 1★ 6c+ 30m
"Avri" extension. Dont clip the anchor, but the bolt on the right. Hard to start; should probably have finished before the ledge. Beware of loose rock. C + Y Remy, 2011

69 And Now for Something... — 3★ 5c+ 18m
...completely different. The steep chimney with fantastic bridging and increasing difficulty. T + S Jekel, 2004

70 Climate Change — 2★ 6b+ 20m
A good sequence up the right edge of the chimney.
T + S Jekel, R Mayer, N Preining, D Bolius, C Kerner, G Linder, V Wallner, 2005

71 Albi Bak — 2★ 7a+ 25m
A sustained tufa wall leads to a spectacular roof. Handle the suspicious-looking block at the start with care. B Girardin, C + Y Remy, 2009

72 Code Quantum — 2★ 7a 20m
The wall, big tufa and pockets. C + Y Remy, 2010

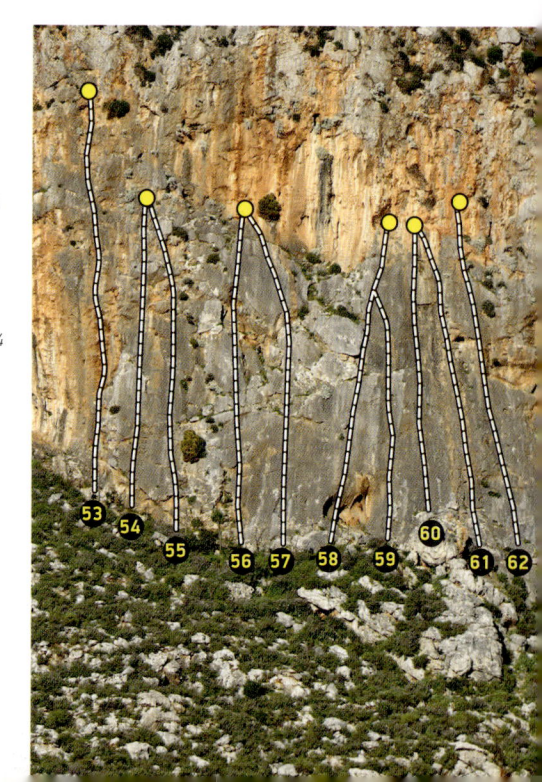

73 **Red Sea Secrets** 2★ 7a 28m
Brilliant climbing on the tufa system followed by a leaning technical wall. *B Girardin, C +Y Remy, 2009*

74 **Fire Wall** 3★ 7b 25m
Top-quality rock with pockets and a tufa. Athletic climbing, with some long reaches and two distinct cruxes. *J Friedrich, G Hommel 2006 (extended by A Theodoropoulos, 2010)*

75 **Hard Primal** 2★ 6c+ 30m
An immaculate wall, but first a roof with a very reachy move if you go direct. *B Girardin, C + Y Remy, 2009*

76 **Klausis** 3★ 6a 30m
At the big hole use the edge and go on to the steeper and harder upper wall. *J Rohrmann, M Rauer, 2008*

77 **Papadopoulos** 2★ 6b+ 30m
Follow the weak line then well-protected crux to the great headwall. *C + Chr Remy, 2014*

78 **Birds Without Arms** 2★ 6a+ 25m
Slab, then wall, then slab again. *C + Chr Remy, 2014*

79 **Birds Without Arms Ext** 2★ 6b 30m
Cross the roof. Impressive but easier than it looks. *C + Chr Remy, 2014*

80 **Lemmy for President** 3★ 6a+ 30m
Slab, wall, and a bulge to finish. *C + Chr Remy, 2014*

Katie on one of her favorite routes, "Avri" 6b. JOHN KOULLIAS

18 ARGINONTA SKYLINE

156

37.013144
26.979585

GRADE RANGE	up to 5b+	5c to 6a+	6b to 7a	7a+ to 7c	7c+ and up
No. OF ROUTES	15	29	34	5	1

KRYPTOS

HAUTE GORGE

ARHI

ARGINONTA

SEA BREEZE

Arginonta Village

The ridge crowning the area of Arginonta has become home to several very good crags in the last few years. The walk-in is a bit longer, but the rock is mostly of excellent quality, the views are stunning, and the feeling of peace and tranquility is priceless.

Haute Gorge, **Kryptos**, **Ovoland**, **Little Verdon**, **Jägerwand** and **Piccalia** are the sub-sectors presented here. The cliffs visible above Red Wall of sector Arginonta are Ovoland and Little Verdon; the cliff closest to the road is Piccalia; the others are not so readily visible. One path mainly goes along the base of the cliff.

Climbing: Various styles on very good rock. Mostly face climbing, but also a short section of overhanging rock with tufas.

Conditions: Sunny and warm. Best for spring, fall, winter, and cloudy days.

Shade: Check each sub-sector. **Exposure**: S

Kids: Most sub-sectors are OK, except **Kryptos**.

Approach: From Masouri, go to Arginonta. Turn right onto the road to Vathy. Drive 2 km and park by a small concrete wall with red marks and the letter "K" (37.013144, 26.979585). Walk uphill, following the red marks to the left of the little gully. After 10 min you can walk up to the base of the first sub-sector, **Piccalia**, or continue on the good path (which goes to the chapel of Panagia Galatiani). Soon after, you are near sub-sector **Little Verdon**. Further, the grey slab of **Ovoland** is left of the big orange overhang. If you walk about 20 minutes longer, you will see **Haute Gorge** to your left (total 60 min). Sub-sector **Kryptos** is further up and to the right (total 75 min).

Walking time: 10-75 min depending on sector.

ARGINONTA SKYLINE SUB-SECTORS

OVOLAND

LITTLE VERDON

JÄGERWAND

PICCALIA

Simon Montmory on "Blame the Machine" 8a (page 165) at sector Little Verdon. CHRIS BOUKOROS

18 ARGINONTA SKYLINE
HAUTE GORGE

37.013144
26.979585

Haute Gorge is a new, serene sub-sector on the highest-quality rock with good potential for more lines. The longer approach is worth your while, and it is almost certain that you will have all the routes to yourself.

Climbing: On bulletproof vertical or slightly overhanging limestone, and routes up to 25-30m long between 6a-7a.

Shade: After 15.00. **Exposure**: E

Approach: As on page 156. Pass below Little Verdon and walk approximately 20 minutes more. When you come to the solitary tree (you will know it when you see it) the crag will be visible down to your left. Walk to the crag; there is no clear-cut path yet. **Walking time**: About 1 hour.

1 La Rondeue a Desbiens 3★ 6a 28m
C Idoux, 2013

2 Hostie 3★ 6a+ 25m
C Idoux, 2013

3 Margi's Prattipower 3★ 6b+ 25m
C Idoux, 2013

4 Silberru Ggamannli 3★ 6c 25m
C Idoux, 2013

5 Pelztierli ♪ 7a 20m
A compact and steep slabby wall. *C Idoux, L Salsotto, 2013*

6 Le Vieux Rom est Amer 3★ 6c+ 25m
C Idoux, L Salsotto, 2013

7 Tabernacle ♪ 6b+ 28m
A slabby wall with an exciting, bulgy finale.
C Idoux, L Salsotto, 2013

8 A la Wok Bar 3★ 6c 28m
C Idoux, L Salsotto, 2013

9 L'Eau S'Pisje 3★ 6c+ 28m
C Idoux, 2013

HAUTE GORGE

18 ARGINONTA SKYLINE
KRYPTOS

160
37.013144
26.979585

Kryptos is something completely different on Kalymnos! Lost in the upper part of the mountain looming above Skalia and Arginonta (590m) and far above Palionisos Bay, the austere **Kryptos** wall is nearly 100m high. Its base is large with overhangs, but the summit is a narrow scramble slab. All routes: Claude + Yves Remy, 2012.

Climbing: The ambiance, rock and climbing style are not at all typical for Kalymnos. The wall is isolated, the foot of the cliff is not cosy (steep/narrow ledges above long slopes), the rock is mostly conglomerate, and at the end of the approach you must go down a couloir, then climb a bit. **Kryptos** has an alpine touch; the rock is strange, scary conglomerate. On all routes here, follow the bolts; do *not* deviate from the line.

ATTENTION: For very experienced climbers only.

Shade: After 14.00. **Exposure**: E

Approach: As on page 156. Pass below Little Verdon and keep going on the path to the long flat pass. (At about 450m, you can see a part of **Kryptos**. Be careful; sometimes the wind at the pass can be very strong, even if there is no wind at the cliff.) Walk to the end of the ridge of the pass. Look for the big letter "K" on the rock. Go down the couloir on your right for about 40m, then follow a ledge (fixed rope) and climb up an easy short pillar (2b) to arrive at the left side of the cliff (fixed rope).

Walking time: 75 min.

1 Born to be Wild   2★ 6a+ 20m
Wall; go up to the big corner.

2 Chiona   3★ 6c 25m
A compact wall. Super.

3 Pumuky   2★ 7b 25m
With a great view over the scary conglomerate sector.

4 Lady Ka-Ka   2★ 6a 25m
A traverse. Strip the QDs on top-rope on your last climb.

5 Dust and Stones   2★ 6b+ 25m
A steep overhang, then go to the left side of the red pillar.

6 Dust and Stones Ext   2★ 6b 35m
Bolts removed. Goes left of a big moving flake.

7 **Mort Subite**   2★   6b+ 35m
A steep overhang, then go up to the middle of the red pillar.

8 **Mort Subite Ext**   2★   7a 35m
Go up to the red pillar.

9 **Sugarland (Unfinished)**   ?★   ? ??m
2012

10 **Russian Plaquette**   2★   6a+ 25m
The first hanger is moving, but it is all solid.

11 **Russian Plaquette Ext**   1★   7a 35m
Bolts removed by the equippers; not a nice climb.

12 **Sponge Rock**   3★   5c+ 15m
An overhang but with big holds.

13 **G3**   2★   6a 15m
"Band of best rock guitarists: Satriani, Vai, Petrucci."

14 **G3 Ext 1**   2★   6c 36m
The crux comes before the 2nd lower-off.

15 **G3 Ext 2**   2★   7a 55m
2012

16 **Dark Desir**   2★   5c 15m
Follow the grey slab.

17 **Slide of Life**   2★   6b+ 36m
Go up to the cave via a short fixed rope.

18 **Slide of Life Ext**   2★   6c 55m
Crux below the lower-off. *2012*

19 **Boneshaker**   2★   6b+ 36m
Right side of this red wall. The fixed rope access is for "Slide of Life" and "Boneshaker".

20 **Boneshaker Ext**   2★   6c+ 55m
There are a couple of hard fingery moves above the 1st lower-off.

21 **Katharos**   2★   6a 20m
From the bottom of the main cliff, go down a bit, then walk up the couloir and the big ramp on the right of the wall (short fixed rope).

22 **Lost World**   2★   5b+ 30m
On the right side of the big ramp-slab.

23 **Lost World Ext**   2★   6a+ 45m
Cross the big roof above the big ramp-slab from the left.

24 **Unfinished**   2★   ? ??m
A line on the red wall.

25 **Master of Puppets**   2★   7a+ 40m
The obvious great overhanging line with an early crux.

18 ARGINONTA SKYLINE
OVOLAND

162
37.013144
26.979585

Ovoland is a small, comfortable sub-sector with flat terrain, refreshing shade from the trees, and a soothing quietness. It features long satisfying routes and friendly bolting, so it is good for relatively new climbers.

Climbing: On slightly off-vertical long grey slabs. Rock is sharp, full of holds and multiple great formations; the longest routes are up to 40m.

Shade: Until 12.00. **Exposure**: SW

Approach: As on page 156. Pass below Little Verdon and then go up to the grey slab to the left of the big orange overhang. **Walking time**: 30 min.

1 **Malista Kyrie** — 2★ 5a 12m
A short climb starting in the little cave. *C + Chr Remy, 2013*

2 **Dirty Free Shop** — 2★ 4c 12m
Start at the right of the little cave. *C + Chr Remy, 2013*

3 **To Salingari** — 2★ 5a+ 15m
A slab with big holds. *C + Chr Remy, 2013*

4 **David Goes to the Pub** — 2★ 4c+ 18m
Another slab climb; follow the left crack. *C + Chr Remy, 2013*

5 **Koukouvas** — 3★ 5b+ 18m
The best of the shorter lines to the left; follow the right crack. *C + Chr Remy, 2013*

6 **Kraftreaktor** — 2★ 6a 25m
Save energy for the last part! *C + Chr Remy, 2013*

7 **Bora Einai** — 2★ 6a+ 28m
Compact rock with many holds. *C + Y Remy, 2012*

8 **Tha Perasei?** — 3★ 6b 28m
Touch the left side of the orange hole. *C + Y Remy, 2012*

9 **Epimetheus** — 3★ 6a+ 28m
Good climbing via the right side of the orange hole to the top. *C + Y Remy, 2012*

10 **Epimetheus Ext** — 3★ 6b 40m
Saves the hard move for the end! 20 QD. *C + Y Remy, 2013*

11 **Hero of the Day** — ♪ 6a 28m
A great route straight up the middle of the steep slab. *C + Y Remy, 2012*

12 **Hero of the Day Ext** — ♪ 6a+ 45m
Another very good, long climb. An 80m rope is *not* enough to lower to the ground. You will have to lower to the first anchor and re-thread. *C + Y Remy, 2013*

13 **Mnemosyne** — 2★ 5b 20m
A nice climb to try to onsight, if you are a beginner, or to warm up on. *C + Y Remy, 2012*

14 **Mnemosyne Ext** — 2★ 5c 28m
Not finished yet, but will go to the lower-off of "Petranella Ext". *C + Y Remy, 2012*

15 **Petranella** — 2★ 4b 22m
A pleasant, steady climb. *C + Y Remy, 2012*

16 **Petranella Ext** — 2★ 5c 30m
A bit steeper, a bit harder. *C + Y Remy, 2012*

18 ARGINONTA SKYLINE

LITTLE VERDON

37.013144
26.979585

Simon Montmory on the crux sequence of "Odious Guppie" 7b.
CHRIS BOUKOROS

Little Verdon is one of the best new crags, with a compact, Verdon-style grey wall and a small red cave with a few tufas to the left. Well-protected from the north wind, it is one of the best places to climb in the winter or on cold spring and autumn days. Routes inside the cave are also protected from the rain.

Climbing: Two different styles. On the left, some very overhanging tufa routes. On the right, Verdon-like, beautiful vertical grey rock offering exquisite face climbing. Unlike in the real Verdon, however, these routes are well-bolted and ideal for those looking to climb grades between 6a-7a.

Shade: Until 12:30. **Exposure**: SW

Approach: As on page 156. **Walking time**: 30 min.

Beatrice Pelissier on the superb "Fanny Ma Reine" 7b+.
CHRIS BOUKOROS

1 Odious Guppie   2★   7b 18m
A hard, crimpy, short route on slopey, somewhat slippery rock. *T Foord-Kelcey, 2011*

2 Tom-Tom Club   1★   7a 12m
Short, with a fingery crux. *N Gresham, S Golley, 2011*

3 Blame the Machine   ♪   8a 28m
A "King" line: very hard "V8" boulder in the middle of a juggy 7a+. Harder if you are short. *N Gresham, S Golley, 2011*

4 Fanny Ma Reine   ♪   7b+ 25m
Steep and athletic on tufas, blobs and pockets, with a spicy traverse finish. *F + F Clarte, C Idoux, 2011*

5 Anazitisi   2★   6b 28m
A natural diagonal line with good holds.

6 Trou Par Trou   3★   6a+ 28m
Continuous slab climbing from hole to hole. Not always obvious. *L Salsotto, C Idoux, 2011*

7 Fioca   ♪   7a 28m
A smooth technical slab with underclings, sidepulls, small pockets. Several obligatory moves. *L Salsotto, C Idoux, 2011*

8 Duro   3★   7b 28m
An immaculate slab full of sidepulls and hard foot smearing. *L Salsotto, C Idoux, 2011*

9 Puro   3★   6c 28m
A compact, balancy slab at its best. *L Salsotto, C Idoux, 2011*

10 Sqale   3★   6c 28m
A technical and sustained slab. *L Salsotto, C Idoux, 2011*

11 Riri   3★   6c+ 28m
A cruxy start and thin, technical wall in the mid-section. *L Salsotto, C Idoux, 2011*

12 Fifi   3★   6b+ 28m
A challenging start then an easier but fun wall. *C Idoux 2011*

13 Loulou   3★   6a+ 28m
Fun, long moves on big pockets and slots; delicate footholds. *C Idoux, 2011*

14 Petra   3★   6b 28m
Stiff crux for the grade; the 1st bolt is too high, and the anchor too far left, but the route is good stuff. *C Idoux, 2011*

15 Filou   2★   6a+ 20m
A dark slab then edge. Balancy, delicate toes. Questionable blocks at the top. *B + C Arnold, A Hafner, C Schmidt, 2011*

16 Zipfelmütze (Bobble Hat)   2★   6a+ 20m
A run-out start, a technical slab with big pockets and a cool end over the bulge. *B + C Arnold, A Hafner, C Schmidt, 2011*

17 Fillo   2★   5a 25m
The further right, the easier.
B + C Arnold, A Hafner, C Schmidt, 2011

18 ARGINONTA SKYLINE
JÄGERWAND
PICCALIA

37.013144
26.979585

Jägerwand is a new small sub-sector on the way to **Little Verdon** and **Ovoland**.

Climbing: On a grey wall and slabs. At the time of writing the routes were still quite new, so they are expected to improve with traffic.

Shade: Until 12.00. **Exposure**: SW

Approach: As on page 156. After you park, walk uphill following the red marks to the left of the little gully. 10 minutes later, walk up to the base of the first sub-sector, **Piccalia**. Continue for 5 more minutes and you are at the base of **Jägerwand**. **Walking time**: 15 min.

1 The Gun   3★ 6a 30m
Wall and slab. *F Heinicke, K Kühnel, R + E + K + P Krug 2015*

2 Unfinished Project   ?★ ?? ?m
F Heinicke

3 Forester   ?★ 5a 22m
J + U Friedrich, 2015

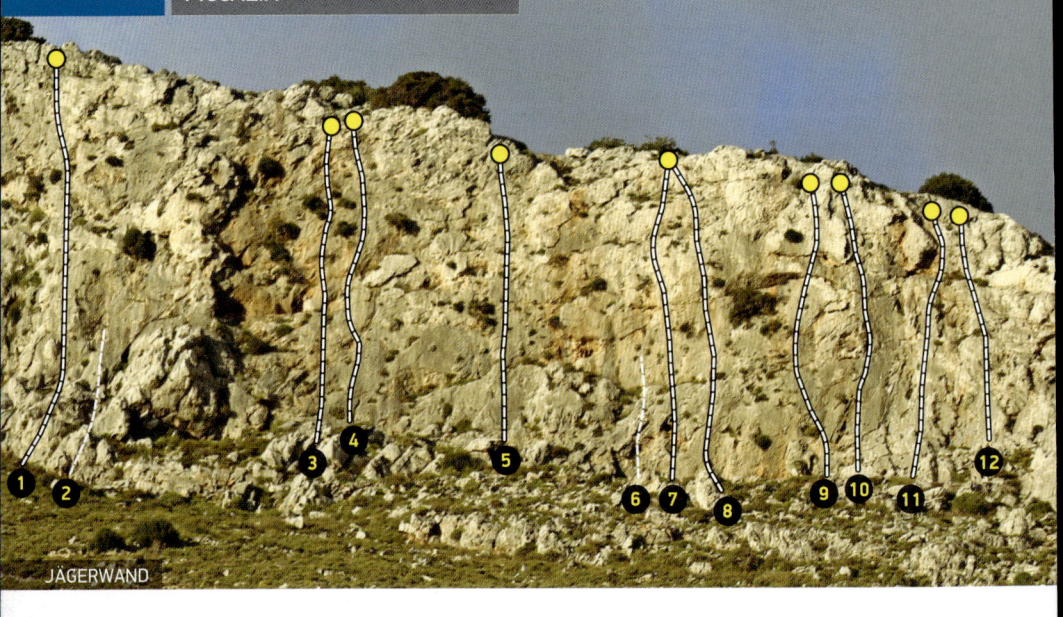

4 Jägermeister   2★ 5c+ 23m
F Heinicke, K Kühnel, R + E + K + P Krug, 2015

5 Bambi   2★ 5c 23m
F Heinicke, K Kühnel, 2015

6 Unfinished Project   ?★ ?? ?m
F Heinicke

7 Blattschuss   2★ 6b 26m
An overhang and wall. *F Heinicke, A Riemer, 2014*

8 Ewige Jagdgründe   2★ 6b 27m
A short edge, wall and bulge. *F Heinicke, A Riemer, 2014*

9 Trophäe   1★ 6a+ 21m
A wall climb with a bulgy finale. *F Heinicke, A Riemer, 2014*

10 Jägerlatein   2★ 5c 21m
Another wall climb.
A Riemer, E Schubert, I Bonikowski, F Heinicke, 2014

11 Dackel Waldi   2★ 5b+ 19m
R + E + K + P Krug, 2015

12 Lockvogel   1★ 5a 18m
A pillar-wall.
A Riemer, E Schubert, I Bonikowski, F Heinicke 2014

Piccalia is a short slab and wall above a small, pretty cluster of trees (a forest by Kalymnos standards!)

Climbing: Short routes on the slab and grey wall. **Piccalia** was first bolted in 2006, but because it needed some rebolting and more cleaning, it was not included in the previous guidebook. In August 2015, this author and George Kopalides were able to correct some bolts and lower-offs and clean the rock. The approach is easy and there is more potential for new routes to the left, but equippers will need to do a lot of cleaning.

Shade: Until 13:00. **Exposure**: SW

Approach: As on page 156. After you park, walk uphill following the red marks to the left of the little gully. 10 minutes later, pass the "forest" and you will see the crag to the right. **Walking time**: 10 min.

1 Hornet ?★ 5b 25m
On the far left; not shown on the topo. *J Friedrich, 2015*

2 Renew ?★ 6b 20m
J Friedrich, 2015

3 Respect ?★ 6c+ 20m
J Friedrich, 2015

4 Loucia 2★ 6c 20m
Intense, with an obligatory crux with small holds and hard footwork. *T + S Jekel, R Mayer, P Wegener, 2006*

5 Piccalia 1★ 6a 20m
A leftward traverse and delicate slab.
T + S Jekel, R Mayer, P Wegener, 2006

6 Ruby 2★ 5c 15m
A smooth start, then a slab with big flakes.
T + S Jekel, R Mayer, P Wegener, 2006

7 Steinwurf 2★ 5b+ 15m
Slab with sharp flakes. *T+S Jekel, R Mayer, P Wegener, 2006*

8 Red Scar 2★ 5c 15m
The technical grey slab finishes on a bulge with small holds. *T + S Jekel, R Mayer, P Wegener, 2006*

9 Bridging 1★ 5b+ 12m
A steep sharp groove. *T + S Jekel, R Mayer, P Wegener, 2006*

10 K2 1★ 5c+ 14m
A steep start, then climbing up a delicate and sharp buttress. *G Hommel, J Friedrich, 2009*

PICCALIA

19 ARGINONTA VALLEY

168
37.013770
26.971809

GRADE RANGE	up to 5b+	5c to 6a+	6b to 7a	7a+ to 7c	7c+ and up
No. OF ROUTES	4	39	17	3	1

Francesca Canciani on "Rintintin" 5c+ at sub-sector Black Buddha (page 176).

Arginonta Valley is a newly-developed area across the valley from the ever-popular red cliff of Arginonta. It was equipped in the context of the major route maintenance program undertaken in 2015/16 and funded by the EU, during which 300 routes in Kalymnos were rebolted and 100 new routes added. This new sector was created to fill the need in Kalymnos for more crags with lots of shade for hot-weather climbing and an emphasis on quality mid- and low-grade routes, plus a quick and easy approach. Both cliffs comprising this new sector, namely **Black Buddha** and **Arginonta Valley**, meet these requirements (with the exception of the longer approach to Black Buddha). They are north-facing, well-bolted, and though originally under thick vegetation, consecutive days of thorough cleaning uncovered quite a few highly enjoyable and varied lines. After climbing, the handful of small friendly shops in Arginonta are perfect for a post-climb drink or a bite to eat.

Climbing: Varied, on slabs full of good holds and some horizontal streaks, vertical walls with small holds and juggy bulges, but also steep overhangs with jugs and some colonettes. All routes were equipped by Aris Theodoropoulos and Claude Idoux unless otherwise noted. Grades are not confirmed yet, as routes are very new and have only had a handful of ascents. We welcome your suggestions about grading.

Conditions: Ideal for climbing on hot days. The approach to sub-sector Black Buddha, though, is in the sun.

Exposure: N

Kids: Both sub-sectors have some suitable areas, though the approach to Black Buddha is much longer. Remember that **kids must always be away from the cliffs and never directly beneath climbers**.

Approach: Check each sub-sector's description.

Natasa Manou on the beautiful technical wall of "Grigna" 6b in the Middle Wall (page 173).

ARGINONTA VALLEY SUB-SECTORS

BLACK BUDDHA

ARGINONTA VALLEY

Parking area

Arginonta Village

19 ARGINONTA VALLEY

ARGINONTA VALLEY
LEFT CAVE

37.013770
26.971809

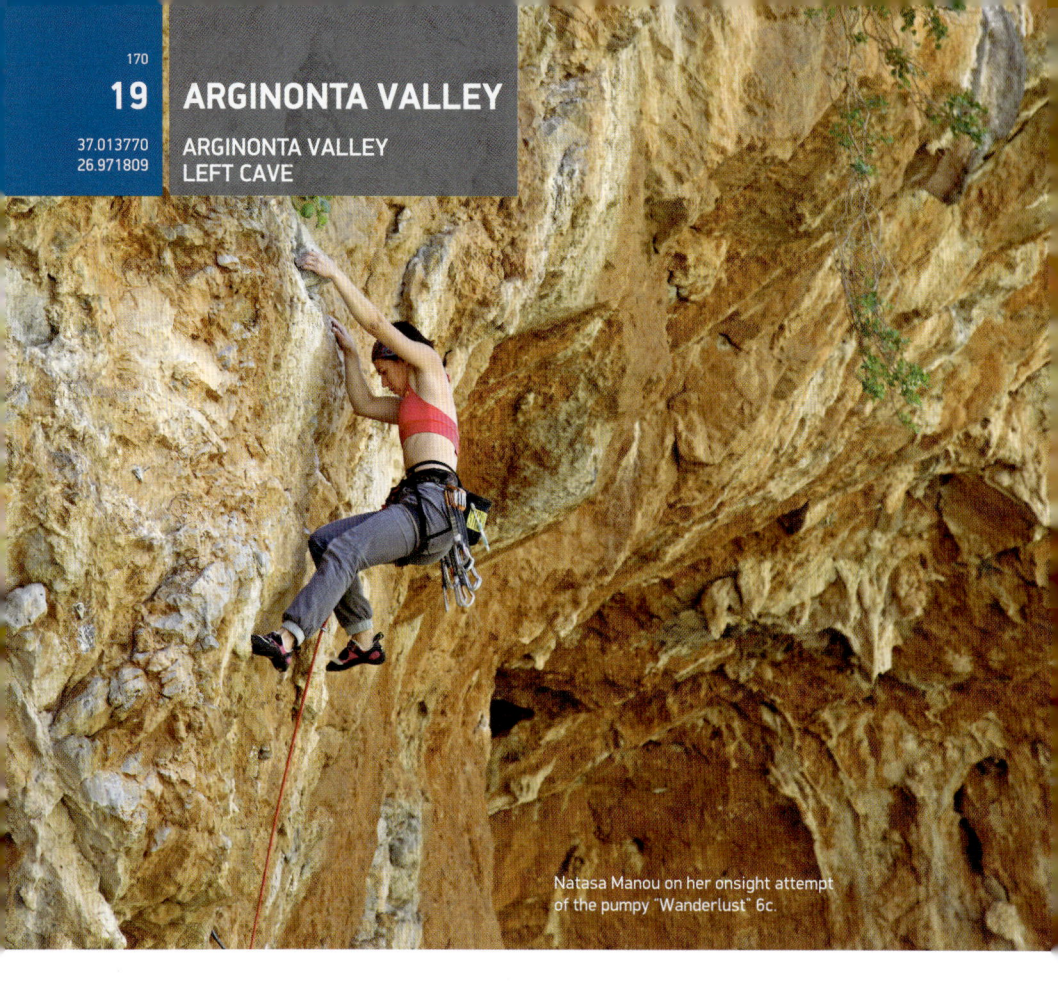

Natasa Manou on her onsight attempt of the pumpy "Wanderlust" 6c.

Sub-sector Arginonta Valley is directly opposite the red cliff of Arginonta, above a valley with centuries-old, beautifully gnarled olive trees. It is perfect for hot days and there is something here for every climber.

Climbing: At three distinct sections offering a bit of everything: steep slabs full of good holds and some horizontal streaks, juggy bulges, but also steep overhangs and some colonettes.

Conditions: Ideal for climbing in summer or hot afternoons. Wake up at your leisure, enjoy your breakfast, and climb in the shade until late. Sub-sectors Middle Wall and Right Wall are often refreshed by a soothing breeze coming from the valley. **Exposure:** N

Shade: After 11:30 (Left Cave + Right Wall) or after 12:30 (Middle Wall) and until the rest of the day.

Kids: The path is very short and there is plenty of space under the shade of the big olive trees. Never let kids sit or play directly beneath the cliffs.

Approach: Go to Arginonta village. Immediately after the small honey shop, turn right. Pass in front of the church and continue on a concrete road for about 200m. The concrete road turns into a bumpy dirt road. Park 50m further, at the clearing with the huge olive trees (37.013770, 26.971809). Walk for a further 100m along the dirt road until you see a wire gate on the right. Go through the gate into the olive grove. Make sure to close the door behind you. Walk up to the cliff through the olive trees for another two minutes. **Walking time:** 5 min.

Left Cave is a small cave with high-quality red rock. Routes are steep, pumpy and athletic, but the jugs are great and there are some tufas, too.

Shade: After 11:30.

1 Arion 3★ 6c+ 15m
Short but steep on tufas and blobs.

2 Unicorn 3★ 7a+ 18m
Amazing and ultra-steep, with huge holds and some tufas all the way to the tricky finale.

3 Diagoras 3★ 7a 18m
Athletic and juggy.

4 Wanderlust 3★ 6c 16m
Steep climbing on blobs and jugs.

5 Pixam 3★ ?? 25m
A steep and roofy project. *Lucas Dourdourekas, 2015/16*

6 Lorreta 3★ 7c 18m
An excellent tufa climb. *Lucas Dourdourekas, 2015/16*

7 Alcyone 3★ 7a+ 20m
A nice red wall with some spaced but good jugs.
Lucas Dourdourekas, 2015/16

19 ARGINONTA VALLEY

ARGINONTA VALLEY
MIDDLE WALL

37.013770
26.971809

Claude Idoux, one of the main equippers of this crag, climbing "Greundzo" 6b.

MIDDLE WALL

Middle Wall is a special black-and-grey steep slab with long routes full of good holds, some horizontal streaks, and several short bulges. There is often a smooth breeze coming from the valley.

Shade: After 12:30.

1 Ahtarmas 3★ 5a 20m
A low-angle slab with good holds.

2 Skafandro 2★ 5c 20m
A steep slab at the end.

3 Hippocrates 2★ 6a 23m
Finishes with a tricky bulge.

4 Alani 3★ 6a+ 38m
Intriguing, long, with some great holds when it steepens.

5 In Vino Veritas 3★ 6b 30m
Again, the upper part steepens.

6 Tricky-Tricky Mana Mou 3★ 6b+ 30m
There is a complex bulge near the top.

7 Patókorfa 3★ 6a+ 30m
A bulge with good holds.

8 Rufixius 3★ 6a+ 33m
A long and intricate wall climb.

9 Greundzo 3★ 6b 33m

10 Grigna 3★ 6b 33m
A fantastic technical wall with some obligatory moves between bolts.

11 Rhythm of the Rain 3★ 6a 33m

12 Thunder Road 3★ 6b 30m

13 Sythas 3★ 5c 30m
An excellent technical wall full of good pockets.

14 Kavourmas 3★ 5b+ 28m
A vertical wall full of jugs.

15 Kamaki 3★ 5b 20m
Another juggy parade.

19 ARGINONTA VALLEY

37.013770
26.971809

ARGINONTA VALLEY
RIGHT WALL

Alex Istatkof flying through the cruxy bulge of "Gasteclou" 6a+.

RIGHT WALL

Right Wall offers varied climbing on sharp slabs, juggy bulges and some fine, short red walls. There is often a smooth breeze coming from the valley.

☁ Shade: After 11:30.

1 Naughty Monkey 2★ 5c 20m
An interesting wall and groove.

2 Naughty Monkey Ext 3★ 7a 35m
An outstanding route up a steep, juggy wall and a crack. Many holds, but which one is best?

3 Bohemian Mermaid 3★ 5c 20m
Slab, flakes, and a steep wall.

4 Bohemian Mermaid Ext 3★ 6c+ 30m
Awesome rock and climbing up the steep groove with a few testing moves.

5 Nargile 1★ 6a m
An easy slab leads to a bulge with good, but sharp, pockets.

6 Rock Tragos 3★ 6a 20m
A steep and enjoyable wall.

7 Damos 2★ 6a+ 20m
One reachy move at the bulge.

8 Ravasaki 2★ 6a+ 20m
A nice headwall on horizontal shelves.

9 Zephyros 3★ 6a 20m
An intriguing upper part.

10 Zephyros Ext 3★ 6c+ 30m
Just before the last bolt of "Zephyros", go right and up to a very technical red wall with small holds.

11 Le Bleu du Ciel 3★ 6b+ 30m
The second part is impressive, up a red wall with some spaced jugs.

12 Ad-Hoc 3★ 6b 30m
Again, an amazing upper part on beautiful red rock.

13 Idoine 3★ 6a 30m
Another striking line on big huecos and an upper groove on immaculate red and brown rock.

14 Gasteclou 2★ 6a+ 30m
An interesting bulge.

15 L'Engeance 3★ 6a+ 33m
A slab and a magnificent headwall.

16 Bancroche 2★ 5c+ 28m
A slab which steepens at the upper part.

17 Chausse-Trappe 1★ 6a 29m
A good but sharp slab.

19 ARGINONTA VALLEY
BLACK BUDDHA

37.014344
26.971145

Paolo Iesu on "Rintintin" 5c+

Black Buddha is high above Arginonta Bay, with beautiful and unusual views over the village and the sea. With many hours of mid-day shade this is another good option for hot days; however, the approach path is in the sun.

Climbing: Quality routes around 6a on grey/black slabby rock full of small bulges and big holds often hiding overhead. All routes were equipped by Claude Idoux in 2015/16 unless otherwise noted.

Conditions: Cool; good for hot days. **Exposure:** N

Shade: From 10:00 to 16:00.

Kids: The path is long and steep, but there are some good areas near or around the cliffs.

Approach: Go to Arginonta village. Immediately after the small honey shop, turn right. Pass in front of the church and continue on a concrete road. Park further along, where the road splits and there is an unfinished stone structure (37.014344, 26.971145). Walk to the right along a faded dirt road, which goes uphill then leftwards, and turns into a path entering a narrow gully. Walk up the gully until you see a cairn on the right. Continue up the steep winding path following the cairns.
See also: photo on page 169. **Walking time:** 25 min.

1. **Psarou** 2★ 5b 20m
The left low-angle arete. *P Alexandris, C Idoux, 2015*

2. **Darko** 2★ 6a 20m
A corner and bulge with sharp holds.
A Istatkof, C Idoux, 2015

3. **Boubou** 2★ 6a 22m
Slab and sharp bulging crack.

4. **Idéfix** 2★ 6a+ 22m
The pillar and hanging groove. A somewhat unbalanced route. Hard climbing past the second and third bolts leads to easier climbing on sharp holds.

5. **Milou** 2★ 6a+ 22m
The groove and nice (but sharp) bulging headwall.

6. **Snoopy** 2★ 6a+ 20m

7. **Scoubidou** 2★ 6a+ 20m
Goes up the left side of the pillar.

8. **Rintintin** 2★ 5c+ 22m

BLACK BUDDHA

9 Arhat   2★ 6a 28m
A pocketed slab interrupted by two short bulges.

10 Nirvâna   3★ 6a+ 35m
A bulge with challenging footwork leads to continuous, pleasant climbing.

11 Jina   2★ 6a 28m
A wall that leads to a jamming crack. Sadly, there are holds in the crack, so no need to jam!

12 Mandala   3★ 6a+ 22m
The rib/slab with underclings and groove to the right with un-obvious pockets.

13 Mandala Ext   3★ 6a+ 32m
A black bulge with big jugs.

14 Vishnou   2★ 5c 24m
Easy slabs lead to a steeper finish with good holds.

15 Ganesha   3★ 6a+ 30m
A nice grey slabby start then several pleasant bulges.

16 Buddha   2★ 6a+ 25m
Climb over a bulge to easy slabs which, in turn, lead to a superb wall and fun overhang.

17 Dharma   2★ 6a 25m

18 Troulalà   2★ 5c 25m

19 Karma   3★ 5c+ 25m
A nice pocketed wall; interesting finale on black rock.

20 Tara   3★ 6a 25m

21 Goussinair   3★ 6b 37m
Several bulges with good holds, if you can find them. 16 QD.

22 Gotta   3★ 6a+ 25m
A wall climb full of good pockets.

23 Push-Pipi   2★ 6b 25m
Climb the left side of the pillar up a fine black wall to a bulging crux with sharp holds.

All routes were equipped by Claude Idoux in 2015/16 unless otherwise noted.

20 SUMMERTIME

37.014994
26.960927

GRADE RANGE	up to 5b+	5c to 6a+	6b to 7a	7a+ to 7c	7c+ and up
No. OF ROUTES	10	13	16	18	12

Hot summer afternoon and looking for cliffs? Well, you found them. The extended area from Kasteli to Arginonta village, with the breathtaking view over the narrow bay, is sector **Summertime** and its four distinct sub-sectors. Starting from the left, they are **Local Freezer**, **Magoulias**, **Summertime**, **Nikoleta** and **Big Shadow**.

Climbing: Everything from gentle slabs, vertical faces and routes for beginners, to insanely overhanging, athletic routes.

Conditions: Shady and cool. Excellent for climbing on summer afternoons, as long as there is at least a slight breeze. In winter, climbing is only possible on sunny mornings.

The lovely Sam Cujes on the classic "Ammohostos Vasilevousa" 6a (page 184).
LEE CUJES

SUMMERTIME SUB-SECTORS

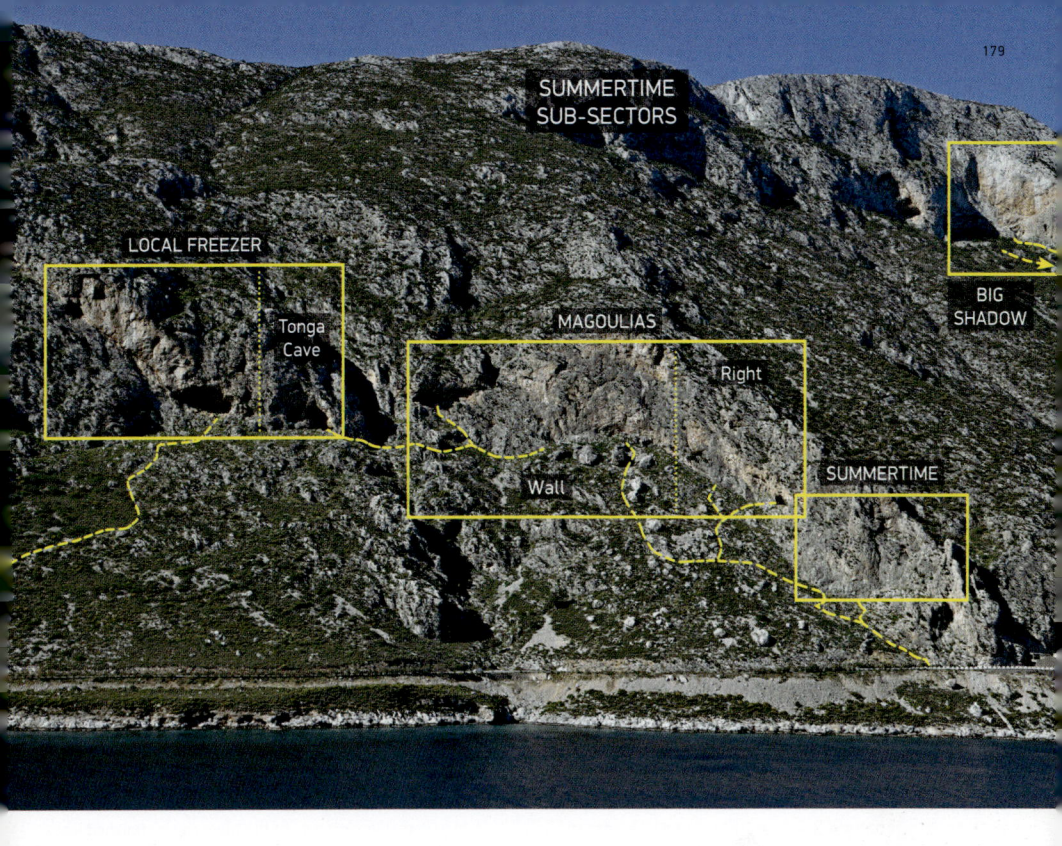

☁ **Shade**: After 13.00 and until the end of the day. **Exposure**: NE

Kids: So-so. The path is steep at parts, but there are some shady spots near the right end of the balcony at Summertime, as well as near Local Freezer, Magoulias Wall and Big Shadow.

Approach: From Masouri, drive towards Arginonta village. Approximately 2km after the big right-hand turn near Kasteli, you will see an abandoned concrete building on the right-hand side. Park there (37.014994, 26.960927). Walk up the steep path following the marks (you may have to scramble up certain bits). The path to Summertime is very short, for the other sub-sectors it is quite a bit longer. **Walking time**: 5-45 min, depending on sub-sector.

Gregor Jaeger on the highly featured rock of "Philotimo" 7a+ (page 181). G. JAEGER ARCHIVE

SUMMERTIME
LOCAL FREEZER

180
20
37.014367
26.962988

Simon Montmory on mega-steep "Blood Bath" 8a+.
NIKOLAOS SMALIOS

Local Freezer is a sector in a very steep cave with stalactites and, rare for Kalymnos, some huge stalagmites. It is located 400m past **Summertime** sector as you head from Masouri towards Arginonta. On the far right (50m) of the crag is **Tonga Cave**, with 3 short overhanging routes. **Local Freezer** faces north, so it is ideal for climbing from May through October. However, it is not good for climbing on humid days with no breeze, especially on the smooth wall with crimps and edges to the left.

Climbing: Very athletic and powerful inside the cave. Technical and varied on the smooth red/white wall to the left. There are no easy routes at the moment, but the rock offers some possibilities. To access the routes further left up the red wall, use the fixed rope starting at the base of "Halara".

☁ **Shade**: After 11:00. **Exposure**: N

Approach: Local Freezer is 400m past sector Summertime (previous page). Drive past Summertime and park close to a goat shelter on the right (37.014367, 26.962988). Walk back rightwards up a path to the cave. **Walking time**: 10-15 min.

Alternate approach: You can also go up to Magoulias Wall and traverse left to Local Freezer from there.

1 Thermopylae   2★   7b+ 30m
A technical and fingery wall with a very bouldery move to gain the final groove. At the top it can be finished a bit further right (as for "Artemisium") at 7b. *A Berry, 2009*

2 Artemisium   3★   7c+ 30m
A Spartan white wall with good rests but a hard crux. You can avoid it via a 7b+ variation (go left into "Thermopylae" then move back right; there is a bolt). *A Berry, 2009*

3 Project   3★   ?? 30m
Free project. *A Berry, 2009*

4 Nostalgia   3★   6b+ 40m
Excellent climbing on highly-featured rock.
G Kopalides, A Theodoropoulos, 2009

5 Odontoglyphida   3★   7c 40m
Technical, slightly overhanging and exposed. Fantastic climbing! *G Kopalides, A Theodoropoulos, 2009*

6 Que Lo Flipas   3★   8a 40m
The immaculate technical wall. *S Sala, G Kopalides, 2009*

7 Kerasma   3★   7c 40m
A powerful and fun start leads to more crimpy terrain. A treat, indeed, which is what "*kerasma*" means.
G Kopalides, A Theodoropoulos, 2009

| 8 | **Halara** | 3★ | **7b+ 35m** |

Long, athletic and reachy. Not exactly relaxed, which is what "*halara*" means. *G Kopalides, A Theodoropoulos, 2009*

| 9 | **Team Sogndal Vertical** | 3★ | **7c+ 20m** |

Very steep + bouldery with a dyno finish. *O K Birkeland 2012*

| 10 | **No More Blood** | 3★ | **8a 20m** |

The steep wall and roof with tufa blobs.
C Daniil, A Mavromatis, 2007

| 11 | **Blood Bath** | ♪ | **8a+ 20m** |

Some big tufas lead to a very steep and bouldery blob section. *C Daniil, A Mavromatis, 2007*

| 12 | **Philotimo** | 3★ | **7b 20m** |

A bouldery "DNA"-like start on steep tufas is followed by a corner/roof. *A Theodoropoulos, G Kopalides, 2009*

| 13 | **Kalymnos Friends** | 3★ | **7b+ 20m** |

An interesting roof with some hard moves.
O K Birkeland, 2012

| 14 | **Super Tonga** | 3★ | **8a+ 18m** |

"Roofy" and very intense! *S Montmory, 2012*

| 15 | **Tonga** | 3★ | **7b 15m** |

A classic gym-like overhanging route. *S Montmory, 2012*

| 16 | **Tonge** | 3★ | **7a+ 12m** |

Short but steep and athletic. *S Montmory, 2012*

TONGA CAVE

20 SUMMERTIME

MAGOULIAS

182
37.014994
26.960927

Magoulias consists of a vertical grey wall plus a gently overhanging orange wall with lots of potential for new single- and multi-pitch routes. On the far left is a small cave, **7a L'Envers**, with a few hard overhanging routes. On the right, just 100m above sector Summertime, is another small cave with two short but quality steep routes. When Summertime is crowded (i.e. often), just walk up a bit further and to the left. **Magoulias** is quieter most of the time due to a longer path and harder routes.

Climbing: Many different climbing styles—sometimes on the same route—on highly featured, good quality rock.

Shade: After 13:00. **Exposure**: NE

Approach: As on page 179. Then, just before you reach Summertime, follow the marks uphill to the left to Magoulias Wall, or turn right where the path splits towards Magoulias Right. **Walking time**: 15 min.

1 7a L'Envers   2★   8b 15m
A great roof with a no-hands rest and surprise at the end. Be careful with the left heel hook; best to avoid it since the fall would be really bad like that. *S Montmory, 2012*

2 Begraveningsplatz   1★   8b+ 15m
A crimpy and intense bouldery passage. *S Montmory, 2012*

3 Finally It's Not 7a   2★   8b+ 15m
Another intense route. Simon is a notorious "underestimator" of grades! *S Montmory, 2012*

4 Agrimi   2★   7a+ 35m
Big tufa wrestling on the 2nd half and a tricky, crimpy finish. *S Montmory, 2012*

5 A Route With a View   2★   7b 40m
An annoying start, but the upper wall gets more interesting and the view is great. *S Montmory, 2012*

6 L'Enfer du Ménage   2★   7b 40m
The crux is very high and the diagonal line creates rope drag. Use long QDs. *S Montmory, 2012*

7 Fred   3★   6b 30m
A nice start on big holes leads to an immaculate wall with hidden handholds. *F Heinicke, A Riemer, 2010*

8 Nikolas   2★   5c 20m
An interesting ramp with a steeper exit.
U Kreiss, F Henssler, C Heinrichs, G Trefzer, 2003

9 Nikolas Ext   2★   7a+ 40m
Saves the hard bit for the end. *S Montmory, 2012*

10 Fotini   3★   6b 25m
A natural groove line with a demanding final wall.
U Kreiss, F Henssler, C Heinrichs, G Trefzer, 2003

11 Honey Ball   2★ 6c 25m
Some varied tufa material offers a teetering moment.
U Kreiss, F Henssler, C Heinrichs, G Trefzer, 2003

12 Toni   3★ 6c 23m
A fine "old school" technical wall with a tremendous climax at the end. *U Kreiss, F Henssler, C Heinrichs, G Trefzer, 2003*

13 Anne   2★ 6b 30m
A long slab with some crimpy and some sloping holds.
U Kreiss, F Henssler, C Heinrichs, G Trefzer, 2003

14 Sabina   3★ 6c+ 28m
Wall climbing with a hard start. *B Girardin, C + Y Remy, 2006*

15 Vlasis House   2★ 6c 28m
The steep and sustained wall.
U Kreiss, F Henssler, C Heinrichs, G Trefzer, 2003

16 K tsi k   3★ 7b+ 20m
An unusual traverse crux and tricky resistance climbing on slopers. *S Montmory, 2012*

17 Vertigo   2★ 7c 20m
Another intense route for the grade. Could use more cleaning. *O K Birkeland, S Montmory, 2012*

18 Shiva + Dimitris   3★ 6a 30m
A long and satisfying slab. *U Rutsch, G Buchs, 2006*

19 Ando Drom   3★ 6b 25m
Technical climbing up a compact grey wall.
U Rutsch, G Buchs, 2006

20 Acon69cagva   2★ 6b+ 30m
Closely bolted, with a sustained finale.
U Rutsch, G Buchs, 2006

21 Didi, Hermana de Alma   3★ 5c 25m
A varied climb with flowing moves on the upper red rock.
U Rutsch, G Buchs, 2006

22 Angry Bird   3★ 7c+ 15m
Very short with a hard, intense start and a strange little upper part. *T Brodahl, L O Gudevang, 2012*

23 Norwegian Friends   3★ 7b+ 15m
Insanely cool with steep tufa climbing. *O K Birkeland, 2012*

Eirik Rakstad on "Angry Bird" 7c+.
LARS VERKET

20 SUMMERTIME
SUMMERTIME MAIN

37.014994
26.960927

The little wall of **Summertime** is hidden away and it evades the afternoon sun. The routes start from a nice shady balcony, and it is a great spot for hot days.

Climbing: On pleasant gentle slabs or vertical faces. The easy routes are good for beginners, and they are quite popular (so they are often occupied).

Shade: After 13:00 and until the end of the day.

Exposure: NE

Approach: On page 179.

1 Salbei   2★ 6a 20m
Sharp rock, quickly easing in angle and difficulty. Nice climbing. *G Hommel, J + F Friedrich, 2004*

2 Friends   1★ 6b+ 20m
A hard, fingery start. *D Stratigos, 2005*

3 Thymian   2★ 4c 25m
An easy route up the ridge then left through bulges. *J + F + U Friedrich, 2004*

4 Asterias   2★ 4c 35m
Long and pleasant with big holds. Not as closely bolted as its neighbors. *A Theodoropoulos, S Montmory, 2012*

5 Ammos   2★ 5a 30m
An exciting slabby start which then becomes easier. *A Theodoropoulos, S Montmory, 2012*

6 Soupia the Great   3★ 5c 20m
A great juggy finish! *A Theodoropoulos, S Montmory, 2012*

7 String   3★ 5b+ 20m
Again, an absorbing upper section. *A Theodoropoulos, S Montmory, 2012*

8 Bikini   3★ 5b+ 20m
Consistent, with good holds. Better than it looks. *A Theodoropoulos, S Montmory, 2012*

9 Salamina tis Kypros   2★ 6a+ 20m
A sharp slab with balancy moves. Don't follow the bolts too closely. *M Hatzipetris, A Andreou, A Theodoropoulos, 2003*

10 Ammohostos Vasilevousa   3★ 6a 20m
Brilliant, sustained climbing on good jugs. You don't want it to end. *M Hatzipetris, A Andreou, A Theodoropoulos, 2003*

11 Maccabi   3★ 6b+ 23m
A continuously challenging wall with a slightly bulgy crux. *A Theodoropoulos, C Kostoglou, and 2 Israeli climbers, 2002*

12 Orea Dana   2★ 6a+ 25m
A fingery wall, some delicate moves and a "thank God" hold. *A Theodoropoulos, C Kostoglou + 2 Israeli climbers, 2002*

| 13 | Yeraki | 2★ 5c 25m |

Use the groove, but don't hide in the crack.
A Theodoropoulos, C Kostoglou, and 2 Israeli climbers, 2002

| 14 | Til Tanit | 2★ 5b+ 25m |

Pleasant and sustained climbing on flakes. A natural line.
A Theodoropoulos, C Kostoglou, and 2 Israeli climbers, 2002

| 15 | Sophia | 2★ 5a+ 25m |

Good, flowing climbing. *A Hedgecock, D Selwyn, 2012*

| 16 | Dorian | 2★ 4c 12m |

Short but on excellent rock.
A Theodoropoulos, C Kostoglou, and 2 Israeli climbers, 2002

| 17 | July | 1★ 4c 20m |

A good warm-up.
A Theodoropoulos, C Kostoglou, and 2 Israeli climbers, 2003

| 18 | Anna | 2★ 4a 20m |

Another one good for beginners.
A Theodoropoulos, C Kostoglou, and 2 Israeli climbers, 2003

| 19 | Leuchtturm | 2★ 5c 22m |

A rock peak with a special view. Interesting climbing which ends with a "shark tooth" wall. *R Hamann, N Rouyet, 2014*

Susy Goldner on "Maccabi" 6b+. LEE CUJES

Arginonta beach is just down the road. JOHN KOULLIAS

20 SUMMERTIME
37.014994
26.960927

NIKOLETA
BIG SHADOW

Nikoleta is a brand-new roadside crag in two steep caves. The rock looked bad and loose from the road, but as it turned out there were parts inside both caves with tufas of characteristically good Kalymnos quallity.

Climbing: On overhanging tufas. Routes were equipped by Giovanni Bettoschi in 2015.

Shade: After 12:00. **Exposure**: NE

Approach: From Masouri, drive towards Arginonta village. Approximately 1km after the big right-hand turn near Kasteli, there is a big unfinished building on the left above the sea. Park by the turn on the right, opposite the road leading to the building (37.017403, 26.952403). Walk rightwards to the cave. **Walking time**: 2 min.

1 Nihil Interit 3★ 7b+ 26m
Bouldery and reachy to gain the tufa, then sustained with positive holds.

2 Omnia Mutantur 3★ 8a? 25m
Handle the stalactite with care; no knee bars. From there, big and unrelenting moves to the chain.

3 Omnia Mutantur Nihil Interit 2★ 8a+? 30m
The link-up with some additional hard moves.

BIG SHADOW

Big Shadow, a relatively new sector, is the "big wall" high above the road connecting Kasteli to Arginonta village. It's hard to miss.

Climbing: On an impeccable wall or steep slabs. There is also one overhanging route on tufas. All routes were equipped by Claude + Yves Remy in 2011*.

Shade: After 11:00 and until the end of the day.

Exposure: NE

Approach: From Masouri, drive towards Arginonta village. Soon after the big turn of sectors Kasteli/Dolphin Bay, on your right-hand side you will see a small concrete building with an antenna. Park there (37.019249, 26.941884). Follow the first three electric poles and the red marks/cairns, then go straight up the left side of the vague ridge. Cross a small band of rocks, then follow small ledges on the left side to the base of the crag.

Walking time: 45 min.

***ATTENTION**: At the time of writing (June 2016) all routes need to be re-bolted. Please check for updates on climbkalymnos.com or email us before climbing.

1 Metralos 2★ 6a+ 30m
A slab and wall with good holds.

2 Cacou 2★ 6a+ 25m
More slab and wall with good holds.

3 Vicking 2★ 6a 25m
Yet again, a slab and wall with good holds.

4 Directos 2★ 6b 30m
The left center line of the wall.

5 Grim 3★ 6b 35m
The line in the middle of the wall.

6 Grim Ext ♪ 6c+ 50m
A striking extension on perfect red rock with good holds. 80m rope mandatory to reach down to the first lower-off.

7 Cosi ♪ 7a+ 30m
An impressive vertical crimpy wall.

8 Taupe the Rop ♪ 7b 28m
Immaculate grey wall pocket-pulling.

9 Rappen 3★ 7a 20m
A steep red wall with small tufas.

21 DOLPHIN BAY

37.018458
26.941812

GRADE RANGE	up to 5b+	5c to 6a+	6b to 7a	7a+ to 7c	7c+ and up
No. OF ROUTES	7	23	3	1	0

Dolphin Bay is a pleasant small crag on a headland near *Kasteli*, with gentle white marble rock in a pretty bay by the sea.

Climbing: Vertical wall climbing on while, crystalline but soft rock for Kalymnos. Some unexpectedly huge holds appear as the angle steepens.

Conditions: Warm. Most routes, especially near the water, can feel soapy. Best for calm winter days or cold, cloudy days in spring and autumn. Not good for windy days or when the sea is rough.

Shade: Until 10.00. **Exposure**: S

Kids: Not good. The approach path is steep and the terrain beneath the cliffs can be dangerous.

Giles Davis climbing "Roufos" 6a (page 190).
SIMON RAWLINSON

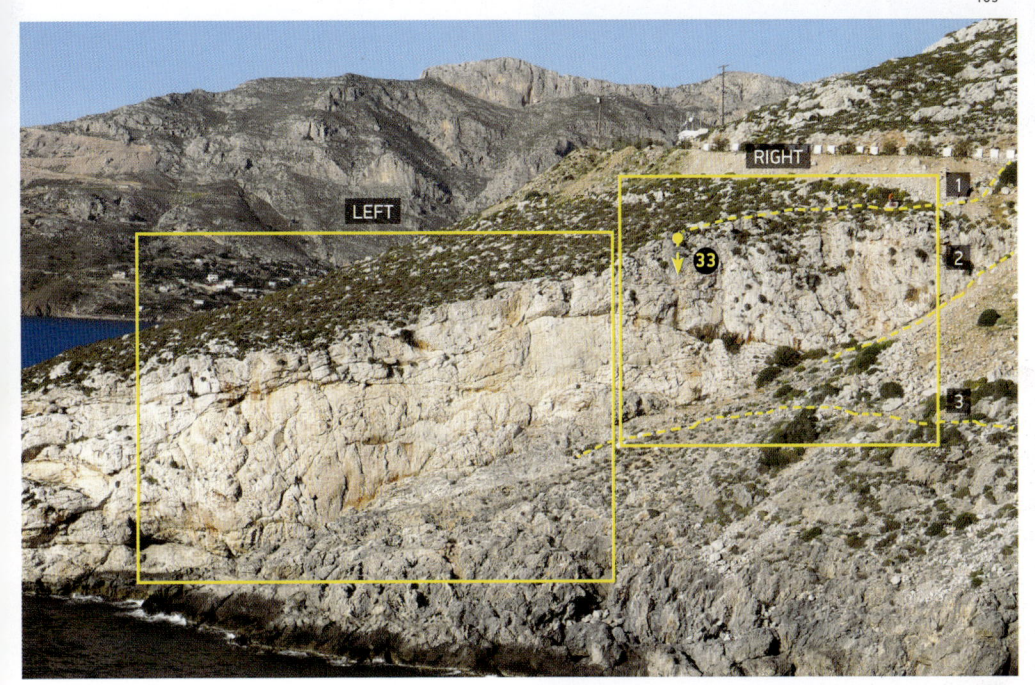

Approach: **1)** From Masouri, go past Kasteli. 50m past Apollo sector, look for the marks on the left side of the road. Follow the marks for 1-2 min to the abseil point "Paula the Seal". Rappel down to the crag. **Time**: 4 min.

2) From the same point on the road, scramble carefully down the scree in the steep gully next to the cliff. This is the trickiest, hardest approach. **Walking time**: 4 min.

3) From the parking area at Kasteli (37.016287, 26.941313) walk down towards Kasteli crag. At the bottom of the dip, turn right. Follow the blue marks to Dolphin Bay. **Walking time**: 10 min.

See also: Crag Panorama on page 197.

ATTENTION: If you climb the 5-6 routes to the far left, watch out for **high waves** on stormy days.

Belay yourself before you belay your leader. There are some bolts at the base of the routes for this reason. The bolts are marked with colors. **If you have not belayed yourself and your leader falls**, you will be torn sideways into a gully with sharp rock close to the sea. On the routes "Siga-Siga", "Tsipoura" and "Koutsoumoura", you can reach a stance at the top and belay your partner from above. This is very convenient if you have rappeled down to the crag.

Sam Cujes is on "Baklava Maniac" 6b (page 191). LEE CUJES

21 DOLPHIN BAY

190
37.018458
26.941812

LEFT
RIGHT

1 Salted Joint 0★ 7a+ 20m
Good rock but caked in salt! Some hard initial moves are followed by easier ones. *G Hommel, J Friedrich, 2009*

2 Too Fat for Tufas 3★ 6a 24m
A fun start leads to much easier slab climbing. *S McDonnell, A Hafner, C Schmidt, 2005*

3 Roufos 3★ 6a 25m
Big holds in the cave; small grips on the final slab. *A Hafner, S Mühlbacher, C Schmidt, 2005*

4 Lavraki 2★ 5b 28m
Start by falling across the gap. Partner must be belayed. *H Weninger C Schmidt A Hafner J Weninger J Weninger 2005*

5 Smineri 3★ 5b 20m
An unusual start, then a groove and slab on good holds. *A Hafner, S Mühlbacher, C Schmidt, 2005*

6 Kavouras ♪ 6a+ 20m
Good technical climbing (though sometimes a bit soapy). *A Hafner, S Mühlbacher, C Schmidt, 2005*

7 Kalymnian Lightning 2★ 6b+ 20m
Crack with occasional holds, no rests and much laybacking. *H Weninger C Schmidt A Hafner J Weninger J Weninger 2006*

8 Barbouni 2★ 6b+ 20m
Another natural line; use the right foot for leverage. *H Weninger C Schmidt A Hafner J Weninger J Weninger 2006*

9 Let There be Rock 2★ 5c+ 20m
Powerful, with three crucial bulges. *C Remy, 2009*

10 Blooming 2★ 5b+ 20m
The wall with big pockets, even on the steep finale. *B Girardin, C + Y Remy, 2008*

11 Iris Production 3★ 5b+ 20m
An interesting start and carefree remainder. *C Remy, 2009*

12 Riglos 2★ 5c 20m
The slab, wall and overhang lead to a crucial reach to the lower-off. *B Girardin, C + Y Remy, 2007*

13 Roussos 3★ 5c 20m
Breeze through the lower section; delight in the second half. *C Remy, 2009*

14 Try Me 2★ 5c 20m
An easy start leads to a steeper wall with good holds. *C + Chr Remy, 2014*

15 Flipper 2★ 5c 20m
An easy start is followed by an overhanging zone on smoother rock. Very nice. *J Friedrich, G Hommel 2006*

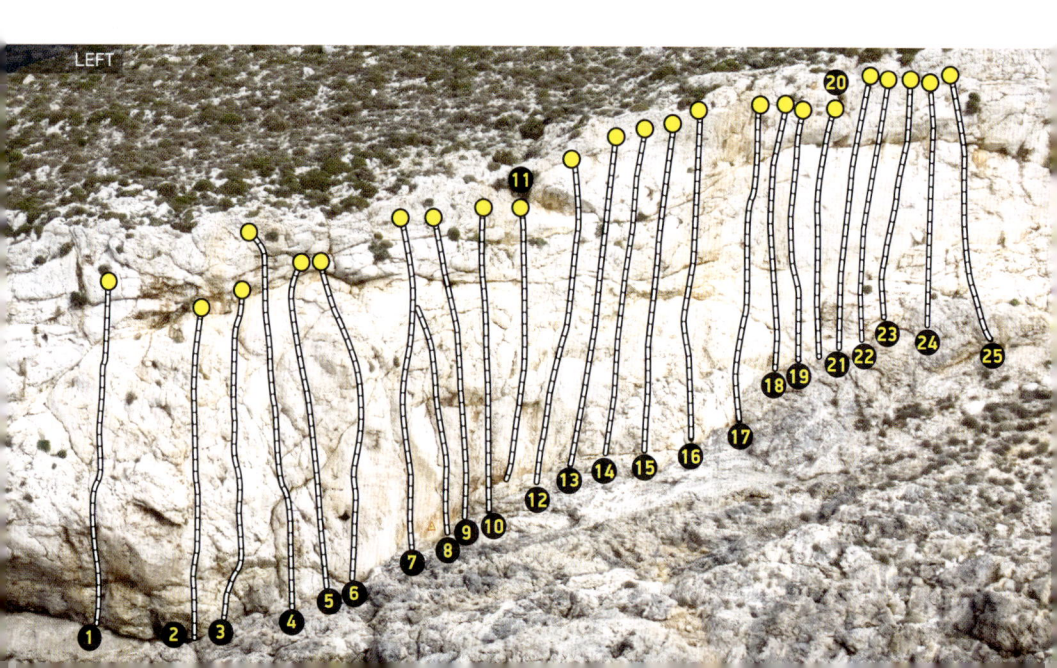

35 Paula the Seal, 20m
Not a route but an airy abseil. Use a back-up knot.

16 Palamida   2★   5c+ 20m
A Hafner, C Schmidt, 2010

17 Koutsoumoura   2★   5c+ 18m
Sustained with a challenging bulge. It's possible to top-out and belay above. *A Hafner, C Schmidt, 2005*

18 Tsipoura   2★   5c 18m
Tackles the same bulge as "Koutsoumoura" but with bigger holds. *A Hafner, C Schmidt, 2005*

19 Siga-Siga   2★   6a 18m
Take care; don't hurry on this one. *A Hafner, C Schmidt, 2005*

20 Baklava Maniac   3★   6b 20m
The intense wall with soft holds, little pockets, and a final juggy bulge. *B Girardin, C + Y Remy, 2009*

21 Dimitra   3★   6a+ 20m
Almost a copy of "Baklava" with some small, reachy holds. *B Girardin, C + Y Remy, 2007*

22 Trokrakhan   3★   6a 20m
A brilliant wall followed by a bulge with good holds. *B Girardin, C + Y Remy, 2007*

23 Lena   3★   6a+ 20m
A superb climb dedicated to little Lena, Simon and Myriam's daughter. *C + Chr Remy, 2014*

24 Under Wisteria Lane   2★   5c+ 20m
A pocketed wall leads to the bulge. *B Girardin, C + Y Remy, 2007*

25 Blind Test   2★   5c+ 20m
The wall then a bulge; big, "soft" holds all the way. *B Girardin, C + Y Remy, 2009*

26 Controlling Crew   2★   5c+ 20m
Again, similar in style though with more "blind" moves. *B Girardin, C + Y Remy, 2007*

27 Coco Rose   2★   6a+ 20m
A challenging but juggy final bulge. *C Remy, 2009*

28 Kiss My...Axe   3★   6a 20m
The wall, followed by an overhang with the good "soft" holds characterizing this sector. *B Girardin, C + Y Remy, 2009*

29 Festival 2009   2★   5c 20m
An interesting finale in an open corner. *C Remy, 2009*

30 Irène   2★   5c 20m
A pleasant enough route with a steady finish. *C Remy 2009*

31 Agelos   2★   5b+ 20m
Surprise! For this wall you need...technique. *B Girardin, C + Y Remy, 2007*

32 Easyland   1★   4c 10m
The slab with big pockets. *C + Y Remy, 2010*

33 Bang-Bang   1★   5a 14m
Another slab with big pockets. *C + Y Remy, 2010*

34 For VIP   1★   5c+ 12m
The wall with pockets and a short crux. *C + Y Remy, 2010*

22 KASTELI

192
37.016287
26.941313

GRADE RANGE	up to 5b+	5c to 6a+	6b to 7a	7a+ to 7c	7c+ and up
No. OF ROUTES	15	17	0	3	0

Kasteli is on the west side of the obvious small peninsula with the cone-shaped hill, right above the sea as you leave Masouri and go north. The ruins of a Byzantine castle, which is said to have been inhabited until the 10th century, still stand at the hilltop along with scattered ruins of old buildings, walls and water cisterns. Sector **Kasteli** is at a serene spot right next to the sea on the northwest side of the hill, an extensive area of steep, rough, but compact slabs of grey limestone. To the south is the beautiful white chapel of *Panayia*, a good spot for a swim after climbing.

Climbing: On sometimes sharp but compact grey slabs. There are several lower-grade routes for beginners, plus a number of demanding vertical slabs.

Conditions: Cool, thanks to lots of shade and proximity to the sea. Not good on very windy days, as it is quite exposed.

Shade: After 15:00 (North Wall); until 13:00-14:00 (Easy Slab + Main Wall); until 16:00 (Back Cave).

Exposure: NW

Kids: Good; an easy path and several flat areas.

Approach: From Masouri, go towards Arginonta. At the bend with a white milestone and a parking area to the left, look for a sign "To Kasteli". Park there (37.016287, 26.941313). Walk downhill across the col following some red marks and cairns. Go around the right side of the hill to the crag. The first sector you come to is North Wall. **Walking time:** 7-10 min.

See also: Crag Panorama on page 197.

Claude Remy on "Pillar of the Sea" 6a+. SIMON CARTER

The **North Wall** features routes on grey slabs and walls. This side is ideal for afternoon climbing.

☁ **Shade:** After 15.00. **Exposure:** S

NORTH WALL

1 **Get a Grip** — 2★ 5c 12m
Wall climbing on good pockets. Easier from the right; maybe 6a straight up. *A Christidis, Y Ernst, 2008*

2 **Tsarouhis** — 2★ 5c+ 15m
A demanding wall with small fingery holds. *A Theodoropoulos, 2000*

3 **Gyzis** — 2★ 5b+ 15m
A pleasant groove, but an awkward start! *A Theodoropoulos, 2000*

4 **Gikas** — 2★ 4c 15m
An excellent short slab for learning to lead. *A Theodoropoulos, 2000*

5 **Pampachoum** — 2★ 6a+ 25m
A sharp wall leads to a red bulge with good slots above. *B Girardin, B Käslin, 2006*

6 **Pillar of the Sea** — 2★ 6a+ 25m
A very well-protected line, but too polished. Don't be intimidated by the steep finale. *S Piskurek, M Wiesenfarth, 1999*

7 **Merci Brothers** — 3★ 6a 25m
Climb the short bulge moving righwards. Save energy for the juggy finish. *B Girardin, B Käslin, 2006*

8 **Shy Talk** — 3★ 6a+ 25m
A hard, smooth slab after mid-height. Hard to clip the chain. *B Girardin, B Käslin, 2006*

BACK CAVE

22 KASTELI — MAIN WALL EASY SLAB

194
37.016287
26.941313

The **Main Wall** is an attractive face above the sea, with routes around 6a on steep, rough grey slabs.

Climbing: Steep and slabby.

☁ Shade: Until 14.00 **Exposure:** W

9 Männer(tor) Tour   2★ 6a 25m
An interesting corner leads to a cruxy finale. Bolting is sparse by Kalymnos standards. *M Biedermann, 2003*

10 Mikros Prigipas   1★ 6a 30m
Long with a very easy mid-section. *A Theodoropoulos, 2000*

11 Nadelkissen   1★ 6a 28m
Bouldery start, then a sparsely bolted ramp to finish. Use a long quickdraw on the ramp's 1st bolt. *J Friedrich, 2003*

12 Ruheloser Pirat   2★ 6a+ 20m
A delicate start, then a crux to reach the ledge. *S Piskurek, M Wiesenforth, 1999*

13 Gefaehrliche Brandung   3★ 6a 20m
Balance up the absorbing crinkly face. Definitely not just another grey slab! *S Piskurek, M Wiesenforth, 1999*

14 Piccolo Diavolo   3★ 6a+ 20m
Absorbing face climbing with good moves to reach the crack. *P Reinih, T Scliffe, J Thielke, M Hiclestoolb, 1999*

15 Hocla   3★ 6a 20m
Very good. Some of the holds are not as positive as you'd hoped. *M Schmed + Team, 2000*

16 Gruselino   2★ 5c 20m
Not as ugly as the name implies; do it! *P Reinih, T Scliffe, J Thielke, M Hiclestoolb, 1999*

17 Gunesli Kiz   2★ 5c+ 20m
Steep, sustained climbing with some intimidating bolting. *P Reinih, T Scliffe, J Thielke, M Hiclestoolb, 1999*

18 Scarabeus   2★ 5b 20m
The brown crack is the key. *P Reinih, T Scliffe, J Thielke, M Hiclestoolb, 1999*

19 Damokles   1★ 6a 22m
Climb the sword then move left. Hard to avoid going over to the next route; artificial. *C Schmidt, R Mayer, A Hafner 2002*

20 Ataolaa   1★ 5a 20m
Steep on good sharp chickenheads. *M Schmed + Team, 2000*

MAIN WALL

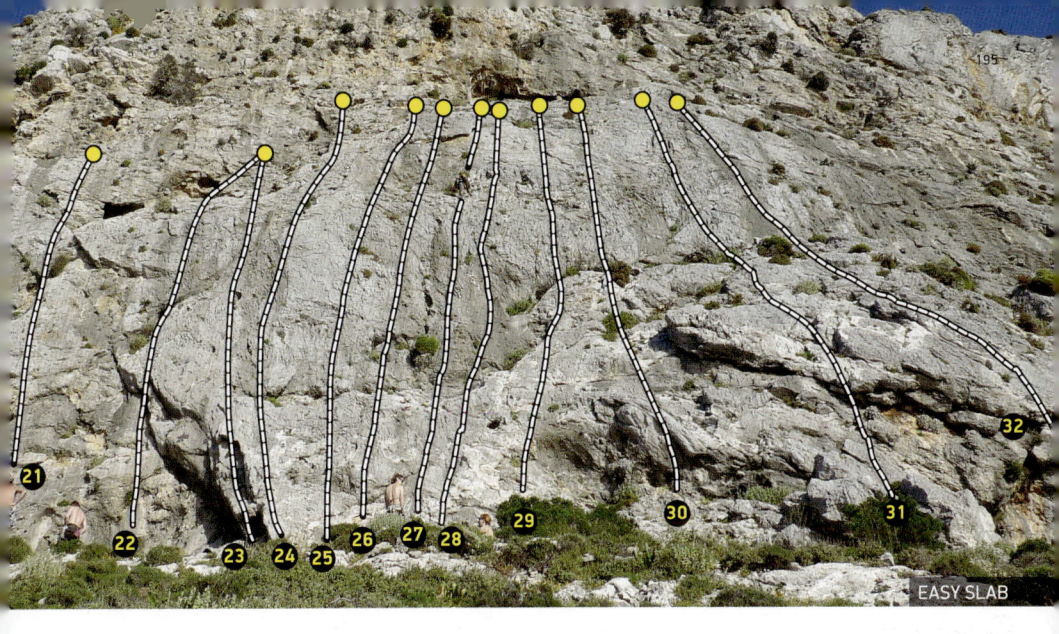

The **Easy Slab** features some lower-grade routes on a rough, off-vertical slab.

Climbing: Some routes are sparsely bolted for the grade.

Shade: Until 13.00 on the right side. **Exposure:** SW

21 Rewithia   2★   5b 20m
Has improved with traffic.
A Hafner, C Schmidt, S McDonnell, 2009

22 Ghecko's Home   2★   5c 20m
Nice, but a bit loose. *A Hafner C Schmidt S McDonnell 2009*

23 Yahurti me Meli   2★   4c 18m
Always keep slightly to the left.
C Schmidt, R Mayer, A Hafner, 2002

24 Psomi ki Elies   2★   4c+ 20m
Good face climbing after an easy start.
C Schmidt, R Mayer, A Hafner 2002

25 Sisyphus   2★   5a 25m
Small chickenheads on a steep grey slab.
C Schmidt, R Mayer, A Hafner, 2002

26 Captain Adonis   2★   5a 30m
Full of good holds and chickenheads. Don't rely on the final not-so-solid blocks. *A Hafner, C Schmidt, 2008*

27 Kokkinidis   2★   4c+ 25m
After the ledge on the right, a slab with good holds. One of the best for the grade. *C Schmidt, A Hafner, H Weninger 2002*

28 A Tight Squeeze   1★   4b 30m
Pleasant, but nothing spectacular. *A Hafner, C Schmidt, 2009*

29 Mathilde   2★   4b 30m
Goes around the rotten rock and then it's nice climbing on the eroded rock. *B Girardin, B Käslin, 2006*

30 Bricounet   2★   4c 30m
The first half is not worthwhile, but it completes the sector. *B Girardin, B Käslin, 2006*

31 Yia ton Kyriako   1★   3c 30m
One of the easiest routes on the island! Take care with the start to reach the slab above. *S Mühlbacher, C Schmidt, 2004*

32 Ligo Akoma   1★   4c 30m
A hard intro then easily to a ledge. The next bolt is hard to clip if you go straight up. A diagonal route; best to strip the quickdraws on top-rope. *S Mühlbacher, C Schmidt, 2004*

22 KASTELI
BACK CAVE

196
37.016287
26.941313

The **Back Cave** is a small cave with short overhanging routes on good holds.

Climbing: Despite the rope, it almost feels like bouldering. The QDs are fixed in place, but take your own because some of the carabiners no longer open.

Shade: After 16.00. **Exposure:** SE

Approach: Go to North Wall (page 183) and then traverse leftwards. **Walking time:** 12 min.

33 A Kapella 1★ 7b 8m
The small overhang above the chapel of Kasteli. Like bouldering indoors, but with a rope. *P Gabarrou, 2002*

34 Bambola Blue 2★ 7b 8m
Again, like a highball (3-bolt) boulder problem.
P Gabarrou, 2002

35 Krotdebiki 1★ 7b 8m
More roped bouldering. *P Gabarrou, 2002*

Dave Reeve on "Pillar of the Sea" 6a+ (page 193). LEE CUJES

CRAG PANORAMA
Dolphin Bay to Jurassic Park

23 NORTH CAPE

37.016216
26.942148

GRADE RANGE	up to 5b+	5c to 6a+	6b to 7a	7a+ to 7c	7c+ and up
No. OF ROUTES	16	25	15	9	4

North Cape is a pleasant and quiet crag, which is seldom very crowded, across the hillside from the famous (and usually very busy) sector Odyssey. North Cape features a long south-facing wall with small interconnected caves and yellow/grey slabs of very good quality, though sometimes sharp. Furthermore, the crag is easily and quickly approachable from the road.

Climbing: On steep slabs and walls with some prickly holds, plus two short but worthwhile caves.

Conditions: Hot, sunny, and very exposed to the wind. The sun comes around early in the day. The two caves are the only areas protected from rainfall.

☁ **Shade:** Until 11:00. **Exposure:** S

Luca Salsotto tries his route "Partiro" 7a+ (page 204)
LUCA SALSOTTO ARCHIVE

Kids: The approach path is short, but the crag is not very good for kids. The only area somewhat suitable is below the Upper Cave.

Approach: From Masouri, go towards Kasteli. Look for the white marker to sector Kasteli on your left. Shortly after that, and immediately after the big right bend in the road, turn off sharply uphill onto a concrete road. Park 80m further, just past the colorful house (pictured above) with the stone wall on the right-hand side (37.016216, 26.942148). Walk up and to the left, following the marks to a telephone pole, then go to the right towards the distinctive grey slabs by the left cave.

Walking time: 5-6 min to the first cave or 12 min to the Upper Cave.

See also: Crag Panorama on page 197.

Left: Günter Hommel painting the name of one of the many routes he and Joachim Friedrich have bolted here.
JOACHIM FRIEDRICH

23 NORTH CAPE
APOLLO
PETER

200
37.016216
26.942148

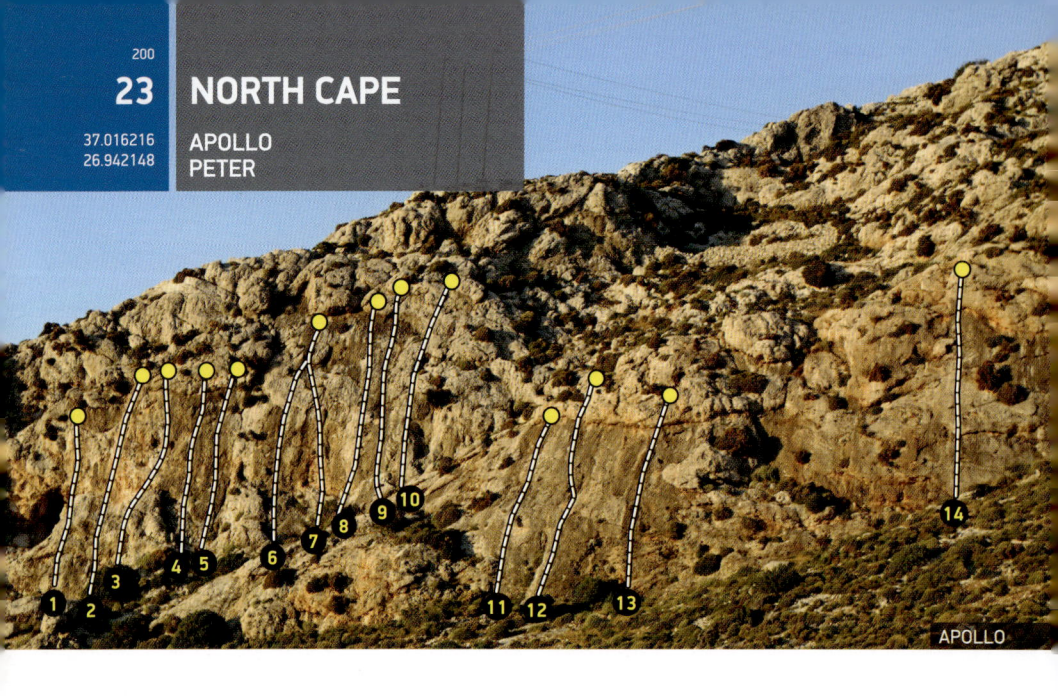

If you don't have much time, **Apollo** is a crag near the road where you can quickly climb pleasant short routes.

Climbing: A solid vertical grey/red wall; a bit sharp.

Shade: Until 12.00. **Exposure:** S

Approach: As you head from Masouri towards Arginonta, about 250m after the big bend in the road and the parking area for Kasteli, look for the "Apollo" sign on the right (37.018208, 26.942040). Follow the marked path which begins by the road. **Walking time:** 2 min.

1 Ugly — 1★ 6b 15m
A few hard moves on the wall. *J Friedrich, G Hommel, 2013*

2 Adonis Apollo — 2★ 6a+ 18m
Steep with an interesting crux on the red wall. *O Steiss, J Rohrmann, 2005*

3 Heike — 1★ 6a 16m
A steep and fingery upper part. *O Steiss, J Rohrmann, 2005*

4 Theo — 1★ 6a+ 15m
An easy slab, short crux and steady finish. *O Steiss, J Rohrmann, 2005*

5 Detlev — 1★ 5c+ 15m
There is a sharp delicate passage, then it gets easier. *O Steiss, J Rohrmann, 2005*

6 Brother — 1★ 5b 15m
Short, sharp and poorly bolted for the grade. *G Hommel, J Friedrich, 2009*

7 Sister — 1★ 5c 20m
A bulging wall then easy slab. *G Hommel, J Friedrich, 2009*

8 Family — 1★ 5a 22m
A steep start then easy angle rock. *J Friedrich, G Hommel, 2013*

9 Dad — 1★ 4c 20m
Two moves at the start, then easy sharp chickenheads. *J Friedrich, 2013*

10 Mum — 1★ 4b 20m
A low-angle slab. *J Friedrich, G Hommel, 2010*

11 Cat — 1★ 4c 17m
Slab; not well-bolted for the grade. *J Friedrich, 2012*

12 Mouse — 1★ 4a 21m
Slab; watch out for some hollow rock. *J Friedrich, 2012*

13 Dog — 1★ 4b 17m
A slab with good rock for the grade. *J Friedrich, 2012*

14 Pig — 2★ 5a 18m
Better than its neighbors, but the finish is a bit brittle. *G Hommel, J Friedrich, 2013*

15 3 Colour — 2★ 5c 22m
Located 150m further right than "Pig". Rock with strong, uncommon features. *G Hommel, J Friedrich, 2015*

Climbing: On some good low-angle grey slabs, but attention: **watch out for large loose blocks.**

Approach: As on page 199 up to the telephone pole. Then, walk up to the left. **Walking time:** 12 min.

1 Peterle — 1★ 4c 35m
Slab with a righward finish from a ramp. Some spaced bolts at the easy part.

2 Petersilie — 1★ 5c 31m
Just for the start; the rest is (s)crappy.

3 Schwarzer Peter — 2★ 5a 30m
Steady compact slab but spaced bolts + suspicious blocks.

4 Peter Pan — 1★ 5a 30m
A grey wall and slab, not well-cleaned and spaced bolts.

5 Peter und der Wolf — 2★ 6a+ 28m
Varied, with an interesting corner at the start.

6 Petrus — 1★ 6a+ 28m
A tough start, then easier flakes and a slab.

7 Zickenpeter — 2★ 7a 22m
A bouldery bulge at the beginning.

8 Salpeter — 1★ 7a+ 12m
Short, fingery and bouldery.

9 Hackepeter — 1★ 6a+ 21m
Unpleasant work in the crack.

Peter is a small crag to the left of North Cape. It features a grey slab with some steeper routes to the right, as well as unusual views of Kasteli. All routes were equipped by Joachim Friedrich + Günter Hommel in 2009 and 2011.

Shade: Until 12.00. **Exposure:** S

NORTH CAPE

MAIN (LEFT, MIDDLE)

37.016216
26.942148

North Cape Main is an extended band of rock that features a little bit of everything: good (though sharp) slabby routes, a couple of small caves, and steep walls and slabs with sharp chickenheads and other features.

Climbing: Varied styles, from delicate slabby climbing to extremely steep, bouldery overhangs and roofs.

Shade: Until 11.00. **Exposure**: S

Approach: See page 199.

1 Mixed 2★ 5c 25m
A nice, though sharp, grey wall + slab.
G Hommel J Friedrich 2011

2 Windy 1★ 5b 19m
A slab with steep finish. *G Hommel, J Friedrich, 2011*

3 Corner 2★ 5b 19m
A nice corner at the upper part. *J Friedrich, G Hommel, 2011*

4 No Fly Zone 1★ 5b 35m
A sharp and blocky rib. Attention when lowering off.
B Viberti, B Ronzino, E Viberti, 1999

5 B.E.B. 2★ 6a 30m
Steep and athletic on nice holes in the headwall.
B Viberti, B Ronzino, E Viberti, 1999

6 Galup 3★ 6b 30m
A technical traverse, then steep and sustained to a crucial finale. *B Viberti, B Ronzino, E Viberti, 1999*

7 Inshallah ♪ 8c+ 15m
A powerful line across the roof of the first cave. Hard bouldering moves from the start! 1st RP was by Nicolas Favresse in 2007. *N Favresse, C Daniil, 2007*

8 Marshmallow 2★ 8a 12m
Short and very bouldery with plenty of opportunities for heel-hooking. *M Bouyoud, 2011*

9 Sposi 3★ 6c 15m
Fun and pumpy big jug-pulling. *2004*

10 To Proto Moro Mou 2★ 5c+ 25m
A quite bouldery start leads to a lovely climb with big pockets throughout. *P Müller, 2001*

11 Seal 2★ 5c 25m
Intricate rock that will improve substantially with traffic.
J Friedrich, G Hommel, 2015

MAIN (LEFT)

MAIN (MIDDLE)

1 Hantsch   3★   7a+ 20m
Enjoyable climbing with a bit of everything. Quite hard to read, though. *2004*

2 Reize   2★   7a 25m
Varied wall climbing. *C + Y Remy, 2011*

3 Seferis   2★   6c 40m
Easy wall and just a few moves at the overhang. Worth it even if just for the view from the "window". *C + Y Remy, 2010*

4 Megastore   2★   6b+ 40m
A steep, sharp slab; not very well-bolted. *C + Y Remy, 2010*

5 Rosso Di Sera   2★   6b 30m
A hard sharp bulge at first, then an interesting wall. *B Viberti, B Ronzino, E Viberti, 1999*

6 Prego   3★   6b+ 35m
Sharp at the start, but then perfect wall climbing with nice chickenheads. *L Salsotto, 2013*

7 Grazie   2★   6a+ 30m
The slab with very small chickenheads. *B Viberti, B Ronzino, E Viberti, 1999*

8 Scanner   2★   6a 30m
A good conglomerate wall, sometimes squeezed. *B Viberti, B Ronzino, E Viberti, 1999*

9 Leone   2★   6a+ 30m
Pleasant climbing on a super-steep slab. *C + Y Remy, 2011*

10 Bolting Day   3★   6a 30m
Nice wall climbing. *B Fara, R Guerin, 2016*

11 Iglu   1★   6b 28m
A grey wall with good moves, but very sharp. *J Friedrich, G Hommel, 2011*

12 Et La Cloche Sonne 3x   2★   7b 25m
The roof with a short crux, then the wall. *C + Y Remy, 2010*

13 Le Mur d'Epicure   2★   7c 25m
A powerful wall with pockets and holes, but an easier final section. Spaced bolts. *F Heinicke, A Riemer, 2010*

14 Ahimsa   3★   7b+ 25m
A striking twin tufa line and the sustained headwall. Spaced bolts. *M Bouyoud, 2011*

Lucas Dourdourekas on "Inshallah" 8c+. NIKOLAOS SMALIOS

23 NORTH CAPE

MAIN (RIGHT, UPPER CAVE)

37.016216
26.942148

North Cape Main continues to the right with a fine-featured grey wall plus a small cave (**Upper Cave**) with steep but excellent routes and rock with beautiful features, small stalactites and tufa pipes. Further right of the cave there is a short, sharp slab.

Climbing: Technical, delicate and slabby on sometimes sharp rock. Athletic and powerful in Upper Cave.

Shade: Until 11:00 (right) or 13:00 (Upper Cave).

Exposure: S

Approach: See page 199. **Walking time**: 12 min.

1 Orca — 1★ 7b 20m
A short, sharp and crimpy wall. *J Friedrich 2013*

2 Polar Bear — 2★ 6c+ 28m
A powerful start, then a pleasant technical wall. *G Hommel, J Friedrich, 2008*

3 Partiro — 2★ 7a+ 25m
A powerful start, then a steep wall. *L Salsotto, 2013*

4 French Connection — 2★ 6a+ 28m
Grey wall climbing with an unusual start. *JN + I Bourgeois, 2009 2010*

5 Ice Age — 2★ 5c+ 27m
Good wall climbing with a steep start. *G Hommel, J Friedrich, 2008*

6 Hawk — 3★ 6a+ 27m
A fine, delicate wall climb with a fingery upper slab. *G Hommel, J Friedrich, 2006*

7 Elk — 2★ 6b 25m
A good wall + a technical crux. *G Hommel, J Friedrich, 2009*

8 Polar Star — 2★ 6b 28m
A well-bolted, sustained and sharp wall. *G Hommel, J Friedrich, 2009*

9 Nordic Walking — 2★ 6a 18m
The climbing is delicate and good, the bolting not so. *J + F Friedrich, G Hommel, 2005*

10 North Light — 2★ 6a 25m
Interesting climbing on pebbles with a thin cruxy wall. *G Hommel, J Friedrich, 2008*

Thomas Michaelides on "Sposi" 6c (page 202). KATIE ROUSSOU

1 Funatiker — 3★ 7a+ 22m
Enjoyable reachy and airy moves on a slightly overhanging wall. *M Schepers, 1999*

2 Saglis — 3★ 8? 12m
Open project. *M Bouyoud, 2011*

3 Mudita — 3★ 7c+ 12m
A short power route. *M Bouyoud, 2011*

4 Helios — 3★ 8a 15m
Exciting and very steep tufa terrain. Bouldery at the crux, where a bit of imagination is needed. *K Oelze, 2000*

5 Nirvana — 3★ 7c 15m
Overhanging endurance climb on good tufas. *K Oelze, 2000*

6 Stachelschwein — 1★ 6c+ 12m
Very short and bouldery. *J + F Friedrich, G Hommel, 2005*

7 Ren — 2★ 5b 20m
Prickly rock with a hard access to the final crack. *J Friedrich, G Hommel, 2010*

8 Karibu — 1★ 6a 21m
A sharp first part, then good holds at the final bulges. *J Friedrich, G Hommel, 2010*

9 Beluga — 1★ 5b 17m
Sharp, again. *J Friedrich, G Hommel, 2010*

10 Whale — 1★ 6a 20m
There is a big loose flake on the right; watch out when lowering. *J Friedrich, G Hommel, 2014*

11 Krill — 1★ 6b 20m
J Friedrich, G Hommel, 2014

MAIN (UPPER CAVE)

24 SCHOOL

206
37.011474
26.943004

GRADE RANGE	up to 5b+	5c to 6a+	6b to 7a	7a+ to 7c	7c+ and up
No. OF ROUTES	11	9	3	0	0

A training crag, for the most part, sector **School** is an area of grey slabs reaching 120m in height. In addition to the single pitches, there are two training multi-pitches suitable for new climbers trying out long routes for the first time. The view from the top of these routes is panoramic, including parts of Kalymnos you don't normally see.

Helmets are strongly recommended.

Climbing: Pleasant on compact grey slabs.

Conditions: Hot and sunny, best for climbing on cloudy or cold days. It is exposed to the rain; however, the rock dries quickly.

Shade: Until 12:00. **Exposure**: S

Kids: The approach is long, but there are several suitable areas near Jungle Book.

Ziwi Richter radiating happiness at the top of "Platon" 5c (page 209). MARKUS SCHAUER

Approach: Use the same path as to sector Odyssey. From Masouri, go towards Kasteli and Arginonta. Immediately after the big right-hand turn in the road at Kasteli, make a sharp right turn onto a steep uphill concrete road around a colorful house. Park off to the side just before the road ends by two big boulders to your left (37.011474, 26.943004). The trail begins between the boulders, near a tall wooden electricity pole. Go uphill for 2 min and then follow the left branch of the path to Odyssey. Traverse along the entire length of Odyssey, until you come to the last route, "Bonnie". From here, follow the trail markers for another 3-4 minutes. Alternatively, you can also go to School via sector North Cape, but there is no established path or trail markers.

Walking time: 20 min to School Right; 24 min to Jungle Book.

See also: Crag Panorama on page 197.

A different angle from the top of "Platon" 5c (page 199).

24 SCHOOL

208
37.011474
26.943004

JUNGLE BOOK
SCHOOL RIGHT

JUNGLE BOOK

Jungle Book is an excellent training sector with many good lower-grade routes, plus a more demanding—but particularly interesting—multi-pitch route. Some impressively long pitches to the right require a 70m rope.

Climbing: On easy-angled compact slabs.

Shade: Until 12:00. **Exposure:** S

Approach: See previous page. **Walking time:** 23-25 min.

1 Mowgli 2★ 5c 30m
A very easy start and good slab. *J Friedrich, G Hommel 2010*

2 Testat 2★ 6b+ 28m
A thin middle wall; two long pulls. *F + X + C Heinicke, 2013*

3 Geröllheimer 1★ 6a 30m
Nice wall climbing with small pockets at the upper part.
X + F + C Heinicke, C + A Riemer, S Hausschild, 2013

4 Dancing Queen 2★ 5c 25m
Move left on the ridge. Sustained, but well-bolted.
Swiss Alpin Club Section Rinsberg (A Kolar, T Schwab, S Meyer, S Bolton, R Kernen, R Felber, Y Hänggi) 2004

5 Drei Strolche 2★ 5b+ 30m
An interesting, delicate long climb. *Swiss Alpin Club, 2004*

6 Heureka 3★ 5c+ 15m
A steep, exhausting bulge, but encouraging bolting (as with most routes here). *Swiss Alpin Club, 2004*

7 Nature Simplicity 2★ 5c+ 15m
Vertical wall climbing on the black flowstone.
Swiss Alpin Club, 2004

8 Oraia Stithi 3★ 6b 110m
Multi-pitch (5c 30m, 6a 30m, 6a+ 30m, 6b 30m). A beauty: a small bulge, small crimpy holds, finger pockets, and a powerful traverse. The last pitch is brilliant but a bit run-out. **Return:** Abseil (4 x 30m) from the anchors to the right of the line. *Guy Abert, L de la Fouchardiere, 2001*

9 Baloo — 2★ 5b 20m
The slab, interrupted by some ledges. The climbing improves as you go up. *Swiss Alpin Club, 2004*

10 The Couch — 1★ 5c 25m
An inconsistent route with only one hard section. *Swiss Alpin Club, 2004*

11 Kaa — 1★ 5a 20m
Not particularly interesting climbing. *Swiss Alpin Club, 2004*

12 Puumba — 1★ 4a 15m
Scrappy and short. *Swiss Alpin Club, 2004*

13 Climbing Wizard — 1★ 4a 13m
A short beginners' route. *Swiss Alpin Club, 2004*

14 Euphorbia Acanthothamnos — 3★ 5b+ 35m
A steep headwall with fingery moves. *A Hafner, C Schmidt, 2010*

15 Laudakia Stellio Stellio — 3★ 5b 35m
Pleasant continuous climbing on water holes. *A Hafner, C Schmidt, 2010*

16 Falco Tinnunculus — 2★ 5a 35m
Walk on and enjoy! *A Hafner, C Schmidt, 2010*

17 Askisi — 2★ 4c 35m
A pleasant long climb. *R Goedeke, 2002*

18 Genista — 1★ 4c 35m
Another low-angle slab, but take care for some loose rock. *A Hafner, C Schmidt, 2010*

19 Mantis Religiosa — 1★ 5a 35m
If you don't use the flake it isn't so bad. *A Hafner, C Schmidt, 2010*

20 Liane — 1★ 6a 32m
A scramble at the start, then a compact slab. *J Friedrich, G Hommel, 2012*

School Right is a long, very easy angled buttress and an ideal sector for learning to climb multi-pitch routes. There are only 3 routes, two of which ("Kalymnos 2000" and "Platon") are very close together to allow a single instructor to oversee 2 climbing parties. The view from the top is unusual and airy.

Climbing: Fine, delicate and slabby.

Attention: Helmets are mandatory.

Shade: Until 12:00. **Exposure**: S

Approach: See previous page. **Walking time**: 20 min.

1 Teacher — 2★ 6b+ 57m
2 pitches (6b+ 30m, 6a 27m). P1: A steep start then easier. P2: A nice compact slab. Descend by abseil from the route (2 x 30m). *J Friedrich, G Hommel, 2012*

2 Kalymnos 2000 — 2★ 5c 120m
Multi-pitch (4c 25m, 5a 25m, 5c 25m, 5b 20m, 4b 25m). Slab climbing with good holds; good for practicing multi-pitch climbing. Descend by abseil from the route (2 x 60m or 4 x 25m). *U Thomsen, 2000*

3 Platon — 2★ 5c 120m
Multi-pitch (4b 25m, 5a 25m, 5b 25m, 5c 20m, 4c 25m). Close to "Kalymnos 2000" and a similar style. Watch out for loose rock on P4. Descend by abseil from the route (2 x 60m or 4 x 25m). *A Theodoropoulos, 2001*

	210						
	25	**ODYSSEY**	GRADE RANGE	up to 5b+	5c to 6a+	6b to 7a	7a+ to 7c	7c+ and up
	37.011474 26.943004		No. OF ROUTES	13	11	23	26	19

Kre Reischel having fun on "Island in the Sun" 7a+ (page 202).
LEE CUJES

The ultimate point of reference on Kalymnos, sector **Odyssey** features something for everyone on some of the finest rock on the island. The crag unfolds along 400m of interconnected caves and walls, with a large variety of routes and styles. Despite the inevitable polishing of some routes, **Odyssey** remains one of the major "star" crags of Kalymnos. Most route names are inspired by Homer's *Odyssey*. Also here is the hardest route on the island, "Los Revolucionarios 9a", first redpointed by Adam Ondra in May 2009.

Climbing: Generally technical and pumpy, but with a great variety of climbs; easy slabby routes from 4a-5c; classic routes on slightly overhanging walls between 6a-6b; highly overhanging, pumpy routes with big pockets at a surprising 6b-6c+ and, as a bonus, power-stamina fests in tufa caves from 7a-8c+.

Shade: Until 14:00-15:00. **Exposure**: NW

Conditions: Mostly cool. In summer the sun comes to routes on the right and in Marci Marc Cave at 15:00. Even a slight breeze makes conditions very pleasant, and cliffs dry fast after the rain. Marci Marc Cave and routes left of "Atena" stay dry. Avoid Odyssey on humid days with no wind; routes on the dark brown rock can feel very greasy.

Kids: Good, with an easy path and suitable flat areas.

Approach: 1) On foot: Walk from Masouri towards Arginonta. About 800m past Elena Village Hotel, there is a row of low buildings on the right. Turn right 20m past them, onto a rough dirt road. Walk up this dirt road to another, smooth dirt road and some houses. Turn right and walk to the parking area of Odyssey, where the path begins between two boulders. **Walking time:** 25-30 min.

2) By scooter/car: Head from Masouri towards Kasteli and Arginonta. Immediately after the big right-hand turn in the road at Kasteli, make a sharp right turn onto a steep uphill concrete road around a colorful house. Park off to the side just before the road ends by two big boulders to your left (37.011474, 26.943004). The trail begins between the boulders, near a tall wooden electricity pole. Go uphill for 2 min and then follow the left branch of the path to Odyssey. **Walking time:** 8 min

See also: Crag Panorama on page 197.

Yuji Hirayama, Caroline Ciavaldini and James Pearson at sector Odyssey during the TNF climbing festival in 2013.

25 ODYSSEY

FETA WALL
ORION WALL

37.011474
26.943004

1. **Bonnie** 1★ 5c 17m
Shares first bolt with "Clyde". A good warm-up, easier from the left. *K Oelze, 1999*

2. **Clyde** 1★ 6b 20m
Another good warm-up, with a delicate sequence before the bulge. *K Oelze, 1999*

3. **Mythos** 3★ 6b+ 32m
Long and varied; a fingery crux above an awkward alcove leads to an easier slab. 60m rope just enough. *K Oelze 1999*

4. **Early Bird** 3★ 7b+ 28m
Athletic tufa climbing, juggy overhangs, tricky slopers and a pleasant finish on gouttes d'eau. *M Dettling, 2012*

5. **Hyma sto Kyma** 3★ 7c+ 25m
Pleasant tufas lead to a testing headwall.
G Koutsoukis, A Theodoropoulos, G Kopalides, 2008

6. **Arugliopoulos** 3★ 7c+ 25m
A steep sloping start then technical, pumpy tufa pinches.

7. **Kulturistika** 3★ 7b 18m
Great tufa action on a slightly overhanging wall. If you can do the "big" move you can do it all! *M Srutek, F Kocis, 2008*

8. **Ya Agori Mu** 2★ 7a+ 17m
Nice climbing on small, somewhat fragile tufas. Don't worry, take it easy! *J Kety, 2016*

9. **Elies** 2★ 7a+ 18m
Pumpy climbing on tufas, pockets and chips. Tricky at the top. *A + S Minneto, 1999*

10. **Feta** 3★ 6c 18m
A short section on small pockets leads to tufa climbing with tons of kneebars. *A + S Minneto, 1999*

11. **Moon Bridge** 2★ 7c+ 18m
Bouldery and technical on thin holds. *A Mavromatis, 2005*

12. **Island in the Sun** 3★ 7a+ 20m
Excellent tufa climbing with nice bridging and some powerful pulls through the bulge. *K Oelze, 1999*

13. **Island in the Sun Ext** 1★ 7b 25m
One hard move to exit from the roof. *K Oelze, 1999*

14. **Lucky Strike** 3★ 7b 20m
A thin start leads to an upper tufa section and an exciting finale. Save some energy for it! *K Oelze, 1999*

15. **Las Gallinas que Entran Por Las...** 2★ 8a 20m
A bouldery start then a sustained headwall. *P Barbero (Direct finish + cleaning by A Theodoropoulos, C Dawson)*

16. **Morfeas** 2★ 6b+ 12m
Short but intense! Learn the art of steep tufa climbing.
K Lambadarios, A Theodoropoulos, 2001

ORION WALL

17 Morfeas Plus — 2★ 7b+ 28m
Powerful and reachy moves.
K Lambadarios, A Theodoropoulos, 2001

18 Los Kukos — 3★ 8c 20m
Short, but with powerful bouldery moves.
C Daniil, A Mavromatis, 2006

19 Pindaro — 2★ 7c+ 30m
Interesting climbing on a big tufa leads to a crimpy headwall. *E Bendinelli, A Longo, 2000*

20 Island Highway — 2★ 6c+ 22m
A very technical, balancy start and a pumpy finish on big but smooth holds. *M Schepers, 1999*

21 Island Highway Ext — 2★ 6c 35m
Easier, though steeper than the first part. Rope drag problems; best to do it as a 2nd pitch. *M Schepers, 1999*

22 Il Gigante e la Bambina — 2★ 6c+ 22m
A hard fingery wall followed by a steeper section on good pockets and a tufa. *D Gozzi, R Gazzera, Nicole, 2001*

23 Satyros — 3★ 6c+ 20m
Long and dramatic, with some reachy moves leading past a pumpy finale. *T Michaelides, L Botelis, 2002*

24 Bubù Pensaci Tu — 2★ 7b+ 23m
A technical crux on slopers; handle the two flakes at the finale with care. *D Gozzi, R Gazzera, Nicole, 2001*

25 Triton — 3★ 7c 25m
A steep power endurance problem and a surprising, unexpected solution. *M Dettling, 2013*

26 Andromeda — 3★ 7c+ 20m
Short but action-packed. Constantly steep and hard climbing on a striking tufa feature. *Y Torelli, 1998*

27 Orion — 3★ 7c+ 20m
A very steep bouldery crux amidst much easier territory. Popular when it was still 8a...! *Y Torelli, 1998*

28 Tagmania — 3★ 8c+ 20m
First ascent by Alex Megos in Oct. 2014. *N Favresse, 2007*

29 Meltemi — 3★ 7b 20m
A fine route with a reachy crux at mid-height.
A + S Minneto, 1999

30 Scylla — 2★ 7c 30m
An excellent sequence at the immaculate upper wall.
A Theodoropoulos, G Kopalides, G Koutsoukis, 2008

31 Paris, Texas — 3★ 7c 30m
Definitive wall climbing with thin moves, unusual for Kalymnos. *A Theodoropoulos, G Kopalides, G Koutsoukis, 2008*

32 Patroclos Reborn — 3★ 7b 30m
A direct but sustained finale on tufa chips and pockets.
A Theodoropoulos G Kopalides L Pouzadoux 2008

33 Daphne — 3★ 7b 25m
Technical climbing requiring balance on smooth and somewhat slippery pockets. *D + F Bessone, A Gamba, 2001*

25 ODYSSEY
MARCI MARC CAVE

37.011474
26.943004

Alex Megos redpoints "Los Revolucionarios" 9a on his 2nd go. CHRIS BOUKOROS

MARCI MARC CAVE

34 Tupac Amaru — 3★ 9? 25m
A blank slightly overhanging wall. Free project.
G Kopalides, A Theodoropoulos, 2009

35 Gora Guta Gutarak — ♪ 8c+ 30m
A power testpiece with a fingery intro crux. First OS placing the QDs by A.Ondra (2009). *C Daniil, A Mavromatis 2006*

36 Los Revolucionarios — ♪ 9a 30m
Still the hardest route here. FA by Adam Ondra (2009), who says you need "power, long arms and a cool breeze. Climb the lower part then move upwards on desperate slopers and pinches". *A Theodoropoulos, G Kopalides, C Daniil, 2007*

37 Lucky Luca — 2★ 7a+ 15m
A tufa boulder problem, then steep but juggy tufas to the first anchor. *Michi + Co. 2000*

38 Lucky Luca Ext — ♪ 8c 30m
Superb! First RP of full extension by Chris Sharma (2006) dynoing at the crux; so harder for the short. *Michi + Co. 2000*

39 Marci Marc — 3★ 7c+ 30m
One of the most beautiful routes of this style. Elegant, unforgiving and exposed! *Michi + Co. 2000*

40 Nadir — ♪ 8b+ 30m
A stellar line, crimpy and sustained. Onsighted by Adam Ondra in 2009. *G Kopalides C Daniil A Theodoropoulos 2007*

41 Amphora — 2★ 7b 20m
Good edges, crimpy finale and some polished holds.
P Raspo, 2001

42 Sirene — 3★ 7c 33m
Builds magnificently to a confusing climax crux at the very end. A 60m rope is just enough. *A Di Bari + Team, 1997*

43 Inti Raymi — 3★ 7b+ 35m
A slightly overhanging wall with a short but shocking crux at the end. *G Kopalides C Daniil A Theodoropoulos 2007*

44 Sardonique — 3★ 8a 33m
A fine boulder problem and fingery crux requiring good conditions. A 60m rope is just enough. *A Ghersen, 2002*

45 Inti Watana — 3★ 8b 35m
A clean wall climb with thin moves and a cool crux.
G Kopalides C Daniil A Theodoropoulos 2007

46 Boom Boom — 3★ 7c+ 30m
Thin wall climbing. *A Theodoropoulos, G Kopalides 2008*

47 Fourtouna — 3★ 7b+ 30m
A brilliant, often overlooked vertical wall climb with two intense crux sections. *Prinz + Geiswinkler, 2000*

216

25 ODYSSEY
IMIA WALL

37.011474
26.943004

48 Odisseo — 2★ 6a+ 20m
Wall climbing, with moves that can be trickier for shorter climbers. *A Di Bari + Team 1997*

49 Mon Amour — 2★ 6a 28m
A good position on the arête. *A Longo, A Sgvazzotti, 2002*

50 Nausicaa Nausicaa — 2★ 6a+ 28m
A very technical slab on small holds and slopers. You will either love it or hate it. *A Di Bari + Team, 1997*

51 Fouska — 2★ 7a 12m
A hard move low down and powerful to clip the chain; can be made easier by bridging. *J Mendez, 2001*

Katie on the juggy finale of "Lestrygon" 6c (page 218).

IMIA WALL

DETAIL 50-54 (right)

NIKOLAOS SMALIOS

52 Gaia   3★ 8b 20m
The definition of "power endurance" on pockets.
You have to skip some bolts to link it. *K Oelze, 2000*

53 Polifemo   3★ 7c 20m
A popular classic. The stretch to the tufa is good value for
the grade, the crimpy end a final test. *A Di Bari + Team 1997*

54 Alfredo Alfredo   3★ 7b+ 20m
Athletic and technical moves lead out right to easier
ground, but save a bit for the finish. *A Di Bari + Team 1997*

55 Why Not   2★ 6b+ 15m
Climb the tufa columns from the left (clips a long way right)
to a powerful move to the upper wall. *M Schepers, 1999*

56 The Beast   2★ 7b 25m
Fingery wall climbing with a very thin, technical crux.
Shares last bolt and chain with "Imia". *K Oelze, 2000*

57 Imia   3★ 6c 25m
Varied and brilliant. An easy start leads past a very delicate
crux to a sustained upper section. *Butbell, Heitner, 1999*

58 Eumeo   1★ 4b 15m
A slab for beginners. *A Di Bari + Team 1997*

59 Argo   2★ 4c 15m
Another easy slab. *A Di Bari + Team 1997*

60 Argo Navis   2★ 6a 25m
A worthwhile extension, slightly overhanging
on good jugs. *N Gresham, 2005*

61 Telemaco   2★ 5b 18m
A good slab with gouttes d'eau requiring good footwork.
A Di Bari + Team 1997

62 Penelope   2★ 6a+ 18m
Good climbing with a hard, athletic mid-section on the
red wall. *A Di Bari + Team, 1997; A Theodoropoulos, 2008*

63 Caribbean Wedding   3★ 6c+ 20m
A technical bridging sequence up the corner. Quite reachy
and harder for shorter climbers. *L Crane, 2004*

DETAIL 50-54

25 ODYSSEY
ITACA WALL
ATENA WALL

218
37.011474
26.943004

64 Lestrygon   2★   6c 22m
Balancy moves left or right of the edge, and an elegant exposed juggy end. *A Theodoropoulos, T Michaelides 2004*

65 Haryvdi   2★   6a+ 19m
Starts with some tricky crux moves, then an easier wall.

66 Mikrotera Kalamarakia   2★   6b+ 15m
A gym-like intro then a crimpy wall. *A + S Minneto 1999*

67 Mermizeli   2★   6b+ 15m
Steep with good holds until an awkward cruxy move over the left of the bulge. *A Theodoropoulos T Michaelides 2000*

68 Poly Retsina No Good   2★   6a 15m
Good pockets + sidepulls, but attention: a loose-looking block sits at the top of the crack.
P Reinih, T Scliffe, J Thielke, M Hiclestoolb, 1999

69 Eurycleia   3★   5b 16m
A fun route with an interesting bulging finale on good holds. *A Theodoropoulos, T Michaelides, 2000*

70 Lotophagos   2★   5c+ 16m
Steady wall climbing on spaced holds.
A Theodoropoulos, T Michaelides, 2000

71 Lotophagos Ext   1★   6c+ 21m
A bouldery sequence, easier from the left, to enter the obvious corner. *A Theodoropoulos, T Michaelides, 2000*

72 Itaca   3★   6c+ 20m
Excellent, steep and technical. *A Di Bari + Team, 1997*

73 Ciao Vecchio 3★ 6c 20m
A delicate vertical start, then steep on big holds. Going direct at the crux involves a 7a move. *A + S Minneto 1999*

74 Ulisse Coperto di Sale 2★ 7a 20m
An entertaining intro followed by a stiff, fingery crux. Not easy to onsight. *A Di Bari + Team, 1997*

75 Calipso 3★ 6c+ 20m
Superb overhanging climbing on jugs. A fast attitude at the top helps. *A Di Bari + Team, 1997*

76 Alcinoo 3★ 7b 20m
Easy climbing leads to a very steep headwall with reasonable but reachy holds. *A Di Bari + Team, 1997*

77 Dionysos 3★ 7a 22m
An impressive, overhanging juggy line with a powerful move at the top. *A Theodoropoulos, T Michaelides 2000*

78 Omiros 3★ 7b 22m
An excellent technical sequence then a tricky finish in a great position. *Y Torelli, 1998*

79 My Name is Nobody 2★ 7c 20m
A bouldery final bulge. *A Theodoropoulos, 2008*

80 Atena 2★ 6b+ 18m
A fine pumpy line, but slippery. *A Di Bari + Team, 1997*

81 Circe 2★ 6b 19m
Nice and technical; hard for 6b. *A Di Bari + Team, 1997*

82 Femio 2★ 6a+ 18m
Sustained, big but polished holds. *A Di Bari+Team 1997*

83 Laertes 3★ 5c+ 18m
Tufa and good jugs. *A Theodoropoulos, T Michaelides, 2000*

84 Nessuno 2★ 5c 18m
Testy moves right of the corner. *A Di Bari + Team 1997*

ATENA WALL

220

25 ODYSSEY
ON THE VERGE

37.011474
26.943004

85 On the Verge — 2★ 3c 18m
All these routes are great for beginners. *N Gresham, 2005*

86 The Naughty Nun — 2★ 4b 15m
A gentle leaning slab. *A Hedgecock, 2014*

87 The Verger — 2★ 3c 16m
A Hedgecock, 2013

88 Second Coming — 1★ 4b 16m
A Hedgecock, 2014

89 Altar Boy — 1★ 5a 14m
A Hedgecock, 2014

90 The Pulpit — 1★ 5a 12m
Just two moves at the start, then easy. *A Hedgecock, 2015*

91 The Mad Monk — 1★ 4b 16m
A Hedgecock, 2015

92 The Kinky Cleric — 1★ 4b 18m
A good low-angle slab for beginners. *A Hedgecock, 2014*

Clipping the chains of "Atena" 6b+ (previous page). At anchors with two opposite carabiners, like this one, always clip both carabiners to prolong their life. While it is easier to just clip one carabiner and go, this drastically shortens the life of carabiners. Please help protect them.

ON THE VERGE

221

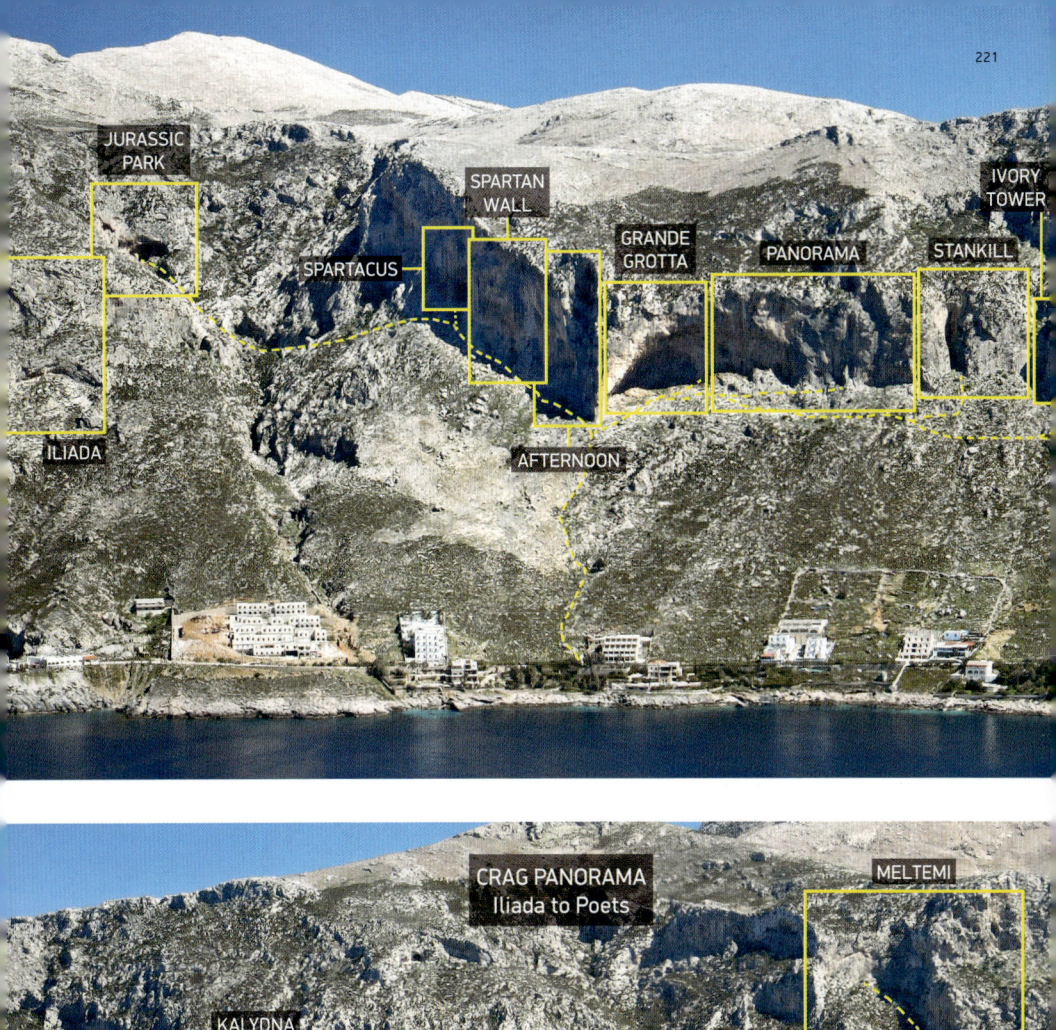

CRAG PANORAMA
Iliada to Poets

MON AMOUR *

A story by Jo Nesbo

I **knew right away there was something wrong with this route**. The wind changed direction just as we stopped in front of it, the temperature dropped sharply and by the time Erik was ready to go, the clouds were already building towers in grey steel against the horizon. We had planned to do the route as a warm-up, the start of a splendid day of cheerful climbing with friends. Little did we know of what laid ahead. Already at the second clip Erik—a 7c climber and progressing—made a tiny sound. As if caught by surprise by something he had not seen nor heard, just felt. But he went ahead. Of course. It was a 6a. After the third bolt I could see him hesitating. After the fourth bolt I could see his knees starting to shake slightly. That happens at warm-ups, most climbers need to warm up mentally too. Still, a 6a … At the fifth I think he said something about the space between the bolts, but I couldn't hear the exact words because of the increasing wind. At the sixth he stopped. Waited. It was strange to see his body, suddenly ridden by a fear I had never seen in this man, so strong and bold that we just call him Erik. Well, that is his name, but nevertheless. He looked around as if he was being attacked by beasts and then, with just a short, sharp yell of warning ("take!"), he tossed himself backwards into thin air, as if mad, desperate to escape these invisible creatures. And he fell towards the ground. Luckily he was tied to a rope that caught him and prevented his body from being smashed to the ancient rocks that make up this mysterious Greek island.

I lowered him down. And as he came closer I saw something in his face I've never seen before. Fright. Bewilderment. Confusion. Not the Erik we call Erik.

"What happened?" I asked. "Let's get away from here," he said. "Why?" "It's … its's … let me do a 7a. I can do a 7a. Just don't make me climb …" We both looked at the name of the route that was painted on the rock in something red that may have been paint. MON AMOUR. MY LOVE.

"I'll have a go," I said and tied myself to the rope.

"Jo, don't," Erik said. "I don't know what, but something happened here. Mon Amour. It got that name for a reason."

After the fourth bolt I could see his knees starting to shake slightly. That happens at warm-ups, most climbers need to warm up mentally too. Still, a 6a...

"Look at the crag," I said. "It's so crowded here we won't find another warm-up-route. Relax, man."

And so I started climbing. And I could feel it as soon as I put my hand I the rock.

I shouldn't have.

The rock was cold as ice. Cold rock? In September in Greece? Good for friction, I told myself and went on. The start felt a bit hard for a 6a, I thought. Maybe that's why we hadn't heard about anybody who had climbed it. Actually we hadn't heard anybody mention the route at all, which is quite strange because it should be a perfect warm-up-route on a crag like this. And the next thought inevitably crossed my mind: shouldn't that be a warning to us? Well, nobody likes under-graded routes, I told myself and went on. I clipped the quickdraw at the fourth bolt. I felt better, more confident. A heard a low rumble. Thunder. I didn't have to turn my head to know that the weather was coming this way. A hint of a crux. I looked at the rock. Sharp. Razor-blade sharp. And it looked as if they had spilt some of the paint here too. And suddenly there were those images in my head. Of someone falling on these rocks. Not me, but somebody else. And not free falling, but sliding down the sharp slab, leaving traces of skin, a torn nipple, a young, beautiful face. I broke a nail on a crimp. Good, that brought me back to reality!

JOHN KOULLIAS

No more ouzo late at night for me! I reached up with my quickdraw, noticed the light had changed, that it suddenly felt like dusk, attached the QD to the bolt and clipped the rope in. At the same moment I felt a gentle touch on my bare shoulder, as if by the skin of a woman's soft hand. A falling leaf, I thought. Or a butterfly. I focused again. I passed Erik's last quick draw. I worked fast now, gained ground. I could feel my inner height measurerer ticking.

There were no bolts.

I looked, I searched. No bolts.

What the f...

I made a quick decision. To go on. Since my only other possible   decision would have been to panic. I was already on a severe run-out, and there was no way I would be able to climb back to the previous quickdraw.

There HAD to be bolts, for God's sake!

And there it was. Suddenly, as if it had sprung out from the rock there and then, right in front of my face. Strange. And it was old. Black and rusty. Looked like something that belonged in another time. Like something that belonged on a chain. A chain that belonged in a cellar. A cellar that belonged in a castle. That chained something or someone that belonged to someone. And in the same instance I heard a voice, it must have come with a gust of the ever-increasing, whistling wind, that said: "I'm leaving you, I love him too much, my love." And since it sounded like the words from a stupid pop song, I figured it must come from a radio brought by a stupid climber. So I looked down. And I could not believe my eyes.

There was nobody there. Nobody. They were all gone.

How could that be, how could a crag be emptied in just a couple of minutes? OK, so bad weather was on its way, but where had they all gone? I couldn't see them walking down the hill either, which should have taken them at least ten or twelve minutes. Maybe there was something wrong with my eyesight, because it looked like the town of Masouri was gone too. And I couldn't see any of the buildings on the nearby island of Telendos, either, just a castle I had never noticed before.

"Let's get away from here," he said. "Why?" "It's...it's...let me do a 7a. I can do a 7a. Just don't make me climb..." We both looked at the name of the route that was painted on the rock in something red that may have been paint. MON AMOUR. MY LOVE.

"Erik?" I said.

No answer. My rope disappeared from sight under a bulge six meters under me. He must be somewhere under there. Of course, where else would he be?

"Erik!" I yelled. "Erik!"

I don't know why I yelled, I was still climbing and he was giving me rope, smoothly and fine, there was not even the slightest feeling of rope drag. Nothing. Just the rope and me.

I know why I yelled. I was scared.

I was scared because I remembered now. I knew why the route was called My Amour. I knew why we had never heard about anybody climbing it. I knew why... TAKE!!!

....

Jo Nesbo is a best-selling Norwegian author, musician, climber, and frequent Kalymnos visitor. His "Mon Amour" story first appeared on 8a.nu in 2012 and was reprinted here with the author's kind permission.

* Mon Amour (6a) is on page 216.

26 OCEAN DREAM

37.011474
26.943004

GRADE RANGE	up to 5b+	5c to 6a+	6b to 7a	7a+ to 7c	7c+ and up
No. OF ROUTES	3	7	6	4	4

A massive cliff in a mountainous landscape, sector **Ocean Dream** features rock of excellent quality and plenty of potential for new routes. Some of the longest, most demanding, and adventurous multi-pitches of Kalymnos are here, along with two extraordinary hard routes atop a balcony where more similar routes could be created. Ocean Dream is worth visiting for the view alone—especially in the winter.

Ocean Dream consists of a **Lower Section**, which also features some multi-pitches, and **Nemo**, featuring fewer routes but also good potential for new lines.

Climbing: Mostly delicate and technical on smooth, easy-angled rock.

Conditions: A warm, sun-lit crag. Best for climbing in cooler temperatures (less than 20°C). **Exposure**: S

Shade: Until 11:00 (left) or 12:00 (right).

Kids: Good, if they don't mind the long approach path.

Approach: From Masouri, head towards Kasteli and Arginonta. Immediately after the big right-hand turn in the road at Kasteli, make a sharp right turn onto a steep uphill concrete road around a colorful house. Park off to the side just before the road ends by two big boulders to your left (37.011474, 26.943004). The trail begins between the boulders, near a tall wooden electricity pole. Start up the path to sector Odyssey, but do not turn left towards Odyssey. Keep going straight up the steep slope following the markings on the right side of the streambed. When you come to the foot of Olympic Wall, traverse leftwards for 5 more minutes.
Walking time: 35-40 min.

See also: Crag Panorama on page 197.

Argyro Papathanasiou on the incredible single orange tufa of "Le Père Noël est une Chiure" 8a+ (page 227).

26 OCEAN DREAM

226
37.011474
26.943005

LOWER WALL
NEMO

The **Lower Wall** features some very good single pitches on smooth low-angle slabs, plus a few worthwhile multi-pitches.

Climbing: Technical and slabby. However, bolts are not always ideally placed.

☁ **Shade:** After 11.00. **Exposure:** S

1 Cardio Palma   2★   8a 125m
Multi-pitch; 7a obligatory. (6c 35m, 7c 30m, 8a 35m, 6c 25m). Pitches 2 + 3 are the highlight. 1st pitch is "Marina". Gear: 60m rope if you walk down afterwards; it is also possible to rappel down using 2 ropes. *G Ongaro, F Palma, 2004*

2 Albert Project   3★   6b 150m
Multi-pitch; 6a obligatory. One of the best multi-pitches. (5a 30m, 5b 30m, 6a+ 30m, 6b 30m, 6b 30m). Continuous technical climbing; walk down afterwards + 20m abseil. Belays are not equipped for abseiling. *G Albert, D Dulac, 2004*

3 Ocean Dream   2★   6a 30m
Good climbing up a compact slab. *U Thomsen, G Schley, 1999*

4 Uomo Senza Qualità   2★   8a 135m
Multi-pitch; 7a obligatory (6a+ 35m, 7b 20m, 8a 35m, 8a 20m, 5a 25m). Gear: 60m rope, 10 QD. Some unique pitches, gut-wrenching exposure and amazing views. Walk down afterwards. *S Pedeferri, M Vago, 2004*

5 Marina   2★   6a 30m
A compact, smooth, technical slab. *R Ferrante, B Vitale 2000*

6 Giuliana   3★   6a 30m
A steep corner and technical slab. *R Ferrante, B Vitale 2000*

7 Sara   2★   6a 30m
Good footwork is necessary. *R Ferrante, B Vitale 2000*

8 Octopus   1★   6a 30m
Slabby climbing on compact rock. *U Thomsen, G Schley 1999*

9 Stachelino   2★   5c+ 25m
Crimps and small footholds. *U Thomsen, G Schley 1999*

10 Zeus   2★   5b 25m
Interesting and compact, but beware of a loose block + flake by the anchor. *Routes #10-12: R Ferrante B Vitale 2000*

11 Calliope   1★   5a 20m
Bolting not so good for the grade. Single bolt anchor.

12 Callisto   2★   4c 20m
Spaced bolts; better climbing from the right side.

13 Francalypso   3★   6c+ 145m
Multi-pitch (5b 50m, 6b 50m, 6a 20m, 6c+ 25m). Gear: 2x50m ropes, 14 QD. Walk down afterwards + 20m abseil, or abseil all the way down. *P Gabarou, F Torre, 2001*

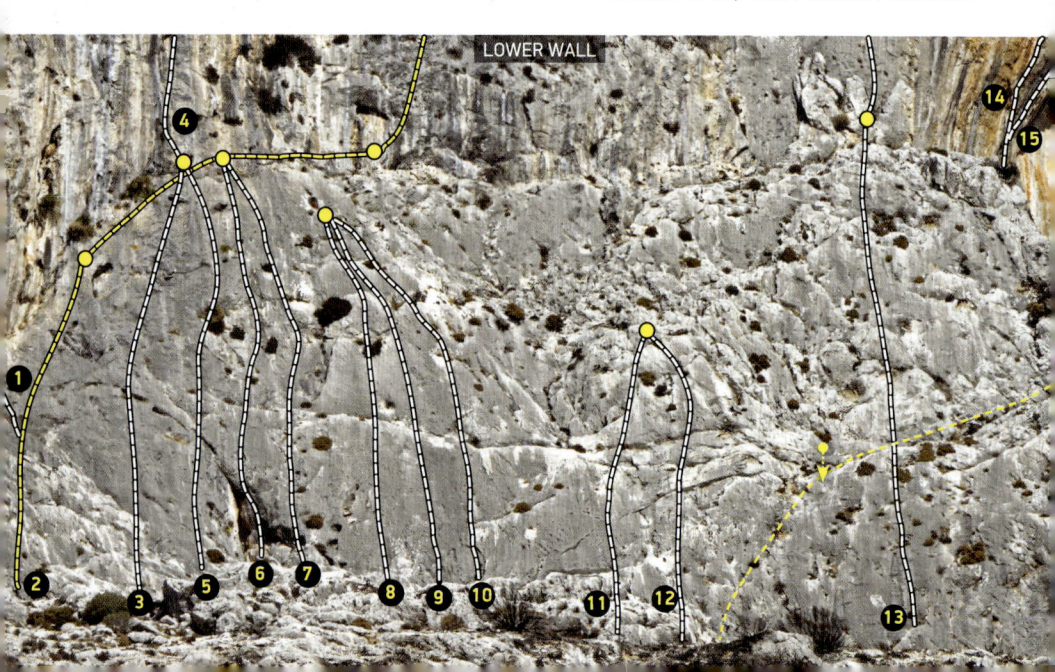

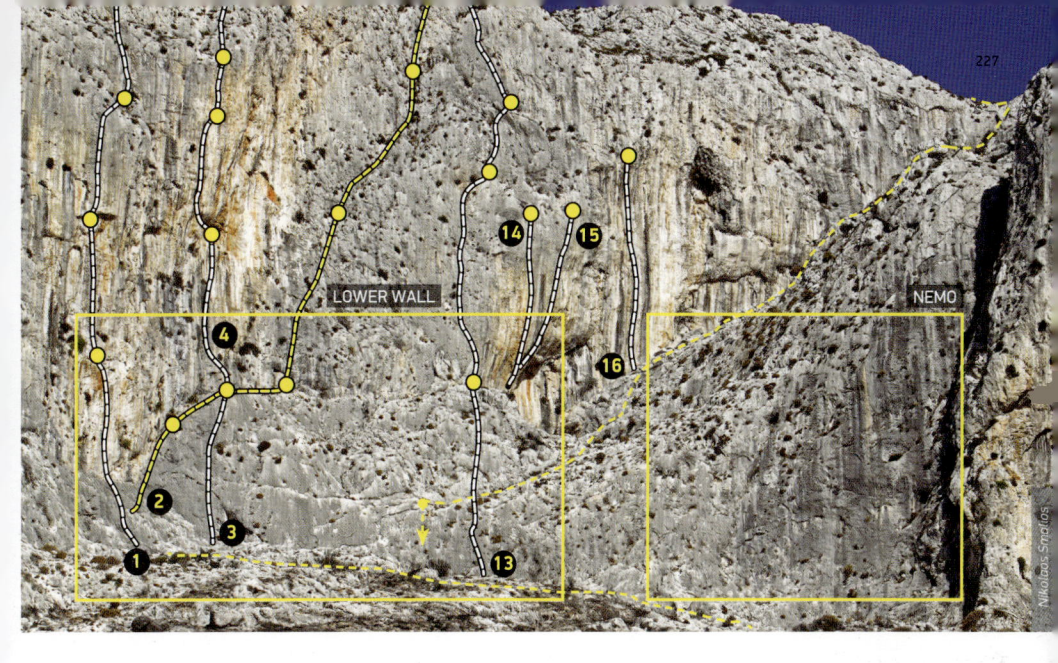

14 **Le Père Noël est une Chiure** ♪ 8a+ 35m
A stellar tufa. Access via "Francalypso". *S Millet, 2006*

15 **Thuladenlos** 3★ 8? 40m
Free project; start as for #14, then go right. *S Millet 2006*

16 **Be Like Water** 3★ 7c 35m
A dream single-tufa climb! *L Halsey, 2011*

17 **Epicure** 3★ 6a 35m
The wall with good holds. *C Idoux, 2009*

18 **Evdokia** 2★ 6b 40m
More good holds and a small overhang. *C Idoux, 2009*

19 **Capucine** ♪ 6c 40m
Has a short, fingery section.
Routes #19-24: C Idoux, L Salsotto, 2009

20 **Engagez-Vous** 2★ 6b 43m
Wall climbing on good holds.
Attention: Loose rock at about 30m high.

21 **Les Portes du Penis Entier** 3★ 6c+ 35m
Quality slab, with a short hard section on monos.

22 **Si T'es Pas Bon Tu Restes...** 3★ 7a+ 35m
... à la maison. Slab with a tricky, short overhanging section.

23 **Pas Penser, Percer** 2★ 7a+ 43m
Nice, technical climbing.

24 **Nemo** 3★ 7b 35m
Strenuous, slightly overhanging climbing on small holds.

Nemo (below) is a dark grey wall with good potential for new long routes.

Climbing: Technical with some spaced bolting.

Shade: After 12.00. **Exposure:** SW

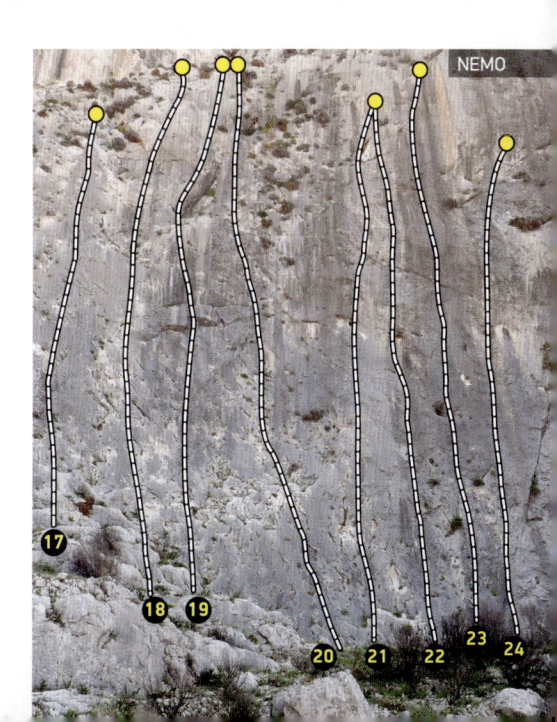

27 OLYMPIC WALL

37.011474
26.943004

GRADE RANGE	up to 5b+	5c to 6a+	6b to 7a	7a+ to 7c	7c+ and up
No. OF ROUTES	0	2	19	8	4

Georg "Gonzo" Hoffmann enjoying "Telendos" 7a+.

A wall of epic proportions looming large over sector Odyssey, **Olympic Wall** features excellent limestone and good potential for new routes, both single- and multi-pitch. Because of the longer approach path, this is not a busy crag. If you go, you will probably enjoy these fine routes all by yourselves.

Climbing: Slightly overhanging rock full of pockets, giant tufa pipes, tufa blobs, stalactites. Stamina and technique can be very useful for some of the monster pitches.

Conditions: Best for early mornings. Exposed to the sun and the rain.

Shade: Until 12:30. **Exposure**: S

Kids: Good, if the long path is not a problem.

Approach: From Masouri, go towards Kasteli and Arginonta. Immediately after the big right-hand turn in the road at Kasteli, make a sharp right turn onto a steep uphill concrete road around a colorful house. Park off to the side just before the road ends by two big boulders to your left (37.011474, 26.943004). The trail begins between the boulders, near a tall wooden electricity pole. Start up the path to sector Odyssey, but do not turn left towards Odyssey. Keep going straight up the steep slope following the markings on the right side of the streambed, until you come to the foot of the massive wall up ahead. **Walking time**: 30 min.

See also: Crag Panorama on page 197.

1. Cantela — 2★ 6b 20m
A red wall, not-so-good rock. *C + Y Remy, 2010*

2. Beta Bloc — 2★ 6c 25m
A steep wall with big holds and flakes. *C + Y Remy, 2010*

3. Défense d'y Voir — 2★ 5c+ 25m
A warm up with an interesting finale. *C + Y Remy, 2008*

4. Alpha — 2★ 6b 25m
A steep start and airy finale. *C + Y Remy, 2010*

5. Kalynette — 2★ 6b+ 27m
A technical wall, sharp at parts. *C + Y Remy, 2010*

6. Le Bite Ne Fait Pas le Moine — 2★ 6c 25m
A hard start and a technical wall. *B Girardin, C+Y Remy 2008*

7. Le Bite Ne Fait Pas…Ext — ♪ 7a+ 40m
A sustained extension with a challenging exit. *B Girardin, C + Y Remy, 2008*

8. Erotik Market — 2★ 6b+ 27m
Very technical. *B Girardin, C + Y Remy, 2008*

9. Il Movimiento Sexi — ♪ 6a 32m
A geologist's fantasy up a black waterstreak and an awesome colorful headwall. Often wet. *H Gargitter Group, 2001*

10. Toutouille — 3★ 6b 30m
A good, fingery climb. *C Idoux, L Salsotto, 2010*

11. Les Ch'tis — 3★ 6b+ 30m
Lovely rock with scattered iron-like knobs. *B Giradin, C + Y Remy, 2008*

12. Saphir — 2★ 6c 31m
Another wall climb. *C + Y Remy, 2010*

13. Sextoys — 3★ 7a 30m
Technical, with a challenging, tricky finish. *B Girardin, C + Y Remy, 2008*

14. Telendos — ♪ 7a+ 30m
Awesome climbing on small tufas and a thin headwall. *H Gargitter Group, 2001*

15. Kalyty — ♪ 7b 25m
Tufas and a cruxy finale. *B Girardin, C + Y Remy, 2008*

16. Galasia Petra — ♪ 8a+ 110m
Multi-pitch (8a+ 40m, 8b+? 40m, 7c? 30m). The boldest line on this excellent wall. Daniel Du Lac ran out of bolts though and didn't finish the last pitch. *D Du Lac, G Albert, 2004*

LEFT

27 OLYMPIC WALL

37.011474
26.943004

MIDDLE RIGHT

17 Laetyan — 3★ 6c 25m
Nice tufas + technical traverse. *B Girardin, C + Y Remy, 2008*

18 Crack — 3★ 7a 25m
A dance between the tufas. *C + Y Remy, 2010*

19 Biloute — 3★ 7a 30m
Technique, tufas and good holds. *B Girardin, C + Y Remy, 2008*

20 Yamas — 3★ 8a 40m
Amazing tufas lead to a hard headwall.
D Du Lac, G Albert, 2004

21 Hogo Fogo — ♪ 7c 35m
Tufas, huecos, and a finale on a demanding vertical wall.
Pizcas, Pavouk, 2008

22 Hellas Rodeo — 3★ 7c+ 40m
A giant single colonette. "Bear-hug" climbing.
D Du Lac, G Albert, 2004

23 Tornado Lou — ♪ 7b 30m
Spectacular tufas all the way.

24 La Moule — 3★ 6c+ 22m
An athletic steep wall and tricky tufa-pinching.
B Girardin, C + Y Remy, 2008

25 Happy Birthday — 3★ 7a 35m
Varied and very technical. *B Girardin, C + Y Remy, 2008*

26 Limonadovy — 1★ 6b+ 30m
Varied wall climbing, but a short section with loose rock.

A British climber on "Biloute" 7a.

27	**Rêve de Femme**	3★	6b 20m

An easy slab leads to a big tufa. *B Girardin, C + Y Remy, 2008*

28 Folly   2★   6b 20m
Some good action right of the giant tufa. *C + Y Remy, 2010*

29 Pingu   1★   6c 20m
Half slab, half overhang; hard final clip. *C + Y Remy, 2010*

30 Saule   3★   7a 30m
Nice, steep, full of tufa flakes and huecos. *C + Y Remy, 2010*

31 Kalygula   1★   6c 20m
Short, athletic tufa climbing, but hard to clip the anchor. *C + Y Remy, 2010*

32 Blue Magic   3★   7b+ 35m
Very steep tufa and roof climbing, then an impressive headwall with huecos. *C + Y Remy, 2010*

33 Mella   2★   7c+ 25m
On the short cliff before Olympic Wall (photo below). Athletic, on tufas and small holds. *S Pedeferri, M Vago, 2004*

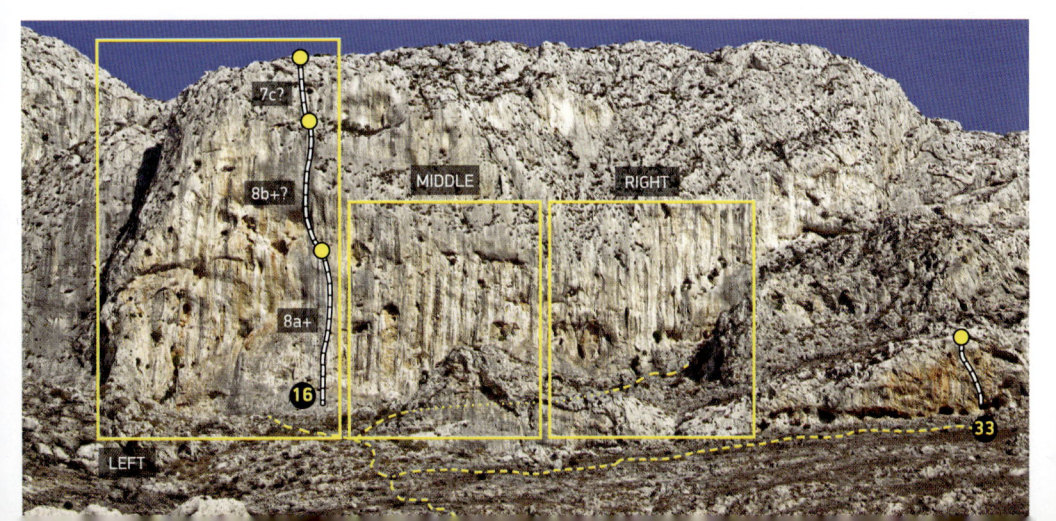

28 ILIADA

232
37.011474
26.943004

GRADE RANGE	up to 5b+	5c to 6a+	6b to 7a	7a+ to 7c	7c+ and up
No. OF ROUTES	7	26	25	10	6

Stefano Pelloni on "Ajax" 5b (page 235). NIKOLAOS SMALIOS

Iliada was originally created as an alternative for when sector Odyssey became too crowded, but before long it had developed a following of its own. Sector **Iliada** is at about the same level as Odyssey and a bit to the right. The quality of rock is just as good, and the extra 10 minutes needed to reach it are perfectly worth it. As in Odyssey, most route names in sector **Iliada** are inspired by the Homeric epic *The Iliad*. The only drawbacks of this crag are that the rock is a bit prickly on the grey walls, and the sun arrives earlier.

Climbing: Something for everyone; slabs, walls, overhanging routes on big pockets, slightly overhanging routes on small stalactites and tufa blobs, and a remarkable cave-roof.

Conditions: Warm and exposed to the weather. On windy days the wind can be quite annoying.

☁ **Shade**: Until 11:00 (Dolonas Cave area) or 13:00 (routes to the right of Polipitis Cave). **Exposure**: S

The happy faces of Megan Ison, Patrick Ison and Rab Pettener against an impossibly blue sea.

Kids: Good; the path is relatively smooth, and there is some suitable terrain around the crags.

Approach: From Masouri, go towards Kasteli and Arginonta. Immediately after the big right-hand turn in the road at Kasteli, make a sharp right turn onto a steep uphill concrete road around a colorful house. Park off to the side just before the road ends by two big boulders to your left (37.011474, 26.943004). The trail begins between the boulders, near a tall wooden electricity pole. Start up the path to sector Odyssey, but do not turn left towards Odyssey. Continue straight ahead until you are the same level as the Odyssey cliff. Now turn right, and traverse along an obvious path marked in red for an additional 10 min. You will first come to **Climbers Nest Wall** on the left. Continue uphill along the base of the cliffs, and you will come to **Dolonas Cave** next. **Walking time**: 18-30 min.

See also: Crag Panorama on page 197.

ILIADA SUB-SECTORS

ILIADA

EMILIO

MUSES

AFGHAN CORRIDOR

28 ILIADA

234
37.011474
26.943004

CLIMBER'S NEST
ILIADA MAIN (LEFT)

Climber's Nest, a grey limestone wall of generally good quality, is the first sub-sector you arrive at to the left of the main cliff.

Climbing: Technical and sometimes fingery.

Shade: Until 13:00. **Exposure**: S

Approach: See previous page. **Walking time**: 18 min.

1 Popi   1★ 6a+ 18m
Plenty of good pockets, but sometimes sharp.
J Rohrmann, O Steis, H Weninger, 2007

2 Thanks to Oswin   2★ 6a+ 20m
A hard start over the "belly" at the beginning; big holds thereafter. J Rohrmann, O Steis, H Weninger, 2007

3 Looser Baby   1★ 6c+ 20m
Just a few hard moves on a thin wall.
J Rohrmann, O Steis, H Weninger, 2007

4 Ibiscus Market   2★ 6b+ 30m
Technical face climb. J Rohrmann, O Steis, H Weninger 2007

5 Crutches   1★ 6b 25m
Good climbing, but a bit squeezed, and tough at the bulge.
H + J Weninger, A Hafner, C Schmidt, 2008

6 Another Day in Paradise   2★ 6a+ 30m
Excellent moves through the holes to a slabby, delicate finale. O Steiss, J Rohrmann, 2005

7 Homer Alone   2★ 6a 28m
A sustained, technical wall. D Musgrove, C Richards, 2007

8 Strike   1★ 5c 25m
Good climbing but a very squeezed line.
H + J Weninger, A Hafner, C Schmidt, 2008

9 Marianna   2★ 5c 25m
A better, slightly more independent line. Sustained but mild.
J Rohrmann, O Steis, H Weninger, 2007

10 Once More   1★ 6a 25m
J Rohrmann, O Steis, H Weninger, 2007

11 5 Star   1★ 6a+ 22m
Some nice slabby moves but a steep, sharp crux. Not a 5-star route… J Rohrmann, O Steis, H Weninger, 2007

12 Restaurant Acrogiali   1★ 5c 30m
There are good holds if you look carefully. Some suspicious-looking blocks at the top; be careful.
J Rohrmann, O Steis, H Weninger, 2007

CLIMBER'S NEST

Iliada's Main Cliff features a great variety of styles and grades, from hard roof climbs and overhangs to phenomenal mid-grade slabs and walls.

Climbing: Everything; pumpy, athletic, technical.

Shade: Until 11:00 (left) or 13:00 (right).

Exposure: S

Approach: See previous page. **Walking time:** 20 min.

1 **Ajax** 3★ 5b 31m
Good climbing up the ridge. At the ledge, be creative.
C + Y Remy, 2003/04

2 **Homer Vision** 2★ 5c+ 30m
Very rough rock and a bit broken near the top. A tricky crux for shorter climbers. C + Y Remy, 2003/04

3 **Diomidis** 2★ 6b+ 30m
Technical moves on small holds and pockets. Good climbing, but a little sharp. C + Y Remy, 2003/04

4 **Ira** 1★ 6c 20m
Take care at the start. C + Y Remy, 2003

5 **Dromos ton Meteoriton** 3★ 8b+ 15m
A hard roof sequence.
V Batsios, N Iatropoulos, C Kritsas 2008

6 **Celtic Dragon** 3★ 8c 30m
A traverse across the entire roof (20 m). Crosses #7, #8 and connects with the slabby finale of "Valley of the Dolls".
F Legrand, 2015

7 **Demon Direct** 2★ 8/9? 15m
Goes left at the 6th bolt of "Demon" and ends with "Dromos". V Batsios, C Kritsas, 2010

8 **Demon** 2★ 8/9? 15m
Another free project; impossible? V Batsios, C Kritsas, 2010

9 **Dolonas** 3★ 7b 15m
The big roof of the cave. Enjoyable, photogenic tufa climbing. C + Y Remy, 2003/04

10 **Valley of the Dolls** 2★ 8a+ 30m
"Dolonas" extension, a powerful sequence. N Gresham, 2009

28 ILIADA
ILIADA MAIN (MIDDLE)

37.011474
26.943004

François Legrand warms down on the impressive roof of "Dolonas" 7b (previous page).

11 **Iliada**   3★   6c   30m
Steep terrain with large pockets leads to an easier but technical headwall. *C + Y Remy, 2003/04*

12 **Athina**   2★   6c   28m
Interesting crimpy wall climbing, with two distinct crux sequences. *C + Y Remy, 2003/04*

13 **Ifigenia**   2★   6a+   25m
A good warm-up, sharp in places. *C + Y Remy, 2003/04*

14 **Lampetia**   2★   6c   20m
Wall climbing with some tricky moves. *C + Y Remy, 2012*

15 **Tefkros**   1★   6a   25m
Goes up the slabby groove with plenty of bridging and up to the small lip. Spaced bolts, though. *C + Y Remy, 2003/04*

16 **Troia**   1★   6a+   35m
Mountain-style pillar climbing. Watch out for loose blocks mid-height on the right. *H-P Bartens, K Hildenbrand, 2003*

17 **Ulysse**   2★   6a   32m
The technical groove with big holds. *C Idoux, 2010*

18 **Agamemnon**   2★   6a+   32m
The grey wall requires some good footwork. *C Idoux, 2010*

19 **Memories**   2★   6c   30m
A fine technical traverse and tricky exit with excellent moves. *C Idoux, 2010*

20 **Mirmidons**   3★   6b+   20m
Very pleasant, with varied climbing styles. Demanding from start to finish. *C Idoux, 2010*

21 **Patrocle**   3★   6b   20m
A tough start and steep but juggy finale. *C Idoux, 2010*

22 **Kalhas**   2★   6b   20m
A short but pleasant slab and small overhang. *C + Y Remy, 2003/04*

23 **Priamos**   2★   6b+   33m
Sharp rock but a pleasant middle section with tufas. *C + Y Remy, 2003/04*

MAIN (MIDDLE)

28 ILIADA

ILIADA MAIN (RIGHT)

37.011474
26.943004

24 Le Grand Retour — 3★ 7c+ 30m
Starts by riding a technical, steep prow; then, it crosses "Oetida" following the logical diagonal to the right on XL tufas at the lip of the cave. Finishes straight up the top of the wall with several technical cruxes! *F Legrand, 2015*

25 Oetida — 1★ 6c 25m
Unusual rock through the small cave leads to a tufa finale. Easier to strip the QD on top-rope. *C + Y Remy, 2003/04*

26 Oetida Ext — 3★ 7a 35m
Rope drag! One solution is to climb and strip the first pitch on top-rope, then lead this extension. *C + Y Remy, 2003/04*

27 Thetida — 3★ 7b+ 30m
A tremendous sustained route: a small roof with big jugs, then a pumpy tufa-covered headwall where things start to get exciting. *C + Y Remy, 2003/04*

28 Mythologie — 3★ 7b+ 35m
Exceptional tufa action on a moderately steep wall then a delicate, fingery finish on small crimps. *C + Y Remy, 2003/04*

29 Penelope — 2★ 6b 25m
A sharp start but a very rewarding finale on good holds. *C Idoux, 2011*

30 Ekavi   3★   6a 25m
A slabby start leads to a nice finish on the black tufa. A short but good intro to tufa climbing. *C + Y Remy, 2003/04*

31 Paris   3★   6c+ 30m
Smart moves on small tufas and good pockets. *Not* named after the French capital! *C + Y Remy, 2003/04*

32 Polipitis   3★   7a+ 25m
A tricky pocketed wall followed by a steep tufa finale. Interesting footwork, too. *C + Y Remy, 2003/04*

33 Zorba le Gros   3★   7b 25m
Outrageous for the grade! A great tufa start and committing headwall on undercuts. *P Collet, 2005*

34 Padroni e Pagliacci   3★   7c 28m
A steep, athletic start leads to the sustained, crimpy upper wall and a grand finale. *S Pedeferri, M Vago, 2004*

35 Nestoras   3★   7a 28m
Incredible features and big pockets go to an out-of-balance fingery bulge. *C + Y Remy, 2003/04*

36 Ektor   3★   6c 28m
A good steep pocketed wall past an obvious sloping ledge. Think laterally. *C + Y Remy, 2003/04*

37 Beautiful Helen   3★   6a+ 30m
A super route which steepens as you go. Moving out left looks terrifying, but isn't. *C + Y Remy, 2003/04*

38 Antilohos   2★   5b+ 25m
A straightforward slab with no real crux; however, some bolts feel far apart for the grade. *C + Y Remy, 2003/04*

39 Menelaos   2★   6a 25m
Mainly easy. At the end, look around for the good holds; going direct is harder (6b). *H-P Bartens, K Hildenbrand, 2003*

François Legrand climbs his new route "Le Grand Retour" 7c+.

28 ILIADA
EMILIO

240
37.011474
26.943004

Emilio is a good, relatively new addition to the right of the main cliff of **Iliada**, with high-quality grey rock. The easier routes can become a bit vegetated during spring; please take the time to clean a bit when lowering. The first four routes comprise an even smaller sub-sector called **Spice Garden**. Most routes here were equipped by Claude + Christine Remy (unless otherwise noted).

Climbing: Pleasant slabby and vertical climbing.

Shade: Until 12:30. **Exposure**: S

Approach: See page 233. **Walking time**: 25 min.

1 Glueck im Unglueck 1★ 5c 30m
Slab and wall. *A Hafner, S Muehlbacher, C Schmidt, H Weninger (The Drilling Gang), 2008*

2 Caper 2★ 4c 30m
A natural line and much more beautiful than it looks. *H + J + J Weninger, 2006*

3 Sage 2★ 5a 30m
A very pleasant slab covered in water pockets. Stiff at the end. *H + J + J Weninger, 2006*

4 Thyme 2★ 5b 30m
Higher up, it's really great. *H + J + J Weninger, 2006*

5 To Kati Alo 3★ 5c 25m
"Something else", with big holes and underclings. *Routes #5–#16 C + Ch Remy, 2011*

6 Kapou Kapou 3★ 5b+ 25m
Pleasant climbing on good holds.

7 Kapou Kapou Ext 2★ 6b 40m
The longest route of this sub-sector; 15 QD.

8 Ta Leme 3★ 5b 25m
Lovely, easy climbing.

9 Ta Leme Ext   2★   6a+ 30m
An athletic small roof and flakes.

10 Emilio   3★   5c+ 30m
Enjoyable climbing to an intricate roof finish.
Dedicated to Emilio Bollini, 1957-2001.

11 Marathon   3★   6a+ 30m
Cool and unusual, with 3 bulges and good but hidden holds.

12 Feideippides   2★   6c 30m
A wall on tufa material and a steep, sneaky finish.

13 Nenikikamen   1★   7b 30m
"We won" (said Feideippides when he ran to Marathon).
A boulder problem with a long reach.

14 Zoei   1★   6c? 28m
6c with one A0 move.

15 Panda Hilti   2★   6c 28m
Left side of the tufa, then a bulge. A bit expo.

16 Glyka Maniak   3★   6c 28m
On the right side of the tufa, a nice flight with slopers and a crack.

Climbers on "Mirmidons" 6b+ (left) and "Patrocle" 6b (right), both on page 237. CLAUDE REMY

28 ILIADA
AFGHAN CORRIDOR
MUSES

37.011474
26.943004

Afghan Corridor is a new sub-sector to the right of **Emilio**. It is a vertical red and grey wall decorated with some beautiful tufa snakes.

Climbing: Absorbing and technical, though there are some sharp holds. All routes were equipped by Giorgio Mallucci + Elisabetta Galli in 2012/13.

Shade: Until 12:30. **Exposure**: S

Approach: See page 233.

Walking time: 28 min.

1. **Babatangi** 1★ 7a 30m
Inconsistent. 25m of 6a climbing with a short crux of a few thin moves.

2. **Oxus** 3★ 7c 27m
Quite technical, rather than steep. Very well-bolted, though the crux is still somewhat obligatory.

3. **Unfinished Project** ?★ ?? ?m
An unfinished line.

4. **Kret** 3★ 7a 20m
Follows the big single tufa. Very technical (and sharp).

5. **Qala-e-Vust** 3★ 6c 30m
Very nice, well-bolted drip-hole climbing.

6. **Qazi-Deh** 3★ 6b 30m
2012

7. **Ishkashim** 2★ 6a+ 30m
Beautiful and homegeneous, quite tricky in parts though.

AFGHAN CORRIDOR

MUSES

Muses is a relatively small sub-sector well to the right of the main cliff, with excellent rock quality. Grey slabs co-exist with red overhangs and stalactites on the left. Route names come from the 9 Muses of Greek Mythology. If you are interested, the names still to be picked are *Thaleia*, *Melpomene*, *Terpsichore* and *Ourania*.

Climbing: On short and tough, but enjoyable, very well-bolted lines.

Shade: Until 12:30. **Exposure**: S

Approach: As on page 233, then traverse rightwards for 3 more minutes from the first cave ("Dolonas") of Iliada's main cliff. **Walking time**: 25 min.

1 Artemis 1★ 6c+ 12m
A pleasant tufa start with a fingery crux at the end.
A + I Ronner, 2001

2 Apollo 0★ 7b 12m
A tufa start leads to a very crimpy, sharp and unpleasant finale. *A + I Ronner, 2001*

3 Erato 3★ 7a+ 17m
Brilliant climbing on the left of the impressive tufa. Some tricky moves at mid-height.
T Michaelides, A Theodoropoulos, 2000

4 Calliope 3★ 7a 17m
A pleasant tufa start then a demanding headwall. Tough and blind at the top. *T Michaelides, A Theodoropoulos, 2000*

5 Efterpe 3★ 6b+ 18m
A worthwhile route with a hard intro, then varied wall climbing. *T Michaelides, A Theodoropoulos, 2000*

6 Polymnia 2★ 6a+ 18m
A stiff start leads to a much easier slab.
T Michaelides, A Theodoropoulos, 2000

7 Cleo 2★ 6a+ 18m
An enjoyable slab with a steeper technical exit.
T Michaelides, A Theodoropoulos, 2000

29 JURASSIC PARK
LEFT

244
37.004151
26.940815

GRADE RANGE	up to 5b+	5c to 6a+	6b to 7a	7a+ to 7c	7c+ and up
No. OF ROUTES	0	0	6	10	5

Jurassic Park is a huge crescent of pocketed wall with tufas high above and to the left of the Grande Grotta, and slightly higher than sector Spartacus. Despite being a small crag with a short climbing season, the rock is so solid and the routes so good that this crag is well worth the walk.

Climbing: Overhangs with holes, huecos and tufa pipes on some of the classiest routes in Kalymnos.

Conditions: Warm and protected from the wind and the rain (on the right). Not good for very hot, humid, or windless days.

Shade: Until 11:00 (left), 13:00 (right headwall) or 15:00 (right cave). **Exposure:** SW

Kids: A long walk, but some suitable areas near the cliffs. Be extra careful with the scramble up the approach gully.

Approach: From Masouri, go towards Kasteli and park by *Hotel Philoxenia* (37.004151, 26.940815). Take the steep uphill path to sector Grande Grotta, then past sector Afternoon to sector Spartacus. From here, the path dips down and left before a rocky scramble up an obvious gully on the opposite hillside, to Jurassic Park. (Alternatively, you can go by way of sector Iliada, but there is no established path.) **Walking time:** 45-50 min.

See also: Crag Panorama on page 221.

Nicolas Favresse on "Labyrinth" 8b (page 247). NIKOLAOS SMALIOS

1 **Fossil Wall**   3★   6c+ 25m
Steep and sustained climbing up the jug-infested wall.
N Gresham, 2010

2 **Pegasus**   3★   7a 25m
Power through an overhang on huge holds to an airy tufa, then to a blind and fingery crux. N Gresham, 2010

3 **Nike**   3★   7a+ 33m
An interesting pocketed wall with a steeper finale.
A + I Ronner, 2001

4 **Dike**   3★   7a 32m
Thought-provoking, despite big pockets to pull on and a tremendous, airy finale. A + I Ronner, 2001

5 **Pterodactyl**   3★   6b+ 18m
Direct start to "Dike". Juggy pockets to the steep rib and an anchor by the bush. Short but worthwhile. L Gresham 2009

6 **Full Wingspan**   2★   7b 32m
A hard move around the overhang then an amazing head-wall with some big reaches all the way to the top. Bolting is not so good. N Gresham, 2010

Left: Patxi Usobiaga on "Rendez with Platon" 8b (next page). NIKOLAOS SMALIOS

29 JURASSIC PARK
RIGHT

37.004151
26.940815

Jelisa Dunbar climbs "Raptor" 7c+. KARL GRUBNER

7 Themelis 3★ 6b 30m
A magnificent pillar with steep jug-pulling and endless letterboxes on the upper wall. You can belay from the ground with a 70m rope. *T Michaelides, A Theodoropoulos, 2001*

8 Cesta do Praveku 2★ 7a+ 28m
Athletic with some long reaches on good jugs. Finish up a tricky wall with some sharp holds. *M + J Srutek, 2010*

9 Houftasaurus 3★ 7b 25m
Another great route on the steep, bulging, juggy walls. Houfta means "jug". *N Gresham, 2010*

10 St Savvas 3★ 7b+ 18m
A steep start leads to a relentless upper wall. *T Michaelides, A Theodoropoulos, 2002*

11 Carnivore 3★ 7c 30m
Pull rightwards out of a small cave to a sustained finale on good but spaced holds. It bites! *N Gresham 2009*

12 Kalinycta Mer 3★ 7b+ 30m
Fantastic, with a reachy sequence. *D Gleize G Ulysse 2009*

13 Raptor 3★ 7c+ 30m
A leaning orange wall leads to a rest before the final fingery crux on the headwall. Classic. *N Gresham, 2009*

14 Atlantis 3★ 8b 30m
A fight all the way to the final move, with a complex crux weaving leftwards at the lip. *N Gresham, 2009*

15 Rendez With Platon 3★ 8b 30m
Every hold is a sinker pocket, but they're all far apart and the line is overhanging all the way! *P Pellet-Perrier, 2001*

16 O Lakos ton Leonton 3★ 8b+ 30m
A direct version of "Labyrinth" with a separate start and finish. FA by Alex Megos (2014). *G Kopalides, C Daniil, 2007*

17 Labyrinth 3★ 8b 25m
A wild outstanding journey across the roof. *N Gresham 2010*

18 Paleolithic Line 3★ 7b+ 17m
A pumpy crux with underclings leads to an upper wall which is no less hard. *M Zanolla, S Moro, 1999*

19 Nicola la Tigre 3★ 7c 16m
Very steep and powerful. Good holds, but stiff for the grade. *M Zanolla, S Moro, 1999*

20 The Sickle 3★ 7c 13m
Just as good as its neighbors. *N Gresham, 2010*

21 Neolithic Line 3★ 7c 16m
Pinch up the single tufa crawling out of the overhangs. A short route, but thank God for that. *M Zanolla S Moro 1999*

30 SPARTACUS

248
37.004151
26.940815

GRADE RANGE	up to 5b+	5c to 6a+	6b to 7a	7a+ to 7c	7c+ and up
No. OF ROUTES	0	3	10	12	4

To the left and higher than Grande Grotta and Spartan Wall, **Spartacus** features fabulous, challenging long routes, most of which carry the signature of Michel Piola. Sector **Spartacus** ranks very high in popularity, so expect it to be crowded during high season. Because of its enclosed shape and limited number of routes, it can feel confined when crowded.

Climbing: On steep orange tufa-streaked walls with smooth slabs on either side. Excellent, pumpy, sustained climbing and distinct cruxes, but some routes are polished.

ATTENTION: Most routes are very long, so your rope must be *at least 70m long*.

Shade: Until 18.00. Exposure: N

Argyro Papathanasiou on "Daniboy" 8a (page 252). CHRIS BOUKOROS

[Photo labels: JURASSIC PARK, SPARTACUS, SPARTAN WALL, AFTERNOON, GRANDE GROTTA, PANORAMA]

Stéphanie Bodet on "Pygmalion" 6b+ (page 251). SAM BIÉ

Conditions: Lots of shade and protected from the south winds. Good for winter, but also for summer climbing on breezy days. **Spartacus** is not good on hot, humid days with no wind: it can get hot and greasy, especially on the dark brown rock.

Kids: The approach is rather long, but there are some decent spots for kids near the cliffs.

Approach: From Masouri, go north and park by *Philoxenia* hotel (37.004151, 26.940815). Follow the steep uphill path starting on the left side of the hotel. Go through a goat gate and close it again. At the big olive tree, go left and up to the big cave. At the left edge of the cave, continue left for 10 min more, past sectors *Afternoon* and *Spartan Wall*. **Walking time:** 25 min.

See also: Crag Panorama on page 221.

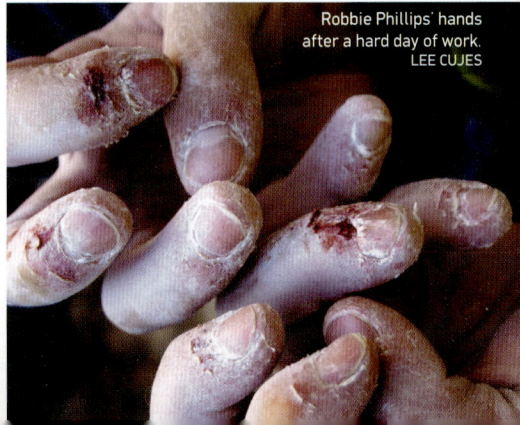

Robbie Phillips' hands after a hard day of work. LEE CUJES

30 SPARTACUS

250
37.004151
26.940815

FAR LEFT
LEFT

FAR LEFT

① 3 Stripes   3★ 5c 175m

Six pitches (4a 35m, 5a 40m, 5b 30m, 5c 20m, 5c+ 20m, 5b 30m). Start just left of Spartacus, left of the fence. Fantastic, pleasant climbing on slabs and walls with big holds. Very well-protected; just bring 14 long QD to reduce rope drag. On the last pitch, there is an extra anchor about 10m from the top. It is recommended you belay there, because if you go directly to the top you will not be able to communicate with your partner because of the wind. Overall, the combination of lower-grade climbing followed by an otherworldly abseil is every mountain guide's dream of an intro to multipitch climbing with clients.
M Leippold, P Keller, U Odermatt 2013

Attention: Be careful not to dislodge any loose stones. They can hurt climbers down below at sector Spartacus.

Gear: 14 long QD | 2 belay devices | 2-3 screwgate carabiners | 2-3 slings | helmets | a single 60m rope (or 2X80m ropes if you plan to abseil down; see below).

Return (walk): Go to the left then down via sector *Jurassic Park* following the blue marks. There are not-so-easy scree sections, so take proper approach shoes. **Time**: 50 min.

Abseil: YOU MUST HAVE 2 X 80m ROPES AND BE EXPERIENCED IN ABSEILING. Walk down to the right for 10 min following the cairns and abseil down the middle of the Grande Grotta. (Tip: You can hide one rope at the base of Grande Grotta. One of you will abseil using the fixed single 80m rope you brought. Then, tie its end to the 2nd rope you left at the cave for your climbing partner to pull up.)

LEFT

RIGHT

2 | Geissen Schnucki   1★ 6a 18m
Sharp rock, so don't tumble. *HP Bartens, K Hildenbrand 2001*

3 | ZiegenPeter   2★ 6a+ 18m
A technical start and long moves on a steep slab. *HP Bartens, K Hildenbrand, 2001*

4 | Astree   3★ 6b 35m
Varied but wandering climbing on a pocketed wall. Good moves on incredible holds. *M Piola, 2004*

5 | Chariots of Fire   3★ 6c+ 35m
A continuously challenging, atmospheric climb. *M Piola 2004*

6 | Vangelis Connection   3★ 6c+ 35m
Sustained wall climbing; run-out in places. *M Piola, 2004*

7 | Pygmalion   3★ 6b+ 35m
An excellent upper wall with good holds. Use long QD to avoid rope drag at the end of the first section. *M Piola, 2004*

8 | Magnetus   2★ 7c 18m
Short and stiff; some fingery moves and sustained pulls. Non-Kalymnian style and bolting. *J Batalla, D Brasco, 2005*

9 | Alexis Zorbas   2★ 7a+ 18m
A crimpy, bouldery exit. *HP Bartens, K Hildenbrand, 2001*

10 | Arena   3★ 7c 35m
A fingery boulder problem leads to magnificent wall climbing on the pillar. *A Theodoropoulos, V Kastanias, 2005*

11 | Jellyfish Pie   2★ 7a+ 30m
Hard to read, with several tricky sections on some tufa blobs, but fun all the way. Easier for the tall. *L Crane, 2003*

12 | Kerveros   2★ 7a 30m
An interesting and unlikely line for the grade, but polished for being so popular. A tricky start then tufa and pockets through exciting terrain. *C Seekircher, S Kolmbauer, 2003*

13 | Kerveros Ext   3★ 7b+ 40m
The leftward extension. *G Kopalides, 2014*

14 | Kerverias   3★ 7b 40m
The rightward extension. *G Kopalides, 2014*

30 SPARTACUS
RIGHT

252
37.004151
26.940815

Unknown climber on "Les Amazones" 6c

15 Neska Polita — 3★ 7c+ 20m
A tricky crux sequence with delicate moves at the lip of the cave. The 2nd part is intertwined with "Kerveros". *A Mavromatis, 2005*

16 Daniboy — 3★ 8a 20m
A Kalymnos classic; a natural line defined by a sequence of pockets and tufa snakes. *D + JB Winkler, M Piola, 2002*

17 Spartacus — 3★ 7b+ 20m
Steep, with unexpectedly good jugs to a demanding crux at the lip. *D + JB Winkler, M Piola, 2002*

18 Spartacus Maximus — 3★ 7b+ 45m
Upper tufa-land! To strip the route with a 70m rope, lower to the 1st anchor, pull your rope from there, then lower again. *S Golley, 2005*

19 Gladiator — 3★ 7b 25m
A bouldery start leads to a steep sequence on blobs, pockets and tufa to a technical exit. *D + JB Winkler, M Piola 2002*

20 Harakiri — 2★ 6b+ 28m
A pumpy gym-like climb on slippery holds. Popular, but polished. *D + JB Winkler, M Piola, 2002*

21 Tzatziki Vikiki — 2★ 7b+ 35m
A short pocketed extension. *D + JB Winkler, M Piola, 2002*

22 King Cobra — 3★ 7c+ 45m
Another extension. Finish "Harakiri" to the right, then good stalactites lead to an obvious single tufa. *N Gresham, 2005*

23 Mon Batchounousougounoudoudou — 3★ 6c+ 30m
A bouldery start; if you sneak from the left, a pumpy sequence at the end of the crack. *D + JB Winkler, M Piola, 2002*

24 Chameleon — 3★ 8a 45m
The streaked, bulging headwall can be climbed as a separate pitch starting from the upper cave. *N Gresham, 2009*

25 Les Amazones — 3★ 6c 30m
A superb but soapy line up tufas to a steep final wall. *D + JB Winkler, M Piola, 2002*

26 Ares — 3★ 7b+ 45m
A sustained exension of "Les Amazones". *N Gresham, 2009*

27 Aphrodisia — 2★ 6c+ 35m
Fine tufa blobs and good pockets. *K Schwarz, M Stofer, 2004*

28 Nabuchodonosor — 3★ 6c 35m
A long, sustained wall climb. *D + JB Winkler, M Piola, 2002*

29 Le 13ème Travail d'Hercules — 3★ 6b+ 35m
Technical, sustained wall climbing with several tricky bits. A bit run-out for the grade. *D + JB Winkler, M Piola, 2002*

253 RIGHT

31 SPARTAN WALL

37.004151
26.940815

GRADE RANGE	up to 5b+	5c to 6a+	6b to 7a	7a+ to 7c	7c+ and up
No. OF ROUTES	8	3	10	8	7

Evan Stevens climbs "The Siege of Thermopylae" 6c+ in the soft glow of early morning. SIMON CARTER

A minimal cliff face with very few features, the immaculate **Spartan Wall** is home to some of the hardest wall climbs on Kalymnos. For old-fashioned vertical climbing it will become one of your favorites. At the base of Spartan Wall Right is a small cave with just two routes called The End Cave.

Climbing: Very long pitches, small crimps and technical, old-fashioned vertical wall climbs.

Conditions: Not good for hot, humid days without wind; the tiny crimps "melt" into the rock.

Shade: Until 14:30. **Exposure:** N

Kids: A long approach, but some OK spots at the crag.

Approach: From Masouri, go north and park by *Philoxenia* hotel (37.004151, 26.940815). Follow the steep uphill path starting on the left side of the hotel. Go through a goat gate and close it again. At the big olive tree, go left and up to the big cave. At the left edge of the cave continue left, past sector Afternoon, for 5 min more. **Walking time:** 25 min.
See also: Crag Panorama on page 221.

1 Tales of Greek Heroes 3★ 6b+ 38m
A direct pitch up the groove in the rib. A 70m rope is just enough. *D Musgrove, 2006*

2 The Siege of Thermopylae 3★ 6c+ 33m
Climb through the niche at half-height before trending right on the technical upper wall. *D Musgrove, K Morgan, 2007*

3 Leonidas 3★ 7a+ 35m
Long and varied; slab, tufas and groove. *D Musgrove, 2008*

4 The Shield 2★ 7b+ 30m
Fingery climbing up the streak; a 60m rope barely reaches the starting ramp. *N Gresham, 2009*

5 Lucifer's Hammer 3★ 6c 30m
Compact, immaculate rock. A 60m rope is OK if the belayer is clipped in at the ramp by the route name. *K Ochsner, 2003*

6 Hippolyta's Belt 2★ 6c+ 30m
The wall + groove; 60m rope just enough. *G McArthur 2009*

7 Xerxes 3★ 6c+ 37m
Great vertical climbing on pockets. 80m rope and 19 QD. *D Musgrove, 2010*

8 Spasspartour 2★ 6b 45m
Multi-pitch (6a+ 30m, 6b 15m). A delicate grey slab leads to a pleasant steeper section on good jugs. With a 60m rope you should belay clipped in at the start. Both pitches are possible in one with a 70m rope. 20 QD plus some long ones to reduce rope drag. *K Ochsner, 2002*

9 Yanap   3★ 7b 50m
Superb, intricate wall climbing to an open corner with good holds. Not too steep with several rests. Can be climbed on a 70m rope: lower off directly to the "Spasspartour" belay to rearrange your rope and continue the descent. 21 QD.
B Girardin, C + Y Remy, 2009

10 Problème Mineur   3★ 6b 32m
The wall and open corner; excellent and enjoyable.
B Girardin, C + Y Remy, 2009

11 Kurva   3★ 7a 38m
A sustained wall + steep finish. *B Girardin, C+Y Remy 2008*

12 Kurva Ext   2★ 7b 42m
A Berry, 2014

13 Layo and Bushwacka   1★ 5c 20m
Start at a short corner 3m left of *End Cave*. Climb this to a ledge and small pedestal at 6m, then up the slab to the broad ledge known as *Space Terrace*. *N Gresham, 2010*

31 SPARTAN WALL

RIGHT

37.004151
26.940815

Argyro Papathanasiou is on "The Path to Deliverance" 7c+.
DYLAN WYER

14 Broken Souls 3★ 7c 30m
This and the next three routes all start from *Space Terrace*. (Use route #13 as the approach pitch; there are good ring-bolt belays to rappel down.) Start by scrambling onto the big pinnacle, then a stunning technical wall climb with some bouldery sections. Gets harder and harder. *N Gresham, 2010*

15 The Poison 3★ 7c+ 30m
Start as for #14 but go right to gain the orange streak. Small crimps, sloping feet, awesome finale. *N Gresham 2010*

16 Fudoshin 3★ 7c+ 30m
An epic adventure up spaced pockets through an overhang to a groove. Sustained and technical. *N Gresham, 2010*

17 Spartakiada 2★ 6c+ 25m
Good climbing but not very good bolting; hard to clip the chain. *M Srutek, F Kocis, 2008*

18 Spartakiada Ext 2★ 7b+ 45m
A long, sustained wall climb. *M Srutek, F Kocis, 2008*

19 Harlem Nights 2★ 7b+ 17m
Short and straightforward apart from one very hard crux move. *N Gresham, 2003*

20 The Beginning at the End 3★ 7b+ 17m
The first route to be climbed in the *End Cave*; a bouldery start to some great tufas and a tricky slab. *N Gresham, 2003*

21 Guest DJ 3★ 9a+? 55m
A very hard project; 80m rope.
L Triay, G Fanguin, A Cherbonnier, 2004

22 Titantrope ♪ 8c+ 65m
A very compact overhanging wall with constant dynos on very small edges and gouttes. 80m rope.
L Triay, G Fanguin, A Cherbonnier, 2004

23 Hibiscus Market Part 1 2★ 6a 25m
Devious and intimidating despite some added bolts.
L Triay, G Fanguin, A Cherbonnier, 2004

24 Hibiscus Market ♪ 8b+ 55m
A thin wall climb with three bouldery sections on tiny crimps. 80m rope needed for the full pitch.
L Triay, G Fanguin, A Cherbonnier, 2004

25 Yo Yo 3★ 5c 30m
A nice, photogenic ramp. *U Odermatt, 2010*

26 Poupakis 1★ 4c 18m
A scramble to the belay cave of #27-#28.
A Theodoropoulos, G Kopalides, 2008

27 The Path to Deliverance 3★ 7c+ 20m
An exciting, technical blank wall. *A Berry, 2005*

28 Spartan Wall 3★ 8a+ 20m
A super-technical, balancy white wall. *A Berry, 2005*

29	**Dulces Suenos**	3★ 5a 20m

A well-bolted leaning wall. *U Odermatt, 2010*

30	**Tigryonak**	2★ 5b 35m

Some nice, unusual parts. *U Odermatt, 2010*

31	**Dimarhos**	2★ 5a 35m

Good climbing on the second half. *U Odermatt, 2010*

32	**Insomnia**	3★ 5b+ 40m

Long and interesting, with good pockets and underclings higher up. 18 QD. *U Odermatt, 2010*

33	**Ojos de Brujo**	3★ 8a 20m

An immaculate wall. *G Kopalides, 2012*

34	**Strange Little Girl**	1★ 4c 17m

Harder at the top. *U Odermatt, 2010*

35	**Motyka Jawa**	2★ 6c+ 45m

A tricky, sharp wall leads to an impressive corner. Don't do it before it is rebolted: Dangerous run-out and bad bolting. *T Pycha, F Kocis, 2010*

36	**Megaburger**	1★ 4c 18m

Good for beginners; harder at the top. *U Odermatt, 2010*

37	**Organizer**	1★ 4b 17m

Step to the right. *U Odermatt, 2010*

32 AFTERNOON

37.004151
26.940815

GRADE RANGE	up to 5b+	5c to 6a+	6b to 7a	7a+ to 7c	7c+ and up
No. OF ROUTES	3	7	8	4	1

A beautiful grey slab to the left of Grande Grotta, sector **Afternoon** features a diverse assortment of climbs from 4a to 7b+. If you can lead 5c-6a you will really enjoy it, but there are also some very good 6b-6cs here. **Afternoon** is a good crag to warm up at before hitting the unreal overhangs of the Grande Grotta next door; furthermore, it is a good, north-facing crag for hot summer days, hence the name.

Climbing: On vertical or slightly off-vertical grey rock. Pleasant slabs (left), quality walls (right), and a few superb long pitches.

Conditions: Cool. A good crag for hot days; but exposed to the rain and the north wind.

Shade: Until 13:30 (left) or 16:00 (right). **Exposure:** NW

Kids: The approach is somewhat long and steep, but otherwise there are several open areas around the cliffs.

Approach: From Masouri go to *Hotel Philoxenia*. Park there (37.004151, 26.940815). Walk up the steep path starting on the side of the hotel. Go through the goat gate and close it behind you. Walk to the lone olive tree, then go left up a steep obvious path to the cave. At the edge of the cave, go left to the grey walls/slabs.

Walking time: 20 min.

See also: Crag Panorama on p. 221.

*Note: The goats at this crag are particularly well-accustomed to people and they will steal food from inside your bag. So always keep your bags zipped shut, and don't encourage the goats.

Lithuanian climber Vytautas Zurauskas gets past the tricky sequence of "L'Uomo che Non Credeva" 6b (page 261).

259

8a

6a+

6c

9

10

16

8

15

The two new multi-pitches shown here are described in more detail on the next page.

ATTENTION: Please be mindful of climbers below when climbing the multi-pitches. If there are climbers at sector **Afternoon** (which is quite popular with beginners) be careful not to dislodge any loose rock.

260

32 AFTERNOON

37.004151
26.940815

3 Energy 4 May 2000   2★ 5a+ 17m
Wall climbing on good holds and a tricky finale on tufa material. *M Schmed + Team, 1999/2000*

4 To Deftero Moro Mou   2★ 5c 17m
A smooth tufa groove with a technical crux but slippery finale. *AM Bader, 2001*

5 The Butcher of Baragwanath   2★ 7b+ 40m
A hard start after 'To Deftero Moro Mou' and continue up the tufa. One bolt poorly positioned out of the climbing line. Needs more cleaning. *G Parry, 2013*

1 Finger Piercing   2★ 4c 17m
Easy scrambling; good for beginners. *A + S Minneto, 1999*

2 Spartan Junior   2★ 7c 35m
Extension up the fingery, very technical wall. *A Berry, 2013*

6 Origano   2★ 5b 18m
Balancy, before an easy final scramble. *A + S Minneto, 1999*

7 Nonno Ringo   3★   5c 18m
A well-bolted, technical climb with an interesting traverse on cauliflower rock. *M Schmed + Team, 1999/2000*

8 L'Amico Ralph   2★   5c 18m
A delicate and pleasant grey slab.
M Schmed + Team, 1999/2000

9 Project   3★   ? 70m
A multipitch project (photo-topo on previous page). Climb "L'Amico Ralph" and follow the tufas to the left of "Beta". The next pitch is a blank wall, and the top pitch is an impressive red wall already redpointed at 8a. *G Parry, 2013*

10 Beta   3★   7b+ 35m
The inevitable extension of "L'Amico Ralph". Awesome, technical tufa climbing. To avoid rope drag, belay from the cave, not from the ground. *B Kauffungen, 2002*

11 L'Uomo che Non Credeva   2★   6b 18m
A sneaky crux sequence above the small tufa. Non-friendly bolting, occasionally. *M Schmed + Team, 1999/2000*

12 Kalo Taxidi   2★   6a+ 20m
Delicate but it bites! Small holds. *A + S Minneto, 1999*

13 Dinosaur Junior   3★   7b 30m
A 2nd pitch for "Kalo Taxidi". From the belay at the mid-height cave, hard pinches on thin tufas lead to continually sustained terrain. *N Gresham, 2003*

14 Blu   2★   6a 20m
Nice, crimpy wall climbing. *A + S Minneto, 1999*

15 Claire   2★   6c 20m
Sustained wall climb with a fingery crux. *P Bate, 2003*

16 Skyhedral   2★   6c 60m
Multipitch (6c 40m, 6a+ 20m; photo-topo on previous page). After "Claire", traverse right then climb up a series of fragile holds. Belay at the small cave. For the last pitch, move left and follow the corner. Descend by lowering off the top pitch then make one or two abseils to the ground. *A Berry, 2013*

17 Bye Bye Doc   3★   6c 25m
Excellent and technical on very small holds.
M Schmed + Team, 1999/2000

18 Jana's Kitchen   3★   6b 25m
A technical climb that reaches and follows a strong feature. The upper groove is tricky. *M Schmed + Team, 1999/2000*

19 Asklipios   2★   6c 22m
Sustained and balancy up a slightly overhanging wall.
T Michaelides, A Theodoropoulos, 2000

20 Panakia   3★   6c 22m
A technical crux on small edges, then good pocket-pulling. Encouraging bolting. *T Michaelides, A Theodoropoulos, 2000*

21 Swiss Baby   2★   6a+ 25m
Committing moves up the slippery second half.
M Schmed + Team, 1999/2000

22 Tsopanakos   2★   6a 18m
Some hard moves at mid-height; an exciting, athletic finale.

23 Tsopanakos Variation   1★   6a+ 22m
Don't clip the 1st anchor but make a strenuous traverse left and then up and back right to reach the 2nd lower-off. *Route #22, 23: T Michaelides, A Theodoropoulos, 2000*

24 My Long Holiday   2★   6c 25m
A bouldery crux to start, then fun reachy moves on sharp but good pockets. *F Amann, H Erber, 2001*

33 GRANDE GROTTA

37.004151
26.940815

GRADE RANGE	up to 5b+	5c to 6a+	6b to 7a	7a+ to 7c	7c+ and up
No. OF ROUTES	1	2	5	7	7

Grande Grotta, the Big Cave, is the trademark of Kalymnos. Its uniqueness and massive scale (up to 50m high) coupled with an unbelievable concentration of huge stalactites make it the most spectacular overhang on Kalymnos.

Climbing: Out of this world, for those who climb hard routes, on red 3-D limestone. Radically overhanging tufas, blobs, and stalactites. Technical and pumpy on hidden holds and features ideal for heel hooks, laybacks, bridging, bear-hugging, bull-riding, thigh locks, kneebars, chimneying and imaginative rest positions.

Conditions: Good for year-round climbing, though spring and fall are best. In winter the cave is protected from the wind and rain, but in late winter/early spring the stalactites can be wet. In summer, climbing is good even on humid days thanks to the big, juggy holds.

Shade: Until 14:30-15:00 on the left.

Exposure: SW

George Kopalides on his phenomenal and widely photographed route "Aegialis" 7c (page 265).

Kids: No. The terrain is steep and there is always the risk of falling rock and breaking stalactites.

Approach: From Masouri go to *Hotel Philoxenia*. Park there (37.004151, 26.940815). Walk up the steep path starting on the side of the hotel. Go through the goat gate and close it behind you. Walk to the lone olive tree, then go left up a steep obvious path to the cave. **Walking time:** 20 min.

See also: Crag Panorama on page 221.

New routes: Climbers agree that no more new routes should be put up in the Grande Grotta, to protect this amazing natural monument.

① Massalia 3★ 6b 100m

A classic multi-pitch (6b 25m, 5c 25m, 5c 25m, 5c 25m). Pitch 1 is very technical and requires good footwork. The quality of climbing improves as you go up to the arch of the cave and the view is stunning. **Return:** Abseil a) From **Grande Grotta** (1 x 80m), 2 x 80m ropes obligatory. b) From **Panorama** (2 x 35m). Walk 150m right. A 70m rope is OK. **A knot in the end of the rope is a must.**
O Didon, G Albert, L Catsoyannis, P Pezzini, 2001

② Zenith 3★ 8b+ 40m

A superb line on the smooth wall to the left of the cave. First RP Alex Honnold, 2011, who says: "A pretty cool route tha feels like a big wall up top. Airy and awesome".
S Montmory, 2011

ATTENTION: There is always the risk of breaking stalactites in the cave.

- Never stand under people climbing in the cave.
- When belaying, it is best to stand near the base of the cliff with your back against the wall.

33 GRANDE GROTTA
LEFT

37.004151
26.940815

3 Aegialis   3★   7c 30m
A mega-classic stamina monster. Surprisingly easy (technically) but hard at the same time, and probably the most photographed sport route on the planet!
G Kopalides, Y Torelli, 1998

4 Kopalization   3★   8a+ 55m
Céuse-style with lots of long traverses.
G Kopalides, C Daniil, 2007

5 Kopalization Extra   3★   8b+ 65m
A bouldery headwall. *G Kopalides, 2014*

6 Zawinul Syndicate   3★   7c+ 30m
A massive journey through impressive terrain, with some "pushy" moves but also good, obvious hands-off rests. To reduce rope drag, unclip the first bolt. *M Troussier, 2002*

7 Aphrodite   2★   7a+ 12m
Short but stiff; a jug parade after a hard reachy crux.
F Amann, H Erber, 2001

8 DNA   3★   7a 20m
Not very long...but the real thing! Serious training on steep indoor walls is a good preparation for this route. The holds are quite big, but there's a strong possibility for "lactic" forearms. *T Michaelides, A Theodoropoulos, 2001*

9 DNA Ext   3★   8a+ 50m
Another monster pitch. A wild sideways sequence off a tufa at mid-height leads to a tricky runout exit to the anchor.
L Triay, G Fanguin, A Cherbonnier, 2004

10 Ivi Ole   3★   7b+ 20m
A two bolt direct variation of "Ivi" featuring a fun dyno off crappy holds to the big hole. *G Kopalides, 2014*

11 Ivi   3★   7a+ 20m
An interesting, excellent primer for gaining confidence in this sector. *2002*

12 Priapos   3★   7c 35m
Priapos is a route from another world! A 3-D stalactite fest, where constant rests can be had by mounting the huge stalactites in the middle of the cave. However, the sections between rests are no joke. Rest well then give it your all and go for the onsight. *Y Ghesquiers, P Pellet, 2001*

13 Super Priapos   3★   8a 55m
A tremendous extension; more of an expedition than a rock climb. An incredible 55m in one pitch with 25 QD. (For the best way to climb this extension see note on the right column). *Y Ghesquiers, P Pellet, 2001*

14 Fun de Chichunne   3★   8a 40m
Everything that is great about Grande Grotta: a mammoth overhanging adventure through 40m of psychedelic tufa roof! You will need 28 QD and tons of energy.
O Didon, G Abert, L Catsoyannis, P Pezzini, 2001

*Note: The route **Super Priapos** (extension of **Priapos**) is a good example of the out-of-this-world climbing in Grande Grotta. It is 55m long with an additional lower-off at 35m. For this route, you will need 24 QD and two 70m ropes.

The following technique is recommended:
With one rope tied normally to your harness, attach the second rope to the main loop of your harness with a screwgate carabiner. As you climb the first pitch, clip in with the second rope (the one attached to your main loop by carabiner). At the first lower-off, clip yourself in (but no resting!) and clip the first rope into a quickdraw. Your belayer should now switch ropes and belay you with the first rope (the one tied to your harness). You can now abandon the second rope and its screwgate. As you continue climbing up **Super Priapos**, clip in with the first rope (the one still tied to your harness). Abseil from the final lower-off to the first lower-off. From there, your belayer can lower you back down to the ground. A 70m rope should be just enough.

A knot at the end of the rope is a must.

Unknown climber on the classic "Priapos" 7c. NIKOLAOS SMALIOS

33 GRANDE GROTTA
RIGHT

37.004151
26.940815

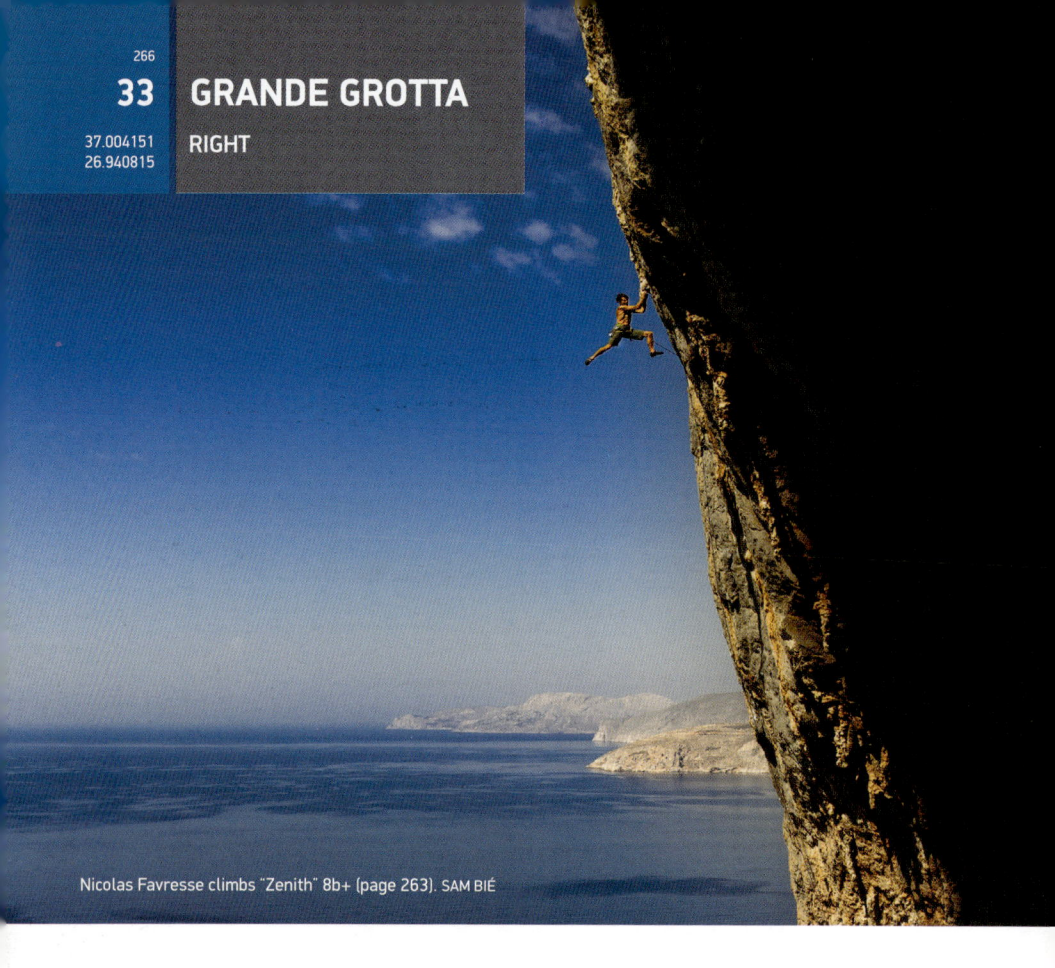

Nicolas Favresse climbs "Zenith" 8b+ (page 263). SAM BIÉ

15 Happy Girlfriend — 3★ 5c+ 15m
A good slab followed by an intro to tufa climbing. When you clip the anchor, turn around and enjoy the best view of Telendos framed by the cave. *A Theodoropoulos, 2008*

16 Elefantenhimmel (Part 1) — 2★ 5a 15m
An unusual stalactite slab. *K + R Ochsner, F Meier, 2001*

17 Elefantenhimmel — 3★ 7a 30m
Continue easily beyond the first lower-off via huge, crazy steep stalactites to some hard final moves. *K + R Ochsner, F Meier, 2001*

18 Punto Caramelo — 3★ 8a 30m
A very overhanging, athletic tufa climb. *C Daniil, A Mavromatis, 2007*

19 Tufantastic — 3★ 7b+ 40m
A long and pumpy fight through the stalactite forest left of "Trela". As with many routes in the cave, it is easier to remove your quickdraws by top-roping the route. *2007*

20 Trela — 3★ 7a 40m
Perfect bolting through 40 very overhanging meters and perfectly amazing tufa formations. Some good rests, despite the loss of the famous giant stalactite. 70m rope. *O Didon, G Abert, L Catsoyannis, P Pezzini, 2001*

21 Monahiki Elia — 3★ 6a+ 25m
An ideal intro to steep tufa climbing. Starts easily with vertical climbing, but even the steep upper half has surprisingly good holds. *A Skevofylakas, K Lampadarios, 2002*

22 Taz — 3★ 6c 27m
A wall of handy blobs leads to a technical hanging groove. An excellent, popular route despite the occasional off-route hold. *A Skevofylakas, K Lampadarios, 2002*

23 KalyPige — 3★ 6c+ 35m
Long and varied climbing on big black tufas. Technical and sustained in the upper section. *M Piola, 2004*

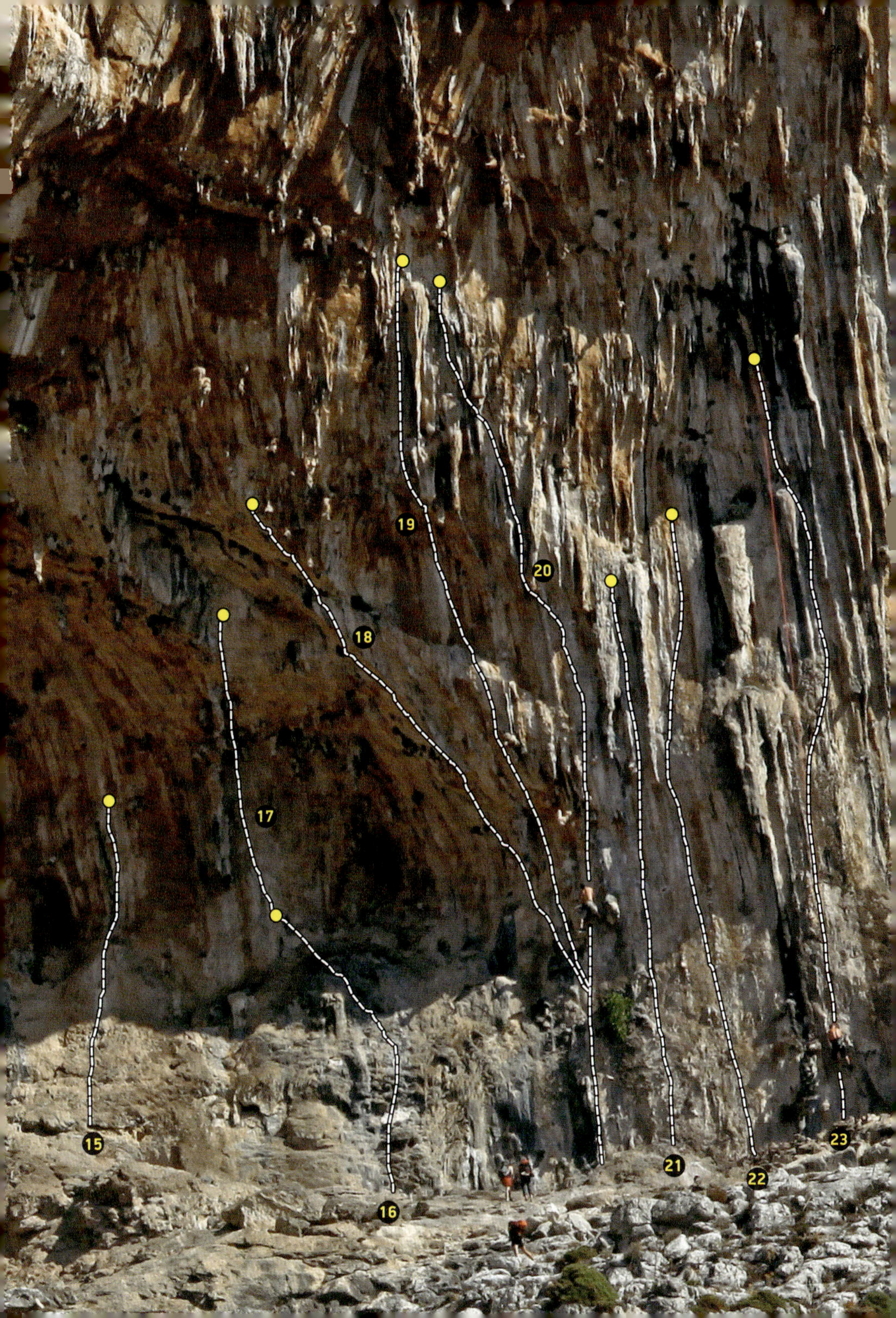
19
20
18
17
15
16
21
22
23

34 PANORAMA

268
37.004151
26.940815

GRADE RANGE	up to 5b+	5c to 6a+	6b to 7a	7a+ to 7c	7c+ and up
No. OF ROUTES	1	3	28	22	4

Panorama is a tufa kingdom. Next to the Grande Grotta, sector **Panorama** consists of a steep red and grey wall, overhanging in parts, with a unique, exposed feel.

Climbing: Technical and sustained, on long pitches of high-quality limestone that comes in all shapes and colors. Sector **Panorama** is not as overhanging as the Grande Grotta, but the climbing is equally 3-dimensional and the variety of routes is greater. The huge, spectacular tufa pipes require *a lot* of stamina.

George Kopalides on the fantastic "Kopakabana Ext" 8a+ (page 271).

LEFT   MIDDLE   RIGHT

Abseil (1 x 80m) 2 x 80m ropes

Abseil (2 x 35m)

GRANDE GROTTA   PANORAMA

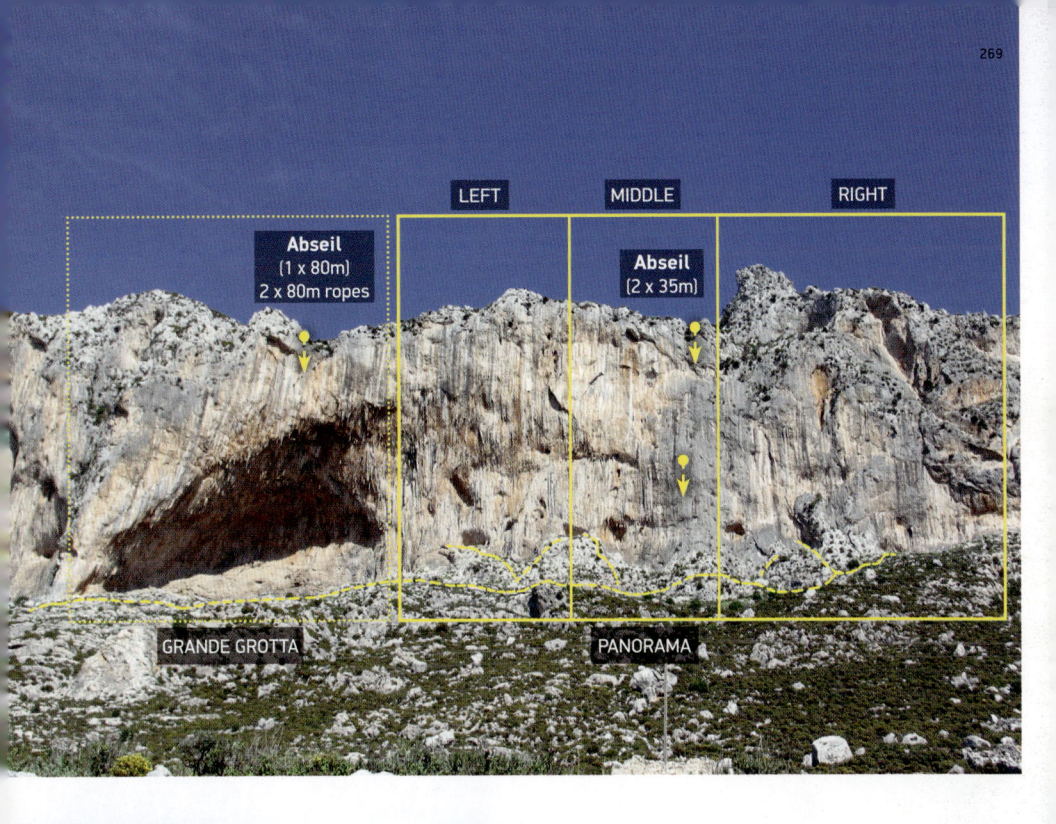

Conditions: Very pleasant and breezy, even on summer mornings. Not good on humid days with no wind; the tufas feel very greasy. The left side is protected from light rain. Tufas may be wet in early spring.

Shade: Until 13:00. **Exposure:** W

Kids: Not good. Steep terrain.

Approach: From Masouri go to *Hotel Philoxenia*. Park there (37.004151, 26.940815). Walk up the steep path starting on the side of the hotel. Go through the goat gate and close it behind you. Walk to the lone olive tree, then go left up a steep obvious path to the *Grande Grotta* cave. Now, traverse to the right and go up to one of the ledges from which the routes start. There is no marked path, and you may need to scramble a bit to reach the base of certain routes. See photo above.

Walking time: 20-22 min.

See also: Crag Panorama on page 221.

34 PANORAMA
LEFT

270

37.004151
26.940815

1 **Rastapopoulos**   3★   6c+ 30m
From the left edge of the shelf (bolt belay), follow steady tufas until established between two columns. Then, let's get physical! Some spaced bolts. *Y Ghesquiers, P Pellet, 2001*

2 **Rastapopoulos Ext**   3★   7b 40m
From the 1st "Rastapopoulos" anchor (and rest) go up and right through even steeper terrain to one of the most expo rests in Kalymnos. On descent, re-thread at the 1st anchor (unless you have an 80m rope). *Y Ghesquiers, P Pellet, 2001*

3 **Aegean Sea**   3★   7a+ 28m
Typical Kalymnos column-climbing, technical and sustained, to a final tricky crux. Hard to onsight.
A Skevofylakas, K Lampadarios, 2002

4 **Papacostopoulos**   3★   8a 55m
Extension of "Aegean Sea" with a hard final wall.
L Triay, G Fanguin, A Cherbonnier, 2004

5 **Cigarillo**   3★   7a 28m
Sustained and varied tufa climbing. *2002*

6 **Where is My Mind?**   2★   7b 28m
Shares the first bolts with "Cigarillo" then goes right on the single tufa. *G Kopalides, 2014*

7 **Panselinos**   3★   6b+ 20m
A very pumpy route with the crux just before the angle eases. The remainder is easier, but still not trivial.
A Skevofylakas, T Michaelides, 2001

8 **Carpe Diem**   3★   6b 16m
A perfect introduction to single-tufa climbing. There are plenty of holds and plenty of bolts. *T Zuber, 2001*

9 **Super Carpe Diem**   3★   7b+ 40m
A fabulous extension with a technical crux. Some bolts are spaced (long QDs are useful) but the holds are good and the rests monumental. *L Triay, G Fanguin, A Cherbonnier, 2004*

10 **Carpe Noctem**   2★   6c+ 20m
G Kopalides, 2014

11 **Commandante Marcos**   2★   7a 25m
A hard start and a broccoli finish.
M Berthoud, M Troussier, 2005

12 **Joggel + Toggel**   3★   6c+ 25m
A testpiece power start to get out from the lip; then, enjoyable climbing up tufa mushrooms. *K Ochsner, 2001*

13 **Joggel + Toggel Ext 1**   3★   7b+ 40m
Much steeper tufa terrain and a bouldery section with one long tufa reach. 24 QD, 80m rope and tie a knot at the end.
L Triay, G Fanguin, A Cherbonnier, 2004

14 **Joggel + Toggel Ext 2**   1★   8a+ 55m
Spaced bolts and sharp edges make a less-than-friendly double extension. *L Triay, G Fanguin, A Cherbonnier, 2004*

Roberta on the fabulous "Super Carpe Diem" 7b+.

15 **Mind Boggle**   3★   7b+ 30m
After a short lunge the route settles down to steep, crazy, pumpy climbing on tufa blobs. 16 QD. *R Prohaska, 2002*

16 **Kopakabana**   3★   7b+ 35m
An obligatory crimpy boulder, then amazing stamina climbing on tufas. *G Kopalides, 2014*

17 **Kopakabana Ext**   3★   8a+ 55m
Another obligatory crux. *G Kopalides, 2014*

18 **Manou Tchao**   3★   7b+ 40m
Shares the first bolts with "Ktulu" then goes out left to tufa heaven. *G Kopalides, 2014*

19 **The Call of the Ktulu**   3★   7b+ 40m
After an easy start, a short bouldery move and then miles of tufa. 18 QD. *C + Y Remy, 2012*

20 **Ktulu Olé**   3★   ?? 55m
A hard project. *G Kopalides, 2016*

21 **Lulu in the Sky**   3★   7a+ 40m
Climb the technical start (or climb up "Aeolia") before breaking out left at the base of the hanging groove, then up a tufa fest in the upper reaches. 70m rope just enough. Dedicated to Lucien Berardini. *M Troussier, 2005*

22 **Aeolia**   3★   6c+ 30m
Demanding, technical climbing up an interesting tufa groove, with many no-hands rests if you can find them.
A Skevofylakas, T Michaelides, 2002

23 **Aeolia Ext**   3★   7a+ 40m
A powerful bulge leads to tufa-land. A 70m rope is just enough. 17 QD. *A Skevofylakas T Michaelides 2002*

34 PANORAMA
MIDDLE

272
37.004151
26.940815

Dani Belisha on "Bitman" 7b. The big stalactite broke in 2015, which pushed the grade up slightly to 7b. NIKOLAOS SMALIOS

24 Gwundernase — 2★ 6c 20m
A great wall with tufa blobs. *K + R Ochsner, F Meier, 2000*

25 Russel Paradies — 3★ 7a+ 60m
Multi-pitch (7a+ 35m, 6c+ 25m). Long and committing. Start as for #23 and continue up and left on steeper and pumpy terrain, but with a couple of rests. To climb it in one long pitch: 22 QD + long slings. **Return**: Abseil (2 x 31m). Walk 60m to the right. **60m rope and knot at the end of the rope obligatory**. *K + R Ochsner, F Meier, 2001*

26 Lothar Scie — 2★ 6b+ 20m
A hard start then easier on small tufas. *M Troussier, 2002*

27 Lothar Là — 3★ 6c+ 35m
A very worthwhile extension on big tufas, good rests, and a hard finale. For Lothar Mauch. *M Troussier, 2005*

28 Steven Up — 1★ 6c+ 20m
Some hard moves on tufa blobs to reach the easier final tufa. *M Troussier, 2002*

29 UP — 3★ 7a 35m
An extension of "Steven Up" with excellent tufa climbing. *M Troussier, 2005*

30 Poupetskaia — 2★ 7a+ 20m
A bouldery start, then an easier wall. *M Troussier, 2002*

31 Uncle Bert — 2★ 6c+ 20m
A steep start followed by a technical wall with small tufas. *R Prohaska, 2002*

32 Steps Ahead — 3★ 7a 35m
Outstanding tufa climbing. *M Troussier, 2005*

33 Uncle Ernie — 3★ 6b 20m
Intricate tufa slab with 2 rest mushrooms. *R Prohaska 2002*

34 Bitman — 3★ 7b 30m
Lovely stalactites at the start then the wall and overhang. *B Girardin, C + Y Remy, 2007*

35 Cyclops — 3★ 6c 20m
A fabulous climb on tufas and pockets. *A Theodoropoulos, T Michaelides, 2004*

36 Neptun kl — 3★ 6c 28m
An easy slab leads to a short roof and the headwall above; nice moves between tufa blobs. *K + R Ochsner, F Meier 2001*

37 Neptun kl Ext — 1★ 7c 35m
A strenuous, ugly extension over a steep bulge. *K + R Ochsner, F Meier 2001*

38 Steinpilz — 3★ 7a 35m
A technical stiff crux, then excellent, delicate climbing on tufas with a tricky finale. *K + R Ochsner, F Meier 1999/2000*

39 Chnosi Family — 3★ 7a 30m
A sustained and slightly intimidating wall with a surprise at the exit. *K + R Ochsner, F Meier, 1999/2000*

40 Tuefeli — 1★ 7b+ 30m
A hard, crimpy wall, with several tricky sections all the way to the top. *K + R Ochsner, F Meier, 1999/2000*

41 Mecki Messer — 2★ 7a+ 30m
Fabulous rock, awkward climbing, a bit sharp and very sustained. Bolting is not great: use a long QD on the 3rd bolt. *K + R Ochsner, F Meier, 1999/2000*

42 Boomerang — 2★ 6c+ 30m
A wandering with good, technical climbing, but take long QDs to avoid rope drag. *K + R Ochsner, F Meier 1999/2000*

273

34 PANORAMA RIGHT

37.004151
26.940815

43 Michis Hohlenfieber — 2★ 4c 15m
A children's route. *M Ochsner (7 yrs old), K + R Ochsner, 2001*

44 Lucido — 3★ 7a+ 40m
A huge technical wall climb with a hard traverse. 18 QD.
B Girardin, C + Y Remy, 2007

45 Reptil — 3★ 7a+ 40m
Excellent climbing left of a huge black tufa. Needs good footwork, strong fingers and endurance! 70m rope.
K + R Ochsner, F Meier 2001

46 Bye-Bye Felix — 3★ 7a 35m
A sustained, varied tufa climb. Use long QDs in the first half to avoid rope drag. 70m rope. *K + R Ochsner, F Meier 2001*

47 Taka — 2★ 6c 30m
A groove and wall with a thought-provoking crux in the upper section. *C + Y Remy, 2012*

48 Arno — 1★ 5c 35m
Inconsistent. A low-angle little pillar with a very short tufa finish. *C + Y Remy, 2012*

49 Elia — 2★ 7a 40m
The lower half is harder. *B Girardin, C + Y Remy, 2008*

50 Hell Est Nique — 2★ 7b 40m
Again, a cruxy lower half. *B Girardin, C + Y Remy, 2008*

51 D.T.F. — 2★ 6c 35m
Sustained, varied moves. A bit sharp at the crux. The final move is also a bit of a shocker! *B Girardin, C + Y Remy, 2008*

52 Eureka — 2★ 6a 25m
A fine slabby warm-up. *Unknown French climbers, 2001*

53 La Vie Selon Gege — 2★ 6b 30m
A vertical wall climb with some spaced, sharp-but-good holds. *B Fara, G Abert, 2001*

54 A Room With a View — 2★ 7a+ 28m
A long, varied climb. Tufas, a technical fingery crux, and a sustained finale to keep you guessing. *D Musgrove, 2006*

55 L'Homme Qui Tombe à Spit — 2★ 7b 35m
Finishes up an easy corner. *B Girardin, C + Y Remy, 2008*

56 La Risée — 2★ 7a 15m
Short but intense, with a bouldery finish.
B Girardin, C + Y Remy, 2008

57 Médical Project — 1★ 6b+ 30m
Varied. Begins with a red wall, then joins a corner. Finale up a smooth slab. *B Girardin, C + Y Remy, 2008*

58 Space Walk 1★ 6a+ 155m

Multi-pitch (2b 15m, 4a 15m, 6a 20m, 6a+ 20m, 5a 30m, walk 20m, 5b 35m). A traversing multi-pitch picking its way to the highest point above Panorama. Both partners must be comfortable in the grade, because bolting is not encouraging and in the event of a fall, you fall down the overhang and it is hard to get back. **Gear**: 70m rope and 14 QDs, including some long ones. **Return**: Abseil down the last pitch (1 x 35m). Walk left as in the photo to use the abseil point above the middle section of Panorama (2 x 35m). Alternatively, you can walk further left to the abseil point above sector Grande Grotta and descend that way (2 x 80m ropes). *G Parry, A Berry, 2014*

Pitch 1, 2b 15m: Make an easy scramble/walk along the ramp to a belay. There are no bolts on this pitch. **Pitch 2, 4a 15m**: Follow the ledge leftwards. **Pitch 3, 6a 20m**: Drop down (clipping a bolt on "Medical Project" to protect your second) and follow the low-angle rock left with just a couple of remotely technical moves to a belay just right of the final groove of "L'Homme Qui Tombe". **Pitch 4, 6a+ 20m**: Follow the groove of "L'Homme Qui Tombe" continuing past its clipper lower-off, then easier to a belay on the slab above. **Pitch 5, 5a 30m**: Follow the big slab up left to the edge of a large ledge/meadow. The belay is set back a few meters. **Pitch 6, 20m**: Walk back through the "meadow" to the base of the final pitch. **Pitch 7, 5b 35m**: Climb a pocketed wall to its top.

35 STANKILL

37.004151
26.940815

GRADE RANGE	up to 5b+	5c to 6a+	6b to 7a	7a+ to 7c	7c+ and up
No. OF ROUTES	2	7	10	2	0

Rick Frugtniet climbing at Stankill. SIMON RAWLINSON

Sector Stankill is a narrow cleft in the rock between sectors Panorama and Ivory Tower, featuring nearly two dozen routes of varying styles.

Climbing: Very sharp rock on the grey walls inside the cleft, but there is better quality rock on the steep red wall further in and on the outer slab + wall to the right.

Conditions: Early sun; exposed to the rain.

Shade: Until 13:00. **Exposure:** W

Kids: Several suitable areas beneath the cliffs.

Approach: From Masouri go to *Hotel Philoxenia*. Park there (37.004151, 26.940815). Walk up the steep path starting on the side of the hotel. Go through the goat gate and close it behind you. Walk to the lone olive tree, then go left up a steep obvious path to the cave. At the edge of the cave, traverse rightwards past sector Panorama to the crag. The crag can also be approached from sector Poets by traversing leftwards under sectors Iannis, Kalydna and Ivory Tower. **Walking time:** 25 min.

1 Titan — 1★ 6a+ 25m
A steep sharp slab. Tricky route finding.
Routes #1-#10: B Girardin, C + Y Remy, 2005

2 Duo — 1★ 6a+ 25m
Sharp, again; the bolts are quite close to "Titan".

3 Stankill — 2★ 6a+ 25m
A sharp, hard finish. Steep for the grade.

4 String — 2★ 4a 15m
Strange but easy climbing up a gully to an anchor out right.

5 Krackholy — 2★ 7c 47m
Small tufas and big huecos lead to a hard headwall.

6 Lyrix — 3★ 7b 45m
Very interesting! Use long QD before the roof and save some energy for the final crux.

7 Zack — 2★ 7a 15m
#7 and #6 in one go=a long great 7b 45m.
20 QD plus some long ones.

8 Plagnolis — 3★ 6c+ 35m
Some hard first moves then a crack and much easier terrain.

9 Tonic — 2★ 6c 25m
A vertical wall; a real tonic indeed!

10 Noynoy — 2★ 6b 25m
Technical and balancy across the sloping shelves.

11 Sibylle — 2★ 5a 28m
A good, steady slab, but spaced bolting. *J Rohrmann, 2008*

12 Hugox — 3★ 5c 25m
Good pocket and crack climbing. *B Girardin, C+Y Remy, 2005*

13 Paulix — 3★ 5c+ 25m
Tricky cracks, some hard clips. *B Girardin, C+Y Remy, 2005*

14 Bobodo — 2★ 6a 25m
A slab with an interesting bulge. *B Girardin C+Y Remy 2005*

15 Gunpowder Plot — 2★ 6b+ 25m
A diagonal slabby line. *A Berry, 2006*

16 Gunpowder Plot Ext — 3★ 6c 40m
Good climbing on *gouttes*. *A Berry, 2006*

17 Paparazzi — 1★ 6c 25m
Interesting, but sharp start. *F+C Heinicke, A+C Riemer 2009*

18 Zaros — 3★ 6b 35m
A varied slab with a tricky bulge. *B Girardin, C+Y Remy, 2008*

19 Zaros Ext — 3★ 6b 40m
Immaculate grey rock. *L Salsotto, 2011*

20 Stelios — 3★ 6a+ 38m
A long, steep slab climb with a slightly worrying flake at the crux. 70m rope. *B Girardin, C+Y Remy, 2008*

21 Justice Is Its Own Reward — 2★ 6b+ 18m
A superb slab pitch; not so friendly bolting. *C Singer 2006*

36 IVORY TOWER

36.999981
26.939005

GRADE RANGE	up to 5b+	5c to 6a+	6b to 7a	7a+ to 7c	7c+ and up
No. OF ROUTES	1	4	8	6	5

Sector Ivory Tower is a distinctive section of the rocky escarpment overlooking Masouri village. It looks like a large stone pillar featuring a characteristic geometric roof on the left, and it enjoys the same trademark view of Telendos as most west-facing crags.

Climbing: Mostly on vertical to slightly overhanging walls. There is a good variety of grades here, along with several worthwhile routes.

ATTENTION: Most routes can be climbed with a 60m rope, however a 70m rope is highly recommended.

Audrey Chaspoul on "The Craic" 7b+ (page 281).
ELODIE SARACCO

Conditions: Shadier than most other crags on this stretch of rock. The routes on white rock are not good for climbing on hot or humid days. The overhanging section offers some protection from light rain.

Shade: Until 15:30. **Exposure:** W

Kids: A long approach, but the terrain near the cliffs is fairly suitable.

Approach: There are two options: a) from sector **Poets**, or b) from sector **Grande Grotta**. Option (a), from **Poets**, is best because it is less steep.

The path to sector **Poets** starts at the north edge of Masouri village, up the steps to the left of "Lambrinos Studios" and above "Mike's Bikes" and "Sofrano" café (36.999981, 26.939005). Start up the path. Walk for approx. 10 min and pass through an old wire fence level with a large white house to the right. Then, turn left along the smooth goat path. After you pass sector **Iannis**, look for the gate through another wire fence. Walk beneath the massive orange wall of **Kalydna**, and then go uphill to **Ivory Tower** following some waymarks and cairns. Do not be tempted to walk up to the crag directly. It is private property and there is a lot of barbed wire. **Walking time:** 25-30 min.

See also: Crag Panorama on page 221.

36 IVORY TOWER

36.999981
26.939005

1 Fainéantdertal — 2★ 8a+ 30m
A nice crimpy climb. *S Montmory, 2014*

2 La Flemme Olympique — 2★ 7b+ 30m
Bouldery with a long reach at the crux. *S Montmory, 2014*

3 Perskindol — 3★ 6b 30m
A very good steep, juggy wall. *B Girardin, C + Y Remy, 2009*

4 Aypa — 3★ 6c 30m
An excellent wall climb with an interesting bulge to gain the hanging chimney. *B Girardin, C + Y Remy, 2009*

5 Schnügu — 2★ 6b 20m
A pleasant diagonal line with an awkward finale. *B Girardin, C + Y Remy, 2008*

6 Am Abgrung — 1★ 6a+ 20m
A slab with a hard headwall. *J Rohrmann, 2008*

7 Attiki — 2★ 6a+ 20m
A slabby start, but save power for the end. *B Girardin, C + Y Remy, 2008*

8 Happiness — 2★ 6c 30m
A pleasant pitch on cauliflower rock to the right of the big roof, but spaced bolts and hard final clip. *A Berry, 2006/07*

9 Happiness Ext — 2★ 7b+ 35m
Thin, technical moves and long stretches. *A Berry, 2006/07*

10 Bloc Volant — 3★ 6b 20m
A diagonal slab climb; unusual, wandering and sustained, with an expo finale. Strip the quickdraws by top-roping the route. *B Girardin, C + Y Remy, 2009*

11 Sidewinder — 3★ 6c+ 30m
An interesting traverse to get through the roof. Don't follow the bolts too literally. Bolting is a bit spaced. There is an extension with bolts but no hangers. *A Berry, 2006/07*

12 Sunrise (Part 1) — 3★ 7a 27m
Really good rock with some tufas. Hard to clip the anchor. *S Montmory, 2011*

13 Sunrise — 3★ 7c+ 40m
Hard boulder problems on vertical terrain. *S Montmory 2011*

14 Café (Part 1) — 3★ 7a+ 27m
A nice slab, but one sharp hole. *S Montmory 2011*

15 Café — 3★ 7c+ 40m
Bouldery, on beautiful, colorful rock. *S Montmory 2011*

16 Anaphylactic Shock — 3★ 7c+ 33m
Tufa and pockets lead to the roof and then a technical groove with some small pockets. *A Berry, 2006/07*

Left: Nicolas Galteri on "Lactic Shock" 7c. ELODIE SARACCO

17 Lactic Shock   3★   7c 36m
From halfway up #16, move right and make long but fun moves on big holds. Pumpy! *A Berry, 2006/07*

18 The Craic   3★   7b+ 36m
A great line. Some fingery moves lead to tufas, big huecos and a layback crack. *A Berry, 2006/07*

19 Poker Face   3★   5b+ 20m
A smooth, very interesting red groove.
B Girardin, C + Y Remy, 2009

20 Arthur   2★   5c+ 20m
A good slab with a demanding finish.
B Girardin, C + Y Remy, 2009

21 Deletime   2★   5c 20m
A corner, steady slab, and steeper headwall.
B Girardin, C + Y Remy, 2009

22 The Silent Way   3★   7c+ 50m
An extension to "Deletime". A tricky start leads to the obvious shallow groove line. *C Woodburn, 2009*

23 Dream Line   3★   7b 20m
The crux is a mantel! Goes way out right at the last bolt, then back left along the break. *A Berry, 2006/07*

24 Dream Line Ext   3★   7c 32m
From the first belay on #23 go through the bulge and up the wall to belay at mid-height. The continuation remains unclimbed (hard). *A Berry, 2006/07*

25 Ivory Tower   3★   8a 50m
Multi-pitch (7b 20m, 8a 30m). A brown and thin white wall.
A Berry, 2006/07

26 Ultimo Bucco   3★   6b+ 25m
An excellent natural flake line on well-featured rock.
G Abert, L Catsoyannis, P Pezzini, 2001

27 Fuga da Guy   3★   6c+ 55m
Multi-pitch (6a 25m, 6c+ 30m). The second pitch goes up a nice wall with a splitting crack. It is possible to climb it as the extension of "Ultimo Bucco".
G Abert, L Catsoyannis, P Pezzini, 2001

37 KALYDNA

36.999981
26.939005

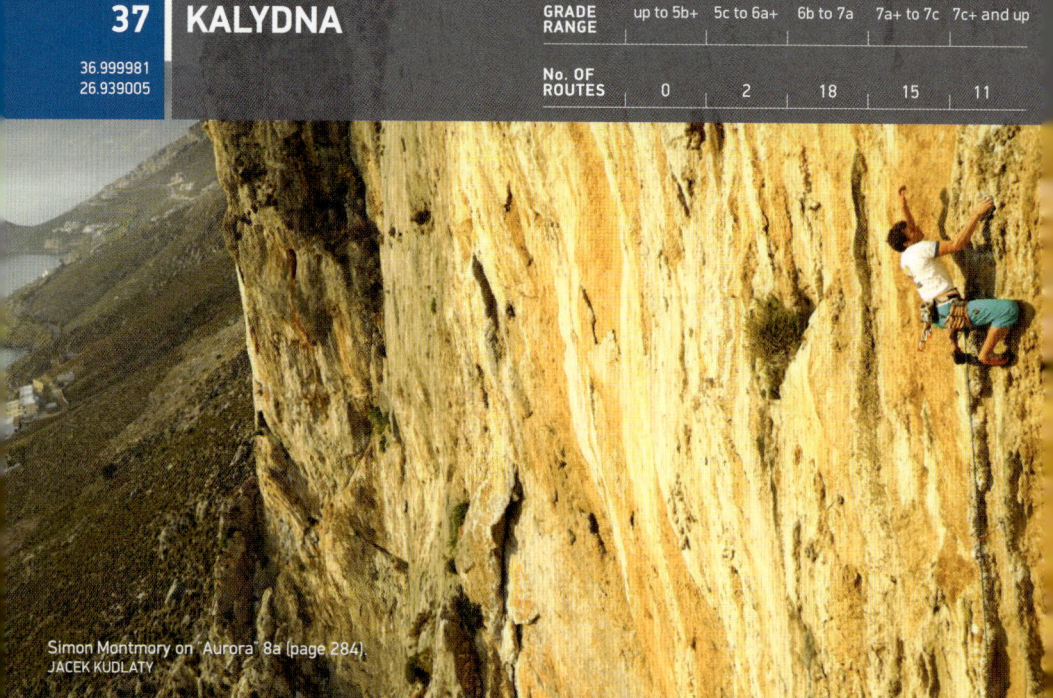

GRADE RANGE	up to 5b+	5c to 6a+	6b to 7a	7a+ to 7c	7c+ and up
No. OF ROUTES	0	2	18	15	11

Simon Montmory on "Aurora" 8a (page 284).
JACEK KUDLATY

Kalydna resembles a giant stone amphitheater. With top-quality limestone, it is best for those climbing grades from 6b and above.

Climbing: Very technical on small holds, pockets, tufas + blobs. Gentle red slabs and vertical or just off-vertical angles. Challenging athletic routes in the right cave.

Conditions: Relatively cool, but on humid days the rock feels soapy. Exposed to the rain.

Shade: Until 13:00 on long routes. Until 14:00-14:30 on single pitches to the right. **Exposure:** W

Kids: Not recommended.

Approach: Via sector Poets. The path starts at the north edge of Masouri, up the steps to the left of "Lambrinos Studios" and above "Mike's Bikes" and "Sofrano" (36.999981, 26.939005). Walk up for approx. 10 min and pass through an old wire fence level with a large white house to the right. Then, turn left along the smooth goat path. After you pass sector Iannis, continue uphill following cairns and waymarks. **Walking time:** 25-30 min.

See also: Crag Panorama on page 221.

① Radom 2★ 6b+ 40m
A prickly intro is followed by a red/white pillar providing exposure and interest. 16 QD. *B Girardin, C + Y Remy, 2009*

② Hype 3★ 7b 32m
A sharp slab leads to the obvious, steep headwall with pockets and tufas. *B Girardin, C + Y Remy, 2009*

③ Spark 2★ 6b+ 30m
The sharp lower wall, then an interesting groove and a tufa finale. *B Girardin, C + Y Remy, 2009*

④ Hot Fuel 1★ 7a 30m
A moment of balance. *B Girardin, C + Y Remy 2009*

⑤ Blevita 1★ 6b 20m
Slab and wall climbing. *B Girardin, C + Y Remy, 2009*

⑥ Avra 2★ 6a 20m
Fingery slab, demanding exit. *B Girardin, C + Y Remy, 2009*

⑦ No name (unfinished) ?★ ? ?m
An unfinished 2- or 3-pitch route. *1999*

⑧ Mami au Grigri 2★ 6b+ 30m
Steep, but with big holds and a technical finale.
B Girardin, C + Y Remy, 2010

9	**Miss Latex**	3★ 6b+ 30m

A steep wall with small holds. *B Girardin, C + Y Remy, 2009*

10	**Bigboo**	3★ 7a 30m

Good; pockets and large holes. *B Girardin, C + Y Remy, 2009*

11	**Mitra**	1★ 7b 120m

Multi-pitch (7b 40m, 7b 45m, 7a 35m). A Verdon-style long climb. *C Ravaschietto, D Bosio, L Tosi, 2000*

12	**Fragment**	1★ 6c 50m

An older multi-pitch (5c 30m, 6c 20m). *P Gasser, 1998*

13	**Yebus**	2★ 6c+ 35m

Good flakes, but run-out bolting for Kalymnos. A tricky and reachy finish. *B Girardin, C + Y Remy, 2005*

14	**Fran-Fran**	2★ 7b+ 32m

A fingery, technical wall. *B Girardin, C + Y Remy, 2005*

15	**Tassir**	3★ 7a+ 28m

A very sustained and technical wall climb with a crucial soapy pocket. *B Girardin, C + Y Remy, 2005*

16	**Tassir Ext**	3★ 7b+ 45m

S Montmory, 2010

17	**Calida**	3★ 6c+ 28m

A wall, quite blind at the top. *B Girardin, C + Y Remy, 2005*

18	**Sickle**	3★ 7a+ 35m

Sustained climbing with a tricky middle and final section. *B Girardin, C + Y Remy, 2009*

19	**Sickle Ext**	3★ 7b 45m

Superb! Goes to the new "Tassir" belay. *C + Y Remy, 2012*

20	**Uschana**	3★ 6c 30m

Slippery, but with good holds and edges. Some balancy, tricky clipping. *B Girardin, C + Y Remy, 2005*

21	**Uschana Ext**	3★ 7b+ 45m

S Montmory, 2010

22	**Golden Oriole**	2★ 6b+ 30m

A squeezed direct line up the ever-steepening wall. *D Musgrove, K Morgan, 2011*

37 KALYDNA

36.999981
26.939005

Christine Remy on "KalyNikhla" 6b.
CLAUDE REMY

23 Aurora (Part 1)   3★   7b 35m
Well worth climbing, but with a runout crux near the end. Belay from ledge at 12m. Total 12m + 35m. *N Gresham, 2004*

24 Aurora   3★   8a 45m
Features every possible style of climbing, and gets harder as you go up. Can be climbed in one giant pitch. Belay from ledge at 12m. Total 12m + 35m + 10m. *N Gresham, 2004*

25 Theodora   3★   6c+ 30m
Crimpy wall with tufa blobs and a tricky, technical crux sequence. *B Girardin, C + Y Remy, 2005*

26 KalyNikhla   3★   6b 25m
A pretty dance up small tufas and blobs.
B Girardin, C + Y Remy, 2005

27 KalyNikhla Ext   3★   7b+ 36m
A bouldery start, then technical and varied climbing up the compact and thin corner. Tricky finish with poor feet.
B Girardin, C + Y Remy, 2005

28 Ixion   3★   7a 25m
Technical with good pockets, small tufas and flakes. Continue to #27 for a nice 7a+ 36m. *B Girardin, C + Y Remy, 2005*

29 To Have + Not To Be Part 1   3★   7c+ 35m
The 1st pitch of the leftward extension of "Ixion", with one delicate boulder problem. *S Montmory, 2009*

30 To Have + Not To Be   ♪   9a? 50m
The full leftward extension of "Ixion". An incredible line up the red streak in the middle of the pillar. Finishes with an extra 10m-long hard boulder problem. *S Montmory, 2009*

31 Unique (Part 1)   3★   7b+ 37m
The rightward extension of "Ixion", part 1. *S Montmory, 2009*

32 Unique   3★   8c+? 50m
The full rightward extension of "Ixion". A bit easier than "To Have + Not To Be." No FA yet. *S Montmory, 2009*

33 Extra   3★   6b 25m
A wall full of pockets, but hard to clip the chain.
B Girardin, C + Y Remy, 2005

34 Nickel 3★ 7a+ 32m
An easy lower wall gives way to a long crescendo of delightful small tufas. *B Girardin, C + Y Remy, 2005*

35 Late Evening Light 3★ 6a+ 25m
A bit broken with ledges in the 1st half, but a steep and interesting 2nd half. *B Girardin, C + Y Remy, 2005*

36 The Mole That Cram Full 3★ 8b 45m
Intense and increasingly harder. *S Montmory, 2009*

37 Triste Saccage 2★ 8b+ 40m
A very hard boulder problem at the lip of the cave roof, but an easier finish. FA by Alex Megos, 2014. *S Montmory, 2009*

38 Fake Friends 3★ 8b 32m
Characterful, strange moves, and hard until the end. *S Montmory, 2009*

39 Trous Dans l'Air ♪ 8b 30m
Awesome line, long reaches, surprise at the end! *S Montmory, 2009*

40 L'Air d'Un Trou 2★ 8b 30m
Nice rock. Again, three boulder problems. *S Montmory, 2009*

41 J'ai du Temps Donc de l'Argent 2★ 7b+ 30m
Stiff and slopey to the upper groove. *S Montmory, 2009*

42 Keep Going 3★ 8a+ 25m
A bouldery routes with pockets, slopers, technical smearing and bridging. *S Montmory, 2009*

43 Life Style 2★ 7b 35m
An overhang. *C + Y Remy, 2010*

44 Kaly Câlins 2★ 6c 25m
The short overhang. You can continue left to "Life Style" for a 6c+ 35m, but the anchor is too far left and it is hard to strip the QDs. *C + Y Remy, 2010*

45 Mamy Nova 1★ 6c 20m
The overhang with big pockets. *C + Y Remy, 2010*

46 Spacy 2★ 7a+ 25m
This overhang has a short crux. *C + Y Remy, 2010*

47 Dart 2★ 6b 35m
A long wall climb. Use long QDs at the start to avoid rope-drag. *C + Y Remy, 2010*

38 IANNIS

286
36.999981
26.939005

GRADE RANGE	up to 5b+	5c to 6a+	6b to 7a	7a+ to 7c	7c+ and up
No. OF ROUTES	0	1	8	6	6

Margarita on "Themelina" 7b+

A remarkable cave with big tufas and stalactites, plus a vertical grey wall and a steep orange wall on either side, sector **Iannis** is a shady, small natural balcony with fantastic views.

Climbing: Exquisite and overhanging, on stalactites and tufas inside the cave and on the wall next to it. Easier warm-ups on the slabs on both sides.

Conditions: Cool, with lots of shade in the cave, which is also protected from the rain. Not good for humid days: routes feel soapy, especially the hard ones.

Shade: Until 15:00. **Exposure:** W

Kids: Good, with some suitable areas near the cliffs.

Approach: Via sector Poets. The path starts at the north edge of Masouri, up the steps to the left of "Lambrinos Studios" and above "Mike's Bikes" (36.999981, 26.939005). Walk up for approx.10 min and pass through an old wire fence level with a large white house to the right. Then, turn left along the smooth goat path.
Walking time: 20 min.

See also: Crag Panorama on pages 221 and 289.

1 Fence Guest 2★ 6b+ 30m
A stiff and long wall with balancy climbing on small holds.
H + J Weninger, Y Saito, 2001

2 Ypakoe 2★ 6c+ 20m
An easy corner leads to a tricky, sharp bulge.
A Theodoropoulos, K Lambadarios, 2004

3 Kalotina 1★ 6a 15m
The short but technical grey slab.
A Theodoropoulos, K Lambadarios, 2004

4 Petranta 2★ 7a+ 25m
Shares the first bolt with "Draconian". A powerful start up the tufas, then some demanding gastons and underclings. To avoid rope drag use long QDs in the first four bolts.
A Theodoropoulos, D Stratigos, A Kokkinos, 2005

5 O Draconian Devil 3★ 8b 20m
An impressive steep start on tufas leads to a nasty rest just before a very tricky boulder problem. Please handle the hanging stalactites with care. N Gresham, 2004

6 Sevasti 3★ 7b 18m
Steep, enjoyable climbing and a wild lurch over the final steepening section. A Theodoropoulos, K Lambadarios, 2004

7 Themelina 3★ 7b+ 18m
A romp-up tufa leads to a short hard section. Can you pinch? *A Theodoropoulos, K Lambadarios, 2004*

8 Super Themelina 3★ 7c+ 33m
A long, exciting extension with stretchy reaches, mainly on short tufas and blobs. Don't miss the famous mono! *A Theodoropoulos, K Lambadarios, 2004*

9 Racomelo 3★ 8b 32m
An athletic tufa leads to the stopper "bloc" section at mid-height. Continue up the massive wall to a very sustained finale. *A Theodoropoulos, C Dawson, 2007*

10 Tufa King Pumped 3★ 7b+ 25m
Begins with a very user-friendly bulge of big blobs, but sucks off all your energy by the time you reach the fingery crux. Try saying the name fast. *N Gresham, 2004*

11 Attitude 3★ 7a 20m
Moves to appreciate on an orange wall. Bolting is not so friendly. *S Montmory, 2009*

12 Attitude Ext 3★ 7c+ 40m
Continues on steep brown rock. Sustained climbing until the very last move! *S Montmory, 2009*

13 Adolf in the Bay 3★ 6c+ 20m
Excellent climbing up a weaving line on a steep wall with big holds and slots. *B Girardin, C + Y Remy, 2009*

14 Adolf in the Bay Ext 2★ 7c+ 38m
Varied climbing up an impressive wall. *S Montmory, 2011*

15 To Manna 2★ 7b+ 20m
Two boulder problems and a technical final wall. *S Montmory, 2011*

16 To Manna Ext 2★ 8a 38m
S Montmory, 2011

17 Verikoko 3★ 7a+ 30m
Wonderfully technical wall climbing. Take care at the ledges. *B Girardin, C + Y Remy, 2009*

18 Sens Unique 3★ 7a 40m
The wall with small ledges. Very pretty rock. *B Girardin, C + Y Remy, 2009*

19 Zagori 2★ 6c 40m
A long and varied wall climb; never too hard. A 70m rope is just enough; tie a knot. *B Girardin, C + Y Remy, 2009*

20 Kalyne 3★ 6b 30m
A nice sequence up an interesting wall. *B Girardin, C + Y Remy, 2009*

21 Yaka 2★ 6b 35m
After the start, a pleasant, technical wall. *C + Y Remy, 2012*

39 POETS

36.999981
26.939005

GRADE RANGE	up to 5b+	5c to 6a+	6b to 7a	7a+ to 7c	7c+ and up
No. OF ROUTES	3	22	46	9	1

Poets is a strip of compact grey slabs directly above the village of Armeos. It is the closest sector to the village of Masouri, so it is perfect for getting a first taste of the rock as soon as you arrive. The main section features perfect grey rock at a vertical or near-vertical angle full of *gouttes d'eau*. Sub-sectors **Coeur D'Armeos**, **Poets Right** and **White Shark** also feature some worthwhile routes in the mid-grades on solid limestone of excellent quality.

Climbing: Old-fashioned, balancy, crimpy climbing. Highly technical routes on a compact grey slab. Most grades range between 6a-6c.

David Reeve on "Sapfo" 6a+ (page 293).
LEE CUJES

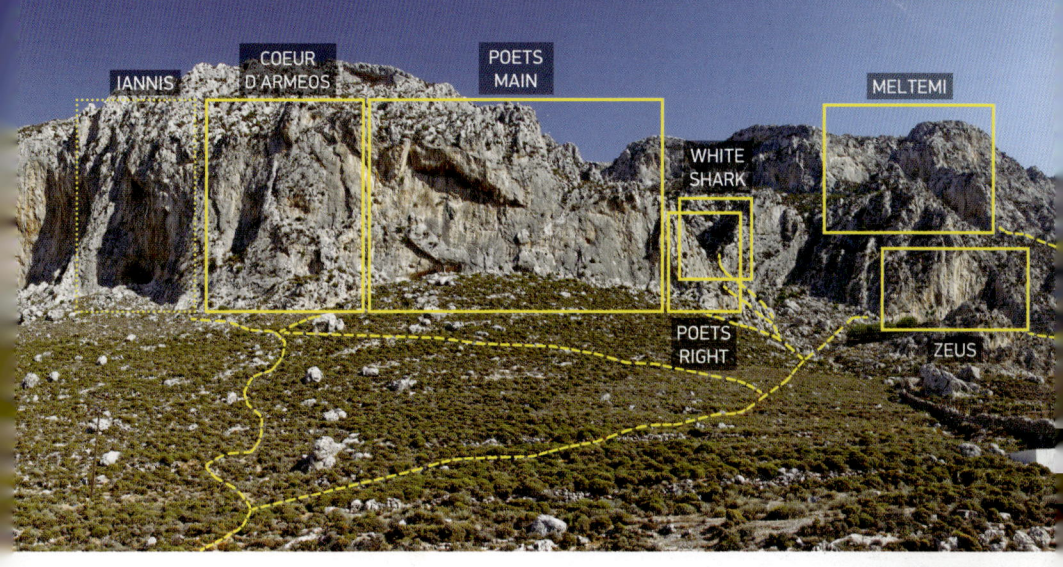

Conditions: Relatively cool. Good for year-round climbing. Exposed to the northwest wind and the rain, but the cliffs dry quickly.

Shade: Until 13:00. **Exposure:** W

Kids: Not bad. The path is well-used and there are a few suitable areas.

Approach: The path to sector **Poets** starts at the north edge of Masouri village, up the steps to the left of "Lambrinos Studios" and above "Mike's Bikes" (36.999981, 26.939005). Start up the path. Walk for approx. 10 min and pass through an old wire fence level with a large white house to the right. Then, turn left along the smooth goat path. **Walking time:** 15 min.

See also: Crag Panorama on page 221.

39 POETS
COEUR D'ARMEOS

290
36.999981
26.939005

1 Scrogneugneu   2★   6b+ 40m
Crumbly and sharp, but good climbing. 18 QD. *C Idoux, 2012*

2 Snouf   2★   6c 35m
Good climbing with an intense bulge on small pockets. 17 QD. *C Idoux, 2012*

3 Reste Haut du Cœur   3★   6b+ 32m
Amazing climbing. A short crux at the start leads to great yellow rock with big pockets. 15 QD. *C Idoux, 2012*

4 Boubou   3★   6b 32m
A hard, fingery start, then fun climbing up a groove with bigger holds. *C Idoux, 2012*

5 Y'a Rien Au Dessus   3★   6b+ 32m
A grey and yellow wall. 17 QD. *C Idoux, 2012*

6 Y'a Rien...(right-hand variation)   3★   6b+ 32m
Shares the 1st half, then goes right. 17 QD. *C Idoux, 2012*

7 Patrick and Bambou   1★   6a+ 20m
Sharp grey rock and a tricky bulge; easier as you go. *C Idoux, 2012*

8 Patrick and Bambou Ext   1★   7a+ 40m
Yellow rock with big pockets and nice moves. 19 QD. *C Idoux, 2012*

Cœur D'Armeos is a new sub-sector to the left of the Poets main wall. It sits atop a small balcony approached by way of a small via ferrata. It is a worthwhile addition with some good routes.

Climbing: Long, technical routes on vertical rock. Good, small (but sometimes sharp) holds and small features. Routes are long; bring 20 QDs.

Shade: Until 12:30. **Exposure:** W

Kids: Not good.

Approach: As on previous page. Then, at the first fork in the path, go left towards sector Iannis. Shortly before Iannis, there are metal rungs in the rock going up 20m to the small balcony. **Walking time:** 20 min.

Pushing, pulling and balancing up the perfect grey rock of sector Poets. NIKOLAOS SMALIOS

COEUR D'ARMEOS

9 Extra tes Restes — 2★ 6c+ 40m
19 QD. *C Idoux, 2012*

10 Dream Thym — 2★ 6b+ 40m
Interesting but sharp. Some creative clipping. 19 QD.
C Idoux, 2012

11 Mytos — 2★ 6b 42m
A special long route with an interesting flake and a demanding headwall. 19 QD. Bon voyage, *Mytos*! *C Idoux, 2012*

12 Propolis — 3★ 6a 70m
Multi-pitch (6a 35m, 5c+ 35m). Newly cleaned and rebolted. A pleasant second pitch up the beautiful flake.
Jeunes FFME Ariege, 2005, C Idoux, 2012

13 Ates Souhaits — 2★ 5c+ 30m
Very easy at the start; not so at the finish. *C Idoux, 2012*

14 Été Indien — 2★ 6a 30m
A very easy start but hard moves at the finale. *C Idoux, 2012*

15 Minos — 2★ 7a 50m
Multi-pitch (3c 20m, 7a 30m). Easy climbing to a ledge, then a 2nd pitch up a crimpy wall with spaced bolts.
B Girardin, C + Y Remy, 2005

16 New Route — 3★ 6c 40m
A compact wall with an easy start up the rib. *C Idoux, 2016*

17 Kavafis — 3★ 6b+ 50m
Multi-pitch (3a 20m, 6b+ 30m). A classic line up a characteristic flake. An easy scramble (one bolt) leads to a second pitch where old-fashioned laybacking leads to a delicate slab at the finale. *A Theodoropoulos, T Michaelides, 2000*

18 Poetic License — 1★ 6b+ 20m
The technical wall steepens to a move right above the overlap to an easier finishing groove. Not well-cleaned.
D Musgrove, 2006

39 POETS
MAIN

292
36.999981
26.939005

Perfect vertical grey limestone full of *gouttes d'eau*.

Shade: Until 13:00. **Exposure:** W

Approach: As on page 289. **Walking time:** 15 min.

1 Damocles — 2★ 6a+ 27m
A recently cleaned, nice, varied and fingery wall.
J Friedrich, G Hommel, 2005

2 Charles Bukowski — 1★ 6c+ 22m
A bouldery crux leads to a pleasant slab. *D Stratigos 2005*

3 Delicatessen — 3★ 6b+ 30m
A bulge with good holds leads to a neat black wall.
Green bolts. *C Idoux, 2014*

4 Iris — 2★ 6b+ 30m
A stiff start on small holds, then a technical slabby finish on flowstone slopers. *C + Y Remy, 2005*

5 Saxonia — 3★ 6a 30m
Nice variety: slab, steep, overhang, tufas. Tough for the first few moves on small holds. *J Friedrich, 2003*

6 The Homeric Verses — 2★ 6a+ 30m
An easy slab to the tufas below a worrying bulge; go around it to the right, then back left. *D Musgrove, K Morgan, 2007*

7 Quando Tramonta Il Sol — 3★ 6a 30m
An interesting line with pleasantly surprising moves in and out of the alcoves above. *1999*

8 Karoubalo — 2★ 6b 25m
A broccoli rock groove with an intriguing crux. Blue bolts.
C Idoux, 2014

9 Dryads — 2★ 6b 25m
A grey slab + some tufa blobs. *B Girardin, C + Y Remy 2005*

10 Mustass — 3★ 6a 25m
A slabby start then tufa climbing with friendly holds. *1999*

11 Styx — 3★ 6a+ 25m
An easy slab leads to a steeper wall with balancy climbing on flowstone and tufas. *B Girardin, C + Y Remy, 2005*

12 Oreads — 3★ 6a+ 25m
A fingery slab and a technical wall with tufas. Sustained, though no real crux. *B Girardin, C + Y Remy, 2005*

13 Palamas — 2★ 6c 32m
A hard pull around a roof leads to a sharp upper wall.
B Girardin, C + Y Remy, 2005

14 Solomos — 3★ 6c+ 35m
Relentless wall climbing with hidden holds.
B Girardin, C + Y Remy, 2005

POETS MAIN

15 Reins Beaux — 3★ 6c 35m
A wall with small holds. *B Girardin, C + Y Remy, 2005*

16 O'Brothers — 3★ 6b+ 20m
A weaving, cunning, and beefier climb. *Y + J Pinon, 2002*

17 Omero — 3★ 7a 25m
The sector's classic saves its surprises for the end. Technical! *A Di Bari + Team, 1997*

18 Sapfo — 3★ 6a+ 25m
Zigzag up the steepening slab with sketchy footwork at the top. *A Di Bari + Team, 1997*

19 Pindaros — 2★ 5a 15m
Not as easy as it looks. Good footwork required. *1999*

20 Alfa — 2★ 5b 16m
A pleasant slab. *C Idoux, 2016*

21 Alceo — 2★ 6c 25m
An easy slab leads to a fingery, cruxy section. *A Di Bari + Team, 1997*

22 Licimnio — 2★ 6c 25m
An easy start leads to an extremely technical finale. Not easy to onsight, but a good RP. *A Di Bari + Team, 1997*

23 Ella L'a — 2★ 7a+ 26m
Old-school thin, technical slab with two cruxes. *C Idoux 2016*

24 Alcman — 2★ 6c 30m
Harder on the steeper upper half. *A Di Bari + Team, 1997*

25 Anacreonte — 3★ 6a 22m
A great route, strenuous and reachy, but a bit greasy due to its popularity. *A Di Bari + Team, 1997*

26 Archiloque — 2★ 6c 27m
C Idoux, 2016

27 Ibria — 3★ 6b+ 25m
A grey slab then a crimpy technical wall. *A Di Bari + Team, 1997*

28 Hipponas — 2★ 7a+ 25m
C Idoux, 2016

29 Ione — 2★ 7a+ 25m
Hard wall climbing on thin holds and crimps. A wandering, sharp line. *A Di Bari + Team, 1997*

30 Poets' Corner — 2★ 5c 20m
A pleasant exercise in bridging. *D Musgrove, J Walker, 2010*

31 Poets' Corner Ext — 2★ 6b+ 35m
A smooth groove + a nice pocketed headwall. *C Idoux, 2016*

39 POETS RIGHT
WHITE SHARK

294
36.999981
26.939005

POETS RIGHT

Poets Right is a small vertical wall around the corner from the main crag. Good photos can be taken here with a picture-perfect view in the background.

Climbing: Technical face climbing on mostly small holds.

Shade: Until 12:00. **Exposure:** SW

Approach: As on page 289. Then, walk to the right side for another minute. **Walking time:** 15-16 min.

1 Oyzo   2★ 5c+ 25m
A steep, sustained slab with small sharp holds.
R Ferrante, B Vitale, 2000

2 Mpyra   3★ 6b 25m
A nice slab climb on a profusion of water pockets.
L Salsotto, A Langenbach, 2014

3 Metaxas   3★ 6a+ 20m
Tricky and fingery at the start; slightly easier on the left.
R Ferrante, B Vitale, 2000

4 MAO   3★ 5c+ 22m
A natural line with good holds. At the top you can follow the buttress or the groove. C Schmidt + Friends, 2004

5 Il Gino   2★ 5c 27m
Long and easy. L Salsotto, A Langenbach, 2014

6 Kalispera   1★ 6a+ 18m
Sustained thin moves at the top. R Ferrante, B Vitale, 2000

7 Kalimera   1★ 6c 18m
Typical wall climb with a hard sequence.
R Ferrante, B Vitale, 2000

8 Disobbedisco!   3★ 6c+ 22m
A cruxy mid-section. L Salsotto, 2014

9 Alsace   2★ 6b+ 18m
A sharp and technical climb. L Salsotto, A Langenbach, 2014

10 E'Tardi   2★ 6a+ 15m
A steep and short slab. L Salsotto, A Langenbach, 2014

Marie-Laure Idoux on "Metaxas" 6a+

WHITE SHARK

White Shark is a small but interesting crag a bit further up and to the right of **Poets** with white/grey rock (some gentle-angled, some overhanging) and two curtains of thin tufas. To the right of the crag is a good, near-vertical grey slab, with only one route at the moment.

Climbing: Technical, on small holds and features.

☁ **Shade:** Until 12:30. **Exposure:** W

Approach: As for Poets (page 279). Then, continue up and to the right for 5 min more. **Walking time:** 20 min.

❶ Troppo 3★ ?? 32m
Troppo is too much! An open project on microholds on the headwall after nice tufa curtains in the lower section. *L Salsotto, 2011*

❷ The Wave 2★ 7a 25m
Very technical moves and a good value for the grade. *S + J Welich, 2004*

❸ Agopuntura 2★ 7b+ 30m
A really nice route on very small and sharp, fingery holds. Good balance is a must. *L Salsotto, A Langenbach, 2011*

39 POETS
ZEUS

296
36.999981
26.939005

Giorgio Mallucci on "Rocklandis" 7b.

Zeus is a compact orange wall further right from Poets, and at a slightly higher level. It is a beautiful venue overlooking a garden with large, old fig trees.

Climbing: Mostly vertical or gently overhanging on a well-featured wall. **Attention**: some routes climb above large ledges. There is the risk of injury in case of a fall.

 Shade: Until 12:30. **Exposure**: W

Approach: As on page 289. When you are almost level with Poets, continue to the right, to a fence with a gate. Go through the gate and close it again. Walk along the fence for 2 minutes until you come to the fig garden with an orange cliff above it. **Walking time**: 18-20 min.

1 Mad Dad   3★   6c+ 30m
The steep wall with big holds...except on the hard bits.
B Girardin, C + Y Remy, 2008

2 Callisto   3★   6c+ 28m
Brilliant climbing on good pockets in the mid-height white wall. Well-protected, go for the onsight! Maybe 7a if you are short. *S Mühlbacher, C Saul, 2003*

3 Rocklandis   3★   7b 30m
Some hard, fingery moves. *B Girardin, C + Y Remy, 2008*

4 Ganymede   2★   6b 28m
A long wall climb with an intriguing final groove.
K Kindernils, K Nagel, 2003

5 Isabel   2★   6c 36m
Good wall climbing leftwards to the final tricky crack. Height-dependent crux and awkward bolting. A 70m rope is just enough. Remember to **make a knot**. *A Brenner, 2004*

6 Blonde, James Blonde   3★   6c 25m
The rough red and white wall full of good holes to a steep finale and the anchor in the middle of nowhere!
B Girardin, C + Y Remy, 2009

7 Blonde   ♪   7c 35m
The airy extension pitch. Pull hard past the first belay to access the complex shallow groove up the headwall. A technical testpiece. 17 QD. *B Girardin, C + Y Remy, 2009*

8 La Mouette Généreuse   2★   6b+ 20m
The wall with big holds and a big blocky ledge at mid-height. *B Girardin, C + Y Remy, 2009*

9 Kalyfornication   3★   6b+ 25m
A red wall with a steep finale on handy tufas.
B Girardin, C + Y Remy, 2009

10 Pipe Cleaner   3★   7b 30m
An elegant tufa. It's not easy getting established on the pipe, and it keeps coming at you. Hard to onsight.
N Gresham, 2004

11 Wild Sport   3★   7c+ 32m
Technical climbing with big moves on the first crux results in a good rest, then on to a tufa with small grips but an easy finale. *V Batsios, N Bredas, 2012*

12 Dura Lex   3★   7b 25m
An easy start leads to an absorbing sequence on the headwall. Smartly bolted; a very worthwhile route.
N Bredas, V Batsios, 2012

13 Demeter   2★   4b 28m
Hard to get onto the ledge, then easier.
S Mühlbacher, C Schmidt, 2004

14 Demeter Ext   1★   5c+ 36m
Climb only as a separate 2nd pitch, otherwise there's too much rope drag. *S Mühlbacher, C Schmidt, 2004*

15 Hefaistos   1★   6c 30m
Long, varied and sustained.
A Hafner, T Hoch, S Mühlbacher, C Schmidt, 2004

ZEUS

39 POETS
MELTEMI

298
36.999981
26.939005

Sarah Peet on "Kalyfornication" 6b+, sector Zeus (previous page). JIM THORNBURG

MELTEMI

Meltemi is a peculiar crag with a mountain feel, further up and to the right of Zeus. The path is long but the view is stunning, and you will likely be alone, even in October.

Climbing: Mountain-style on some routes. There is one route up a corner and the rest are on vertical walls. The four recent additions on a compact slab are worth the long approach, though.

Shade: Until 12:30. The route "Pounenti" faces north and stays in the shade until 14:00 **Exposure**: SW

Approach: Go to Zeus (previous page). Walk to the right end of the cliff, and follow the marks and cairns uphill. Some scrambling is needed. **Walking time**: 50 min.

1 West Way — 0★ ?? ?m
Unfinished. Two pitches. *D Stratigos, 2005*

2 Siroco — 1★ 6c 30m
D Stratigos, 2005

3 Ob Ladi — ♪ 6a+ 30m
A fine steep slab. *C Idoux, 2013*

4 Ob Lada — ♪ 6a+ 30m
An amazing thin slab. *C Idoux, 2013*

5 Cent Plomb — 3★ 7a 32m
A steep and crimpy slab. *C Idoux, 2013*

6 Super Super — 3★ 7a 60m
Overhanging with big tufa and a small roof. *C Idoux, 2013*

7 Pounenti — 3★ 6b+ 30m
A very technical corner, unusual for Kalymnos. *D Stratigos, 2005*

8 Agnes — 0★ ?? ?m
Unfinished. Two pitches. *D Stratigos, 2005*

9 Thermopyla — 1★ 6b+ 60m
Two pitches with a hard trad feel and a photogenic traverse on the 2nd pitch. *D Stratigos, 2005*

40 GERAKIOS

36.992986
26.934002

GRADE RANGE	up to 5b+	5c to 6a+	6b to 7a	7a+ to 7c	7c+ and up
No. OF ROUTES	8	45	24	5	4

"Pépite Haut" 6a (page 307), one of many beautiful mid-grade routes expected to be classic at Trois Ilots, a major new sector.

Yet another long area of cliffs above the upper road and the village of Myrties, on the west coast of Kalymnos, sector **Gerakios** includes sub-sectors **Rainbow Wall**, **Upper Cave**, the **Main** cliff and **Trois Ilots**. Most sub-sectors are excellent recent additions and expected to become quite popular.

Climbing: Almost all Kalymnos styles, from steep caves to technical wall climbing.

Conditions: Warm and sunny. Good for winter climbing, or in the early morning in summer. Exposed to the rain, though.

Shade: Until 12:30 at all sub-sectors **Exposure:** S

Kids: OK. The path is long but the terrain beneath the cliffs is fairly suitable, mostly at sub-sectors Gerakios Main and Trois Ilots.

Approach: From Masouri, drive to Myrties village and then onto the upper road which goes back around from Myrties to Armeos. Park just before the first big right-hand turn (36.992986, 26.934002). The path begins immediately to the right of the house as shown above. Go through some gates, and make sure you close them behind you. When you arrive at the first band of cliffs, traverse to the right for **Gerakios Main** and **Trois Ilots**, or go up and slightly to the left for **Upper Cave** and **Rainbow Wall** sectors. Walking time: 15-35 min.

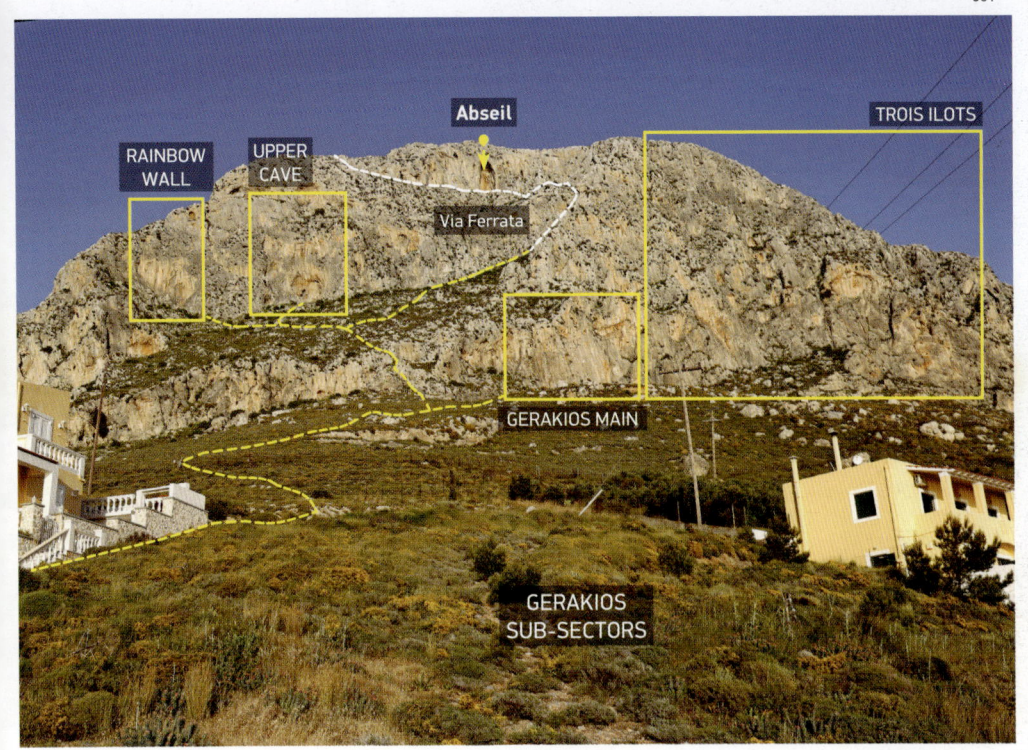

Via ferrata: A relatively short via ferrata (a mountain route equipped with fixed cables and ladders) was equipped by Claude Idoux in 2008 above sector Gerakios. A via ferrata sounds fun and relatively simple, but don't let that distract you from its inherent danger. Following a via ferrata still requires care, common sense, good physical shape and some climbing knowledge.

Gear: 70m rope, harness, energy absorber with "Y" lanyard, helmet (some gear is available for rent at climbing shops in Masouri, but ask ahead of time).

Approach: Follow the trail leading to sector Gerakios. When you are level with crag, do not turn right. Continue up and slightly to the left. **Walking time**: 45-50 min to the starting point of the via ferrata.

Description: The first 70m of the route is grade 3 climbing with bolts, and the remainder of the route has a fixed stainless steel cable. There are ladders to help you through the hard bits.

A little extra: when you get to the top (if you have time), make an airy 35m abseil (for the fun of it) from above the cave where there's an abseil station. Then, repeat the last portion of the via ferrata to get back to the top!

Return: From the top, start your descent by going south through a small gorge. Stay to the left the whole time. Then, you will find a relatively smooth path leading down to meet the path of sector Symplegades. Wind your way back down the lanes to the main road and Myrties and so back to your starting point.

Total time: 4-5 hours

Peta Barrett climbs "Ergo" 7b (page 303). SCOTT HAILSTONE

40 GERAKIOS

36.992986
26.934002

**RAINBOW WALL
UPPER CAVE**

Rainbow Wall, on the upper left of Gerakios, was established by Hannes Webhofer and Bruno Schneider in 2014. The name was chosen because this wall is so impressive and colorful, especially when touched by the sun.

Climbing: A good variety of styles and grades, plus a very worthwhile 3-pitch route. Attention, though: don't climb the 3-pitch if there are people at the base of the cliffs.

Approach: See page 300. At the level of Gerakios Main, go up and to the left. **Walking time**: 35 min.

1 Moonshine Dihedral   3★   6b 30m
Alpine style with outstanding moves and good bridging action.

2 Hansi-Mansi   2★   7a 23m
A somewhat sharp grey slab leads to interesting moves all the way. One of the cruxes is easier for the tall, and footwork options can be limited.

3 Desperado   2★   7c+ 20m
A technical slab on the 1st half gets you to the intense upper part with some powerful moves.

4 Rainbow Warrior   3★   8a+? 30m
A massive undertaking up this consistent, very technical and always challenging yellow wall.

5 Rainbow Dancer   ♪   8a+ 25m
A slightly overhanging wall on colorful rock. Finger power-pulling on several mono pockets with no feet, then complex moves all the way to the chain.

6 Utopia-Rainbow   3★   6a+ 18m
Versatile climbing on interesting rock formations; gets progressively harder towards the top.

7 Pressure Drop   2★   7b 30m
A technical slab leads to a black tufa, then to steeper ground and a bouldery crux on thinner holds.

8 Opportunista   3★   7c 26m
An easy corner leads to steeper terrain with two distinct cruxes. *2015*

9 Crossroads   2★   6b+ 20m
Fun start on big holds, then technical with flakes + pockets.

10 Crossroads 2   2★   5b 10m
A variaton on low-angle rock with good holds.

11 Born to Run   3★   6b+ 60m
Multi-pitch (6b+ 20m, 6a+ 20m, 5c+ 20m). P1: Very technical pocketed wall with a hard crux. Left or right? P2: A bit sharp and some spaced bolts. Needs traffic. P3: Fantasy-land on smooth grey/orange rock! One of the best in its grade.

12 Looking 4 Space   2★   6a+ 20m
Fine grey wall climbing; delicate moves near the top.

UPPER CAVE

Upper Cave is a large cave above the original sector. It was equipped in 2012 by Claude + Yves Remy, and some hard lines were recently added in the middle.

Climbing: On overhanging, athletic terrain in the middle, and technical walls on either side.

Approach: As for Rainbow Wall. **Walking time**: 30 min.

1 Losing my Religion　　　　2★ 7a 40m
An old multi-pitch project. P1 features an amazing layback crack. The initial easy slab is runout. Take long QDs to avoid rope drag. *2005*

2 Axa　　　　2★ 6a+ 25m
A slab with a crux on "stinky *gouttes d'eau*" and a steep large flake at the finale. *C + Y Remy, 2012*

3 Emi　　　　3★ 7a+ 28m
More *gouttes d'eau*, a crack and flakes. *C + Y Remy, 2012*

4 Tatoo　　　　2★ 6b 15m
A short quality wall with a technical end. *C + Y Remy, 2012*

5 Amra　　　　2★ 7b 25m
A steep wall and a nice, cruxy single tufa. *C + Y Remy, 2012*

6 Ergo　　　　3★ 7b 25m
Steep, juggy and athletic. *C + Y Remy, 2012*

7 No Name　　　　3★ ?? ?m
G Kopalides, 2014

8 No Name　　　　3★ ?? 30m
G Kopalides, 2014

9 Zavara Katranemia　　　　♪ 8a 25m
The super-steep but juggy line. A tricky start is followed by brilliant roof work to the big hole, then a distinct crux with desperate moves. *A Theodoropoulos, G Kopalides, 2012*

10 Native　　　　1★ 5b 15m
Short, but a good warm-up. *C + Y Remy, 2012*

11 Lola　　　　3★ 6c+ 35m
A diagonal start leads to the magical vertical centerpiece with surprisingly good slots. Excellent. *C + Y Remy, 2012*

12 Voltric　　　　2★ 6c+ 33m
The steep wall with a technical, thought-provoking section. *C + Y Remy, 2012*

13 Super Mami　　　　2★ 6a 33m
An impressive wall with sharp rock forms. *C + Y Remy, 2012*

40 GERAKIOS

304

36.992986
26.934002

UPPER CAVE
GERAKIOS MAIN

UPPER CAVE

George "Jorge" Kopalides on the crux sequence of "Zavara Katranemia" 8a (page 303). CHRIS BOUKOROS

GERAKIOS MAIN

Gerakios Main is a grey and white/orange vertical wall on crimpy, crumbly medium-quality rock. The view, however, makes it worth a visit.

Climbing: Balancy and technical slab climbing.

Approach: As on page 300. **Walking time**: 15 min.

1 Drill 2★ 6b+ 24m
A slab with a bulge at the end. *J Friedrich, G Hommel, 2012*

2 Pita-Rita 3★ 6a 23m
Well-featured red rock. *J Friedrich, G Hommel, 2012*

3 Sharp 1★ 6a 24m
Well-eroded rock with big, sharp holds.
J Friedrich, G Hommel 2011

4 Needle 2★ 6a+ 26m
Fingery rock with unusual features. *J + F Friedrich, 2013*

5 Beach House 2★ 6c+ 33m
Hard single pulls on the lower part of a nice yellow wall.
17 QD. *F + X + C Heinicke, A + C Riemer, 2013*

6 Climbing House 1★ 6a 25m
Left of the crack. *G Hommel, J Friedrich, 2011*

7 Stefanos 2★ 5c 25m
A ridge on the left of the big groove, with an interesting finish. *B Viberti, B Ronzino, E Viberti, 1999*

8 Chimney 2★ 5b 30m
The big unusual groove. *G Hommel, J Friedrich, 2014*

9 Zio Gio 1★ 5c 20m
Some delicate moves. *B Viberti, B Ronzino, E Viberti, 1999*

10 Little Gio 1★ 6a+ 20m
Several cracks with good holds and a steep finish.
B Viberti, B Ronzino, E Viberti, 1999

11 Titis Blues 3★ 6b+ 25m
A well-bolted pocketed wall. *B Fara, 2015*

12 Open Book 3★ 6a+ 28m
A nice open corner/groove. *G Hommel, J Friedrich, 2013*

13 Reader 2★ 6a 29m
Interesting face climbing. *G Hommel, J Friedrich, 2014*

14 Trip 2★ 5b 28m
A crack with good holds. *G Hommel, J Friedrich, 2015*

15 Flag 2★ 6a 22m
A white slab then easier groove. *G Hommel, J Friedrich, 2014*

16 Grueffelo 1★ 6b+ 23m
Needs more traffic. *T Jekel, M Hensel, 2014*

17 Hannah 2★ 6a 23m
A direct line; pleasant climbing. *T Jekel, M Hensel, 2014*

18 Port 1★ 5c 23m
Starts right of the goat gate. Very rough rock.
J Friedrich, G Hommel, 2011

40 GERAKIOS
TROIS ILOTS (LEFT)

36.992986
26.934002

Stamatis Agadakos on the photogenic "Sandy Kilo" 6a

Yiannis Chrysochoou on the fantastic "Crystal Line" 6a (p. 311).

Trois Ilots is a recently developed sub-sector with all the qualtiies of a popular crag. It is an extended band of rocks further right of Gerakios Main. The cliffs are fairly vertical but they were very vegetated and thus "hidden" from the eyes of most equippers. However, the persistent and stubborn Claude Idoux found the time and patience to clean the lush rock and reveal a small treasure: the quality of the rock hiding underneath is exceptional, and some of the best routes in Kalymnos in the mid-grades (6a-6b) are here, so it will appeal to the majority of climbers visiting the island.

Climbing: Technical and requiring good footwork on well-bolted, well-cleaned routes and an amazing variety of rock types. Additionally, there are two multi-pitches going all the way to the top of the cliff face.
All routes were equipped by Claude Idoux from 2014 to 2016 unless otherwise noted.

Approach: As on page 300, then traverse rightwards from the main crag. **Walking time**: 20 min.

TROIS ILOTS LEFT

1. Délice Choc — 3★ 5c+ 35m
A nice long groove.

2. Pépite Haut — 3★ 6a 35m
A wall with a thin crack and green bolts.

3. Sandy Kilo — 3★ 6a 36m
A wall and crack with several small bulges.

4. Allez Gros — 2★ 6a+ 23m
A nice slab and a delicate final wall with a thin crack.

5. AP. Wall — 2★ 6a+ 36m
Long and homogeneous, with big holds when you need them. 18 QD.

6. Rowan — 2★ 6a+ 35m
Technical climbing with an intricate finale on a yellow wall and pink bolts.

7. Express Haut — 3★ 6a+ 30m
An excellent technical wall with a short, athletic finish.

8. Léa Rico — 3★ 6a 30m
A slightly overhanging middle section, but juggy.

9. G.D. Gaz — 3★ 6a 30m
A technical start, bulge and wall with good holds. Red bolts.

10. Pétain Coup — 3★ 6b 32m
A pleasant start, balancy mid-section, and steep tufa finish.

11. Kipetetropvitechie — 2★ 5b+ 30m

12. Rita T — 2★ 6a 28m
Y Zoidis, 2015

13. Kitsos E — 2★ 5c 23m

14. New Route — 2★ 5c 24m

15. New Route Ext — 3★ 6a+ 40m

40 GERAKIOS
TROIS ILOTS (MIDDLE)

36.992986
26.934002

1 3ème âge — 3★ 5a 30m
A good warm-up on an enjoyable slab.

2 Ginette — 3★ 5b+ 30m
Wonderful slab climbing.

3 Chirlipipi — 3★ 5c+ 30m
An excellent groove and good holds up a steep red wall.

4 Epidixias — 3★ 5c 30m
An amply featured slab/crack to a steep final section on good holds.

5 Pornogeros — 3★ 6b 35m
A slabby start and an intimidating athletic final wall on good, but spaced, holds. Follow the blue bolts.

6 1995 — 3★ 6b 30m
The lovely main groove leads to an intricate headwall.

7 1995 Ext — 3★ 6c 40m
Climb up the massive red wall, but don't follow the bolts blindly. Use long QDs from the 1st pitch to avoid rope drag.

8 Cuni Lingugus — 3★ 6b+ 32m
The striking pillar. Amazing climbing and an airy finale.

9 Cumulo Sinus — 3★ 6b 32m
Nice moves on good quality pockets and flakes all the way.

10 Prosciutto + Champagne — 3★ 6a 20m
An absorbing technical groove that gets harder as you reach the top. Follow the green, white and red bolts.

11 O Claire de l'Anus — 2★ 6a+ 32m
Fingery climbing, and it needs your best footwork.

12 Les Pros Se Tâtent — 3★ 6a+ 35m
A steep start which eases off at the upper part, but still pleasant climbing.

13 Les Copains d'Abord — 3★ 6a+ 200m
Multi-pitch, 5 pitches (6a 33m, 6a+ 35m, traverse via static rope, 6a+ 38m, 5c 35m, 6a 25m). P1 and P2: Sustained slabs. P3: A clever chimney. P4 and P5: Slab climbing. **Return**: Abseil down the route "Modeste". 80m rope required. Alternatively, you can walk back down by way of sectors Ourania and Symplegades.

14 Minion — 3★ 5c+ 30m
Face climbing with some good foot movement.

15 Jolie Emilie — 2★ 5c 26m
A good warm-up; a couple of bulges to keep you focused.

16 Modeste — 3★ 6b+ 190m
Multi-pitch, 6 pitches (5b 35m, 6a 25m, 6b+ 25m, 6b 25m, walk 20m, 5c 20m, 6a 40m). **Return**: Abseil down P6 (1 x 40m) and P5 (1 x 20), then walk 20m to the abseil points to the left of the route (2 x 40m).

All routes above were equipped by Claude Idoux in 2013.

"La Jolie" Emilie Idoux on "1995" 6b.

Proud papa Claude Idoux with daughter Emilie.

TROIS ILOTS MIDDLE

40 GERAKIOS
TROIS ILOTS (RIGHT)

36.992986
26.934002

Stamatis Agadakos on the testing moves of "Qeen Couine" 6b

TROIS ILOTS RIGHT

1. Eh Ma Tomme — 3★ 6a+ 30m
A wall which eases off in the mid-section to steepen again at the end.

2. L.H.O. — 3★ 6b+ 35m
A delicate finish with hidden holds.

3. Pouce Twalda — 3★ 6b+ 25m
Steep start with hidden pockets and an interesting finish.

4. Crystal Line — 3★ 6a 35m
Impressive, with a great variety of rock and a small hidden crystal treasure.

5. Tétonne Pas — 3★ 6a+ 22m
Wall climbing which gets progressively harder. Follow the blue bolts.

6. Gabou — 3★ 6b 25m
Great climbing on rock with an intense personality.

7. Lafete Alm — 3★ 6a+ 30m
Well-spaced flakes at the middle. Follow the red bolts.

8. Qeen Couine — 3★ 6b 30m
More climbing up an interesting wall and the short crack/groove at the end.

9. L.A.O.T.C.O. — 3★ 6b 40m
Much variety and an impressive juggy finale.

10. Oxèo — 3★ 5b 25m
A steady ridge.

11. La Raie Publique — 3★ 6a 30m
This route starts higher up, from a huge wedged block. First, climb the route "Oxèo", then lower to the big flat block. Clip yourself there to belay your partner on this route, which is a mountain-style corner/chimney.

12. Bises to Kate — 3★ 6a+ 40m
An old-school steep slab with blue bolts.

13. Ari Cover — 3★ 6a+ 37m
A sustained wall and slab climb with white bolts.

All routes above were equipped by Claude Idoux in 2015.

41 OURANIA

36.985664
26.938151

GRADE RANGE	up to 5b+	5c to 6a+	6b to 7a	7a+ to 7c	7c+ and up
No. OF ROUTES	8	11	16	7	1

HUMP PISTE

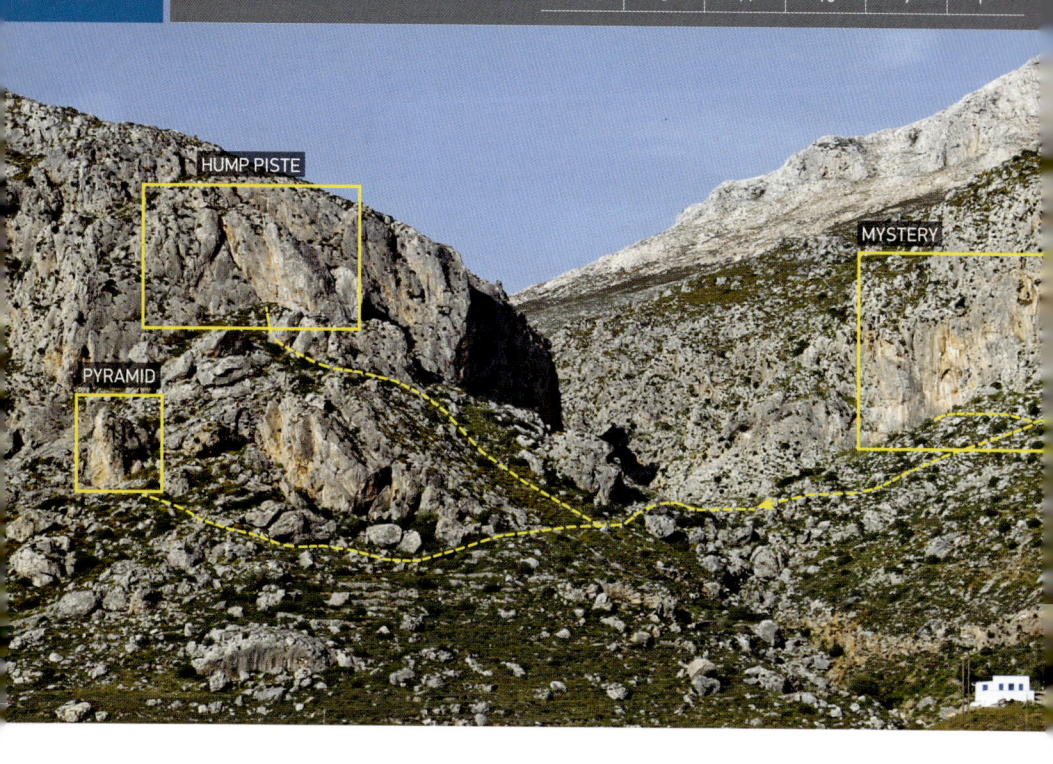

MYSTERY

PYRAMID

Sector Ourania has an impressive large cave at its center that really catches the eye. To its left are sub-sectors **Mystery**, **Hump Piste** and **Pyramid**, and to its right is the popular crag **Symplegades**. Many routes at sectors **Ourania** and **Mystery** have been put up by Michel Piola, an equipper known for creating routes of high aesthetic value.

Climbing: Overhanging with big holds inside the cave. Sustained and technical on the outer walls.

Conditions: The cave stays in the shade until late afternoon and it is protected from the rain. The walls, though, only get shade in the morning.

☁ **Shade:** Until 13:00-16:00. **Exposure:** W

Kids: There is some suitable terrain near Mystery and Pyramid. Ourania cave may sound like a good place for kids, but it is actually covered in layers of goat poo.

Approach: From Masouri, drive in the direction to Pothia (the port town). When you get to the top of the steep zig-zag turns, just after a big home on the left that looks like a castle, turn off left towards Kamari onto a narrow road. On the 3rd road, turn left. This is a very narrow uphill concrete road. At the first junction, turn left again. Continue uphill until the narrow road levels off at a big gate. Park there without blocking the road (36.985664, 26.938151. The owners of the property have graciously installed a small side-gate for climbers to go through. Please open and close it again behind you. Walk up the final portion of the uphill road to a big house. There is a barbed wire fence on the left-hand side with a small gate. Go through the gate and close it again behind you. Walk straight along the well-defined path until it splits: the uphill branch to the right goes to sector Symplegades; the branch straight ahead goes to Ourania (cairns). When you arrive below the cave, turn right and follow an unclear path to the cave, or continue straight ahead to go to Mystery, then further left to Hump Piste and Pyramid. **Walking time:** 15-20 min.

Pyramid is large and distinctive pyramid-shaped boulder with just one route.

Climbing: The rock quality is good; it is quite similar to the rock at sector Symplegades.

☁ **Shade:** Until 13:00. **Exposure:** W

Approach: Go to sub-sector Mystery. When you are level with Mystery, cross the gully and traverse leftwards to the boulder. **Walking time**: 20-22 min.

#	Route	Stars	Grade	Length
1	Sehnsucht	2★	6c	18m

Schwarzbart + Klaus, 2003

41 OURANIA

314
36.985664
26.938151

HUMP PISTE
MYSTERY

Hump Piste is a new little sub-sector on a short grey wall and low-angle slabs. All routes were equipped by Joachim Friedrich and Gunter Hommel.

Climbing: Technical face climbing on sharp grey rock. Good for easy climbs between 3c-6a.

Shade: Until 11:30. **Exposure**: S

Approach: Go to sub-sector Mystery. When you are level with Mystery, cross the gully. Go through an open gate and follow the red marks to a rock niche after about 200m. **Walking time**: 22-25 min.

#	Route	Stars	Grade	Length
1	**Hump** — The steep pillar. 2015	1★	6b	24m
2	**Bingo** 2015	1★	6a+	28m
3	**Bang** 2015	1★	5c+	22m
4	**Poem** 2015	2★	6b+	22m
5	**Channel** — The steep pillar. 2015	1★	5a	20m
6	**Film** 2015	1★	6c	16m
7	**Script** 2015	1★	6b	16m
8	**Novel** 2015	1★	6c+	16m
9	**Story** 2015	1★	6a+	18m
10	**Song** 2015	1★	5c	30m
11	**Word** 2015	1★	5b	30m
12	**Rest** 2015	1★	3c	30m
13	**Light** 2015	1★	3c	25m
14	**Sparrow** 2015	1★	4a	15m
15	**Duck** — On the back of the big boulder. 2015	1★	6a	18m
16	**Goose** 2015	1★	5c	17m

Mystery is an interesting small cliff with highly-featured red and grey limestone.

Climbing: Very pleasant and technical on vertical or slightly overhanging rock.

Shade: Until 13:00. **Exposure**: W

Approach: See previous page. **Walking time**: 15-18 min.

1 Bouc et Mystère   1★   7a+   27m
A fingery wall. *M Piola et al. (P Strappazzon, B Therre, F Amman, M Balliger, T Genecand, V Leuchsner), 2004*

2 Katifellx   2★   6c+   27m
M Piola et al. (see #1), 2004

3 Zickenschule   1★   6b+   18m
Short, stiff and sharp. *M Creutz, 2004*

4 Mystère et Boule de Gomme   2★   5c+   30m
Long and sustained; sharp in places. *M Piola et al., 2004*

5 Diedre Oublie   3★   6a+   30m
An absorbing corner with some delicate moves in the middle. *B Fara, R Guerin, 2010*

6 Klettern Paradise   3★   7b+   25m
Fabulous rock, very technical. *M Piola et al. (see #1), 2004*

7 Stranger in Paradise   3★   7a+   25m
Good, technical and sustained. *M Piola et al. (see #1), 2004*

8 Paradise Artificial   2★   7a+   25m
Challenging with a fingery technical crux. *M Piola et al., 2004*

9 Olymbiakos   3★   6c   35m
An interesting pocketed wall leads to a crimpy finale. *M Piola et al. (see #1), 2004*

10 Aquarella   2★   7a   30m
A good slab, then a steeper fingery headwall. Spaced bolts. *M Creutz 2004*

11 Haralampos   1★   6c   35m
A couple of hard moves at the bulge. *B Fara, R Guerin 2011*

12 Farapopoulos   2★   6b   35m
A technical wall, harder at mid-height. *B Fara, R Guerin 2011*

13 Tufa's Story   3★   6b   25m
A compact slab leads to an unlikely tufa finish. Hard for the grade. *M Piola et al. (see #1), 2004*

14 Son Venthous des Windes   2★   7a   25m
A nice pillar with a crimpy finish. *M Creutz, 2004*

41 OURANIA

OURANIA

36.985664
26.938151

Ourania is a huge cave that stays in the shade until late afternoon. In Greek, *ourania* means "divine". And while the rock quality may not, in fact, *be* divine—by Kalymnos standards, anyway—the routes here are certainly worth a visit. Furthermore, there is still potential for new, hard routes inside the cave, and easier ones on the outer walls.

Climbing: Technical but pumpy inside the cave, on routes that often feel "airy". Some new easier slab and wall climbs have been added on good rock outside the cave, but they need traffic to improve.

Shade: Until 16:00 inside the cave. Until about 13:00 on the wall to the left. **Exposure**: NW

Approach: As on page 312. **Walking time**: 15-18 min.

1 Grenzpfeiler   2★   **7a ??m**
Two pitches. Some scrambling (not easy) is required to get to the base of the route. P1 goes up a good wall.
P2 follows an airy pillar. *B Arnold, G Mueller, 2006*

2 Pet   1★   **5b 21m**
J Friedrich, G Hommel, 2014

3 Fact   1★   **5b+ 27m**
J Friedrich, G Hommel, 2014

4 Act   1★   **6a+ 25m**
J Friedrich, G Hommel, 2014

5 Fun   1★   **5c 22m**
A slabby climb. *J Friedrich, G Hommel, 2014*

6 Ego   1★   **5c 25m**
Finishes on big holes. *J Friedrich, 2014*

7 Stone Bakery   1★   **5a 25m**
A low-angle route full of features. Will improve with some traffic. *J Friedrich, G Hommel, 2014*

8 Terra Incognita   2★   **7a+ 25m**
A hard corner sequence. Very technical. *M Piola, 2004*

9 Ourania   3★   **7c+ 20m**
The black overhanging wall. Really good punchy climbing with a killer last move. *M Piola, 2004*

10 Star Wars   2★   **7b+ 18m**
Suspicious-looking rock, but good, athletic climbing. Better than it looks. *M Piola, 2004*

11 Captain Caveman   2★   **6c+ 18m**
A bulging wall which is very steep, but on mostly big holds and good underclings. *N Baker, K Morgan, 2008*

12 Facatelendos   3★   **6b+ 25m**
A bit stiff for the grade. It helps to "think laterally".
M Piola, 2004

13 Sponge Beach   2★   **7b+ 20m**
Good climbing, but some holds are sharp. *M Piola, 2004*

Unknown climber on "Ourania" 7c+. MICHEL PIOLA

Glenn Sutcliffe is on "Terra Incognita" 7a+. NEIL FOSTER

42 SYMPLEGADES

36.985664
26.938151

GRADE RANGE	up to 5b+	5c to 6a+	6b to 7a	7a+ to 7c	7c+ and up
No. OF ROUTES	3	15	21	0	0

Two massive limestone walls facing each other, with a perfect plateau in between: this is the popular sector **Symplegades**. A peculiar work of nature, and a unique crag here on Kalymnos. The locals used to call this peak "The Castle", suggesting that it was used as such in the past. There are signs of old dwellings at the highest point of the north crag; there is also a very impressive cave-like crack at the beginning of the route "Valery + Thomas". It runs through the crag with two exits on the south face, and pottery shards inside the crack indicate that it was likely used as a hiding place in the past. Fantastic rock aside, sector **Symplegades** is attractive for families with kids, too, as the flat terrain and long hours of shade arguably make it the best crag in Kalymnos for families.

Nazo Canitez on the classic "Drama" 6a+ (page 323).

Climbing: Very pleasant, on unusual fluted limestone full of creases and little holes. Routes of amazing quality on mostly vertical or slightly overhanging well-featured rock, with holds almost everywhere. A perfect crag for gaining some confidence in leading routes (the angle is not so steep, and the bolting is very friendly). There is plenty of potential for new routes, especially in the lower grades (4 and 5) on the northeast face (to the right of the route "Octana", with shade in the afternoon—something Kalymnos climbing still needs).

Conditions: Cool and shady, great for hot days. Not good on days with strong wind: the opposing rocks tend to channel the wind and amplify it.

Shade: Almost all day. When the sun comes to one side, the other side goes into the shade. The routes to the left as you enter (#1-21) are in the shade all morning until about 13:00. The routes to the right as you enter are in the sun all morning and come into the shade after about 13:30. **Exposure**: N,E,S

Kids: Perfect. The path can be steep at parts but it is short, and there are plenty of suitable protected areas on flat terrain.

Approach: From Masouri, drive in the direction to Pothia (the port town). When you get to the top of the steep zig-zag turns, just after a big home on the left that looks like a castle, turn off left towards Kamari onto a narrow road. On the 3rd road, turn left again. This is a very narrow uphill concrete road. At the first junction, turn left again. Continue uphill until the narrow road levels off at a big gate. Park there without blocking the road (36.985664, 26.938151). The owners of the property have graciously installed a small side-gate for climbers to go through. Please open and close it again behind you. Walk up the final portion of the uphill road to a big house. There is a barbed wire fence on the left-hand side with a small gate. Go through the gate and close it again behind you. Walk straight along the well-defined path until it splits: follow the blue marks uphill to the right. A few minutes later you will enter the crag between the Left Slab and the North Face. (If you follow the path straight ahead at the point where it splits, it takes you to sector Ourania).

See also: Crag Panorama on page 312.

Walking time: 10-12 min.

42 SYMPLEGADES
LEFT SLAB
MAIN WALL

320
36.985664
26.938151

The **Left Slab** is the first section of rocks to your left as you arrive at the crag. Route #1, "Pyrsos", stands alone around the corner just before the left slab.

1. Pyrsos — 1★ 6b 35m
A mountain-style route that feels more like trad climbing, even though it is bolted. *D Stratigos, 2005*

2. Mike's Bikes — 2★ 6a 15m
A wandering line. Climbing is a lot more interesting than it looks, but the bolting is not great for the grade. *O Steiss, J Rohrmann, 2005*

3. Isidora — 2★ 6c 30m
A technical wall, overhang and crack. *C Idoux, L Salsotto, 2009*

4. Carlo Juliani — 2★ 6a 16m
A pleasant, sustained face climb on unusual rock with pockets and tufa holes. *A Theodoropoulos, D Yialouris, A + E Gazis, K Patarias, 2002*

5. Anemodarmeni — 2★ 6a 20m
A good flake then a little tufa and a technical bulge. *A Theodoropoulos et al. (see #4), 2002*

LEFT SLAB

MAIN WALL

Ole Karsten Birkeland climbs "Ermix" 7a (left), and Myriam Caissy is on the classic "Drama" 6a+ (right). Both routes on page 323.

42 SYMPLEGADES
MAIN WALL

36.985664
26.938151

6 Climbers' Nest 3★ 6a 28m
Long + varied. Interesting features and everything from face climbing to bridging. *O Steiss, J Rohrmann, 2005*

7 Rabat 3★ 6c 45m
The extension of "Climbers' Nest" goes up a technical pocketed wall. Fine climbing with good positions. Use 22 long QDs to avoid rope drag. *F Heinicke, A + C Riemer, 2007*

Tania Matsuka flashes a smile *and* the route "Homo Sapiens" 6c.

8 K.V.R. 3★ 6b 30m
An awesome wall with good holds leads to a steep, "space walking" finale with good jugs. *O Steiss, J Rohrmann, 2005*

9 Phineas 3★ 5c 22m
Amazing for the grade! Not very solid-looking rock, but in fact it is an overhanging jug-fest with massive holds plus bridging. *H Bartu, A Odermatt, U Neu, A Neiger, 2002*

10 Neanderthal 2★ 6b 18m
A tough start followed by some interesting, unusual climbing up the right edge of the cleft. *A Theodoropoulos, 2010*

11 Homo Sapiens 3★ 6c 20m
Great, varied climbing. A steep start on good jugs, a crux, and technical edge climbing. *G Ermeidis, G Zavouras, 2002*

12 Kamari 3★ 6c+ 20m
A steep, sustained start with a delicate wall above. *G Ermeidis, G Zavouras, 2002*

13 Katsaplias 3★ 6c+ 20m
Technical and varied climbing on pockets with great moves that need a positive approach. *G Ermeidis, G Zavouras, 2002*

14 Ermix 3★ 7a 20m
A demanding sequence on slightly overhanging rock with a "Thank God" jug at the end. *G Ermeidis, G Zavouras, 2002*

15 Kiria Rita 3★ 6c+ 20m
Squeezed, but sustained and full of pockets. *2006*

16 TNT 3★ 6c 20m
Delicate and sustained pocket-pulling. Interesting until the very end. *G Ermeidis, G Zavouras, 2002*

17 Bubuki 3★ 6b+ 25m
Wall climbing with big jugs on the steep bit and a hard technical headwall. *H Bartu, A Odermatt, U Neu, A Neiger, 2002*

18 Drama 3★ 6a+ 20m
A technical and delicate wall. *G Ermeidis, G Zavouras, 2002*

19 Opera 3★ 6b 20m
Excellent, technical, and sustained climbing up a good pocketed wall. *J Seidel, 2005*

20 Musical 3★ 6a+ 26m
A brilliant pocketed route with a short, interesting bulge. *J Friedrich, F Heinicke, 2015*

21 Ivan 2★ 5c 25m
An interesting start at a crack, though rock is quite loose in places. Exit up a demanding corner. *A Theodoropoulos et al. (see #4), 2002*

MAIN WALL

41 SYMPLEGADES

324
36.985664
26.938151

DONNER
EAST FACE, NORTH FACE

22 Gourmet 2★ 6b+ 15m
Short but tasty all the way. *2006*

23 Donner 2★ 6c 8m
Bouldery up a short, juggy wall. *2006*

24 1-2-3 ABC 3★ 2a 4m
The easiest bolted route in the world? The perfect playground for the youngest kids where they can top out and easily walk down a corridor to avoid the rappeling problem. *J Larssen, F Lundqvist, 2015*

25 Obolus 2★ 6b+ 15m
A technical finger crack. *F Heinicke, A + C Riemer, 2007*

26 Igel 2★ 6c 20m
A good balancy climb with an expo finale on a pocketed headwall. *O Steiss, J Rohrmann, 2005*

27 Iason 2★ 6b+ 20m
Sustained wall climbing on good but spaced pockets. *H Bartu, A Odermatt, U Neu, A Neiger, 2002*

28 Skorpios 3★ 6a 20m
Varied slab climbing that keeps its interest as you weave through the bolts. *G Ermeidis, G Zavouras, 2002*

DONNER

29 The Double Twins 3★ 5b 20m
A nice and easy groove that gets harder and more technical for the feet towards the top. *J Larssen, F Lundqvist, 2015*

30 Cleaner 1★ 5c 22m
An easy start but not-so-easy finish on small holds. *J Friedrich, G Hommel, 2014*

31 Broom 1★ 6a 22m
A nicely sustained initial wall. *J Friedrich, G Hommel, 2014*

32 Pretty 3★ 5c 18m
A juggy warm-up. *J + U Friedrich, 2015*

33 Josi 1★ 6a+ 18m
The fingery wall. *B Arnold, M Creutz, 2003*

34 Vasilis 3★ 5c 20m
A wide corner crack offers a nice change in style. An unusual climb for Kalymnos, and a stiff one at that. It does not get easier as you go. *A Theodoropoulos, D Yialouris, A + E Gazis, K Patarias, 2002*

35 Philoxenia 2★ 6a 20m
A good, easy wall interrupted by two breaks and a cute move to reach the halfway ledge. *O Steiss, J Rohrmann 2005*

36 Valery + Thomas 2★ 5b+ 20m
Pleasant climbing up the groove, with a delicate transfer to a flake. Bridging and slab climbing combined. *O Steiss, J Rohrmann, 2005*

37 Octana 3★ 6b 20m
A sustained and technical finger crack, unusual for this kind of limestone. *A Theodoropoulos, D Yialouris, A + E Gazis, K Patarias, 2002*

EAST FACE

NORTH FACE

43 AUSTRIANS

36.968861
26.934604

GRADE RANGE	up to 5b+	5c to 6a+	6b to 7a	7a+ to 7c	7c+ and up
No. OF ROUTES	0	1	3	5	1

On a natural balcony near Kandouni, **Austrians** features 10 routes on mid-quality rock (by Kalymnos standards) but a nice shady location.

Climbing: Short but powerful overhanging routes in a small cave, a yellow wall and a short, interesting roof.

Kids: An easy path, but poor terrain near the cliffs.

Conditions: Cool, good for summer. Exposed to the rain.

Shade: Until 16:00. **Exposure:** W

Approach: Go to Kandouni Beach (36.968861, 26.934604). Follow the path starting at the left end of the beach below the church. Walk 150m then go off the main path and follow the red marks to the left. **Walking time:** 15 min.

1 Pax — 2★ 6a+ 10m
Short and steep. *1999*

2 Glasperlenspiel — 1★ 7b 20m
Steep with a tricky exit from the lip. *1999*

3 Orca — 1★ 6b+ 25m
A sustained, fingery wall. *K Oelze, B Hertner, 2000*

4 Red Tears — 2★ 6b+ 10m
Short but tough and unforgiving. *K Oelze, B Hertner, 2000*

5 Gemini — 2★ 7b 20m
Steep and varied with 2 small bulges and a sharp exit. *1999*

6 Alamgest — 1★ 8a 20m
Short, bouldery and sharp. *1999*

7 Happy Birthday Magic — 1★ 7c 15m
A good tufa start to a bouldery finish. *S Weber, 1999*

8 Broken Hammer — 1★ 7a+ 15m
A tricky and sharp final bulge. *S Weber, 1999*

9 NRG — 2★ 7b+ 20m
A steep start then a sustained wall. *K Oelze, B Hertner, 2000*

10 Gibt's Doch Garnet — 2★ 6c 20m
An interesting wall climb with a steep start. *S Weber, 1999*

Eureka (Boulder Traverse) 2★ 7a+

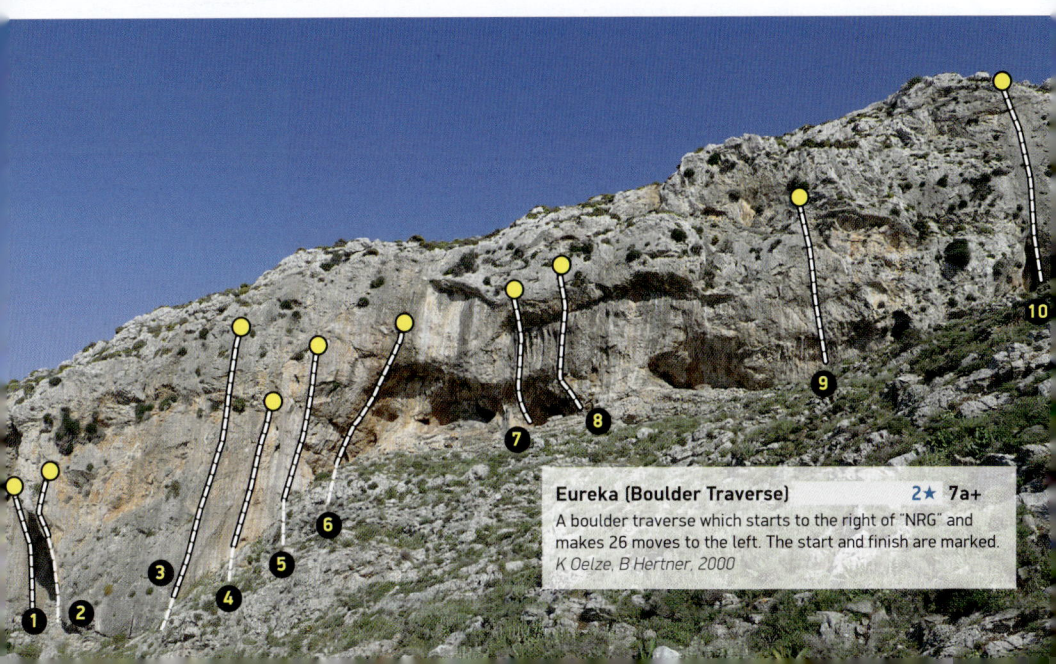

A boulder traverse which starts to the right of "NRG" and makes 26 moves to the left. The start and finish are marked.
K Oelze, B Hertner, 2000

44 MONASTERY

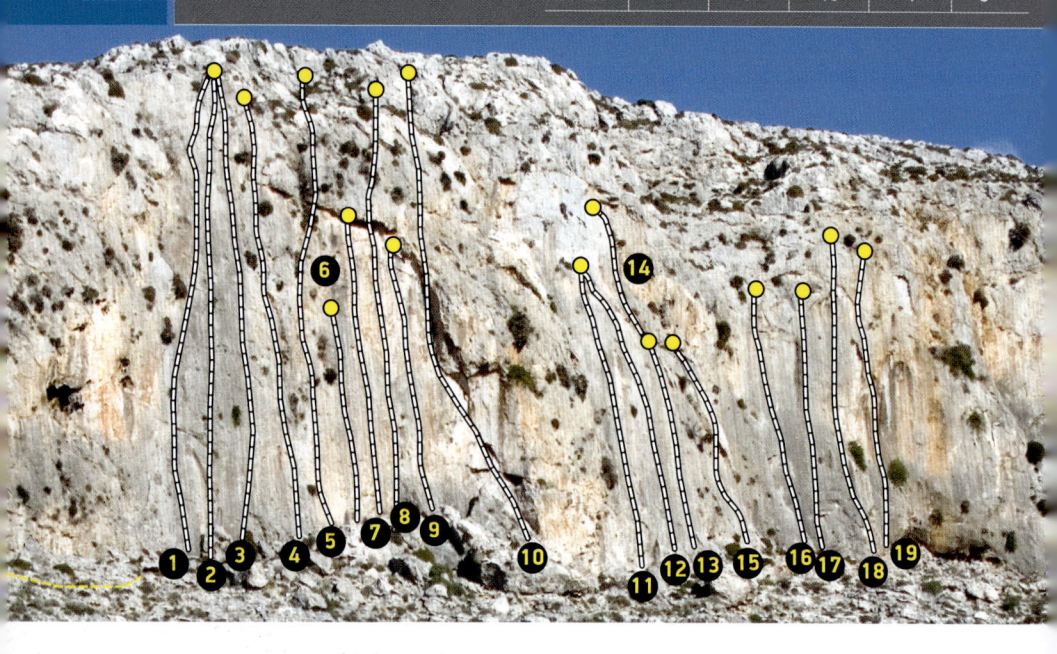

36.968861
26.934604

GRADE RANGE	up to 5b+	5c to 6a+	6b to 7a	7a+ to 7c	7c+ and up
No. OF ROUTES	1	7	16	1	0

Situated in a sheltered area formed by an open streambed, **Monastery** is an out-of-the-way crag with well-bolted routes on solid grey walls.

Climbing: On a high-quality grey wall; slabby on the left, more vertical on the right. Routes are well-protected.

Conditions: Hot and sunny; good for climbing in winter or on cloudy days. Exposed to the rain.

Shade: Until 12:00. **Exposure:** S

Kids: A long path, but some good areas at the far right.

Approach: Go to Kandouni Beach (36.968861, 26.934604). Follow the path starting at the left end of the beach below the church. Walk about 2km, then look for a cairn and yellow marks on the left marking a secondary path going left. Follow this path up a ridge (8-10 min) to the cliffs on the left of an open valley leading to the sea. If you see a white chapel (St Photis) you've gone too far. Go back and look for the cairn/yellow marks.
Walking time: 30 min.

See also: Crag Panorama on page 327.

1 Petoiva ♪ 6a+ 25m
Long, varied, with all the quality ingredients: a slab, a crack, bulges. *B Viberti, B Ronzino, E Viberti, 1999*

2 Idoufix 2★ 6c 30m
Stiff wall to start, then easier. *L Salsotto, 2011*

3 Mythos 3★ 6b 25m
An excellent bouldery part, then a sustained balancy wall. *B Viberti, B Ronzino, E Viberti, 1999*

4 Cresme 3★ 6b 22m
Steep wall climbing, sharp holds, a hard bouldery section. *B Viberti, B Ronzino, E Viberti, 1999*

5 Bau Bau 2★ 6c 25m
A hard start; then easier, but still steep. *L Salsotto, 2011*

6 Prep 2★ 6c+ 15m
A short fingery wall. *B Viberti, B Ronzino, E Viberti, 1999*

7 Aftershave 1★ 6b+ 20m
Biting! *B Viberti, B Ronzino, E Viberti, 1999*

8 La Gina 2★ 6c+ 25m
A cruxy crimpy red wall; then easier over the roof.
L Salsotto, A Langenbach, 2011

9 Ragh 2★ 6b 17m
A technical wall climb. *B Viberti, B Ronzino, E Viberti, 1999*

10 Amita 3★ 6a 25m
A mountain-style crack; love it or hate it. *C + Y Remy, 2003*

11 Octopodi 3★ 5c+ 20m
Surprisingly nice on tufas and jugs.
Routes #11-#15: B Viberti, B Ronzino, E Viberti, 1999

12 Privato 3★ 5b+ 20m
Steep but excellent: every hold is a jug.
Tricky to clip the anchor.

13 Luna Calante 2★ 5c 18m
Technical. The further right, the easier.

14 Luna Calante Ext 1★ 6a 25m
A run-out extension, easier from the right using the corner.

15 Baby 1★ 5c+ 15m
Poor, short, one hard move and a bit loose.

16 Tabacco e Venere 3★ 6a+ 20m
Always difficult, always technical. Hard for the grade.

17 Il Soffio de Eolo 3★ 6b+ 25m
A fingery wall with an impressive black tufa higher up.

18 Charybdis 1★ 7a 27m
Fingery, on sometimes sharp and painful crimps.
F Heinicke, A Riemer 2005

19 Wetterlluchten 2★ 6c 23m
Wall with a hard mid-section. *F Heinicke, A + C Riemer 2007*

20 Pipo 3★ 6b 20m
A wide crack leads to tough laybacking through the bulges.
C + Y Remy, 2003

21 Coky 3★ 6c 20m
Tough but nice on small, sharp pockets. *C + Y Remy, 2003*

22 Nikita 2★ 6c+ 17m
A fingery wall with a hard, tricky finale.

23 L'Orsetto 2★ 6c 17m
The sharp and sustained wall.

24 Sherpani 2★ 6b 22m
A sharp but well-pocketed wall.

25 Task Force 2★ 7c 21m
Steep on good pockets, hard and fingery, then eases off.

Climber on 'Tabacco e Venere' 6a+.

45 SAINT PHOTIS

36.968861
26.934604

GRADE RANGE	up to 5b+	5c to 6a+	6b to 7a	7a+ to 7c	7c+ and up
No. OF ROUTES	0	15	21	13	12

Saint Photis is a quaint whitewashed chapel on the southwest coast of Kalymnos, with a crag of the same name towering next to it. Sector **Saint Photis** was originally created by the Remy Brothers in 2002, and more recently acquired new hard lines equipped by Simon Montmory, automatically elevating this charismatic crag to new heights, as one might say.

As importantly, perhaps, Simon and this author voluntarily rebolted most of the old lines at sector **Saint Photis**. The old lines were equipped with FIXE bolts from 2002 with AISI-303 stainless steel, which is not suitable for marine environments.

The setting of both crag and chapel is beautiful and peaceful, on a secluded balcony overlooking the sea in the area of Kandouni.

The crag features four distinct sub-sectors: **View of Chapel** (left of the little white chapel), **Chapel Wall** (just to the right of the chapel), **Icare** (in the background, above and to the right) and **Spiders** (the far right wall at the same level with the church).

Sector **Saint Photis** is often energized by a cool sea breeze, and after climbing you can relax in the chapel's courtyard and use water from the well to make coffee.

Perfect timing: Simon Montmory on "Kardamo" 8a (page 337) as the Olympic Air turboprop takes off from the Kalymnos airport.
FRED LABREVEUX

45 SAINT PHOTIS
VIEW OF CHAPEL

36.968861
26.934604

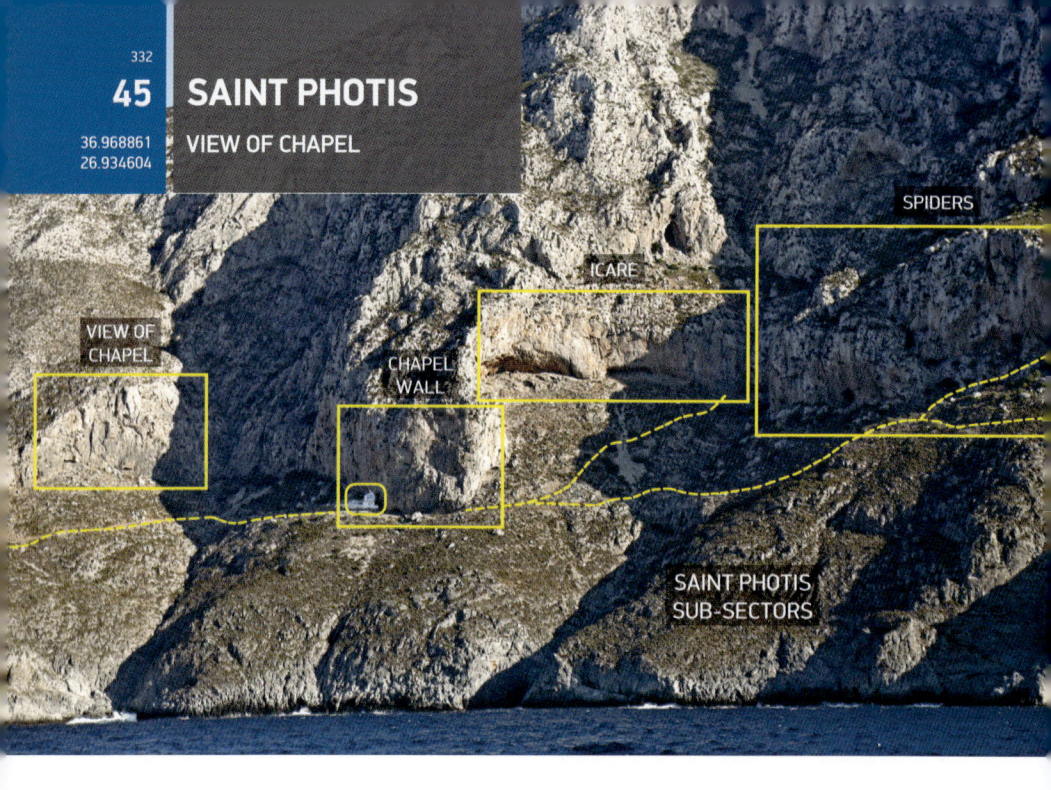

Climbing: On vertical walls and relatively high-quality rock. In the upper section in the big cave with stalactites are some top-quality hard routes at absurdly overhanging angles. The hardest routes were graded by Alexander Megos, who flashed or climbed most of them on his second go. So they may actually be even slightly harder, since he is one of the two climbers with the best onsight in the world (9a at the time of writing...!)

Conditions: Good for year-round climbing, except on very hot or humid summer days. The routes in Icare Cave are also protected from the rain.

Shade: Until 13:30 at View of Chapel; until 14:30 at Chapel Wall; until 14:30 inside Icare Cave (or 13:30 on the wall to the right of the cave and at routes #17 + #18); until 16:30 at Spiders; all day at Spiders Left.

Exposure: W

Kids: The path is good and enjoyable (though long), but the only area suitable for kids is the courtyard outside the little whitewashed church.

Approach: From Masouri, drive to Kandouni beach and park there (36.968861, 26.934604). Alternatively, you can take the Masouri-Pothia bus, which makes a stop at Kandouni. As you face the water, go to the left end of the beach (south). A smooth and very scenic path starts there. The path goes to the chapel of St. Photis parallel to the sea. (The chapel is not visible at this point.) Walk along the path for approximately 25 min, or 2km. At some point the path splits (there is a cairn). Continue straight ahead (the left branch of the path goes to sector Monastery). Walk another 10 min, until you arrive at the tiny white chapel, then to sub-sectors View of Chapel and Chapel Wall. Sub-sector Icare is around the corner to the right (5 more minutes; steep). **Walking time**: 35 min.

See also: Crag Panorama on page 326.

CHRIS BOUKOROS

VIEW OF CHAPEL

View of Chapel is a nice grey wall to the left of the little white church.

Attention: The sub-sector is quite new and routes have not been climbed much yet. It still needs traffic. Some big blocks were dislodged, but in August 2015 Jürgen Rohrmann cleaned some of the routes and removed the bolts from the routes "Mareike" and "Mareike Ext", which used to be between routes #5 and #6. The routes are better cleaned now, but be aware and know that the sector still needs traffic.

Climbing: Good and technical on a vertical wall.

Shade: Until 13:30. **Exposure**: W

Approach: See left. Then, before you get to the little white church, go left. **Walking time**: 35 min.

1 Martin   2★ 5c 18m
A bouldery start, then good bridging. *K Bartetzko, 2013*

2 David   2★ 6a+ 20m
Climbing on the edge. *K Bartetzko, 2013*

3 Miss Experience   2★ 6a+ 20m
Delicate face climbing. *A Schall, 2013*

4 Paul + Paula   2★ 6b 22m
Technical bridging and wall. *A Schall, 2013*

5 Supernicki   2★ 6a 20m
Pleasant face climbing. *A Schall, 2013*

6 Elisabeth   2★ 6a 22m
Good face climbing. *M Rauer, 2013*

7 Jux   1★ 5c 22m
Similar to #6 but easier; sharp holds. *M Rauer, 2013*

8 Pik   2★ 6b+ 22m
Starts hard. *K Bartetzko, M Rauer, 2013*

9 Faulpelze   2★ 6a+ 22m
Varied, enjoyable climbing. *J Rohrmann, 2013*

10 B.B.   2★ 6b+ 38m
Long, varied and committing. *K Bartetzko, 2013*

45 SAINT PHOTIS
CHAPEL WALL

36.968861
26.934604

Chapel Wall is a pretty natural balcony overlooking the sea, with vertical brown rock on the left and a grey pillar on the right.

Climbing: On a vertical wall of relatively good quality. The brown rock can sometimes feel soapy or slippery.

Shade: Until 14:30. **Exposure**: W

Approach: See previous page. The cliff is just to the right of the white chapel. **Walking time**: 30 min.

1 Danone   2★   6b 27m
An intimidating and sustained wall. Sometimes greasy. C + Y Remy, 2002

2 Diablerets   2★   6a+ 27m
A hard start. This was the Remy Brothers' first route in Kalymnos, dedicated to their climbing club in Switzerland. C + Y Remy, 2002

3 Omega   2★   6c 25m
A good wall climb; quite fingery. C + Y Remy, 2002

4 Picorama   2★   7a+ 25m
A steep start and a demanding final wall on good orange rock. C + Y Remy, 2002

5 George Livanos   1★   6a 40m
Long and a bit loose with spaced bolts. Dedicated to the famous French climber of the 1950s and '60s who was originally from Greece. A 70m rope is just enough if you belay from the level of the 1st bolt. Don't forget to tie a knot at the end of the rope. C + Y Remy, 2003

6 Kalenka   1★   6a+ 40m
A 70m rope is just enough if you belay from the level of the 1st bolt. Don't forget to tie a knot at the end of the rope. C + Y Remy, 2003

CHAPEL WALL

335

Watching Simon Montmory climb "Diablerets" 6a+.

45 SAINT PHOTIS
ICARE (LEFT)

36.968861
26.934604

Alex Megos on "Pro Bro" 8b+. SAM BIÉ

Here's Alex again on "Beginner Sis" 8b. SAM BIÉ

Icare is a bit further up and to the right of the white chapel. It is a zone of Kalymnian-quality rock, i.e. excellent, with a large cave and vertical walls. The cave is "Megos-Land": it features out-of-this-world lines for those comfortable in the 7c-8c range, and the limestone walls are good for technical routes mainly between 6a-7c, but some hard 8th grade lines are also to be found here.

Climbing: Mostly hard, on a technical vertical wall and a cave with rock of superb quality.

Shade: Until 15:00 inside the cave; until 13:30 on the wall to the right. **Exposure**: W

Approach: See page 332. After the little white chapel, walk up and to the left.

Walking time: 35 min.

ICARE LEFT

1. Anarrihisi — 2★ 7a 40m
A nice, long wall and slab climb. *S Montmory, 2012*

2. To Doraki — 3★ 7c 25m
Beautiful rock and a little surprise! *S Montmory, 2012*

3. Want a Beautiful Life — ♪ 8a+ 25m
A perfect wall with superb holds and moves!
S Montmory, 2012

4. Mal au Cœur — ♪ 8b+ 35m
Another very steep and fun climb. *S Montmory, 2012*

5. Beginner Sis — ♪ 8b 20m
S Montmory, G Kopalides, 2012

6. Pro Bro — ♪ 8b+ 35m
The extension of "Beginner Sis". Very steep!
Maybe even harder. *S Montmory, G Kopalides, 2012*

7. Les Mains Oranges — ♪ 8b+ 35m
A steep climb with an amazing orange headwall. One of the best in its grade, though the grade may be harder. *S Montmory, 2012*

8. No Remorse — 3★ 8a+ 15m
Bouldery, sustained, and committing until the very end.
B Girardin, C + Y Remy, 2007

9. Sans Le Figuier — 3★ 8a+ 30m
Extension of "No Remorse". Again, a fantastic athletic line with fun climbing and an interesting finale.
S Montmory, 2012

10. Bye Bulli — ♪ 8a+ 30m
A bouldery start, then easier. *S Montmory, 2012*

11. Kardamo — ♪ 8a 30m
A stellar endurance route. The start is weird; best to pre-clip the first two QDs. *S Montmory, 2012*

45 SAINT PHOTIS
ICARE (RIGHT)

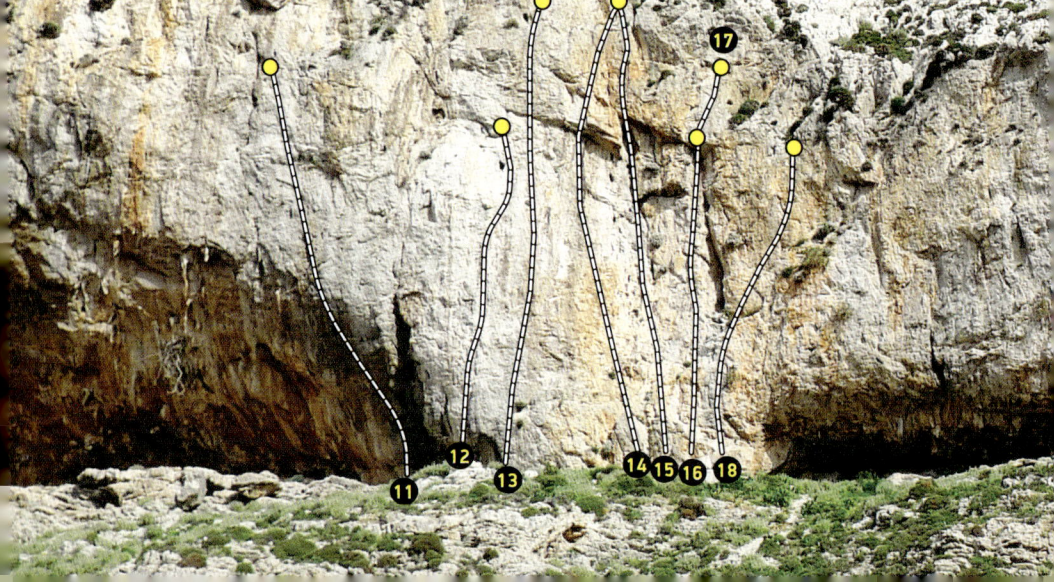

36.968861
26.934604

The man himself, Simon Montmory, on "Kardamo" 8a (page 337). CHRIS BOUKOROS

ICARE RIGHT

12 Icare ♪ 7a+ 20m
The sub-sector's namesake is a short but fabulous climb, with moves on a steep wall and on smooth holds. *C + Y Remy, 2002*

13 Eftace 2★ 7c 25m
An interesting wall and slab climb. Well-bolted. *S Montmory, 2012*

14 Erag 1★ 7a 25m
Strenuous moves on crimps and a hard, bouldery crux. *C + Y Remy, 2002*

15 Cartier 3★ 6a+ 25m
Excellent and varied. *C + Y Remy, 2002*

16 Antarctic 2★ 6a 20m
The crack and small overhang. Not bad! *C + Y Remy, 2002*

17 Antarctic Ext 1★ 6c 30m
The extension pitch is short and bouldery. *S Montmory, 2012*

18 Hydria 1★ 6c+ 22m
The hard, crimpy headwall. *C + Y Remy, 2002*

19 Bim Bam Boom 3★ 8a+ 25m
An amazing tufa boulder passage. *S Montmory, 2012*

20 Ruhetag 3★ 8b+ 25m
It means "rest day" in German, because it was Alex Megos's day to relax. Ha ha, good one. *S Montmory, 2012*

21 The One 2★ 7c+ 20m
A hard but really cool boulder passage. *S Montmory, 2012*

22 Howl Lala 3★ 7b+ 25m
An interesting...appetizer. *S Montmory, 2012*

23 Boulderaki 2★ 7b 15m
A nice little boulder problem, as the name implies. *S Montmory, 2012*

24 Vikos 2★ 6b+ 27m
Worthwhile all the way on good orange and white rock. *C + Y Remy, 2003*

25 Oups 1★ 7a 27m
A sharp, crimpy climb, but with some interesting moves. *S Montmory, 2012*

26 Captain Corelis 2★ 7a 27m
The technical wall. *C + Y Remy, 2003*

27 L'Endurance 1★ 7a 27m
The crimpy wall leads to a sometimes sharp crack. *C + Y Remy, 2003*

28 Primo 2★ 6b 27m
Unusual for Kaly; follow the crack + corner. *C+Y Remy 2003*

29 Speckknödel 2★ 5c 20m
Pleasant easy climbing. *A Schall, 2013*

30 Iki Kampai 2★ 6b+ 24m
One hard move in the middle. *J Rohrmann, 2013*

45 SAINT PHOTIS

340
36.968861
26.934604

SPIDERS

SPIDERS LEFT

SPIDERS MIDDLE

Spiders is a very peaceful place with a unique view to the south face of Telendos.

Climbing: On vertical or slightly overhanging white and brown rock, with smooth, sometimes slippery holds.

Shade: Until 16:00-16:30. **Exposure**: NW

Approach: See page 332 for the path to Saint Photis. When you get to the chapel, don't go left to the cave but follow the main path. You will see a cairn and red marks on a little path to your left. Follow the marks to the cliff.

Walking time: 40 min.

SPIDERS RIGHT

1. Isihia — 3★ 6b+ 25m
Really nice after the 2nd bolt. For safety, re-clip the 2nd bolt from the route to the right. *S Montmory, 2015*

2. Sweat and Dust — 2★ 6b 25m
Hard to onsight, as it is on unusual white rock. *S Montmory, 2015*

3. Wish You Were Here — 2★ 6b+ 35m
Use a long sling or QD at the middle part to avoid rope drag. *S Montmory, 2015*

4. Shade — 2★ 6a+ 35m
S Montmory, 2015

5. Alberto Dubito — 2★ 6c 35m
Good climbing on a steep, crimpy pillar. *S Montmory, 2015*

6. Iremi — 3★ 7c 30m
An interesting passage on unusual holds. *S Montmory, 2015*

7. Relax — 2★ 7b+ 30m
Bouldery at first, then easier. *S Montmory, 2015*

8. The Story of the TE-6A — 1★ 6a 28m
A technical wall. Be careful, the beginning of the route is always sandy. *N Szawrowski, 2014*

9. Saganaki — 2★ 6c 25m
Starts together with "The Story...", then follows the crack on the right. *N Szawrowski, 2014*

10. La Chute du Calife — 2★ 7b+ 30m
Another technical route. *N Szawrowski, 2013*

11. A Mon Étoile — 2★ 7c 30m
A technical and powerful line. *N Szawrowski, 2013*

12. Utopist — 2★ 7b+ 30m
A steep tufa and pumpy pockets lead to a tricky finale. *N Szawrowski, 2013*

13. The Dreamer — 3★ 7c 30m
Shares the first five bolts with "Utopist", then follows the tufa on the right until a bouldery move. *N Szawrowski, 2012*

14. Afrodiane — 1★ 7b 18m
A bouldery, athletic start leads to pleasant climbing. *N Szawrowski, 2013*

46 PYTHARI

36.955577
26.943662

GRADE RANGE	up to 5b+	5c to 6a+	6b to 7a	7a+ to 7c	7c+ and up
No. OF ROUTES	2	4	3	1	0

Pythari is the name of a stunning, untouched location in the south of Kalymnos, and home to the remote monastery shown in the photo.

Nera is a small sub-sector featuring only 10 routes. There is potential for more routes of all grades. Keep in mind that because of the crag's remote location you will need a full day to get there, climb, and return.

Climbing: On an excellent grey slab on the left and very good, steeper red rock on the right.

Conditions: Best for fall, winter and spring. Exposed to the rain.

Shade: Until 11:30. **Exposure**: S

Kids: A very long approach but good terrain near the cliffs.

Approach: From Pothia, go to Vothyni village; from there to *Agia Aikaterini* monastery, then to *Kefala Cave* via a dirt road. Park there, and follow the trail to *Agios Andreas* chapel. Traverse along very faint goat paths parallel to the sea. You will see the crag on the right. **Walking time**: 60 min.

Alternate approach: From Masouri, drive towards the airport and Argos village. Do not turn right at the final turn toward the airport, but continue straight to the back of the village (SW). Park here: 36.955577, 26.943662. An uphill dirt road begins behind a large gate. Go through and close the gate again. Walk up to the end of the dirt road. At the top of the hill is a chapel. From there, follow the marks down the narrow gorge towards the left/south side of Pythari Bay. **Walking time**: 60 min.

1 Lin Xerios — 2★ 6b 28m
G Hasenfratz, M Burger, M Nolte, 2007

2 Manolis — 3★ 5b 28m
G Hasenfratz, M Burger, M Nolte, 2007

3 Dango — 3★ 5a 28m
G Hasenfratz, M Burger, M Nolte, 2007

4 Frederiki — 3★ 6a+ 28m
G Hasenfratz, M Burger, M Nolte, 2007

5 Linaria — 3★ 6a 28m
G Hasenfratz, M Burger, M Nolte, 2007

6 Hike — ?★ 5c 24m
J + U Friedrich, 2015

7 Sfiri Koftero — 2★ 7a+ 28m
G Hasenfratz, M Burger, M Nolte, 2007

8 Walk — ?★ 6b 21m
J + U Friedrich, 2015

9 Irene — 2★ 6a 18m
G Hasenfratz, M Burger, M Nolte, 2007

10 Kali — 1★ 6c+ 18m
G Hasenfratz, M Burger, M Nolte, 2007

343

47 PSILI RIZA

36.978695
26.947488

GRADE RANGE	up to 5b+	5c to 6a+	6b to 7a	7a+ to 7c	7c+ and up
No. OF ROUTES	0	0	8	6	14

Created specifically for The North Face Kalymnos Climbing Festival 2012, **Psili Riza** was the venue for the *PROject Competition*, with 27 very technical wall climbs equipped mostly by Simone Moro and Jacopo Larcher in 2012. Located above the village of Panormos, the crag has sweeping views across Linaria, Kantouni and the sea; a nice change from the usual Telendos view. If you are determined to avoid the October crowds at popular crags, then walk the hour-long path to this crag to enjoy almost complete privacy.

Climbing: Old-school style, not typical for Kalymnos, on vertical or slightly overhanging walls with small features, crimps, and the occasional tufa blob. Routes need more cleaning, brushing and traffic to improve, which is a bit difficult since the faraway location makes **Psili Riza** a seldom-visited crag.

Conditions: Hot and protected from the north wind. Ideal for winter (routes stay dry except immediately after strong rainfall). Also good for late fall and early spring on dry days with low humidity and and around 15°C.

Shade: Until 13:00 (spring, summer) or until 10:30-11:00 (fall). **Exposure**: S

Kids: Some suitable areas, but a very long approach.

Anna Mikushkina on "Cottero" 8a+/b (page 346). SAM BIÉ

The North Face festival days, September 2012. NIKOLAOS SMALIOS

Approach: The crag is inland, high above the village of Panormos. From Masouri, take the road to Pothia (the main port). Go past Elies village and the big super market ("ΣΜΑΛΙΟΣ") on the right. 300m after the super market, turn left. Follow the main road uphill and park in front of *Agios Panteleimon* monastery (36.978695, 26.947488). If access through the monastery is open, walk to the end of the road inside (past the buildings and up the steps to the right up to the bell tower). Go out through the gate and close it again. Then, turn left uphill and go through a small gate in the fence. Close it again. Follow the path with red marks and cairns. After 40 min, the uphill trail traverses slightly leftwards and comes to the foot of the massive cliff. If access through the monastery is closed, start at the parking lot and traverse rightwards around the monastery until you come to the start of the marked trail. **Walking time**: 60 min.

Yuji Hirayama on "Jonas" 8a+ (page 346). SAM BIÉ

47 PSILI RIZA

346
36.978695
26.947488

1 Sunrise ?★ 7b+/c 25m
S Moro, 2012

2 X Ray ?★ 8a/8b 25m
S Moro, 2012

3 Rewind ?★ 8c? 25m
S Moro, 2012

4 Goofy ?★ 7c/8a 22m
S Moro, 2012

5 Drill Story ?★ 8a? 22m
S Moro, 2012

6 Tizi ?★ 7c 18m
S Moro, 2012

7 Jonas ♪ 8a+ 18m
A fabulous line up a single white tufa pipe. S Moro, 2012

8 Schatz 3★ 7c 25m
An overhang with long reaches on somewhat dirty holes, then a fantastic techinal wall on great rock. S Moro, 2012

9 Whit and Whitout 2★ 7a+ 30m
C Idoux, 2012

10 Matt 2★ 6c+ 30m
C Idoux, 2012

11 Matt Ext ?★ 6c+ 40m
C Idoux, 2012

12 Matt Ext #2 ?★ 6c+ 65m
C Idoux, 2012

13 Full ?★ 7a+ 30m
C Idoux, 2012

14 Kurt ?★ 6b+ 31m
C Idoux, 2012

#	Route	Rating	Grade	Length
15	**Fruit Ninja**	?★	8b+?	25m
	J Larcher, 2012			
16	**Boboule Barquette**	?★	9a+?	25m
	J Larcher, 2012			
17	**Early Birds**	?★	8b?	25m
	J Larcher, 2012			
18	**Le Vent Nous Portera**	?★	8b+	25m
	J Larcher, 2012			
19	**Sandmann**	?★	9a?	27m
	S Moro, 2012			
20	**Cottero**	?★	8a+/b	28m
	S Moro, 2012			
21	**Pumf**	?★	8c+?	30m
	S Moro, 2012			
22	**Jeune et Con**	?★	8a+/b	30m
	J Larcher, 2012			
23	**Il Re della Pioggia**	?★	8b+?	25m
	J Larcher, 2012			
24	**Sexy Grip**	?★	?	25m
	M Bort, 2012			
25	**Melissa**	3★	7c	25m
	A great slab: boulder at the start, then fingers and movement on almost virgin rock. Spaced bolts. J Larcher, 2012			
26	**Camilla**	?★	6c	23m
	M Bort, 2012			
27	**Cialvrina**	?★	6c/+	35m
	C Idoux, 2012			
28	**Dédé Genère**	?★	6b+/c	40m
	C Idoux, 2012			
29	**Ravouette**	?★	6b/+	35m
	C Idoux, 2012			

48 DODONI

36.965513
26.962318

GRADE RANGE	up to 5b+	5c to 6a+	6b to 7a	7a+ to 7c	7c+ and up
No. OF ROUTES	0	3	5	6	0

Castle of Hora

DODONI

A beautiful inland venue, sector Dodoni is in a valley above *Hora* and offers superb views of its medieval castle. *Dodoni* was a significant worship site in Northern Greece in antiquity. In modern-day Greece it is an ice cream brand, so many route names (like "Chocorelo") are a testament to one of the equippers' famous sweet tooth.

Climbing: On sharp grey slabs, gentler red rock and some worthwhile routes on vertical rock.

Kids: Good. Families can combine Dodoni with a visit to the Castle of Hora.

Conditions: Warm and protected from the coastal winds, but exposed to the rain. Good for sunny winter days.

Shade: Until 13:30. **Exposure:** SW

Approach: Sector **Dodoni** is near *Pothia*, the island's main port, specifically on the east side of the obvious little valley to the east of *Hora Castle*. Getting there is a bit complicated, but we will do our best to explain. From Masouri, drive towards Pothia. Before Pothia is Hora. As you approach Hora (just after a large cemetery on your right), there is a small roundabout. Do not follow the main road (which goes right towards the port) but go straight ahead. The road narrows and winds through Hora. About 900m further, there is a school building on the right. 100m past the school, turn left. This will bring you to the public Olive Press (there is a sign in Greek; see photo below). Park behind the Olive Press (36.965513, 26.962318). Follow the uphill alley on your right, until it goes slightly to the right again (approx. 30m further). At that point, continue straight leaving the alley and walking on a well-defined footpath. Again, the path goes to the right 4-5 min later. Do not go right. Continue straight ahead to the cliffs. **Walking time:** 10 min.

1 Maria — 2★ 6a+ 28m
Technical, long, persistent. Not easy to find the best solution. *Chr, C + Y Remy, 2002/03*

2 Theo the Snail — 2★ 6a+ 32m
A squeezed, thin and technical slab. *C Idoux, T Panou, 2010*

3 Anna — 3★ 6a 28m
Good holds when you need them! Don't give up. Superb. *Chr, C + Y Remy, 2002/03*

4 Themelina — 2★ 6b 28m
Steady; one thin pull near the top. *Chr, C + Y Remy, 2002/03*

5 St George School — 3★ 6b 31m
A good technical wall. Big holds on the steep finish on the right! *Chr, C + Y Remy, G Hatzismalis, 2002/03*

6 Chocorelo — 3★ 6c 28m
Excellent sequences up the central groove. A tricky exit; a long reach is helpful. *Chr, C + Y Remy, 2002/03*

7 Gouter — 2★ 6c 25m
An interesting wall climb with good crimps at the crux. *C Idoux 2007*

8 Apple — 3★ 6a+ 28m
Most climbing styles in one route. Long and sustained, with a tricky finale. *Routes #8-#15: Chr, C + Y Remy, 2002/03*

9 Yogo Berries — 2★ 6b 28m
Thin, runout moves level with the small ledge.

10 Dodoni — 3★ 6b 28m
Varied; delicate then strenuous.

11 Parfait — 2★ 5c 28m
Nice climbing on good holds, with a tricky move at the stunning finale.

12 Mocha — 1★ 5b 25m
Needs more cleaning near the top.

13 Game Boys — 1★ 5a 25m
A good warm-up.

14 Stratsiatela — 0★ 6a 15m
A wall, arête and bulge. Sharp!

15 Nuts + Berries — 1★ 5a 15m
The right arête of the wall; fingery and sharp.

49 VATHY

350
36.974754
27.026700

GRADE RANGE	up to 5b+	5c to 6a+	6b to 7a	7a+ to 7c	7c+ and up
No. OF ROUTES	0	1	4	2	0

HOOK

PUERTO ESCONDIDO

Vathy village, also called Rina, is built at the end of a beautiful narrow fjord on the east coast, with limestone walls of excellent Kalymnos-quality on each side. About 100m from the harbor on the left wall is the route "Hook". It begins from the water and goes up a red overhang. A few meters after "Hook" and above the water is Daskalio Cave, where prehistoric artefacts (Neolithic and mid-Minoan) have been found. The cave was used as a hideout and ritual site in the past. Steps carved into the rock lead to the entrance of the cave behind a fig tree, approximately 15m above the water. On the fjord's right wall, as you face the sea, there is a crescent-shaped white cliff visible from the harbor. Three new routes were bolted there by Claude Idoux in 2013 with the help of Aris Theodoropoulos, and the old route "Puerto Escondido" was rebolted and cleaned. Routes here also start from the water, but you can clip yourself in and belay your partner from narrow ledges at the foot of the cliff.

Conditions: The sea is always calm thanks to the narrow fjord. Check each description below for sun/shade.

Kids: Vathy is ideal, as you can combine fantastic swimming and playing by the rocks or the pier.

Approach: From Masouri, drive to Arginonta then turn right onto the road to Vathy. When you get to the harbor at Vathy (36.974754, 27.026700), you will need to rent a boat or use a canoe or kayak. The routes are about 100-150m from the jetty on either side of the fjord.

On the **Left Side** of **Vathy Fjord** is the route "Hook" (about 100m from the harbor) and further in, about 150m from the harbor, is a small but pretty **Deep Water Solo (DWS)** crag.

☁ **Shade**: Until 10:00. **Exposure**: S

Hook   3★ 7c ?m
A 2-pitch project (7c, 7b?). Begin from the water in the middle of the large overhanging red cliff. Belay from the boat, which should be tied not only to the rock, but also with an anchor in the opposite direction to the sea current. If you climb the 2nd pitch, the best descent is to climb a little further for a few easy meters and then walk left to the village. This is better than abseiling, as it keeps your ropes dry. *I Riva, A Gelfi, 2001*

Deep Water Solo (DWS)
Because Kalymnos has thousands of very attractive sport climbs, DWS has not been developed much at all; it's rather something to do for fun on a rest day. DWS routes are between 8-12m high and they are listed below starting from the left of the small cave:

1. Left bulging lip of the cave: 5c
2. Traverse to the right: 7b
3. Roof on the lip: 8b?
4. Small roof, sharp finish: 7b
5. Big huecos: 6a
6. Bulging wall: 6a

Evi Kostopoulou having fun at Vathy fjord. PERIKLIS RIPIS

DEEP WATER SOLO (DWS)

49 VATHY
PUERTO ESCONDIDO

352
36.974754
27.026700

The first part of "Socratic Swimming Lessons". RACHEL SAMPSON

Puerto Escondido is is a crescent-shaped white cliff on the fjord's right wall. Three new routes were bolted there by Claude Idoux in 2013, with the help of Aris Theodoropoulos, and the old route "Puerto Escondido" was rebolted and cleaned. Routes start from the water, but you can clip yourself in and belay your partner from narrow ledges at the foot of the cliff.

Climbing: Technical, vertical, or mildly overhanging wall.

Shade: Until 13:00. **Exposure**: W

1 Tremeur   2★   7a   30m
A steep yellow start leads to an easier grey wall.

2 Bigaud   2★   6c+   30m
A wall, small tufa and crack.

3 Puerto Escondido   2★   6c   30m
A technical grey wall with a bulging section after mid-height. *I Riva, A Gelfi 2001*

4 Taupette   2★   6b   30m
A wall with small tufas and a steep finish on well-spaced pockets.

5 Socratic Swimming Lessons   3★   6a+   250m
A sea-level traverse along the short rock wall on the right-hand side of the fjord. The first 250m or so are long and easy, with a short 6a+ section. To return, either climb back along the wall or swim back into the harbor. *T Chubb, 2002*

6 Socratic Swimming Lessons Ext   3★   7a+   350m
The 2nd section grows increasingly difficult with a series of moves around 7a+, depending on the length of your arms and the water temperature! A low overhang on good holds, a blank corner, and a small cave/chimney. *T Chubb, 2002*

Rosa Duepas on "Puerto Escondido" 6c.
DAVID MUNILLA

50 E.T.

354
36.981285
26.991046

GRADE RANGE	up to 5b+	5c to 6a+	6b to 7a	7a+ to 7c	7c+ and up
No. OF ROUTES	0	3	16	3	4

KOUKOUVAS

MAIN BUTTRESS

E.T. CAVE

One of the best crags for climbing on hot, sunny afternoons, **E.T.** sits in the fertile valley of Vathy near a village called Metochi and it overlooks the fjord of Rina, the sea and the coast of Turkey. From a distance the main buttress looks exactly like Spielberg's E.T., hence the name. (Can't see it? The three caves on either side and at the foot of the cliff form the eyes and mouth, respectively.) Sector **E.T.** features three sub-sectors: **Koukouvas**, the **Main Buttress**, and **E.T. Cave**.

Climbing: Delicate and balancy requiring good footwork on smooth low-angle or clean-cut walls full of good pockets and slots. Powerful, on very steep terrain in the cave. Long, sustained lines with an alpine feel, despite dense bolting. Some 6a-6b routes here are outstanding for the grade. On the 2-pitch routes, descend by abseil. Bolting can be spaced on easy sections of the routes.
Gear: 80m rope and **16-18 QD** are obligatory.

Kids: A long approach but many flat areas near the cliffs.

Conditions: Very cool. Ideal for afternoon climbing on hot days in spring, summer and fall. Make sure you bring a long-sleeved top or windbreaker for belaying. (However, the approach path is in the sun.) Not good for windy days, as it is exposed to all except the south winds.

Shade: After 12:00-12:30. **Exposure:** NE

Approach: From Masouri, drive to Arginonta. Turn right towards Vathy. Pass the col and drive down to Metochi hamlet. At the entrance of Metochi, opposite the football field, take the narrow road to the right of the cemetery. Follow the road to the first junction (~ 400m) and turn right onto a dirt road. The cliff is straight ahead. Park where the road levels (36.981285, 26.991046). Continue on foot along the same road as it gets rough and starts to ascend. Pass behind a stone cistern. Close the gate behind you and walk 150m. Go right and walk uphill along the fence. When you reach a gate, climb over it using the stepping-stones and continue to the crag. There are cairns along the way. **Walking time:** 20 min.

Chloe Zubieta on "Iris" 6a+ (page 356). MAX NANAO

Koukouvas is a compact and well-bolted black and grey wall away from the crowds.

Climbing: Technical and pleasant on a vertical wall full of handy pockets and big holes. Bolted by Claude Idoux in 2012, all routes are well-protected.

Shade: After 10:00. **Exposure**: N

Approach: At the 2nd fence gate (see left page), 100m before the Main Buttress, walk 10 more min to the left up an unclear path with cairns. **Walking time**: 30 min.

1 Zupp Le Pinguin — 3★ 6c 25m
A wall with pockets.

2 Ouh Punaise — 2★ 6b+ 25m
A hard wall at the finale.

3 Balla Linda — 3★ 7b+ 30m
Second pitch; an impressive steep slab with a morpho move.

4 Sylvie — 2★ 6c 20m
Fingery at the end.

5 Jako — 3★ 6c 20m
Excellent headwall with slots and small pockets.

6 Manu — 2★ 7a 20m
A steep wall with some hard monos and pocket-pulling.

7 Et Defi Fit — 3★ 6c 20m
Thin climbing on fingery small pockets. Smearing helps.

8 Titi — 3★ 6b+ 20m
A juggy wall with a couple of reachy moves.

9 Paty Fifty — 3★ 6b 20m
A sustained pocketed wall with no easy foot placements.

10 Lin des 100 — 3★ 6b 20m
Nice moves on a steep headwall full of good holds.

11 Le Defi a Lisou — 3★ 6a 17m
A delightful slotted, pocketed grey slab.

KOUKOUVAS

50 E.T.

MAIN BUTTRESS
E.T. CAVE

356
36.981285
26.991046

12 Daisy — 3★ 6b 61m
Multi-pitch (6a 30m, 6b 28m). Pitch 1: A slab full of pockets leads to a clean-cut corner.

13 Anemone — 3★ 6b+ 63m
Multi-pitch (6a 30m, 6b+ 28m). The slab and well-defined wall.

14 Iris — 3★ 6a+ 30m
The perfect, mountain-style, pocketed wall.

15 Orchid — 3★ 6c+ 72m
Multi-pitch (6b 30m, 6c+ 35m). Pitch 1: An amazing wall with "thank God" slots.

16 Ibiscus — 3★ 6b+ 72m
Multi-pitch (6b+ 30m, 6b 35m). Absorbing, reachy and devious. Tricky for the grade.

17 Poppy — 3★ 7b 20m
A very steep, wonderfully sustained pocketed wall.

18 Rose — 3★ 6b 38m
A thin traverse, then pockets.

19 Lily — 3★ 6b 35m
A tricky start leads to easier terrain.

20 Snowdrope — 3★ 6a+ 78m
Multi-pitch (6a 38m, 6a+ 40m). A slabby wall with good holds. 16 QD.

21 Silver Bells — 2★ 6b 35m
Another long, curving line. *D Musgrove, G Peel, 2014*

The **Main Buttress** was first equipped in April 2010 by the inexhaustible Claude Idoux, a resident of Kalymnos who has bolted dozens of good routes. He equips natural lines and dedicates a great amount of time to thoroughly cleaning the vegetation, dirt and loose rock. Unless otherwise noted, all routes below are by C. Idoux.

☁ **Shade:** After 12:00–12:30. **Exposure:** NE

Approach: Previous page.

E.T. CAVE

E.T. Cave features hardcore, mega-steep tufa and pocket-pulling.

☁ **Shade**: All day. There is no wind in the cave, though, so it can be hot and stuffy during the warm months.

Exposure: N

Approach: See page 354. Scramble up to the obvious cave right of the main buttress. **Walking time**: 25 min.

22 Project 3★ ? 25m
Still a project. *L Halsey, 2011*

23 Megalomania 3★ 7b+ 14m
Start on the ledge; a technical crux then steep, juggy climbing on stalactites. *N Gresham, 2011*

24 Rebellion 3★ 8a+ 18m
A lower wall and tufa then a very steep crux sequence on widely-spaced sloping holds. *N Gresham, S Wadsworth 2011*

25 Uprising 3★ 8b 25m
Twisting tufas, crux and headwall. *N Gresham, L Crane, 2011*

26 Tyrant 3★ 8a+ 25m
The classic of E.T. Cave is a great mix of styles. Both pumpy and powerful at the same time. *N Gresham, 2010*

27 Dura Mater 3★ 8a+ 23m
The lower slab leads to a steep tufa and good rest. Then a hard crux and sustained rightwards finish. *N Gresham, 2010*

Simon Montmory climbs "Uprising" 8b. CHRIS BOUKOROS

51 JE T'AIME

36.997302
26.984322

GRADE RANGE	up to 5b+	5c to 6a+	6b to 7a	7a+ to 7c	7c+ and up
No. OF ROUTES	19	13	11	3	2

Sector Je T'Aime is a southeast-facing crag just off the road connecting the villages of Arginonta and Vathy. It's a peaceful crag far from noisy Masouri, with not just overhangs but quite a few easy routes, too, as easy as 3c. Sector **Je T'Aime** presents opportunities for equippers to re-equip and change many of the existing lines; see "Note to equippers" on right page for more details.

Climbing: On rock of medium quality by Kalymnos standards. Climbing is varied on compact vertical or slightly overhanging walls, and there is some slabby climbing on the Far Right Wall.

Conditions: Cool and shady, good for hot days. Protected from the north wind.

Shade: In the afternoon, after 16:00.

Exposure: SE

Kids: OK, if they can make it up the first part of the path (fixed rope). There are some good areas around the cliffs.

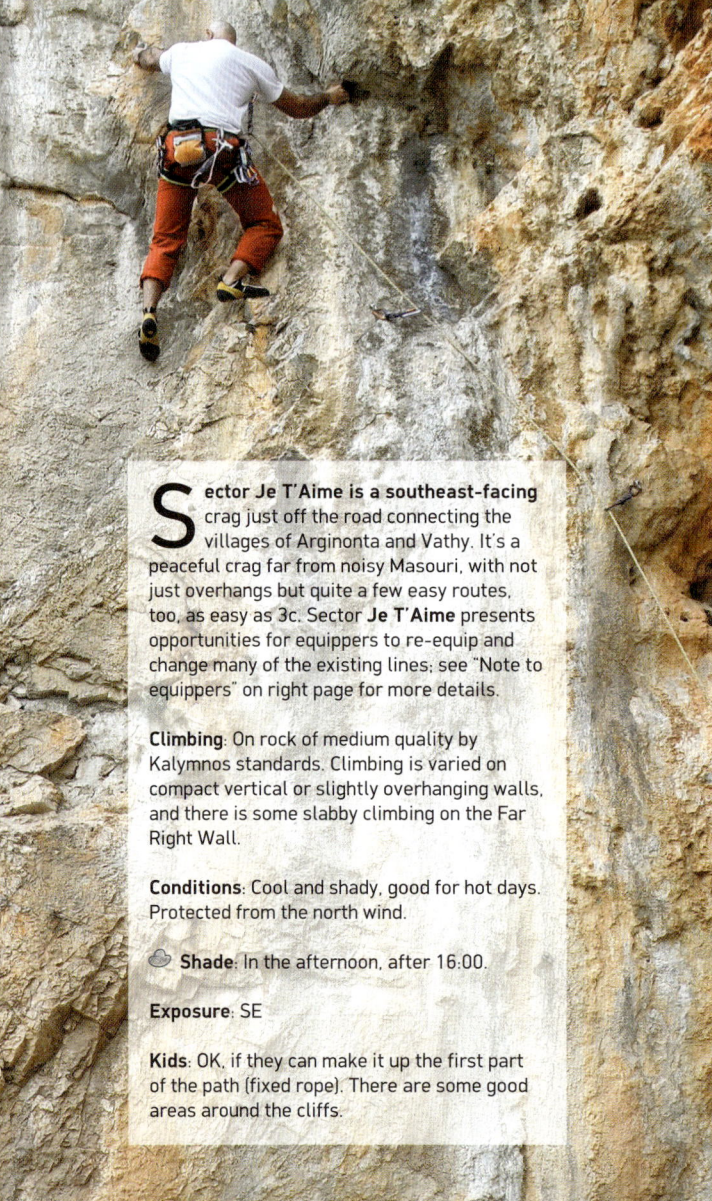

Aris on "Kalytube" 7b+ (page 361). JOHN KOULLIAS

Approach: From Masouri, drive to Arginonta. Then, turn right onto the road to Vathy. Drive to the top of the road then start driving downhill. Park approximately 800m past the col with a hunters' shelter (36.997302, 26.984322). You will see the ciffs on the right. Walk up the fixed rope to the crags. **Walking time**: 3-10 min.

*****Note to equippers**: Many of the routes at **Je T'Aime** are free projects marked with (**??**). Most of these were bolted from the top in 2008 and need to be rebolted (bolts were badly placed, the routes were never cleaned properly, and the bolts used then were of poor quality). If you are interested in equipping lines in Kalymnos, the free projects at **Je T'Aime** are a good possibility. You are free to go ahead and rebolt any of these lines, including changing the line of the route if you want, then make a free ascent, determine the grade and pick a new name for the route. You have the consent of the original equipper, and your name, the route's new name and the grade will replace the original ones.

An official rebolting program was scheduled to be completed in 2015. However, at the time of writing the bolts have still not been replaced. All routes at **Je T'Aime** dating from **2008** are on the list for rebolting. Be aware of this, and please check the condition of the bolts before you start climbing.

Vathy fjord, a stunning place to visit before or after climbing at Je T'Aime. JOHN KOULLIAS

51 JE T'AIME
FAR LEFT SLAB
LEFT WALL

360
36.997302
26.984322

The **Far Left Slab** is 100m further left of the **Left Wall**.

Shade: After 16:00. **Exposure**: SE

Approach: Up the fixed rope, then to the far left.

Walking time: 5 min.

1 Amour   1★   5c   21m
A steady grey slab. *J Friedrich, G Hommel, 2013*

2 Ma Cher   2★   6a+   20m
Fingery slab climbing. *J Friedrich, G Hommel, 2013*

3 Amant   1★   6a+   21m
A steep start, then easier balancy wall climbing with small holds. *J Friedrich, G Hommel, 2013*

FAR LEFT SLAB

Climbing "Kalytube" 7b+ (left) and "Katelis" 6c (right).
JOHN KOULLIAS

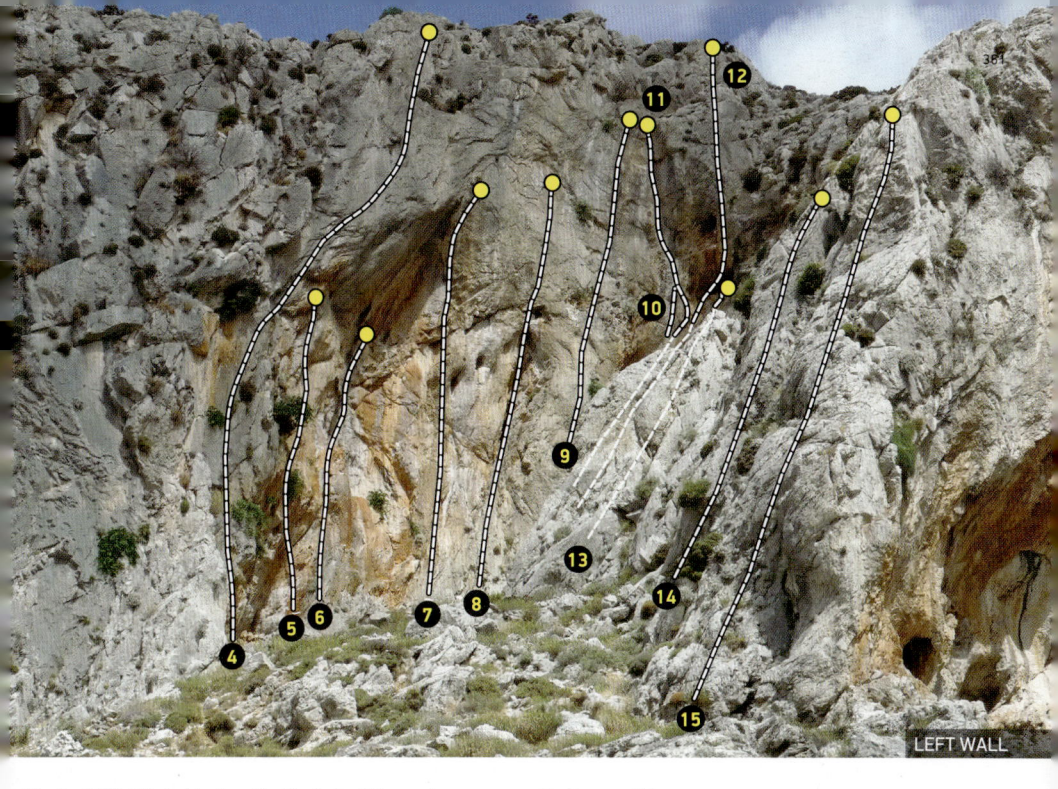

The **Left Wall** is behind and to the left of the main crag.

Climbing: Varied; from slabs, to vertical, to slightly overhanging walls.

Shade: After 16:00 (or 13:00 in the middle).

Exposure: SE

Approach: Go up the fixed rope, then to the left.

Walking time: 5 min.

4 Tas Kebab ?★ ?? ?m
H Orfanoudakis, 2007/08

5 M + P Kuragio ?★ ?? ?m
H Orfanoudakis, 2007/08

6 Hotel Kamari 2★ 6c 18m
H Orfanoudakis, 2007/08

7 Anita ?★ ?? ?m
H Orfanoudakis, 2007/08

8 Nadir Bar ?★ ?? ?m
H Orfanoudakis, 2007/08

9 Paratragudo ?★ ?? ?m
H Orfanoudakis, 2007/08

10 Katman 1★ ?? 30m
A desperate variation of "Kaly Tube". *H Orfanoudakis 2007/08*

11 Kalytube 3★ 7b+ 30m
The orange tube leads to a small cave. Then, exciting moves swing left into the demanding technical groove.
A Theodoropoulos, 2008

12 Katelis 2★ 6c 27m
A good long route, but with a bulging, height-dependent crux. *H Orfanoudakis, 2007*

13 Cherry 1 0★ 5b 21m
Starts on the right of the gully. A nice start, but then poor rock that needs more cleaning and bad anchor placement.
J Friedrich, G Hommel, 2012

14 French Kiss 1★ 5a 27m
A low-angle slab with an easy scrambling finish.
J Friedrich, G Hommel, 2012

15 Nice 1★ 4c 28m
A slab, sadly not so nice, interrupted by some unclean blocky ledges. *J Friedrich, G Hommel, 2012*

LEFT WALL

51 | JE T'AIME
MAIN WALL

36.997302
26.984322

The **Main Wall** is a long U-shaped cliff featuring compact red overhanging rock on the left, scrappy rock in the back, and grey walls and slabs to the right.

Note to equippers: There are many open projects here waiting to be rebolted and renamed.

Climbing: Athletic + steep, also vertical and low-angle.

Shade: After 13:00 (left) or 16:00 (right).

Exposure: SE

Approach: On page 359. **Walking time**: 3-5 min.

1 Cyborg   3★   8a+ 30m
The powerful steep start leads to a marvellous, but testing, orange wall. *A Theodoropoulos, H Orfanoudakis, 2010*

2 Tsila   3★   7c+ 30m
A fantastic line up the middle of the wall. Powerful climbing through steep terrain is followed by a technical wall on small crimps and sidepulls. Not easy to onsight; enjoy looking for the holds! *H Orfanoudakis, 2007/08*

3 We Are the Road Crew   2★   7a+ 30m
Spaced bolts on the wall and overhang; fingery, but a nice sequence. *B Girardin, C + Y Remy, 2007*

4 Vas o Paraskevas   2★   6b+ 20m
An interesting wall climb with reachy, crimpy moves. *H Orfanoudakis, 2007/08*

5 Schizofrenis Dolofonos   ?★   ?? ?m
H Orfanoudakis, 2007/08

6 Ça Va   2★   6a 20m
Not just another 6a slab. *J Friedrich, G Hommel, 2012*

7 Karvelopaido   ?★   ?? ?m
H Orfanoudakis, 2007/08

8 Malamo   0★   6b+ 20m
Poor rock; dirty up the groove. *H Orfanoudakis 2007/08*

9 Erotikos   ?★   ?? ?m
H Orfanoudakis, 2007/08

10 O Erastis Sou   2★   6a 20m
Not just another 6a slab. *H Orfanoudakis, 2007/08*

11 Mavri Kardia   ?★   ?? ?m
H Orfanoudakis, 2007/08

12 MD Sport   ?★   ?? ?m
H Orfanoudakis 2007/08

13 Voilà   2★   6c 22m
An enjoyable wall with a delicate middle section. *J Friedrich, G Hommel, 2013*

#	Name	Stars	Grade	Length
14	Lanterne	2★	6b+	24m

A tough upper red wall. *J Friedrich, G Hommel, 2013*

15 Clan — ?★ 7a+ 20m
F + J Friedrich, 2015

16 Rue — 2★ 6b 27m
Interesting 1st part, then easy. *J Friedrich, G Hommel, 2013*

17 Flower — 1★ 5b 25m
A wall; not very well cleaned. *J Friedrich, 2014*

18 Pip — ?★ 5c 25m
J Friedrich, 2015

19 Cherry 2 — 1★ 6a 25m
A nice start, then blocky rock. *J Friedrich, G Hommel, 2014*

20 Phönix — 1★ 5b 25m
Also a nice start. *J Friedrich, G Hommel, 2014*

21 Fritz — 1★ 6a+ 25m
A tough bulge at 2/3 height. *J + U Friedrich, G Hommel 2013*

22 Helene — 1★ 5a 28m
A short bulge, then steady. *J + U Friedrich, 2012*

23 Flirt — 1★ 4c 24m
Adventurous! *J Friedrich, 2014*

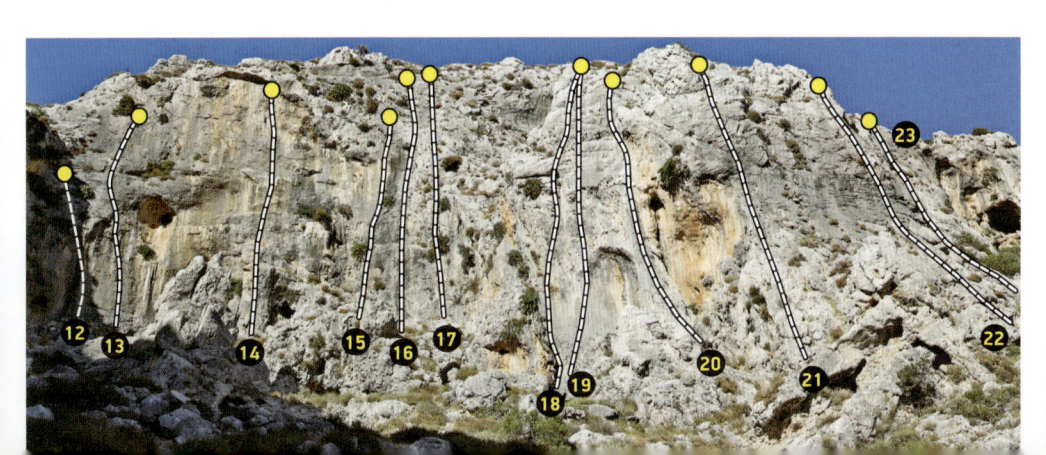

MAIN WALL

364

51 JE T'AIME
FAR RIGHT

36.997302
26.984322

Simon Montmory seduced by "Tsila" 7c+ (page 362). JOHN KOULLIAS

FAR RIGHT

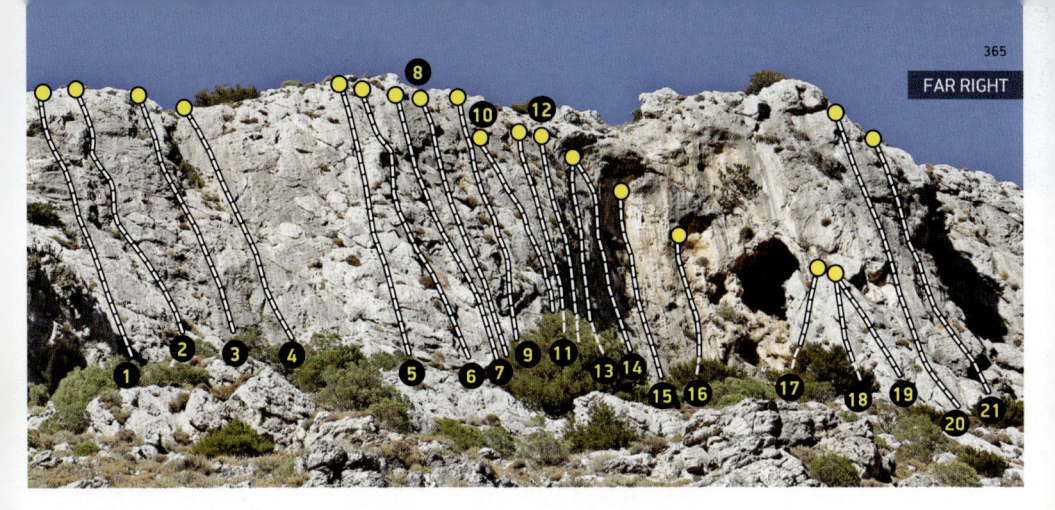

The **Far Right Wall** is a long sheer of slabs and walls about 100m to the right of the U-shaped main cliff.

Climbing: On the left, very low-angle slabs with some suspicious flakes. On the right, better quality vertical grey and red walls.

Shade: After 18:00. **Exposure**: S

Approach: On page 359. **Walking time**: 10 min.

1 Petit — 1★ 4b 30m
Climbing at a very easy angle. *J Friedrich, G Hommel, 2013*

2 Affaire — 1★ 5a 30m
J Friedrich, G Hommel, 2013

3 Sinistre — 1★ 5b 25m
J Friedrich, G Hommel, 2013

4 Ami — 1★ 4b 27m
A slab, not very clean. *J Friedrich, G Hommel, 2011*

5 Dirty Harry — 2★ 3c 35m
A long rib climb. *2009*

6 Magnum Force — 1★ 4b 33m
J Friedrich, G Hommel, 2011

7 Love Me — 2★ 5b+ 35m
Consistent climbing with an interesting pull at the end.
K Kühnel, F Heinicke, 2010

8 Quickie — 1★ 5a 25m
J Friedrich, G Hommel, 2011

9 Brussels By Night — 2★ 5b 25m
Good, but spaced bolts for the grade. *2009*

10 Say You're Sorry — 2★ 5c 25m
J Friedrich, G Hommel, 2013

11 Nordstern — 2★ 6a 26m
A technical wall.
I Bonikowski, E Schubert, A Riemer, F Heinicke, 2014

12 2 Spring — 2★ 6a+ 25m
A steep wall. *G Hommel, J Friedrich, 2015*

13 Mika — 2★ 6b 20m
B Girardin, C + Y Remy, 2008

14 Hilti Sister — 2★ 6c 20m
A hard move to cross the overhang.
B Girardin, C + Y Remy, 2008

15 Fat End — 3★ 6b+ 22m
That's a good name for it. *G Hommel, J Friedrich, 2014*

16 Kiss — 3★ 6a 18m
Short but a good value for the grade. *J Friedrich, 2014*

17 Rachel — 2★ 4a 24m
A clean slabby wall up the rib, with very dense bolting.
A Hedgecock, 2014

18 Grumpy Cavemen — 1★ 3c 20m
An easy leaning slab. *A Hedgecock, 2014*

19 The Sound of the Hound — 1★ 4a 20m
Steady climbing on a good grey wall. *A Hedgecock, 2014*

20 Fortune — 2★ 6a 30m
A long, technical grey wall. *J Friedrich, G Hommel, 2014*

21 Surprise — 2★ 6b 28m
A wall with a bulging middle. *J Friedrich, G Hommel, 2014*

52 JULIAN

366
36.998420
26.992513

GRADE RANGE	up to 5b+	5c to 6a+	6b to 7a	7a+ to 7c	7c+ and up
No. OF ROUTES	11	4	0	0	0

Climbers on "Fraese" 4c. CHRIS CRAGGS

A **grey wall located midway along the road** from Arginonta to Vathy, **Julian** offers alternate views of the islands of Pserimos and Kos and the Turkish coast. By Kalymnos standards it is not a top crag, however the equippers have improved the bolting and it is good for leading easy routes. Still, some routes are squeezed too closely and rock can be dubious at parts.

Climbing: On slabby grey limestone.

Kids: An easy path, but the terrain beneath the cliffs is not good. Keep the kids further away.

Conditions: Warm and sunny. Good for cold winter days or cloudy days year-round. Exposed to the wind.

Shade: Until 10:00. **Exposure:** SE

Approach: From Masouri, go to Arginonta then turn right on the road to Vathy. Drive to the highest point of the road. You will see something like a lookout shelter or kiosk on your left. Park on the turn just before the shelter (36.998420, 26.992513). From there, walk back about 50m until you see a smooth path leading gently uphill, marked with cairns and some faded yellow marks. Watch out for beehives. **Walking time:** 8-10 min.

Meet Julian. Here, he leads "Hessga" 5a at eight years of age. JÜRGEN ROHRMANN

1 **George and Katina**　　　2★　5c 16m
A technical, clean slab with small holds. *O Steis, 2013*

2 **Julian's First Step**　　　3★　5b 18m
A good delicate slab. *J Rohrmann, O Steis, H Wenninger 2007*

3 **Thanks Petra**　　　2★　6a 18m
More technical slab climbing on small holds.
O Steis, J Rohrmann, H Wenninger, 2007

4 **Angi**　　　2★　5c 15m
One hard move at mid-height.
J Rohrmann, O Steis, H Wenninger, 2007

5 **Escorial**　　　2★　5b 15m
J Rohrmann, O Steis, H Wenninger, 2007

6 **Vathy View**　　　2★　5a 20m
Another pleasant grey slab.
J Rohrmann, O Steis, H Wenninger, 2007

7 **Hessga**　　　2★　5a 20m
Good rock with big jugs.
J Rohrmann, O Steis, H Wenninger 2007

8 **SVK**　　　2★　4c 20m
Easy going on good holds. Nicely sustained and well-bolted.
O Steis, J Rohrmann, H Wenninger, 2007

9 **George Fatolitis Studio**　　　2★　5b 15m
At the small roof, look carefully and you'll find the hold.
O Steis, J Rohrmann, H Wenninger, 2007

10 **Netti**　　　1★　5a 18m
Handy flakes on the right.
J Rohrmann, O Steis, H Wenninger, 2007

11 **Fliege**　　　1★　4b 18m
At the slab go right; otherwise, a 5b move to gain the next good holds. *O Steis, J Rohrmann, H Wenninger, 2007*

12 **Fraese**　　　1★　4c 18m
J Rohrmann, O Steis, H Wenninger, 2007

13 **Spinner**　　　1★　4a 18m
A well-protected corner with an occasionally trickier move.
H + J Wenninger, A Hafner, C Schmidt, 2008

14 **Fisch**　　　1★　4a 18m
Another well-protected route for beginners.
H + J Wenninger, A Hafner, C Schmidt, 2008

15 **PB**　　　1★　5c 20m
This route is around the corner to the right. The first 5m are difficult (barn-door problem) with small holds. Descend by walking off. *H + J Wenninger, A Hafner, C Schmidt, 2008*

53 ROCKLAND

36.997195
26.993550

GRADE RANGE	up to 5b+	5c to 6a+	6b to 7a	7a+ to 7c	7c+ and up
No. OF ROUTES	3	8	13	8	0

Hate crowds? Then you will love **Rockland**, a vertical to slightly-overhanging red wall with mid-grade routes overlooking the stunning fjord of *Pezonda*. All routes were equipped by Boris Girardin and the Remy Brothers in 2008-2009.

Climbing: On sometimes sharp, crumbly red limestone.

Conditions: Sunny and warm. Good for cold/cloudy days.

Approach: From Masouri, go to Arginonta then turn right on the road to Vathy. Before the pass, you will see the cliff down left. Park just before the kiosk/shelter (36.997195, 26.993550). Follow the level path with blue marks eastwards until you come to the top of the cliff. Go down to the crag via a large ramp at the left side with a fixed rope. **Walking time:** 25-30 min.

1 Wasp — 1★ 5c 18m
The wall to the left of the fixed rope. *2008*

2 Trudi — 2★ 5a 20m
A slab with plenty of good holds. *2009*

3 Accès — 2★ 3a 20m
The ramp with a fixed rope. *2008*

4 Mum Treck — 2★ 5c 20m
Hard to reach the lower-off. *2008*

5 Amytiville — 1★ 6a+ 20m
Crux at the roof; upper part/anchor same as "Daddy". *2008*

6 Daddy Short Legs — 1★ 6a+ 20m
Varied climbing. *2008*

7 GR 69 — 1★ 6a+ 20m
More varied climbing. *2008*

8 The Book of Olga — 1★ 6b+ 25m
The wall, overhang and slab. *2009*

9 Shantaram — 1★ 6a+ 25m
Varied (and a highly recommended book). *2008*

10 Class Heroes — 1★ 6c+ 25m
The overhang with big holds. *2008*

11 Sex Made Me Stupid — 1★ 6c+ 25m
The wall crosses "Birgit" then goes to the same belay. *2009*

Shade: Until 12:00. **Exposure:** S

Kids: Not good.

12 Birgit   2★ 6b 25m
Varied; stiffens at the roof and remains so. *2009*

13 Howdini   1★ 7a+ 30m
Hard to reach the tufa...then very technical. *2009*

14 Do You Want My Rectification?   1★ 7c? 30m
Easier (but scary) if you don't go straight at the crux. *2008*

15 Fahmîdî   1★ 7a 30m
A steep and tough start followed by wall climbing. *2008*

16 Labor Vincit   1★ 7b+ 20m
The wall and overhang on very sharp rock. *2009*

17 Lefteris   0★ 7b+ 20m
Starts easy then gets trickier; some sharp incut edges. *2008*

18 Olympic Airlines   1★ 7b 20m
Almost everthing, from slab to tufa and steep wall. *2008*

19 OA 136 + 736   1★ 7b 30m
Overhang, then wall; a cruxy intro. *2008*

20 Bitotest   2★ 7b+ 30m
Overhang, then wall; hard start and mid-section. *2008*

21 Panta Psila   2★ 7a 33m
Overhang then wall; crux at the start. *2008*

22 Bokhado   3★ 6c 33m
Steep, on spaced but big holds and a sharp headwall. *2008*

23 Skif the Rock   1★ 7a 20m
Overhang, then wall. *2008*

24 Mikri Gata   1★ 7b+ 20m
Wall and overhang on very sharp rock. *2009*

25 Kee Man   1★ 7b 20m
A very sharp wall. *2009*

26 El Bulli   2★ 6a+ 20m
The steep wall with big, crumbly holds. *2008*

27 Kiss By Death   1★ 6c 33m
More overhanging wall climbing. *2008*

28 Koukourouznick   1★ 6c 20m
Also on the overhanging wall. *2008*

29 Koukourouznick Ext   1★ 7b+? 33m
Goes to the anchor of "Kiss By Death". *2008*

30 Unfinished Project 30   ?★ ? ?
2009

31 Ferran Adrià   1★ 6b 25m
A wall and slab climb. *2009*

32 Beatings Will Continue   1★ 5c 25m
The wall and slab. 6a if you exit left, 5c if you go right. *2009*

33 Until Morale Improves   2★ 5b 25m
The wall and slab. *2009*

54-66 TELENDOS

36.990969
26.931268

Telendos is a small, quiet island opposite the northwestern shores of Kalymnos, to which it was originally joined until a big earhtquake in 554 AD. The channel separating the two islands is 700m across, and getting to **Telendos** takes only 10 minutes by boat from the Myrties jetty (36.990969, 26.931268). At the tiny harbor you will find a lovely hamlet with picturesque fish tavernas and cafes. In summer, the last boat back is around midnight. Life on the island, without asphalt and cars, has its own laid-back rhythm. There are some lovely beaches for swimming and an organized beach for nudists at the northeast end of the island. Lots of quality crags and a few very worthwhile, popular long multi-pitches, are here to add to the sheer pleasure of visiting **Telendos**.

"**Kalymnos is not the only island of interest to climbers here**. The ever-present **Telendos Island** is impossible to ignore and your belayer's head will inevitably be crooned in that direction when it shouldn't be. Like a giant magnet, your eye constantly flicks back to its direction as if it were true north. The cone shaped island is also a sundial by which you measure the passing of the day: illuminated by the soft morning light, you watch the shadows lengthen, and the end of your climbing day is marked by the glowing orange sun melting into the sea behind it. Telendos has incredible new route potential on big cliffs but, with so much to do on Kalymnos, the ten-minute ferry ride has been enough to slow development until recently. Now Telendos has several sectors ready and rearing to go along with some moderate multi-pitch sport routes—which complement the range of otherworldly experiences…"

--Monique Forestier

(Excerpted from Simon Carter's book "World Climbing: Rock Odyssey" and reprinted with permission from the authors).

JOHN KOULLIAS

54 TELENDOS
THREE CAVES

36.990969
26.931268

GRADE RANGE	up to 5b+	5c to 6a+	6b to 7a	7a+ to 7c	7c+ and up
No. OF ROUTES	1	7	12	6	3

Paul Schall on "Totem Pole" 7b+ (next page). GREGOR JAEGER

You can't miss the unmistakable form of the Telendos **Three Caves** as you look at the small cone-shaped island from Masouri. They sit far above the village of Telendos, and naturally a crag was established there in 2007.

Climbing: The rock is not top-quality by Kalymnos standards, however there are some excellent routes here at all levels: some steep routes on holes and small tufas inside the caves, and more vertical routes on the outer grey walls, which can be sharp, though.

Conditions: Good for climbing on summer afternoons, though the long approach is in the sun. Several routes are very well-protected from the rain.

Shade: After 13:00. **Exposure:** E

Kids: Not a good approach (long and steep). But the terrain inside the caves is fairly suitable for kids.

Approach: From the harbor of Telendos, follow the well-marked footpath towards the northern beaches. Walk 100m past the last building (hotel) and turn left (37.003383, 26.924395). Follow the blue signs uphill for 20 min. **Walking time:** 30 min.

GYMNASIUM

Gymnasium is a huge roof, but most of the routes are outside on vertical, sharp, steep walls.

Climbing: Very good, athletic and pumpy inside the cave. All routes were equipped by Gaetan Raymond in 2007 unless otherwise noted.

Shade: After 13:00. **Exposure**: E

1 Dément — 1★ 6c 35m
What the name implies!

2 Princess — ♪ 7c+ 35m
An amazing overhanging voyage on pocketed rock. Elegant moves, progressively harder, just like a competition route.
A Theodoropoulos, G Kopalides, 2007

3 Impossible is Nothing — 3★ 8b? 32m
All kinds of moves in one route, including a one-finger pocket.

4 Un Don du Ciel — 2★ 7b 25m
Beautiful tufas and an easy, overhanging finale.

5 Chaleur — 1★ 6b 20m
A slightly overhanging start and finish with an easy, yet attractive, middle section.

6 Lara Pa — 0★ 6b 20m
Amazing rock on a steep wall, but too sharp for the fingers.

7 Fromage — 0★ 6b+ 20m
Same rock, same pain: like a sharp cheese-grater.

8 Bloody Fingers — 0★ 6b 20m
Continuous difficulty. If you can, climb it wearing gloves!

TELENDOS

374
54
36.990969
26.931268

THREE CAVES (BARBAROSSA, TOTEM POLE, FOR TELENDIAN)

Barbarossa is the smaller narrow cave in the middle. It is much more interesting than it looks; some routes here are hidden gems.

Totem Pole is the lower-right cave with a big column resembling a totem pole.

Climbing: At Barbarossa, climbing is varied and technical. At Totem Pole, climbing is aesthetically pleasing if you like steep routes.

Shade: After 13:00. **Exposure:** E

9 To Kapsouli 1★ 6b 35m
Sharp again. It's better to go right at the top into the gentler white corner. *G Raymond, 2007*

10 Barbarossa 3★ 7a+ 20m
A tricky entry onto the red wall followed by steep but easier climbing through the caves. Two rare slopers just where you don't want them. *A Theodoropoulos, G Kopalides, 2007*

11 Comandante Jorge ♪ 7b+ 20m
The technical vertical wall is followed by athletic climbing on tufas. Slap in those knee bars. *A Theodoropoulos, G Kopalides, 2007*

12 Titi 2★ 6a 18m
Varied climbing on steep but juggy rock. *V Serra di Migni, E Jimenez, 2007*

13 Merinos 2★ 6a+ 18m
Excellent face climbing; not so easy route-finding. *V Serra di Migni, E Jimenez, 2007*

14 Regina 3★ 5c 20m
Good climbing on steep, sponge-like rock. *A Theodoropoulos, G Kopalides, 2007*

15 Reginald 2★ 6a 20m
Strange pocketed rock with a crunchy grip. *F Heinicke, A Riemer, 2007*

16 Summer Wine 3★ 6a+ 18m
Pleasant wall climbing on good pockets. Gorgeous view! *A Theodoropoulos, G Kopalides, 2007*

17 Totem Pole ♪ 7b+ 20m
Very steep finish on big tufas. *A Theodoropoulos, G Kopalides, 2007*

BARBAROSSA

TOTEM POLE

FOR TELENDIAN

18 Roofopoulos ♪ 8a 20m
Athletic climbing on very steep but pocketed rock and roof; superb swings and toe hooks! First RP by the unforgettable Chloé Graftiaux, 2007. *A Theodoropoulos, G Kopalides, 2007*

19 Scooby-Doo 3★ 7b 20m
An easy start followed by a tricky traverse right and a very steep and much harder final section between the tufas. *A Theodoropoulos, G Kopalides, 2007*

20 Viva Fidel 2★ 6b 18m
A cool route on the steep pocketed wall. *A Theodoropoulos, G Kopalides, 2007*

21 Odysseas the Donkey 2★ 6a+ 18m
Steep for the grade, with good holds leading to a tricky finale in the cave. *A Theodoropoulos, G Kopalides, 2007*

22 Kane to Bam! 1★ 6c 30m
You are not here to sleep!

23 Et Bim! 1★ 7a 30m
As above...but in French.

24 Fatsa Karta ston Levante 2★ 5c 25m
The only crack in the Telendos caves. Finish on the slab, not via the crack.

25 Helene the Teacher 2★ 6b+ 25m
A surprising route with big holds to a peculiar finish.

26 Little Fun 2★ 5b 17m
A good route for beginners with a steep finale. *A + C Riemer, C + F Heinicke, 2009*

27 Brutalisation 1★ 7a+ 20m
A very beautiful steep wall, but the name is a clear warning!

28 Gresivaudan 1★ 6c 15m
A slight overhanging start to an easy finale.

29 Mazette 0★ 6b 30m
Again, bizarre rock..but we are on Telendos, after all.

For Telendian is the lower sub-sector, a small gorge. It is dedicated to the very kind people of Telendos!

Climbing: Mostly wall climbing with good, sharp pockets,

☁ **Shade**: After 14:00. **Exposure**: SE

All routes at sub-sector **For Telendian** were equipped by Geatan Raymond in 2007 unless otherwise noted.

55 TELENDOS
NORTH FACE

376
36.990969
26.931268

GRADE RANGE	up to 5b+	5c to 6a+	6b to 7a	7a+ to 7c	7c+ and up
No. OF ROUTES	0	0	2	0	0

Telendos North Face is an impressive north-facing crag, at parts reaching a height of 150m and offering lots of scope for excellent new routes. There are only two long routes here at the moment.

Climbing: Mountain-style with difficult route-finding, despite being bolted throughout.

Conditions: You can climb here year-round.

Shade: After 15:00 for "Gelitokit". After 09:00 for "You Crack Me Up". **Exposure:** N

Kids: No.

Approach: There is no marked path yet. From the harbor of Telendos, follow the path to the beaches on the right side (N) of the island. When you reach the last one, Paradise Beach (the nudist beach: 37.006474, 26.923166), walk up the hillside for about 15 minutes. Follow the ridge above the Three Caves. 400m before you reach the last cave ("Gymnasium"), turn right. You will see a red pillar with two big cracks in front of you. The route "Gelitokit" takes up the white wall to the right of the right-hand crack. For the route "You Crack Me Up", continue traversing to the right along the base of the cliff.

Walking time: 45-50 min from the harbor of Telendos.

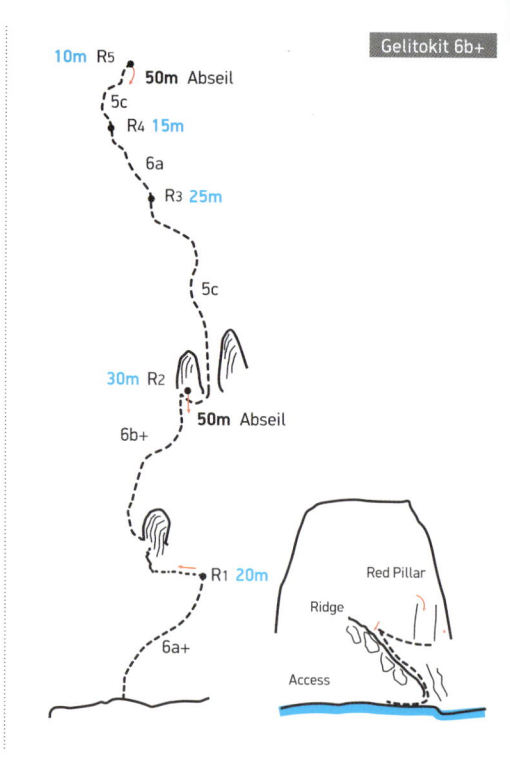

Gelitokit 6b+

TELENDOS NORTH FACE

① Gelitokit   1★   6b+ 100m

Multi-pitch (6a+ 20m, 6b+ 30m, 5c 25m, 6a 15m, 5c 10m). Bolted throughout, but not really sport climbing; instead, a full alpine day out! The rock is loose in places and **helmets are necessary**. P1: Climb the slabby white wall right of the red pillar and a big crack system to the 1st belay in a big cave. P2: The hardest pitch: a big technical overhanging off-width crack to the left of the cave. P3, P4, P5: The final three pitches go up the wall outside the cave to finish 15m below the peak. **Note**: The 4th belay is hidden behind a rock on the left.

Return: Abseil down the route as shown on the diagram.

See also: Diagram on the left.

I Riva, A Gelfi, 2001

② You Crack Me Up   2★   6b+ 130m

Multi-pitch; 6b+ obligatory (6b+ 35m, 6b+ 25m, 6b+ 30m, 6b+ 20m, 6a+ 20m). An obvious crack at the north face of Telendos. Again, a serious route with an alpine feeling. Very consistent and demanding for the grade. You need to be solid for the grade and experienced in these kind of multi-pitch climbs. The 2 last pitches can be linked together if needed. P1: A slightly overhanging, 35m monster corner. P2: A crack with a small roof at the end. P3: A small overhang and big flake. P4: A small roof and slab. P5: Wall climbing. FA by Tiia Porri, Hannes Webhofer (2013).

Gear: 80m rope; long slings; 15 QD; helmet; locking carabiners; cellular phone.

Return: Option a) Walk down "Wings for Life" descent path (2 hours; see next page). Option b) Abseil down the route (80m rope, auto-block knot, knots at the end of the rope!)

Hannes Webhofer, Bruno Schneider, 2013

56 TELENDOS
ST CONSTANTINE

378
36.990969
26.931268

GRADE RANGE	up to 5b+	5c to 6a+	6b to 7a	7a+ to 7c	7c+ and up
No. OF ROUTES	0	5	14	7	5

ST CONSTANTINE SUB-SECTORS

- Underworld
- Descent path
- St Constantine Chapel
- Purgatory
- Falcon Kingdom
- Miltiadis
- Eros
- To Irox
- St Constantine jetty

Saint Constantine is a tiny white chapel amongst scattered medieval ruins on the northeast side of Telendos. Three crags, each quite different from the other, were recently equipped on the untouched, wild terrain surrounding the little chapel: **Falcon Kingdom**, **Purgatory** and **Underworld**.

Climbing: On a smooth technical wall (Purgatory); a sharp grey wall (Falcon Kingdom); and a steep athletic cave (Underworld).

Conditions: Afternoon shade, so it is good for afternoon climbing in spring, summer and autumn.

Shade: After 14:00. **Exposure:** NE

Kids: No.

Approach: a) By boat. Ask the boatmen at the Myrties jetty for transit to and from St Constantine. When you disembark at St Constantine jetty, follow the steep direct path (cairns) to Falcon Kingdom as shown in the photo. **Walking time:** 20 min to Falcon Kingdom.

b) On foot. Start from Telendos village and follow the trail that goes north parallel to the coast. When you are at the level of Falcon Kingdom (up to your left), leave the main path and follow the steep direct path up to Falcon Kingdom (cairns). **Walking time:** 60 min.

c) On foot or by boat following the **main path** going to St Constantine chapel, which is clear and visible whether you take a boat to the St Constantine jetty or walk from Telendos village. Instead of going up the very steep path directly to Falcon Kingdom, follow the smooth clear path that goes past sector Miltiadis, then turn left to Falcon Kingdom and Purgatory or up past the chapel to Underworld. **Walking time:** 30 min from St Constantine jetty.

PURGATORY

Purgatory is a small but quality sector established by Hannes Webhofer in 2014-2015.

Climbing: On a vertical and slightly overhanging wall with Lambda-style rock quality, but steeper and more demanding. Needs some traffic, and helmets are advised.

Shade: After 13:00. **Exposure:** NE

Approach: As for Falcon Kingdom (left page), then continue up towards the left for another 2 min.

Walking time: 22 min from the jetty of St Constantine.

1 Little Wing   2★   6c 26m
An interesting, versatile climb. Gets progressively harder.

2 Stone Free   3★   6b 35m
A long, sustained and adventurous climb.

3 Purple Haze   3★   7a+ 35m
A testpiece with demanding/technical moves all the way on a slightly overhanging wall.

4 Hey Joe   ♪   7b 27m
Starts along a big flake to the right, then a powerful move over a small bulge, and then the fun begins on a demanding wall all the way to the chain! Thank God it's not longer.

5 Foxy Lady   2★   7a 27m
An outstanding versatile climb, except the first two clips.

Yannis Zoidis cleaning at Falcon Kingdom (p. 381). MAURO ROSSI

Italian climber on "Magic Fingers" 8a+ (p. 381) HANNES WEBHOFER

56 TELENDOS
ST CONSTANTINE (FALCON KINGDOM, UNDERWORLD)

380
36.990969
26.931268

Falcon Kingdom is a long band of grey slabs and orange rock with big huecos and small tufas on the right. Routes #1-#8 were equipped by Mauro Rossi, Francesco Vaudo, Ros Gadina and Yannis Zoidis in 2014. Routes #9-#17 were equipped by Mauro Rossi and Yannis Zoidis in 2015.

Climbing: Mostly on technical grey slabs and walls with *very* sharp holds. Routes are very new and holds definitely need more cleaning from sharp/crumbly bits.

Shade: After 13:00. **Exposure**: NE

Approach: See previous page.

Walking time: 20 min from the jetty of St Constantine.

1 Dihedral Wall — 2★ 6b 28m
A nice corner leads to a sharp slab.

2 Piccante Con Urlo — ?★ 7a 24m
2014

3 Monastiri — ?★ 6b 24m
2014

4 Geraki — ?★ 6a+ 25m
2014

5 Trybi — ?★ 6a+ 25m
2014

6 Alisfakia — ?★ 6b 23m
2014

7 Alisfakia Ext — ?★ 7a+ 43m
2014

8 Yellow Scorpion — 1★ 6a 23m
A slab with very sharp pockets.

9 Old Warriors — ?★ 6b+ 25m
2015

10 Trypani — ?★ 6a+ 25m
2015

11 Gruviera — 1★ 6b 20m
A chossy slab, needs more traffic. 2015

12 Petazzone — ?★ 6c 27m
2015

13 Aggeliki — ?★ 6c 30m
2015

FALCON KINGDOM

14 Origano ?★ 6c 25m
2015

15 Panagia Kyra Psili 3★ 6b 20m
A steep slab then a nice orange groove with tufas.

16 Panagia Kyra Psili Ext 3★ ?? 40m
2015

17 Supernova 3★ 7c 40m
One of the best wall climbs. 2015

18 Lizard King 3★ 7a 30m
Flakes, tufa blobs and a demanding slab. H Webhofer, 2015

19 Cratilo 1★ 6a+ 35m
A vegetated slab and wall. G Mallucci, E Galli, 2012

UNDERWORLD

Underworld is the remotest crag on Kalymnos, a "lone wolf" crag for true adventure seekers created by Hannes Webhofer in 2012. The approach is long and exposed, but once there, you will enjoy one of the coolest places on the island with fabulous views and a unique atmosphere.

Climbing: As hard as it sounds! Insane overhanging cave climbing with good holds and some big tufas as well.

1 Out of This World 2★ 7b 20m
The warm-up. Hard to get up to the gigantic flake. Harder if you are short, and best to strip the QDs on top-rope.

2 The Ferry Man 3★ 8a 20m
Steep climbing up a nice tufa to a massive undercling, then right up a crack/dihedral to a bulge with a thin tufa.

3 There and Back 3★ 8b? 20m
A pure line. A wicked technical start gets you to steep tufaland before the crimpy crux throws you off.

4 Hades ♪ 7c+ 20m
A hard-but-doable start up a thin flake and big tufa before a complex move tests your skills; then, a technical headwall.

Shade: After 13:00. **Exposure**: NE

Approach: Adventurous. It takes about 90 minutes to hike from Telendos village in the sun, first to the chapel of St Constantine (page 368), then slightly uphill and left along a narrow, exposed goat trail.
Walking time: 90 min from Telendos village; 50 min from the jetty of St Constantine.

5 Copper Girl ♪ 7c 20m
A steep start (for safety, clip the 2nd bolt first then try the move) then very steep ground with brilliant sequences all the way to the anchor and dense bolting.

6 Magic Fingers 3★ 8a+ 20m
Demanding moves on very steep terrain. Folks loved it!

7 Elena Elena ♪ 8b 20m
A mind-blowing line along the lip of the cave, good jugs at the first clips, then complex technical moves on steep ground. Very dense bolting throughout.

382						
57	**TELENDOS**	GRADE RANGE	up to 5b+	5c to 6a+	6b to 7a	7a+ to 7c	7c+ and up
36.990969 26.931268	MILTIADIS	No. OF ROUTES	14	11	4	1	0

A radiant Renée Guerin on "Oikos" 5c (page 385). BRUNO FARA

Another good addition to the crags of Telendos, sector **Miltiadis** is a grey wall and slab in a pleasant setting to the left of sector Eros and along the trail leading to the chapel of St Constantine. Most routes at sector **Miltiadis** have been equipped by the well-known French equipper Bruno Fara and his wife Renée Guerin from 2009 to 2015, unless otherwise noted.

Climbing: Sustained and technical, on a well-featured vertical grey wall. Some routes, though, have very sharp rock and edges.

Conditions: Good for year-round climbing; climb in the sun or shade according to the season.

Shade: After 13:00. **Exposure:** NE

Kids: Good. The approach is very easy, and the area below the cliffs is well-suited for kids. After climbing, you can walk up to the picturesque chapel of St Constantine (*Aghios Konstantinos*), a further 10-15 min.

Bruno Fara caught in the drilling act. RENEE GUERIN

CRAG PANORAMA
Miltiadis to Pescatore

MILTIADIS
EROS
GLAROS
IROX
PESCATORE

Approach: a) On foot. Go to Telendos village. Follow the path heading north towards sectors Eros, Irox and Pescatore. Then turn left and up onto the path to St Constantine chapel for 150m; walk up to the obvious cliff. **Walking time:** 40 min.

b) By boat. Arrange for a boat to drop you off at the landing spot for St Constantine chapel. Now, just walk along the well-defined path, which turns sharply to the left at some point to the chapel. **Walking time**: 10 min.

c) By boat. If the boat lets you off at sector Irox, take the path up to the left. Before sector Eros, continue to traverse towards the right. **Walking time**: 15 min.

Beautiful, fit, happy people after a full climbing day in Telendos!
OLA BRAHAMMAR

57 TELENDOS
MILTIADIS

384
36.990969
26.931268

1 Rita Restaurant — 2★ 6a 36m
A wall with good sharp pockets. *2009*

2 Sficonis — 2★ 5c+ 36m
A brutal start. *2009*

3 Catsika — 2★ 5c+ 38m
Sustained and fingery. 18 QD. *2009*

4 Emmanuele — 2★ 6a+ 38m
Intricate moves on very sharp chickenheads. *2009*

5 Diana — 3★ 6b 38m
Good character with a steep start. *2009*

6 Creation 2010 — 3★ 7a 38m
A hard, steep wall with small holds at mid-height. Very well-protected. *2010*

7 Et Voilà — 2★ 7a+ 25m
A tough start leads to an easier wall.
M Moulin, N Szawrowski, *2009*

8 Papous kai Yiayia — 3★ 6c 30m
The steep wall between two black streaks. Hard for the first 10 meters, then sustained but much easier. *2011*

9 Sebasti — 2★ 6a 30m
The start is on the ledge below the right cave. A steep wall start is followed by slabby climbing on sharp rock. *2011*

10 Telendos Star — 3★ 5a 30m
A long sharp slab with good pockets. *2011*

11 Ritaxi Boat — 2★ 4c 28m
An interesting final groove, steep and sharp. *2011*

12 Miltos — 2★ 5a 32m
Pleasant, with an unusual finale on the sharp ridge. *2011*

13 Epetios tou Okhi — 2★ 6a 30m
One hard move at the bulge. *2011*

14 Papy Rebel — 2★ 6a 30m
A very sharp slab, and still a bit snappy. Sustained at the lower part, a one-move crux, then easy. *2011*

15 I Aniksi — 2★ 5b 30m
Again, very sharp rock. *2012*

16 Entre Deux — 2★ 5c+ 25m
2012

LEFT

17	**I Dhiakopes**	1★ 4c 25m

Up the sharp groove. *2012*

18	**To Kalokeri**	1★ 5b 25m

A sharp wall climb. *2012*

19	**Xrisostomos**	1★ 5a 25m

A steep start, then slab. *2012*

20	**Pio**	2★ 5b 25m

Again, a steep start then easier. *2012*

21	**Triti**	2★ 5b 23m

Some early sustained bulges lead to easier ground. *2012*

22	**Trentième**	3★ 5a 22m

Nice for the grade, with a few harder moves after the third bolt. *2013*

23	**Harry Potter**	1★ 4c 22m

A Hedgecock, 2013

24	**MILFtiadis**	1★ 3b 18m

A beginner's route. *A Hedgecock, 2013*

25	**Vamos a Samos**	1★ 6c 26m

Inconsistent. The first five meters are hard (overhang), then after going to the left it is 5c. *2014*

26	**Pythagorio**	2★ 6a+ 26m

The start is easier on the right of the bolt line using some holds from "Oikos"; perhaps hard for the grade for a few meters, but after going left it is 5c. *2014*

27	**Oikos**	2★ 5c 25m

A hard start then a grey slab with good holds all the way. *2012*

28	**Astypalea**	2★ 5c 25m

A nice grey slab climb with good holds. *2013*

29	**CVHM**	2★ 5b 25m

An easy start, then splendid climbing on a steep grey slab. *2013*

30	**The End**	2★ 4b 18m

A lovely easy slab and crack finish. *2015*

58 TELENDOS

EROS

36.990969
26.931268

GRADE RANGE	up to 5b+	5c to 6a+	6b to 7a	7a+ to 7c	7c+ and up
No. OF ROUTES	0	3	10	5	2

Eros is a massive limestone amphitheater which rises to a height of 70m at parts and features many new routes in addition to a dazzling sea view. If your plan is to climb at sector Irox but you find it too crowded, head up to **Eros** instead (8-10 min more) and you won't regret it!

See also: Crag Panorama on page 383.

Chloé Minoret on "Eros Telendos" 7b (page 388). ELODIE SARACCO

Climbing: On overhanging, gym-like, pumpy routes in the middle. On vertical or slightly overhanging and technical routes on the right and left. The rock is friendly, with big slotted pockets and gentle on the hands. Most recently (2013-15) Claude Idoux added 12 new quality lines graded between 6a-6c and 32-40m long. Thus, **Eros** now also has the popular mid-grade routes it was missing. The equipping is still underway, so more new lines are expected in the near future.

Conditions: Cool and shady, good even for summer climbing. Not good on very hot, humid days.

Shade: After 12:00. **Exposure**: NE

Kids: There is a natural balcony at the base of the cliffs which may be suitable for kids. However, if you plan to bring kids along, the best way to come is to take the boat to Irox and walk from there (see option "c" below).

Approach: a) From Telendos village, follow the coastal path north towards sectors Irox and Pescatore. At the point where the path makes a sharp left turn uphill (to the chapel of St Constantine), you continue straight ahead. Follow the waymarks for 10 more minutes. **Walking time**: 45 min.

b) Arrange for a boat to drop you off at the landing spot for St Constantine chapel. Then, follow the well-defined path. At the point where the path makes a sharp left turn uphill to the chapel, continue straight ahead. Follow the waymarks for 10 more minutes. **Walking time**: 15 min.

c) Arrange for a boat to take you to sector Irox. Follow the path to the left of Irox. After 3 minutes, the path splits: follow the left branch uphill to sector Eros. (The right branch goes to sector Glaros). **Walking time**: 15 min.

Claude Idoux on "Poka" 6b (page 389).

58 TELENDOS
EROS

388
36.990969
26.931268

1. Zorba — 2★ 8a 35m
Steep first part, then technical and crimpy. *G Raymond, 2008*

2. Kava Aris — 2★ 7c+ 28m
The wall, also technical and crimpy. *G Raymond, 2008*

3. Panagia — 2★ 7a+ 26m
6c obligatory, hard to reach the anchor. *G Raymond, 2008*

4. Aphrodite — 2★ 6c+ 25m
Super-steep and pumpy climbing with two tricky spots. *M Stofer, M Schuh, C Voth, G King, 2001*

5. Ina Lill — 2★ 7a 20m
O K Birkeland, 2015

6. Nymph — 3★ 7a 20m
Steep and pumpy, with fun moves on slightly greasy jugs. *M Stofer, M Schuh, C Voth, G King, 2003*

7. Mira Que Tinc — 3★ 7b+ 20m
A beautiful and varied route with a hard dyno crux on fantastic rock. *C Rossell, D Brasco, 2005*

8. Eros Telendos — 3★ 7b 35m
Athletic climbing on big holds. Incredible style! A bouldery section in the lower half is followed by a crimpy wall. *M Stofer, M Schuh, C Voth, G King, 2001. Extended by G Raymond, 2008*

9. Adonis Telendos — 3★ 7a+ 35m
Awesome tufas provide unexpectedly good holds in the 1st half, then a crimpy, spiky wall. *M Stofer, M Schuh, C Voth, G King, 2001. Extended by G Raymond, 2008*

10. Tremendos en Telendos — 3★ 7b 28m
A technical and pumpy steep wall with sharp rock at the top. *B Puig, D Brasco, 2005*

LEFT

#	Route	Grade	
1	3 Ilots	♪	6c 32m

A pumpy search for a myriad hidden pockets. *C Idoux, 2013*

2 Lucky Eva — 3★ 6b+ 32m
Steady, enjoyable climbing, just a bit pumpy. *C Idoux, 2013*

3 The Fight of a Woman — ♪ 6a+ 40m
A reachy move at the start, then a fantastic pocketed wall; of the best in its kind on Kalymnos. *C Idoux, 2013*

4 Poka — 3★ 6b 40m
A stiff start then an excellent pocketed wall. *C Idoux, 2013*

5 Mignon — 3★ 6b 40m
A steep wall climb full of good holds. *C Idoux, 2013*

6 Grognon — 3★ 6b 40m
Search for the hidden treasure of pockets. *C Idoux, 2013*

7 Ninja — 3★ 6a+ 35m
C Idoux, 2013

8 Il Passatore — 3★ 6a 40m
Gripping wall climbing, pleasantly steep for the grade. *C Idoux, 2013*

9 Tamalou — 3★ 6b+ 40m
A sustained pocket climb. *C Idoux, 2015*

10 Gébobo Là — 3★ 6c 40m
Pumpy and technical. *C Idoux, 2015*

11 Project 1 — ?★ ? 35m
C Idoux, 2015

12 Project 2 — ?★ ? 35m
C Idoux, 2015

RIGHT

59 TELENDOS

IROX

390
36.990969
26.931268

GRADE RANGE	up to 5b+	5c to 6a+	6b to 7a	7a+ to 7c	7c+ and up
No. OF ROUTES	16	5	11	3	3

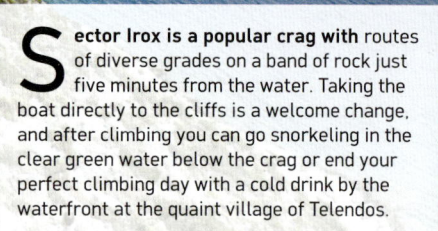

Sector Irox is a popular crag with routes of diverse grades on a band of rock just five minutes from the water. Taking the boat directly to the cliffs is a welcome change, and after climbing you can go snorkeling in the clear green water below the crag or end your perfect climbing day with a cold drink by the waterfront at the quaint village of Telendos.

Climbing: Extremely varied, from pleasant easy-angles to massive overhangs. The easy routes can be sharp, whereas the hard ones offer more athletic, juggy climbing.
Unless otherwise noted, all routes at Irox were equipped in 2007 by Swiss guides Peter Keller + Urs Odermatt.

Conditions: Cool and shady. Good for all seasons except winter. Avoid damp days with no wind if you plan to crank hard.

Shade: After 14:00. **Exposure**: NE

Kids: Good, especially since you can combine it with a boat ride and swim. However, be careful when getting off the boat onto the rocks. Also, beware of goats walking above the cliffs; they may dislodge stones.

Derek Cheng is pretty relaxed on "Magma" 6c (page 392).
OLA BRAHAMMAR

Approach: a) By boat. Ask the boatmen at the jetty at Myrties for transit to and from Irox, or check the back section of this guidebook. It is best to make arrangements in advance, and the bigger your party is, the smaller the fee per person. **Walking time**: 5 min.

b) On foot: Start from Telendos village. Follow the trail going north, parallel to the coast. When you arrive beneath sector Eros, the path splits. Follow the right branch down to Irox (the left branch goes uphill to sector Eros). **Walking time**: 50 min.

See also: Crag Panorama on page 383.

1 Sally's Boat Trip — 2★ 3c 15m
Ideal for learning how to lead.

2 Primerov — 2★ 3c 10m
A short slab, good for children.

3 Captain Jack — 1★ 4a 12m
Pleasant and easy climbing on not-too-sharp holds.

4 Pantelis Sea Jump — 2★ 5b+ 15m
An airy excursion, not without interest particularly at the final horizontal crack.

FAR LEFT

59 TELENDOS
IROX (MAIN)

36.990969
26.931268

5 Cuobo — 2★ 7c 15m
An interesting bouldery start, short but powerful. Easier if you are tall.

6 Aphrodite — 3★ 8c+ 20m
Steep and bouldery. FA by Beni Bilaser, 2014. *2008*

7 Irox — 3★ 8a+ 20m
A "freakin' awesome line". Steep, powerful and reachy.

8 Marmornei — 3★ 7c+ 20m
A bouldery start on tufas is followed by a testing blind headwall.

9 Helvetx — 3★ 7a 36m
Superb but well-spaced holds lead to a brief crouching rest position, before committing to an "easier than it looks" vertical crack to the final roof and spiky finish.

10 Kyprios Angel — 3★ 7a+ 30m
A long and committing line, varied and sustained.

11 More Than Mode — 2★ 7b 27m
A very technical wall with a bouldery crux.

12 Magma — 3★ 6c 25m
A fantastic single-tufa climb. The "expedition" to Irox is worth it for this route alone!

13 Xymox — 2★ 6c+ 18m
Short but tough.

14 The Magic Circle — 2★ 6a+ 18m
Stiff, with a bouldery start.

MAIN

15 Sole Fish   2★ 6b 30m
Nice balancy moves at the mid-height traverse.

16 Swordfish   3★ 6c 27m
Starts with hard tufa pulling, then a sustained grey wall.

17 Hollenfieber   1★ 7a+ 27m
Sharp as hell.

18 Yorkshire Pudding   2★ 6c+ 27m
Good climbing but very sharp and painful at the crux bulge.

19 28 at 40   2★ 5c+ 30m
An enjoyable wall. A bit broken but plenty of good climbing.

20 The White Rose   2★ 6a 20m
A pleasant line leading up to the left side of a dubious block. Step right above it to a tricky finish.
D Musgrove, C + S Richards, 2007

21 Ingleton   3★ 6b+ 27m
A little sharp, but very good moves and position.

22 Dionesis   1★ 6b+ 26m
A few crumbly holds add interest, and a painful top-out tests the resolve.

23 Menecis   2★ 6b+ 20m
Fingery, but good moves on sharp holds.

Souvlaki kalamaki on Telendos. GREGOR JAEGER

59 TELENDOS
IROX (RIGHT)

36.990969
26.931268

Vladek Zumr on "Magma" 6c (page 392). RAINER EDER

24 Evangelia 2★ 5b 25m
Balancy and pleasant.

25 Anastasia 3★ 5a+ 25m
Pleasant technical wall climbing; tricky finish for the grade.

26 Mo An 2★ 5a 25m
2007

27 Memories of Dorothy 1★ 5a 30m
A sharp slab with good holds, but there is some loose rock.
A Hedgecock, 2012

28 Sevasti 2★ 4b 30m
2007

29 Wind Chime 1★ 5a 28m
A short bulge, a scrappy part then a slab. *A Hedgecock, 2015*

30 Evdokia 1★ 5c 20m
A short overhang followed by awkward moves leads to easier ground.

31 Evoula 1★ 4c 20m
The easy but sharp ramp.

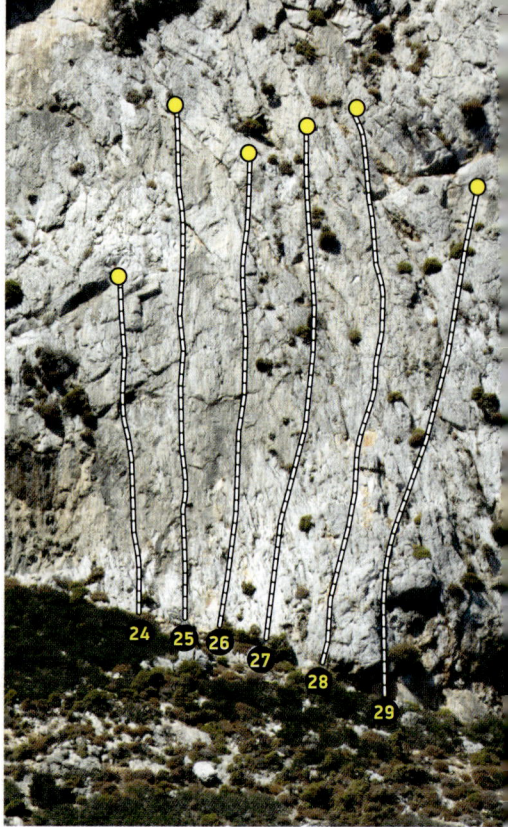

32 Kiriaki 1★ 5a 20m
2007

33 Niki 2★ 5a 20m
A must for every newcomer.

34 Iason 2★ 5b 20m
Stepping left at half-way keeps the route reasonable.

35 Maria 1★ 5a+ 20m
Again, a sharp slab but pleasant climbing.

36 Popi 1★ 5b 20m
A cheese-grater slab with a final tricky step to the right.

37 Taxi Boat 2★ 6c+ 20m
50m to the right and up from "Popi". A steep juggy wall leads to the big hole followed by a demanding shadowy exit.
F Heinicke, A Riemer, 2007

38 Crossing 1★ 7a 22m
A hard start leads to a technical and fingery wall.
F Heinicke, A Riemer, 2007

All routes by Peter Keller + Urs Odermatt (2007) unless otherwise noted.

RIGHT

Samantha Lawson on "Ingleton" 6b+ (page 393).
OLA BRAHAMMAR

60 TELENDOS
GLAROS

36.990969
26.931268

GRADE RANGE	up to 5b+	5c to 6a+	6b to 7a	7a+ to 7c	7c+ and up
No. OF ROUTES	2	2	6	4	5

Another stunning crag on Telendos, Glaros is situated on a natural north-facing balcony and features some gems in the harder grades and unique rock with ledges and smooth holds.

Climbing: On the left, a smooth grey wall with easier routes but unique features for the grade, like slopers and downward holds. In the middle, slightly overhanging climbing on solid white tufa pipes. And on the right, a smooth 45-degree overhanging cliff with white, orange + black stripes. Huge holds, but.how long can you *really* last at the angle?

Conditions: Cool and shady all day. Not good on humid days with no wind or on days after rainfall.

Shade: Until 17:00 far left; all day everywhere else. **Exposure:** N

Kids: No. Risky approach and sloping terrain beneath the cliffs.

Approach: a) **By boat via sector Irox**. Follow the path to the left of Irox for 3 minutes, until it splits. Follow the right branch along an exposed ledge above Irox. You will soon come to a fixed rope: use that to go up to the balcony of Glaros. **Walking time**: 15 min from Irox.

b) **On foot**: Start from Telendos village. Follow the trail going north, parallel to the coast. When you arrive beneath sector Eros, the path splits. Follow the right branch down to Irox. Shortly before Irox, follow a ledge with cairns and marks up to Glaros. **Walking time**: 60 min.

See also: Crag Panorama on pages 383 and 403.

Chloé Minoret climbs "Maylen" 7b. ELODIE SARACCO

1 Dirty Dog — 3★ 5a 25m
Consistently interesting. Good footwork is a plus.

2 Heather — 2★ 5b+ 25m
Just pleasant.

3 Claudia — 3★ 5c+ 25m
A tricky crux.

4 Ingvild — 3★ 6a+ 25m
Unusual climbing on a nicely slotted wall.

5 I-Climber — 2★ 6b+ 30m
Athletic for the grade.

6 Kyra — 2★ 6b+ 25m
Intimidating for the grade, but good holds appear when you need them.

7 PhanX — 2★ 6b 25m
An interesting wall with good holds.

8 Laruna — 3★ 6b+ 25m
Another brilliant juggy parade.

9 Schiza — 3★ 7a 25m
The sustained and tricky wall with a demanding bulge/exit.

10 Contador — 3★ 7a 20m
A spectacular tufa climb with some big but hard-to-reach jugs.

11 Contador Ext — 2★ 7a+ 25m
A tricky boulder problem. Can you hook?

12 Maylen — 3★ 7b 30m
The smooth black line on a 45° overhang on huge jugs. Very slippery in wet conditions.

13 Breakfast on Pluto — 3★ 7c+ 30m
Very powerful and aggressive; good fun, but only when there is no seepage.

14 Glaros — 3★ 8a+ 30m
All kinds of perfect holds on a brilliant 40° overhang.

15 Tipota — 3★ 8c+? 30m
A project in the Sharma climbing style.
Q Chastagnier, G Raymond, 2008

16 Apagorevmeno Oniro — 3★ 9a? 30m
Another project which will be very, very hard.

17 Barabuk — 3★ 8b+ 30m
Many hard bouldery moves; fantastic.

18 Storm PU — 2★ 8a+ 20m
A hard boulder problem.

19 Trollgod — 3★ 7b+ 25m
You do indeed need the power of a Troll. Brilliant!

All routes were equipped by Peter Keller + Urs Odermatt in 2008 unless otherwise noted.

61 TELENDOS

PESCATORE

36.990969
26.931268

GRADE RANGE	up to 5b+	5c to 6a+	6b to 7a	7a+ to 7c	7c+ and up
No. OF ROUTES	1	9	16	4	6

Pescatore, a fine wall up to 30m high with large stalactites, tufa pipes and an immaculate austere face, is just around the corner form sector Irox. The beauty of the coastal landscape is further enhanced by the view of Leros Island and the north coast of Kalymnos from a different angle. The absence of houses and signs of civilization is a big plus.

Climbing: The left side features excellent routes in the 5c-6c range on a beautiful smooth wall. Further right, harder routes which often start off with tough moves on stalactites, though they sometimes end on sharp rock of lesser quality. On certain routes on the right side, bolts are not always ideally placed.

Conditions: Not good for humid days with no wind. When the sun arrives you can go further up to Glaros (10 min) or down to Irox (5 min) to continue climbing.

Shade: Until 16:00. **Exposure**: NW

Kids: Good, mainly to the right of the crag.

Approach: a) **On foot**. From Telendos village, follow the pretty coastal trail north towards sector Irox. Traverse along the foot of the cliffs. Where Irox ends, walk up briefly to the right. **Walking time**: 60-65 min.

b) **By boat**. Go to sector Irox and walk up and around to the right. **Walking time**: 10 min.

See also: Crag Panorama on page 383 and 403.

Maria Intze on "Petrula" 6a.

THE MAGIC ROUNDABOUT

The Magic Roundabout is a recent addition to Pescatore, but not a very good one. It is a short white wall with razor-sharp rock; however, it can improve with traffic or if the routes are better cleaned from crumbly sharp bits.

☁ **Shade:** Until 13:30. **Exposure:** NW

Approach: As for Pescatore, then to the left up a gully with scree (see page 403). **Walking time**: 13 min.

1 G.T.C.   1★   6a+ 20m
A fingery wall with a hard bulge on prickly, crumbly rock.

2 Mr Rusty   0★   6c 20m
Similar to #1 with a harder bulge. Watch out for the big suspicious flake at the end with a bolt on it (last one before the anchor).

3 The Magic Roundabout   2★   6b 20m
Well-bolted and nice climbing on vertical flakes. Can use more traffic/cleaning.

4 Lucia   0★   7a 20m
A bouldery start on razor-sharp holds.

5 Brian the Snail   1★   6b 20m
A bulge not well-protected, then a fingery sharp wall.

PESCATORE LEFT PILLAR

The nice **Left Pillar** of Pescatore features excellent varied climbs from 5c-6c and up to 30m long. Approach as described on left page.

☁ **Shade:** From 11:00-16:00. **Exposure:** NE

1 Pelagia   3★   6b+ 25m
Athletic start, tufa, wall and crack; a fascinating climb.
V Serra Di Migni, 2014

2 Vendetta   3★   6b 30m
A weaving, steep line with big holds and a tremendous finale on compact rock. *B Fara, R Guerin, 2011*

3 Petrula   1★   6a 35m
A hard final wall. *2012*

4 Lucas Bad Boy   2★   5c 32m
Well-protected crux on the the intimidating final wall.
B Fara, R Guerin, 2008

5 Hot Roc   3★   5c 32m
Exposed and impressive for the grade. Gets harder as you go, so it makes an excellent warm-up. *B Fara, R Guerin, 2008*

6 Agelica Babis Bar   3★   6b+ 30m
The wandering line up the steep orange wall offers dance-like moves. *B Fara, R Guerin, 2008*

61 TELENDOS
PESCATORE (MAIN)

400
36.990969
26.931268

7 Farabutto   2★ **6c+ 25m**
A fingery grey wall leads to a crimpy boulder on the slightly overhanging orange wall. *C Idoux, L Salsotto, 2009*

8 Forza 99   2★ **6b 25m**
Good moves up the mid-height wall. *G Mallucci, E Galli, 2008*

9 Karabolas   2★ **6a 28m**
A neat slab requiring good footwork, with a tough crux at the start. *V Serra di Migni, 2007*

10 Rita   3★ **6a 28m**
A fingery and sustained slab with excellent tiny holds; one of the best in this style. *V Serra di Migni, 2007*

11 A l'Ovest di Kaboul   3★ **6a+ 28m**
A technical and sustained slab with an intriguing finale. *G Mallucci, E Galli, 2008*

12 Leane   3★ **6a+ 30m**
A pleasant line up the orange groove. Constant effort needed from bottom to top. *B Fara, R Guerin, 2008*

13 Axel   3★ **6a 20m**
Very pleasant for the grade, with some thin moves. *B Fara, R Guerin, 2008*

14 Easy   2★ **5b 20m**
A warm-up for this sector. *G Mallucci, E Galli, 2008*

15 Adios Chloé   2★ **6c 32m**
Dedicated to Chloé Graftiaux. *V Serra di Migni, 2010*

16 Zoidis   3★ **8a 25m**
Boulder problem at the beginning, then a beautiful single tufa with a sloppy exit. The final boulder is a bit easier, but reachy! *V Serra di Migni, 2010*

17 Amores Perros   3★ **7c+ 25m**
A stellar line with great technical climbing on a slightly overhanging, smooth wall blessed with small tufas and concretions. *G Kopalides, 2007*

18 Il Y Avait de Laure Dans ma Vie   3★ **8c+? 30m**
Very technical and bouldery wall with tiny holds and bad crimps. Somewhat engaged bolting. *T Anquetil, 2010*

19 Aegena   3★ **8a 25m**
A beautiful, arched orange wall with two distinct sections. *S Montmory, 2008*

Chloé Minoret bridges on the huge stalactites of "Y Viva Pancho Villa!" 7a. ELODIE SARACCO

PESCATORE MAIN

20 Queen Potha — 3★ 8a+ 25m
An amazing route with a hard boulder problem on beautiful rock. *S Montmory, 2008*

21 Scooter Fun — 2★ 8a? 20m
The huge stalactite followed by a desperate wall with small crimps. *Q Chastagnier, 2008*

22 Miltiadis — 3★ 7b 20m
A full-body fight to reach the tufa...then very technical, with a sustained finish. *S Montmory, V Serra di Migni, 2008*

23 Y Viva Pancho Villa! — 3★ 7a 15m
A bouldery start and bridging on huge stalactites! *V Serra di Migni, 2008*

24 Aboneros el Chilli — 3★ 7b 20m
A hard start; are you flexible for some good stalactite action? *V Serra di Migni, 2007*

25 Padelis — 3★ 7b+ 20m
A steep tufa masterpiece which only succumbs to an intense fight. Some bolts feel poorly positioned. *V Serra di Migni, E Jimenez, G Kopalides, 2007*

26 Zorba's Restaurant — 3★ 7a+ 15m
A powerful start, then a technical stalactite-corner. *V Serra di Migni, 2008*

27 OTR — 3★ 7a 25m
Some tufa wrestling and hugging followed by technical moves on water pockets. The finale is sharp and the bolting isn't great. *V Serra di Migni, E Jimenez, G Kopalides, 2007*

28 Tequischiapan — 3★ 7a 20m
More great tufa climbing leads to a tricky headwall. It is possible to finish either left or right of the bolts... but which is easier? *V Serra di Migni, 2007*

29 Plaka — 0★ 6c 18m
A fingery wall climb with just one hard move...really hard. Bad bolting. *V Serra di Migni, 2008*

30 Issili — 1★ 6c 18m
A technical wall with a hard finish. Bad bolting. *V Serra di Migni, E Jimenez, G Kopalides, 2007*

31 Mafalda — 3★ 6b 15m
An excellent warm-up on small tufas with a tricky finish. At the exit, think laterally. *V Serra di Migni, E Jimenez, G Kopalides, 2007*

62 TELENDOS
LAMBDA

36.990969
26.931268

GRADE RANGE	up to 5b+	5c to 6a+	6b to 7a	7a+ to 7c	7c+ and up
No. OF ROUTES	11	12	15	3	0

Lambda is a sublime crag in Telendos, far above the sea, with about 40 fantastic extra-long routes up to 50m on vertical or slightly overhanging rock of outstanding quality. The concentration of first-class climbs at **Lambda** is very high, and some routes here are probably among the best in their grade in Kalymnos and Telendos combined.

Climbing: Long routes! Do not come here with anything less than an **80m** rope. There are many 40- and 50-meter long routes, but they are not so steep. Typically, the first half is on sharp grey rock and the second half is on orange rock with well-spaced pockets and big jugs. The rock has surprisingly good friction with positive holds, and it is a little heaven for 6a-6c lines.

Aurélie Lacombe on "Hot Chili Young Love 6c+ (page 404). MAX NANAO

CRAG PANORAMA
Pescatore to Lambda

LAMBDA
GLAROS
The Magic Roundabout
PESCATORE

Gear: 18-24 QD and an 80m rope, **always with a knot tied at the other end.**

Conditions: Morning shade and a cool breeze. Windy in the afternoons. Climbing at **Lambda** combines well with sectors Glaros and Irox.

Shade: Until 13:30. **Exposure**: NW

Kids: Not bad, though the approach is long.

Approach: Go to sector Irox (see page 390). From Irox, go right to Pescatore, traverse past the length of Pescatore to the right, then go uphill along the path marked with blue to the obvious cliff. **Walking time**: 25 min.

Chloe Zubieta on "Lava" 6a+ (next page). MAX NANAO

What does a Swiss banker have to do with it?

A good portion of **Lambda** was equipped thanks to a Swiss banker named Simi. Urs Odermatt tells the story:

"Simi isn't really a climber at all, but as a true-blooded Zermatt man, he loves the mountains. He at least knows the Matterhorn and a few nearby 4000ers fairly well. But instead of learning a proper trade and becoming a mountain guide, he left the heart of Switzerland and moved to the 'province' of Zurich, where he now earns a fortune with other people's money. But his home and his family-run hotel remain in Zermatt.

"Why am I telling you this? Because I met Simi in Kalymnos. We climbed a few routes together, and Simi was fascinated by the incredible atmosphere there. 'Something special is being created here, climbing routes are being hewn out of stone and hard work, bringing enjoyment to lots of people and a source of income for the local people' he says, spontaneously deciding to sponsor a new sector to be named after his sister's hotel. Of course, no one believes that there will be more guests in the Simi Hotel (Lambda) in Zermatt because of this sponsorship deal!

"But a Swiss banker sponsoring a climbing sector just like that is almost as fairytale-like as the climbing here itself."—Urs Odermatt, Swiss Mountain Guide

62 TELENDOS

404
36.990969
26.931268

LAMBDA

1. KV Brig — 1★ 5b 15m
Routes #1 and #2 are 200m to the left, high up. See previous page. Just one hard move. *K Schefer, 2012*

2. D'Sezz — 1★ 5b+ 20m
Less holds than you would expect. *P Ziegler, 2012*

3. Stafel — 2★ 6b 25m
Precise technical climbing. Needs more traffic.

4. Lambda — 3★ 6a+ 30m
Smooth rock, nice balancy moves and smart route-finding.

5. Lambda Capital (Lambda Ext) — 3★ 7a+ 50m
Extension of "Lambda". A 50m stamina monster up the entire face. Very well-protected; save QDs in the lower part.

6. Hot Chili — 3★ 5c+ 25m
A nicely sustained warm-up.

7. Hot Chili Young Love — 3★ 6c+ 40m
Extension of "Hot Chili". Long, with a pumpy finish. Save QDs on the first pitch to avoid rope drag.

8. Lava — 3★ 6a+ 30m
A smooth and balancy flowstone slab with 1-2 spaced bolts.

9. Eruption — 3★ 7a 50m
Extension of "Lava". A magnificent long route on gentle, compact rock. A steep first part, then a sustained headwall with nice moves on rounded jugs and pinches.

10. Meiggeren — 3★ 6a 30m
Pleasant and sustained, without very hard moves.

11. Aroleid — 1★ 5c 20m
Nice and easy, but ends early due to too soft rock above.

12. Progressive Rock Part 1 — 3★ 6a 30m
Fabulous! A long and technical climb that gets harder as you progress.

LEFT

13 Progressive Rock Part 2   3★ 6c 40m
A committing but juggy, bulging final wall.

14 Progressive Rock Part 3   3★ 7b 50m
Progressive until almost the last move, which comes when you get pumped! Save QDs to avoid rope drag.

15 Dom   ♪ 6b 40m
Another monster pitch! Fun climbing and an exciting finale.

16 Fiirhelzer   3★ 6b 30m
A pleasant warm-up with an interesting upper part.

17 Arbzug   2★ 6b+ 40m
A long and technical climb.

18 Gerwitscht   3★ 6c 40m
When good holds stop, think right. Well-protected and long.

19 Chardonnay   3★ 7a+ 40m
A quality, varied climb, with 5m of steep climbing on some little edges.

20 El Alamein   ♪ 6c 40m
A classic Lambda monster. A pocketed wall leads to a corner with smooth rock.

21 Marinelli   1★ 4b 20m
Very easy and well-protected. Good for children.

22 Hotel Simi Basement   2★ 4c 20m
Approach for #23, but worthwhile for kids and beginners.

23 Hotel Simi   ♪ 6b+ 50m
A mega-pitch with outstanding juggy climbing and smart route-finding. Gets harder as you get high!

24 Schwjieschwanz   3★ 6a 40m
First, a black/grey slab; then neat red juggy rock.

25 Schwjieschwanzerrected   3★ 6b+ 50m
The extension on the roof and the intimidating red rock.

26 General   3★ 6b 40m
Brilliant climbing on delightful rock. It gets steeper (and harder) as you go.

27 Telendos Star   3★ 6a+ 35m
A great, classic climb that transitions from slab, to face, to overhang.

28 Nordend   2★ 6a 30m
A warm-up dark grey slab leads to a steeper wall with some demanding bulges.

All routes on Lambda left were equipped by Urs Odermatt and Markus Leippold in 2012, unless otherwise noted.

1 Flauschi   3★ 6b+ 30m
Technical, with thought-provoking moves. *Y Wright, 2012*

2 Rolfi   1★ 6b 32m
Technical first part, sustained second part. *Y Wright, 2012*

3 Hermetje   1★ 6b 30m
Sharp and inelegant. *Y Wright, 2012*

4 Maxim   1★ 6a 20m
A nasty crux on sharp rock. *H-P Hoidn, U Odermatt, 2014*

5 Johan   1★ 5b 20m
Not great but still worthwhile. *H-P Hoidn, U Odermatt, 2014*

6 Cresta Rey   2★ 5a 20m
Steep + juggy with a hard end. *U Odermatt, M Leippold, 2012*

7 Barbara   2★ 5b 20m
Easy moves on very nice rock. *U Odermatt, M Leippold, 2012*

8 Isabel   2★ 5b 20m
A technical crux in the middle. *H-P Hoidn, U Odermatt, 2013*

9 Emilie   2★ 5a 20m
Easy and very nice climbing. *H-P Hoidn, U Odermatt, 2013*

10 Eggen   2★ 5b 20m
Again, pleasant climbing. *U Odermatt, M Leippold, 2012*

11 Nuria   1★ 5c 20m
Quite technical for the grade. *H-P Hoidn, U Odermatt, 2013*

12 Ze Seewjnen   2★ 5b+ 20m
Interesting, on very solid rock. *U Odermatt, M Leippold, 2012*

63 TELENDOS
PRINCESS CANYON

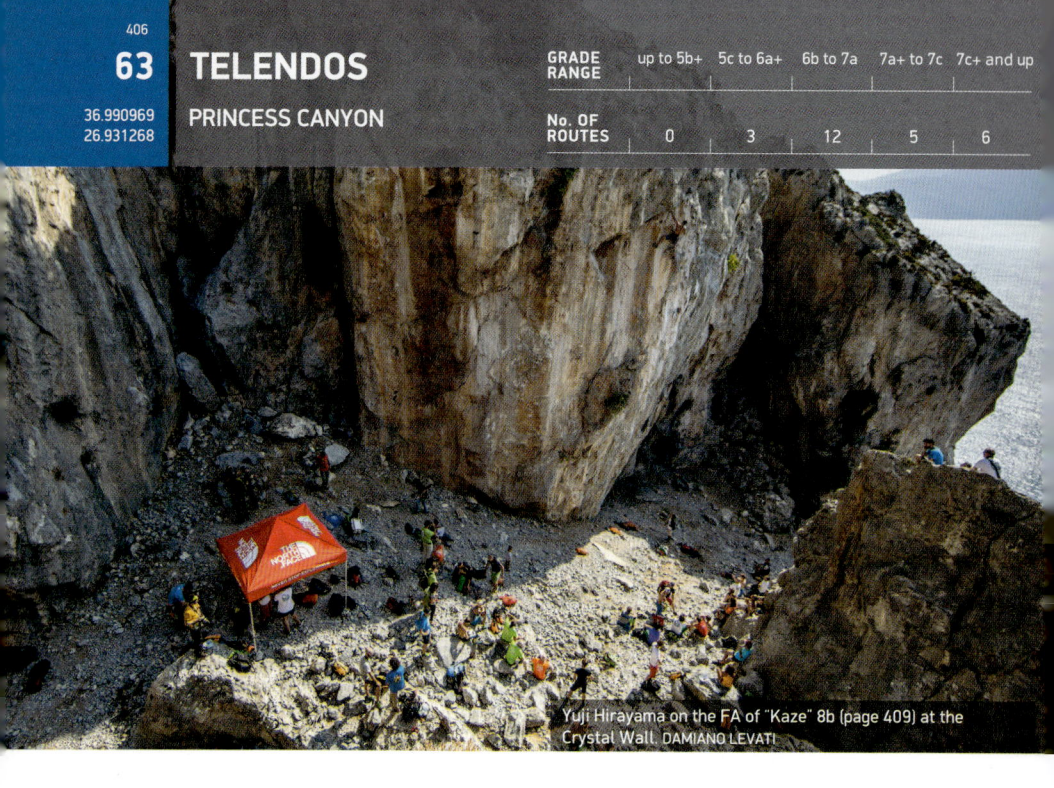

406
36.990969
26.931268

GRADE RANGE	up to 5b+	5c to 6a+	6b to 7a	7a+ to 7c	7c+ and up
No. OF ROUTES	0	3	12	5	6

Yuji Hirayama on the FA of "Kaze" 8b (page 409) at the Crystal Wall. DAMIANO LEVATI

Princess Canyon is a secluded, faraway gorge tucked away in the Telendos South Face and surrounded by stunning wild beauty and incredible views of Kalymnos and the sea. It is the "Symplegades" of Telendos, since these two crags with walls of excellent rock facing each other have many similarities. But Princess Canyon is much larger and the approach is long and intimidating, the cliffs are higher, the gorge longer, and the potential for new routes is major. 15 new routes were added in October 2014 by James Pearson, Caroline Ciavaldini and Jacopo Larcher for The North Face. These new routes saw their first ascents during the 2014 TNF Festival by the Climbing Legends (Gerhard Hörhager, Yuji Hirayama, Jean-Baptiste Tribout, Patxi Arocena, Ben Moon and Boone Speed). Alex Megos, a future legend perhaps, also freed some of the routes.

Climbing: On top-quality slabs and slightly overhanging, fully pocketed walls.

Conditions: In theory, once you are inside the gorge you can be in the shade all day. But this is only true for certain routes. In the afternoon the only shade is beneath the big north-facing boulders (The Waxy Wall, Black Stripe). Therefore this crag is best for climbing on mild winter days, in spring, or in autumn.

Kids: Only for older kids with mountaineering experience. The approach is long and hard, and there is scrambling. The terrain inside the gorge, though, is relatively level.

Shade: All day at certain parts. **Exposure:** S, N

Approach: Start from Telendos village. As you face the village, walk to the left towards Hochlakas Beach. When you come to the ancient temple overlooking the beach, continue along the trail parallel to the southern coastline; there are blue and some yellow marks. Follow the markings and cairns past the huge cave of Crescendo, until you come to a point almost directly beneath the also distinctive Crystal Cave. Here, start walking slightly uphill following the yellow marks. The trail eventually needs some easy scrambling, and with the help of a fixed rope you will come to the narrow mouth of Princess Canyon. **Walking time:** 1 hr 45 min.

Alternate approach (by boat): Take a boat to a point beneath Crystal Cave. Walk straight up towards the cave for about 25 min, then slightly uphill toward a band of cliffs. Traverse over these to a clearer path leading to the mouth of Princess Canyon. **Walking time:** 40 min.

See also: Crag Panorama on page 412.

Yuji Hirayama trying the route "Alani" 8b+ (page 409).
MATTEO MOCELLIN

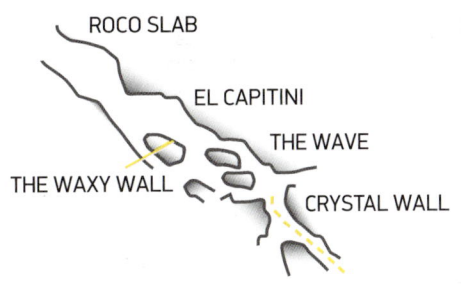

ROCO SLAB

ROCO SLAB
EL CAPITINI
THE WAVE
THE WAXY WALL
CRYSTAL WALL

1 Roco 2★ 6a 26m
C Idoux, 2009

2 Aladinde 2★ 6a+ 28m
C Idoux, 2009

3 Boubou 3★ 6b 30m
C Idoux, 2009

4 Nic Le Grec 2★ 6a 32m
C Idoux, 2009

63 TELENDOS
PRINCESS CANYON

408
36.990969
26.931268

3 Moon Speed — 3★ 6c+ 30m
A wall with many pockets and features.
J Pearson, C Ciavaldini, J Larcher, 2014

4 Pan — 3★ 8a+ 35m
J Pearson, C Ciavaldini, J Larcher, 2014

5 Flo Scarfaloni — 2★ 6b+ 25m
Steep climbing on beautiful holds. C Idoux, 2009

6 Toutou is Dead — 3★ 6c+ 25m
Amazing climbing on a slightly overhanging wall with continuously unexpected good holds. C Idoux, 2009

7 Betty Bella — 3★ 6c+ 25m
C Idoux, 2009

8 Luka K. — 2★ 6c+ 25m
C Idoux, 2009

9 Le Bi Mobile — 3★ 6b 28m
Big holes, beautiful route. C Idoux, 2009

10 Moby Nique — 3★ 6c 28m
C Idoux, 2009

11 Vade Retro de Tarace — 2★ 6c 53m
Multi-pitch (6b+/6c 28m, 6a+ 25m, project). P1 has a pleasant start and a boundary section in the middle. C Idoux, 2009

12 Au Nom de la Grosse — 2★ 7a 25m
C Idoux, 2009

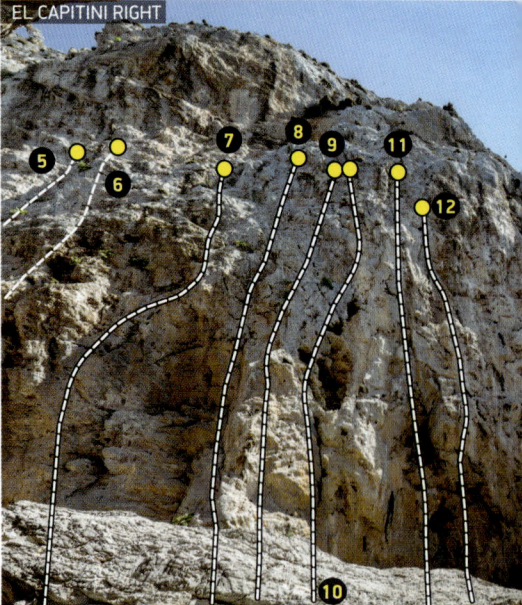

ROCO SLAB
EL CAPITINI
THE WAVE
THE WAXY WALL
CRYSTAL WALL

1 Sylvie Moon — 3★ 7c 30m
A steep wall. J Pearson, C Ciavaldini, J Larcher, 2014

2 Project — ?★ ?? 30m
J Pearson, C Ciavaldini, J Larcher, 2014

EL CAPITINI LEFT

EL CAPITINI RIGHT

#	Route	Stars	Grade	Length
1	Dinosaur Trail	2★	8a	15m

J Pearson, C Ciavaldini, J Larcher, 2014

2 B of the Bany — 2★ 8a+ 15m
J Pearson, C Ciavaldini, J Larcher, 2014

3 Alani — 2★ 8b+ 18m
FA Alex Megos. *J Pearson, C Ciavaldini, J Larcher, 2014*

4 Tsuki — 3★ 7a 12m
J Pearson, C Ciavaldini, J Larcher, 2014

---

1 Mikro Bruno — 2★ 7c 15m
Left of the black stripe.
J Pearson, C Ciavaldini, J Larcher, 2014

2 Fakir — 2★ 7b+ 13m
On the edge of the tiny tower.
J Pearson, C Ciavaldini, J Larcher, 2014

3 The Wave — 3★ 7c 13m
Overhang and short crimpy wall.
J Pearson, C Ciavaldini, J Larcher, 2014

4 Mythos + Legends — 3★ 7a+ 15m
J Pearson, C Ciavaldini, J Larcher, 2014

5 Kaze — 3★ 8b 17m
FA Yuji Hirayama. *J Pearson, C Ciavaldini, J Larcher, 2014*

6 Kamaki — 3★ 8a 17m
An easy start on big holes, then a testing wall.
J Pearson, C Ciavaldini, J Larcher, 2014

7 Charakas — 3★ 6c 17m
A good warm-up for this crag.
J Pearson, C Ciavaldini, J Larcher, 2014

THE WAXY WALL

THE WAVE

CRYSTAL WALL

64 TELENDOS
CRYSTAL CAVE

36.990969
26.931268

GRADE RANGE	up to 5b+	5c to 6a+	6b to 7a	7a+ to 7c	7c+ and up
No. OF ROUTES	0	0	3	8	3

Crystal Cave is like the Grande Grotta of Telendos; a maze of huge stalactites on the wild and beautiful south face of the little island. All routes were opened from the bottom by Gaetan Raymond and his friends from Grenoble, France.

Climbing: Trademark Kalymnos-style 3D climbing on huge tufas and stalactites.

Gear: 100m rope; at least 25 QD for the longer routes; long slings; helmet and cellular phone.

Conditions: Sunny, so best for winter climbing.

Shade: Until 10:00. **Exposure**: S

Kids: No.

Approach: Start from Telendos village. As you face the village, walk to the left towards Hochlakas Beach. When you come to the ancient temple overlooking the beach, continue along the trail parallel to the southern coastline; there are blue and some yellow marks. After one hour, you will arrive at a distinctive-looking tree. The trail markers are now red, and will guide you uphill toward the cave, which you still cannot see at this point.
Walking time: 1 hr 30 min.

Alternate approach (by boat): You can take a boat to the bottom of the cliff and walk straight up the steep slope for "only" 30 minutes, which may feel like a lot longer. **Walking time**: 30 min.

See also: Crag Panorama on page 412.

Olivier Michellod on the impressive "Typhoon" 7c+. SIMON CARTER

1 Telendos ô Telendos (Part 1)   3★   6c 35m
A surprising and wonderful first pitch.

2 Telendos ô Telendos   ♪   7c 60m
A stellar extension traversing the stalactites. 26 bolts and the first anchor at 35m. 100m rope required.

3 The Nose of the Princess (Part 1)   3★   6c 35m
A superb first pitch for the grade.

4 The Nose of the Princess   ♪   7c 55m
Extension on the impressive overhanging wall above. 22 bolts. The first anchor is at 35m. Two ropes needed, although a 70m is enough if the belayer goes onto the upper ledges to lower the climber to the mid-belay.

5 George's   ♪   8a+ 60m
A terrifying and amazing route: preserve energy and nerves for the finale. 2 ropes (100m), 25 QD.

6 Avis   ♪   7b+ 55m
Varied climbing, continuously surprising. 100m rope required.

7 Sunrise   ♪   7b 45m
Huge tufas and a potato field of stalactites! Exceptionally long and still a little fragile. 100m rope required.

8 Stalas   2★   6b 35m
For those who thought they were only here to belay! 100m rope required.

9 Sea View   3★   7c 40m
An incredible location. Long slings + 100m rope required.

10 Nectarios   3★   7b 40m
Another beautiful journey. 100m rope required.

11 Es Pontas   ♪   7c 30m
A roof with a view! An amazing traverse across the arch. 100m rope required.

12 Typhoon   3★   7c+ 40m
A link with "Vespa", which perhaps needs more traffic (and may have gotten harder after holds breaking). 100m rope required.

13 Vespa   ♪   7c+ 40m
Another outrageous route! Sustained climbing on tufas and stalactites.

14 Flying Dutchman   3★   7b 40m
The only vertical route here, but with a bouldery crux.

Routes #1-#4 by Gaetan Raymond (2007). Routes #5-#14 by Thibault Saubusse, Quentin Jaillard, Quentin Chastagnier, Gaetan Raymond (2008).

65 TELENDOS
SOUTH FACE

36.990969
26.931268

GRADE RANGE	up to 5b+	5c to 6a+	6b to 7a	7a+ to 7c	7c+ and up
No. OF ROUTES	0	2	2	3	4

Labels on photo: Princess Canyon, Crystal Cave, Wild Country, Eterna, Wings for Life, Crescendo

The South Face of Telendos is a gigantic face rising above the wild southern coastline of Telendos. It is best known for its increasingly popular multi-pitch routes that unfold through an unmatched landscape over the deep blue of the Aegean Sea: **Wild Country**, **Eterna**, **Wings for Life** and **De Charbyde en Cila**. Between them the intimidating **Crescendo**, a wild cave adorned with stalactites for experienced climbers.

Climbing: Hardcore alpinists may think these multi-pitches are over-protected and lacking in continuous difficulty compared to classic long routes they have climbed in the Alps, but unplanned bivouacs have frequently happened on the South Face, or even on the return path! Despite being fully-bolted, don't forget: these multi-pitches are, above all, long alpine-style routes on a huge face. As such, they must be approached with the seriousness and respect reserved for mountain climbing. Treating them as laid-back "holiday climbs" is naive and can be downright dangerous.

Gear: A helmet, backpack with food and water, headlamp, jacket and cellular phone are all absolutely necessary.

Conditions: Sunny, so it is very important to start early in the morning. During hot months it is best to climb on very windy days.

Shade: Until 11:00. **Exposure:** S

Kids: No.

Approach: Start from Telendos village. As you face the village, walk to the left towards Hochlakas Beach. When you come to the ancient temple overlooking the beach, continue along the trail parallel to the southern coastline; there are blue and some yellow marks. When you arrive below the huge cave of Crescendo, turn right and start walking uphill. **Walking time:** 1 hr 30 min.

CRAG PANORAMA
Princess Canyon to Inspiration

De Charybde en Cila

INSPIRATION

Alternate approach (by boat): You can take a boat to the bottom of the cliff and walk straight up the steep slope for "only" 30 minutes, which may feel like a lot longer.
Walking time: 30 min.

Return: The descent is marked by cairns. When you finish your route, walk up to the top ridge of the mountain, turn right for a short way, then descend on the other side (north). Look carefully for the small cairns leading to the chapel of St Constantine. From there, a well-defined path leads back to the village of Telendos.

Walking time: Anywhere from 2 hours to all night!

Another alternative is to find out whether one of the Telendos boatmen have scheduled trips to sector Irox. If so, you can walk down to Irox and catch the boat there. It will save you about an hour's walk.

Francis Haden and Gordon Jenkin on the ridge of the South Face of Telendos after climbing their route "Eterna". DONNA KWOK

65 TELENDOS
SOUTH FACE (WILD COUNTRY, ETERNA, WINGS FOR LIFE)

414
36.990969
26.931268

1 Wild Country 3★ 6a+ 265m
Multi-pitch; 9 pitches (5a 30m, 5a 25m, 6a 35m, 5c 35m, 5c 35m, 6a+ 20m, 6a 30m, 5b 30m, 5c 25m). A long and very popular multi-pitch. Far more serious and intimidating than its "sister" route "Wings for Life". All the pitches are interesting and quite sustained, but the bolting is good. The sixth pitch is the crux pitch and the climbing is very good, indeed.
P Keller, U Odermatt, 2010

2 Eterna 2★ 6b+ 265m
Multi-pitch; 11 pitches (5b 40m, 6b+ 25m, 5c 20m, 4b 15m, 5c 25m, 6a+ 25m, 6b+ 25m, 6a 35m, 4c 10m, 6b 25m, 6b 25m, 5m). A bit harder than its neighbor, "Wild Country", Eterna is another climber-friendly, accessible and very well-bolted long route equipped with titanium glue-in bolts. Throughout the 11 pitches, 124 bolts plus nine titanium ring sets have been used for an optional abseil descent. In the words of the equippers, "Eterna" is "a continuous sea of small chickenhead holds leading up over a couple of bulges on a near-vertical wall of orange. Two pitches of fantastic climbing interspersed with a wild hanging stance that pushed the sky away". *F Haden, G Jenkin, 2014*

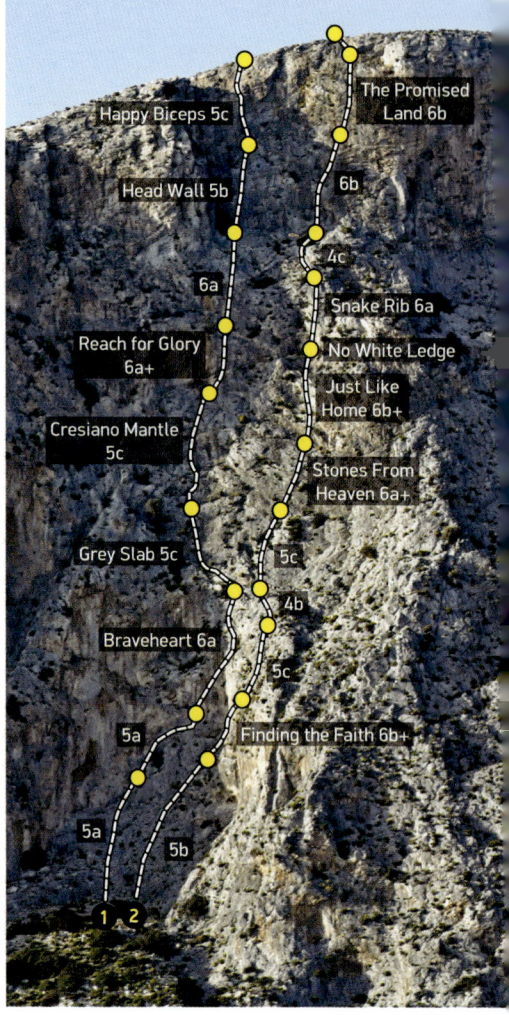

Donna Kwok on the last pitches of "Eterna" 6b+. FRANCIS HADEN

The Promised Land 6b
Happy Biceps 5c
Head Wall 5b
6b
6a
4c
Snake Rib 6a
Reach for Glory 6a+
No White Ledge
Just Like Home 6b+
Cresiano Mantle 5c
Stones From Heaven 6a+
5c
Grey Slab 5c
4b
Braveheart 6a
5c
Finding the Faith 6b+
5a
5b

③ Wings for Life   2★ 6a 250m

Multi-pitch; 11 pitches (5a 20m, 5b 30m, 5b 10m, 4b 30m, 4c 20m, 5b 20m, 6a 30m, 5b 20m, 6a 20m, 5b 20m, 5a 30m). A multi-pitch epic following a buttress along a gigantic cave. The first half of the route is fairly broken, but the upper portion earns its stars as it leads directly above the daunting overhangs through a goutte-and-chickenhead zone. It can't get any more exposed than this! Incredibly, the level of difficulty never gets harder than 6a. From Telendos village, follow the track along the south coastline until a high cave is visible with a monster rib coming down its right-hand side. Hike up to a point where the rib can be accessed (obvious cairn). Follow the rib for many pitches on very sharp rock (well-bolted). A very awkward steep corner finally lands one below the headwall. Technical climbing now leads up and left into hyperspace (hanging belay). At the top, throw away your climbing shoes, massage your feet, bring up your partner, then walk up to the main Telendos ridge. Turn right along it until small cairns lead down the far side, heading towards the small chapel on the north slope. Turn a small cliff to its right. From the chapel, head down more easily to the coast path back to Telendos village. A major day out. 18 QD plus gear for the belay points.
P Keller, U Odermatt, 2008

Paul Walters on the crux pitch of "Wings for Life".
SIMON RAWLINSON

65 TELENDOS

416
36.990969
26.931268

SOUTH FACE (DE CHARYBDE EN CILA, CRESCENDO)

Serge Crocfer moves up the fantastic airborne corner of "De Charybde en Cila" 6b+

Airborne Corner 6b
6a
6b+
6b+
6b
walk
6b
6a

④ De Charybde en Cila 3★ 6b+ 215m

Multi-pitch; 8 pitches (6a 25m, 6b 30m, 6b 35m, 6b+ 35m, 6b+ 35m, 6a 20m, 6b 30m). A newer multi-pitch with more continuous and sustained climbing compared to its neighboring routes. P1: An easy start and hard wall before the anchor; 11 QD. P2: Traverse rightwards; a challenging, slightly overhanging wall on small sharp holds. Hard for the grade; 11 QD. P3: A leftward traverse and walk. P4: A smooth vertical wall; 14 QD. P5: Slightly overhanging; 14 QD. P6: A consistently interesting slab; 13 QD. P7: Attention, loose blocks above the anchor; 13 QD. P8: An "airborne" exit. The icing on the cake! 13 QD. The final anchor is a bit further up, behind a big wedged block. The view from the top is unbelievable—even for those who take the beauty of Kalymnos for granted!

Approach: From the village of Telendos, go southwest to the beach of Hochlakas. At the Paleochristian chapel, go right (yellow marks). A bit further, pass through a goat gate. Walk uphill for 150m. You will see a large cairn marking a junction of trails. Keep straight ahead (right) following the yellow marks. The route starts opposite the solitary olive tree that grows practically at the foot of the cliff. **Walking time**: 60 min.

Return: Walk north following the cairns and then the red marks to the chapel of St Constantine and the village of Telendos (2 hours). Make sure you stay on the path and do not try to find short cuts.

Note: Abseiling down the route is possible, but not recommended.

C Idoux, A Langenbach, 2012

Crescendo is a sub-sector inside one of the colossal stalactite-adorned caves on the south face. It's a very wild crag with some exceptional routes, for very experienced climbers only: approaching the crag via an 80m fixed rope up a vertical wall with loose rock, belaying on an exposed ledge, and finally, the return to the cliff base, are all inherently dangerous.

Climbing. Very steep on stalactites or big jugs and tufa blobs.

Conditions: A good spot for early spring, late autumn, and perfect for sunny winter days.

Shade: Until 11:00 and after 16:00. **Exposure**: S

Gear: 80m rope and very long quickdraws are absolutely necessary. Helmets are also mandatory the whole time (when climbing, belaying and approaching the crag).

Approach: Go to the South Face of Telendos (page 402). As you go uphill towards the cave, keep to the right and follow the trail markers. On the fixed ropes use auto-protection such as a Grigri. (If this isn't obvious, you should not be climbing at Crescendo.)

Walking time: 2 hrs (or 1 hr by boat).

Return: You can reach the bottom of the first fixed rope via a 40m abseil. From there, descend using the fixed ropes, as the angle becomes gentler.

① Lancelot   3★   7b+ 35m
Classic Grande Grotta-style tufa climbing. *G Raymond, 2010*

② Perceval   3★   7b 35m
Steep action on tufas and big stalactites. Requires very long quickdraws. *G Raymond, 2010*

③ Crescendo Pitch One   3★   8a 35m
A crack, big jugs, and small stalactites. *S Montmory, 2010*

④ Crescendo Pitch Two   ♪   8b 50m
Steep overhanging climbing. The perfect endurance challenge! *S Montmory, 2010*

⑤ Crescendo Pitch Three   3★   8b+ 65m
S Montmory, 2010

⑥ Do It Now or Never (Variation)   3★   7c+ 40m
Climb to the left after the stalactite. Funny moves and fun falls! *S Montmory, 2010*

⑦ Do It Now or Never   3★   7c 40m
Steep, but with big jugs. No hard moves, just endurance. *S Montmory, 2010*

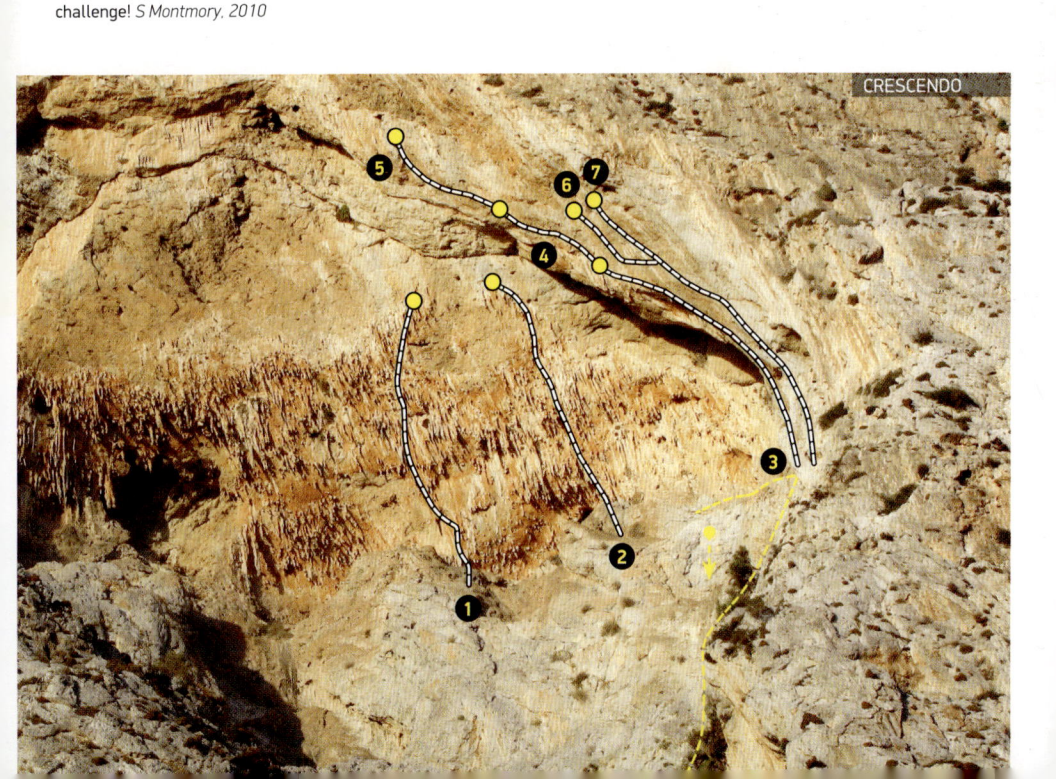

CRESCENDO

66 TELENDOS

INSPIRATION

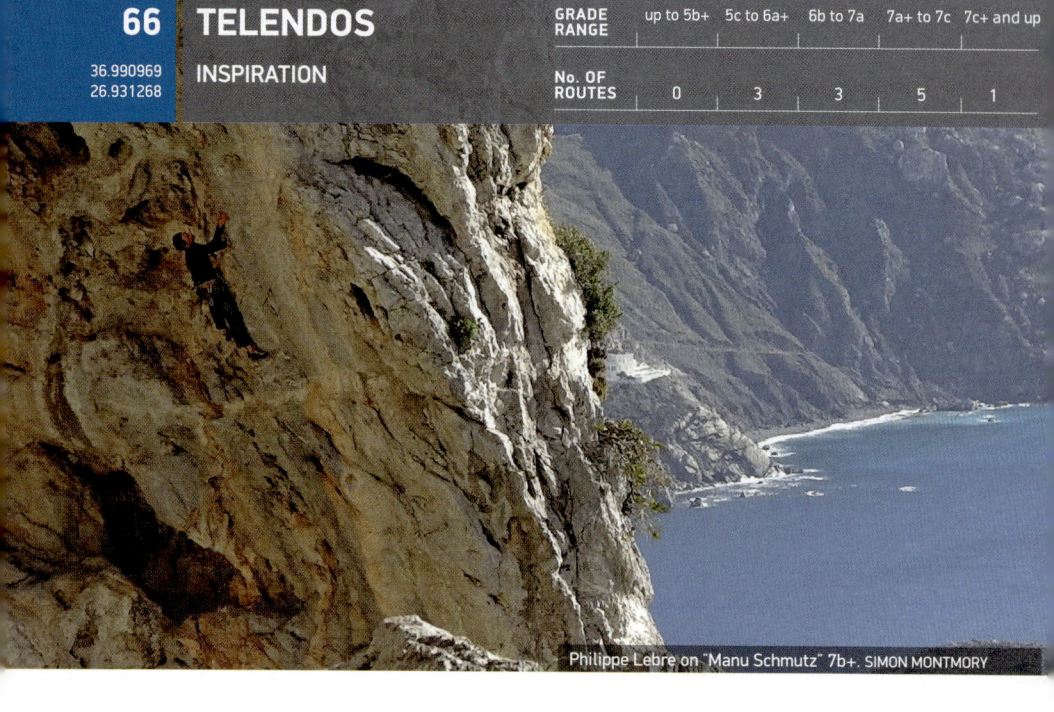

36.990969
26.931268

GRADE RANGE	up to 5b+	5c to 6a+	6b to 7a	7a+ to 7c	7c+ and up
No. OF ROUTES	0	3	3	5	1

Philippe Lebre on "Manu Schmutz" 7b+. SIMON MONTMORY

Inspiration is one of the most impressive and untouched places in Telendos. The cliffs with prominent features like a large arch, stalactites and huge holes are worth seeing either way, not just for the climbing! The unique landscape feels like a miniature Getu Valley in China, only in this case with an Aegean backdrop.
To reach the ledge where some of the routes start, you must climb a 2a+ and pass through a big hole of rock. Then you discover some amazing 80-90m pillars with tufas and huecos. The second arch to the right has a hole near the spot where you belay—from there, with a 15m rappel you can even explore a potential new sector.

Climbing: Steep athletic tufa climbing on mostly good rock. **Gear**: 80m rope, long QDs, and helmets at all times.

Conditions: Best for spring and autumn. **Exposure**: S

Shade: Until 13:00 (left) or 16:00 at "Manu Schmutz".

Kids: No.

Approach: As for the route "De Charybde en Cila". Walk from Telendos village following the yellow waymarks. The crag will be obvious up to the right.
Walking time: 50-60 min.

See also: Crag Panorama on page 412.

Here's Simon Montmory equipping "Evolution Ext" 7b+.

1 Alpinstil — 2★ 7c+ 150m
Multipitch (7a 64m, 7c+ 45m, 6b+ 25m). A new bold line which breaches the huge Inspiration Cave. Not at all "Kalymnos-style" given the runouts between bolts; falls up to 15m need to be taken into account. **Return**: At the top, walk right for 250m to a cairn. The first abseil station is 2m below the rim. Down-climb to the abseil station, rappel down (1 x 25m), then a second rappel (1 x 60m) to the big ledge at the bottom of "Manu Schmutz". From here, follow the fixed rope back to the start.
R Schaeli, M Kementer, J Reinmueller, 2015

2 Cheburaska — ♪ 6c+ 45m
An amazing route behind the huge "Inspiration" arch.

3 Inspiration — 3★ 7b 150m
Multipitch; 6c+ obligatory (6b+, 6c, 7b+, 6c, 6b+). It is close to an amazing arch surrounding the ground at more than 100 meters. The rock is excellent, except the tufa part (needs some traffic) and the view is amazing. Steep rock from start to end, and P3 is a "DNA"-style climb! **Conditions**: not good for humid, damp days. **Shade**: until 13:00. **Gear**: 16 QD; helmet. **Return**: **a)** Walk. At the top of the wall, walk to the right in the direction of Masouri (15 min). When you reach the top, turn right and follow the yellow waymarks down for 30 min more. **b)** Abseil as for the route "Alpinstil".

4 Le Pilier — 3★ 7c 40m
The characteristic pillar with beautiful holes.

5 Evolution — 3★ 6a+ 25m
The route to the right of the characteristic pillar.

6 Evolution Ext — 3★ 7b+ 40m
Cool climbing on very good quality tufas.

7 Best-of-5 — 2★ 5c 20m
Very nice slab climbing in a unique setting.

8 Discovery — 2★ 5c+ 20m
More good slab climbing.

9 Discovery Ext 1 — 2★ 6c 40m
2012

10 Discovery Ext 2 — 3★ 7b+ 60m
A great adventure finishing on a single tufa!

11 Yannis Loves Rita — 2★ 6c+ 30m
At the right cave, with shade until 16:00.

12 Manu Schmutz — 3★ 7b+ 35m
An interesting mix of different climbing styles.

Routes #2-#12 were equipped by Simon Montmory in 2011-2012.

Kalymnos...in other words

Photos and stories of Kalymnos by other climbers and friends

1 "It's not all about the climbing... OK, it really *is* all about the climbing"

[Kalymnos] still surprises us; we are stil uncovering its many secrets. In spring Kalymnos is green! It's hard to believe when you visit in prime climbing season September through November, when a large portion of the island looks like a barren rocky desert but after the rains of winter the island is blooming with wild flowers. Yep, those brown swaying pincushions that even the goats won't touch are brilliant purple puff balls in April!

OK, it really *is* all about the climbing ... until after fighting your way through a strenuous Kalymnian tufa pump-fest you find a little escape pod, an eye of the storm.

Sitting in one of these no hands, often no feet rest positions, time disappears and it's suddenly all about the resting. In normal sport climbing you smash it out to the top, have a quick look at the view, lower down and start all over again. The long Kalymnian routes however, give themselves over to long introspective pauses on the wall. Time disappears, have you been resting for 3 mins or 30? Has your belayer fallen asleep? Do you really want to leave your perch, it's soooooo meditative...ooohmmmm .....

—*"It's not all about the climbing..."*
www.thetravelingclimber.com

Has it been 3 minutes or 30? Peta Barrett doesn't seem too bothered on "Por Una Sociedad ..." 7c+ (page 49). SCOTT HAILSTONE

Jonathan Siegrist glistens his way through the limestone forest of Grande Grotta. PERIKLIS RIPIS

2 "It's much better to work as a mountain guide in Kalymnos than in Chamonix"

Q: What did you think during your first visit to Kalymnos?

Urs: It's much better to work as a mountain guide in Kalymnos than in Chamonix.
Peter: Uahhh puahh yeahhh, let's move this island to the lake of Zurich!

Q: How many times have you visited Kalymnos since? Any funny stories from your visits?

Urs: Maybe 15 times? There is always a funny story, but I will never forget that we almost didn't find the way back to Telendos by boat after we had a drink or two…
Peter: I can't remember how many times we visited Kalymnos [but] all the times were very funny. Somehow Yannis, the ferryman who helps us a lot in every situation, was always involved. The story where Yannis crashed with his boat into the jetty, told us and our clients laughing that he has lost his propeller, is unforgettable.

—"Q + A with Swiss guides Peter Keller and Urs Odermatt"
www.climbkalymnos.com

3 "Kalymnos always ends up being a big party"

Kalymnos…what climber hasn't heard of this limestone mecca in the middle of the Aegean Sea? It's all been said, but here's our version.

This was Janine and I's third visit in the last few years. Simply put, we love it. The remarkable thing about Kalymnos is that the whole package is perfect. The climbing, island, food, prices, weather, and of course the Greeks themselves—the ideal hosts to the thousands of visiting climbers from all over the world. What other climbing destination has so many routes stacked on top of one another? With grades for everyone, side by side, 5c and 8a climbers can be equally entertained at the same walls. This year we noticed that, unlike previous years, Americans have discovered Kalymnos as well. It was great to both run into old friends and make new ones. Kalymnos always ends up being a big party.

—Dan Patitucci
www.patitucciphoto.com

A jubilant Emmanuela Kostaki lowers from "Sevasti" 7b (page 286). PERIKLIS RIPIS

Raw power oozes out of Chris Flowers on "Neolithic Line" 7c (page 247). LUKE MILNES

4 "Kalymnos has climbing coming out of its climbing"

I'm pumped, insanely pumped, with my legs wrapped around a twisted stalactite, frantically swapping hands, shaking out, trying to get a little something back. I contemplate the next sprint through the bewildering three dimensional tufa jungle—and I'm only halfway there. But then, feeling like a cheeky monkey, a smile creeps across my face as I realise that life doesn't get much better than this (...) I feel like I've cashed in all of my frequent flyer belay bunny points, passed through the pearly gates, and gone straight to heaven.

Kalymnos has climbing coming out of its climbing. Line after line after luscious bolted line, over 2000 of them on blue ribbon quality limestone, spread over 64 unique sectors each with its own breathtaking view over the Aegean. To complete the package are the short approaches, delectable restaurants, swish studios, idyllic (well, rocky) beaches and an international melting-pot of climbers. The only thing missing is having more time, that's for sure.

—Monique Forestier from "World Climbing: Rock Odyssey"
www.onsight.com.au

One of multiple ways to rest on the sculpted limestone of Kalymnos. PERIKLIS RIPIS ARCHIVE

5 "Goats are not interested in you in particular, unless you are holding a banana peel"

There's one (goat) in every photo! There may be no sharks in the ocean but there are roving packs of goats trotting around the island. They are not interested in you in particular, unless you are holding a banana peel, but step away from an open climbing bag at any given crag and it is open season on your lunch. It would not be unusual to see four or five of these guys, head down in a backpack like a family of hyenas in the belly of a dead zebra. There is a particularly well horned, brunette nanny goat that likes to hang out on the corner of the Grotta so she can survey for an open backpack at three different sectors without moving! Naughty goat!

Speaking of the Grande Grotta, seen from Telendos at the end of the day it is an upside down golden forest of stalactites and tufa blobs. I never get sick of looking at it whether I am climbing in it or not, it draws the eye from all directions.

—"It's not all about the climbing..."
www.thetravelingclimber.com

The goat mafia on the lookout. NIKOLAOS SMALIOS

"Eurycleia" 5b (page 218) ticked, yeah! PERIKLIS RIPIS

Nobody glams up a can of tuna at the crag like the fabulous Nantis Alber.

François Legrand smooth as ever on the stellar "Gegoune" 7c (page 105), in one of the photos shortlisted for the cover of this book.

6 "It's the warm handshakes of new friends you meet on the main street after a long day of pulling on some of the best tufas in the world"

...But Kalymnos is much more than a perfect climbing destination. It's a warm hillside pungent with wild herbs. It's the hidden beach with crystalline water and gentle waves you can claim as your own. It's a scooter ride over a windy mountain pass. It's the local delicacy tucked behind the eggs at the mini-super, or the smiling faces welcoming you into your new favorite restaurant, or the kitten that waits for you each morning at the café. Most of all, it's the warm handshakes of new friends you meet on the main street after a long day of pulling on some of the best tufas in the world.

—*Jim Thornburg, "The Call of Kalymnos"*

"Kalymnos times a million". CHEYNE LEMPE

Gabrielle Nobrega encountering "some of the coolest tufas on earth" on "Aurora" 7b (page 284). JIM THORNBURG

It's not Kalymnos...
but it's still Greece!

Meteora
Mouzaki
Patra's area
Varasova
Leonidio
Kyparissi
Crete
And many more crags

Greece Sport Climbing: The Best Of

For the first time, a selection of the best sport crags in Greece collected in one guidebook.

Written by Aris Theodoropoulos and published by Terrain Editions, with the same clear photo-topos, beautiful color photos, practical tips, user-friendly layout and in-depth knowledge of climbing as its best-selling sibling, the Kalymnos guidebook.

climbgreece.com

NAO® New version

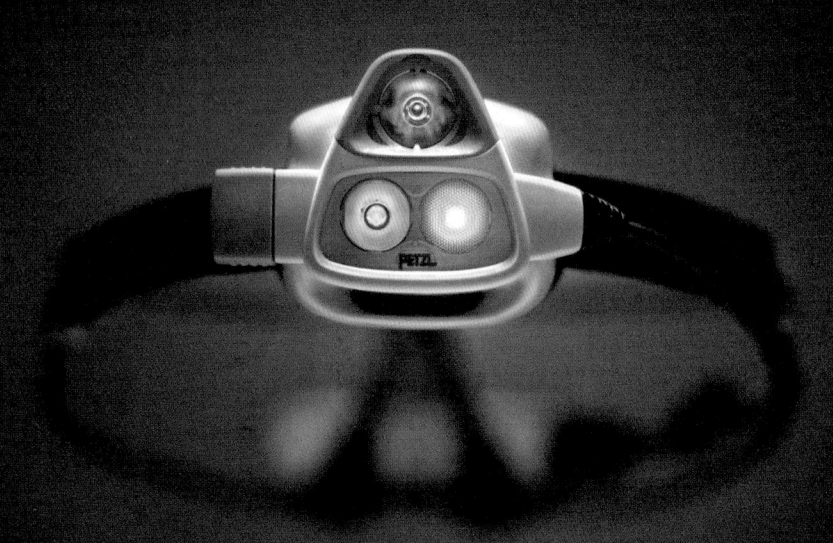

Onboard computer with REACTIVE LIGHTING.
Focus on the trail ahead.

Intelligent, ultra-powerful headlamp with rechargeable battery
Thanks to REACTIVE LIGHTING, the NAO automatically adapts light output and beam type to the ambient light. Reduced manipulations, optimized burn time, and greater comfort for intense endurance activities. Light output: 575 lumens.
www.petzl.com

Photo © www.kalice.fr

PETZL®

Access
the
inaccessible

wildsport KALYMNOS

all about climbing ...& not only!

E9
PETZL
FIVE TEN
STERLING
LA SPORTIVA
innovation with passion
SALEWA
Black Diamond
Chillaz
SALOMON
Beal
BUFF
GRIVEL
ABK
TEVA
CMP
CU AT THE WALL
REEF
8b+
climbOn

1
MAIN STREET
MASSOURI VILAGE
KALYMNOS
GREECE
+30 22430 48644

2 StockHouse
ARMEOS
MASSOURI
KALYMNOS
GREECE
+30 22430 47048

www.climbing.gr | info@climbing.gr

Routes.8a.nu

60.000 members
3,6 million ascents
82.000 ascents in Kalymnos

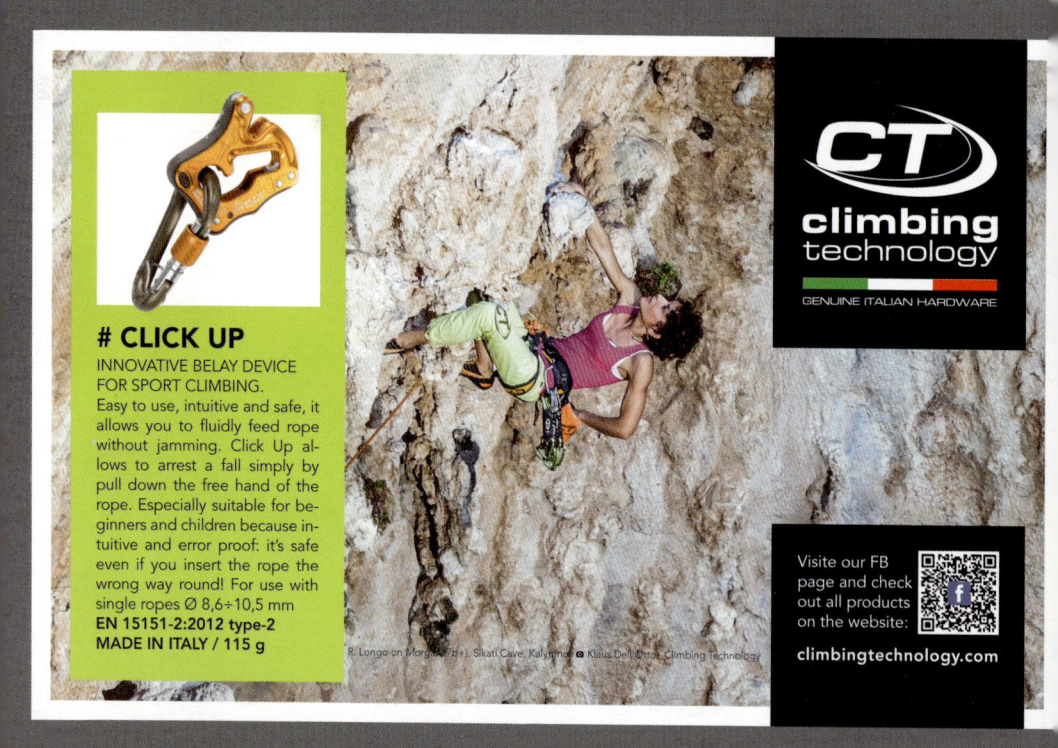

CLICK UP
INNOVATIVE BELAY DEVICE FOR SPORT CLIMBING.
Easy to use, intuitive and safe, it allows you to fluidly feed rope without jamming. Click Up allows to arrest a fall simply by pull down the free hand of the rope. Especially suitable for beginners and children because intuitive and error proof: it's safe even if you insert the rope the wrong way round! For use with single ropes Ø 8,6÷10,5 mm
EN 15151-2:2012 type-2
MADE IN ITALY / 115 g

R. Longo on Morgana (7b+), Sikati Cave, Kalymnos © Klaus Dell'Orto_Climbing Technology

climbing technology
GENUINE ITALIAN HARDWARE

Visite our FB page and check out all products on the website:

climbingtechnology.com

CLIMB ROCK

1mation – disturb the ordinary
1mation.com
action | fashion | on demand

BUFF

MAMMUT

EDELRID

TRESPASS – www.trespass.ie EXPLORE THE OUTDOORS

CT climbing technology

wdx Wind x-treme

TENAYA

ROCKIT CREAM

SALEWA

climbOn Incredible Skin Care

Montano

MILO of climbing

FERRINO

LIZARD POWER GRIP FOOTWEAR

Masouri central road (opposite Plaza Hotel)
TEL: (0030) 6946 129 300   email: themipoulla@gmail.com

"I eat my Tzatziki on the rocks"
- BRUNO THE CHALKBAG -

8b+ 8BPLUS
8BPLUS.com #EATMORECHALK

ESSENTIAL TOOL

ABK
THE BOULDERING COMPANY
Lazy BRAND
TYPICALLY FRENCH
ABK NO TE HARÁ MÁS FUERTE PERO SI MÁS GUAPO

PANTERA V
GABRIELE MORONI

CLIMBERS GO FISHING

ScooterFun

www.scooterfun.gr

Scooterfun scooters rentals Kalymnos

Masouri, Kalymnos
Tel. +30 22430 47744
Email: mansc1972@gmail.com

...more than a scooter rentals shop

Celebrate gravity!

The world has turned upside down to celebrate gravity!

Eleven – fully anodized quickdraw with 11 kN breaking load. Tanga & Keylock for maximum safety. Made in Tirol.

TEAMATHLETIN CATHY LAFLAMME

AUSTRIALPIN.AT

onlineshop: www.ziwi.at ... made in Tirol, Austria
Wildsportshop, Massouri

ziwi.at

Chillaz
search & respect
every day challenge

Kampi Almyra megali Almyra mikri

Renowned for its stunning backdrops, you will come across the ideal spot for.... **Deep water solo!**

waternative
kalymnoskayakcentre

Only **a short kayak ride** away from three of the most secluded, picturesque beaches on kalymnos Island.

*all beaches accessible only by water

Vathi (Rina), 85200 Kalymnos - tel. +30 22430 31132
www.kalymnoskayak.gr - info@kalymnoskayak.gr

Hop on one of our motor or sailing boats
for a trip to the best spots of Dodecanese. Day trips and longer tours are available.

Rent a BOAT & explore
the charming beaches of Plati and Pserimos Islands.

*Boating licence is not required.

ZLAG! Board

Train smart - climb hard!
www.zlagboard.com

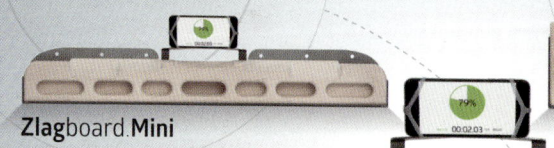

Zlagboard.Mini

Zlagboard.Vario

Zlagboard.Pro

Efficient, automatic training with Zlagboard and App. Find your level, follow the **training plans** by professional trainers like **Patxi Usobiaga** or **Gimme Kraft** and improve your performance!

OutDoor INDUSTRY AWARD 2014

ISPO AWARD WINNER 2015/2016

| measure | train | analyse | compete | share |

SUNRISE at Masouri square

call us (+30) 22430 47783

rate us on tripadvisor

breakfast sweet crepes coctails main meals omelettes desserts soft drinks sandwiches side order & dips traditional pita milk shakes salads coffees spirits wines drinks beers

AEGEAN TAVERN at Masouri ☎ 2243047146 - 2243023790

aegean tavern kalymnos ✉ aegeantavernkalymnos@hotmail.com

We invite you to visit our family restaurant, where you can explore Greek food culture and dinning, over the sea and with a **panoramic view of the island of Telendos**. With our 50 years international experience and innovations on Greek cuisine, like the establishment of the **Kalymnian salad (Mermizeli)** in the menu and the **sponge diver's meal (Kavourmas)**, we will connect you with our roots.

You will enjoy local dishes like **Kalymnian Dolmades** and lamb from the oven, fresh fish and seafood specially cooked, accompanied by a variety of Greek quality wines. We use local products and cook with **extra virgin olive oil**. We keep our high standards and quality thanks to the love that we receive from our customers through the years.

George Pizanias

Executive chef, Member of the Culinary Institute of America (CIA) and the Chef Club of Cyclades and Dodecanese with certification in 'Aegean Cuisine'

ethereal snack n coffee

- we are located at **Masouri**
- call us at **(+30) 22430 48781** for free delivery
- send us an email at **info@ethereal-kalymnos.gr**
- visit our web site at **http://www.ethereal-kalymnos.gr**
- follow us on facebook at **Ethereal snack n coffee**

Enjoy your coffee or natural juice with fruits of your choice from our own vitamin bar with home made snacks and sweets

WiFi hotspot

ethereal is using packaging made from sugarcane, and pla, giving you the chance to make the most **eco** friendly choice while exploring the **magnificent nature** of Kalymnos.

CLIMBERS' MASSAGE
THERAPEUTIC/SPORT/RELAXATION

REHABILITATION/EMPOWERMENT
ORTHOPEDIC/SPORT CONDITIONS

KINESIOTHERAPY / ELECTROTHERAPY / ULTRASOUNDS

DIMITRI CHALIKOS
Certified Physiotherapist/Kinesiotherapist

Located in Armeos, Kalymnos / Serves all areas of the island.

For appointments:
Mobile: +30 697 289 7152
Email: chalikosdimitrios@yahoo.gr
http://climbkalymnos.com/massage

Lambrinos Studios

Open year-round with special prices for climbers, our fully equipped studios feature Wi-Fi access, private balconies with breathtaking views and a friendly family environment.

Armeos, Kalymnos, 85200 Greece
tel: +30-2430-22110, +30-2430-47231
lambrinosstudios@gmail.com

http://climbkalymnos.com/lambrinos-studios/

tripadvisor

Rita Kokkinidis

Restaurant

Massouri / Armeos, Kalymnos Tel: +30 22430 47202, +30 22430 29146
Mob: +30 6984 311050, +30 6983 646913 E-mail: halikos@yahoo.com

Harry's Paradise
APARTMENTS & RESTAURANT

Restaurant - Accommodation - Gardens - Meditation

http://harrys-paradise.gr

harrys@klm.forthnet.gr +30-2243040062 +306973766279

CAFE - RESTAURANT - TAVERNA RITA
FRIENDLY FAMILY BUSINESS For Over 30 Years

TRADITIONAL GREEK CUISINE & FRESH LOCAL SEAFOOD

Rooms & Studios to Rent

BOOKINGS & INFORMATION
Tel: (+30) 22430-47927
Email: Telendosrita@Gmail.com
Www.Telendos-Rita.com
 Rita Zoidis

RITA'S, TELENDOS, KALYMNOS, GREECE, 85200

RITA, YIANNIS and PETROULA Offer You a Very Warm Welcome...

OPEN From APRIL 'til NOVEMBER

SWISS CHAMPS PREFER BEST MOTO

BEST MOTO
THE NR1 SCOOTER RENTAL OF KALYMNOS

www.bike-rental.gr
bike-rental@bike-rental.gr
0030-22430-48724
Massouri center.

To Best Moto, where professionals work for you. The only rental company where knowledge and quality goes together. The place where the staff is working hard to satisfy you in any way. Our demands are high as well as your wishes. For this we offer a fleet of scooters and bicycles. Quality vehicles for quality people.

Imagine owning your property in Greece...

Why dream? We have unique properties for sale in Kalymnos island

Tel: +30 22430 22221   +30 6942 445319   www.prekashomes.gr

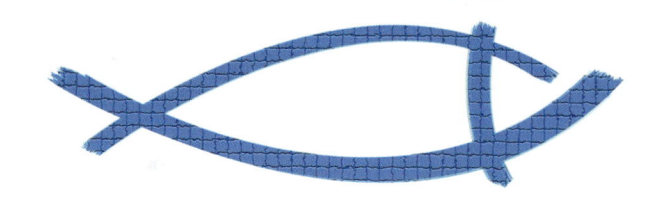

AZUL
Wine Bar - Art Gallery

eat - drink - feel the difference

Greek wine selection
speakeasy cocktails
Mediterranean cuisine

Armeos Kalymnos | visit us: www.azul.gr | follow us: www.facebook.com/azulkalymnos

Nadir Rock Café

After-climb at Nadir Rock Café

Join the **atmosphere** Have a chat *after* **climbing**. **Relax** and **enjoy** the tunes. **DANCE** Play a game of **pool** or **dart** with **Chilled beer** great **cocktails** tasty **food** and **pop corn** for our **people**.

Hotel Kamari

Situated 500 metres from both Myrties Beach and Panormos Village in Kalymnos, the family-run Hotel Kamari features a traditional Greek restaurant and free Wi-Fi. Rooms open to a private balcony overlooking the Aegean Sea and the sunset.

You can relax in the terrace, use the common outdoor kitchenette or have **BBQs in the garden**.

The **climbing sectors** Ourania and Symblegades are within a walking distance. **Physiotherapy treatments** can also be arranged.

Free private parking is available.

Myrties, Kalymnos | Tel: +30 2243 047278 | www.kamarihotel.gr | kamari92@otenet.gr | / Hotel-Kamari-Kalymnos

TAVERNA ILIAS
PALIONISSOS

Feel free to climb our mountains and discover a wide variety of climbing routes. Taste our traditional dishes and variety of fresh fish **directly from our fishing nets**.

Enjoy and have fun on our water slide and dive into crystal clear waters. Relax while having your coffee or breakfast admiring the magnificent view of Palionissos.

Tel: +30 22430 28862   Email: basilikoulailias@gmail.com

Free parking available

GELATERIA ARTIGIANALE ITALIANA
Authentic Italian *Gelato*
Made fresh on the premises

MIKE'S BIKES
The best way to see Kalymnos

Tel.: +30 - 22430 - 47137   Mobile: +30 693 9663365
Email: mikesbikes@klm.forthnet.gr
www.kalymnos-info.com/mikes-bikes
Armeos Kalymnos. (located 300 meters north of Masouri square, beneath "Poets" sector)

Tsopanakos Restaurant

Tsopanakos is a restaurant, run from a shepherd family of Kalymnos Island. Is based at Massouri, under of the famous sector "Grande Grotta" and next to the most important climbing sectors as "Odyssey".
Kalymnian specialties, meat from our stock breeding, roasted mince Grilled sea food and fresh fish. Local cheese from *our production*

**ECONOMICAL PRICES
ALL YEAR OPEN!**

Armeos - Masouri Tel. +30 22430 47929

Tania Matsuka

Certified climbing instructor
(French national diploma)

Learn, improve and enjoy climbing on Kalymnos from Spring until Autumn

- Beginners, Intermediate
- Family, Children & Private
- Multi-pitch

Info & Bookings

www.climbmediterranean.com
Tel. +30 6987586251
taniamatsuka@hotmail.com

CLIMB MEDITERRANEAN

www.marmot.eu · facebook.com/marmot.mountain.europe
Marmot PRO: Stefan Glowacz, Location: Verdon, FR
📷 Frank Kretschmann

Marmot®
FOR LIFE

Der Bergsportspezialist im Raum Zürich

Klettergurt, Abseilbremse und einen Helm hätte er bei Ruedi Bergsport kaufen können...

WWW.RUEDI-BERGSPORT.CH
Top Sortiment – Kompetente Beratung – Tiefe Preise

Birmensdorferstr. 55 | 8004 Zürich | Tel. +41 (0)44 241 58 52

Paradisio – Vluchadia • Kalymnos

Aegean cuisine with a Twist...
Snacks-Drinks right on the "Vlyhadia" beach

- www.facebook.com/Paradisiokalymnos
- https://instagram.com/paradisiovlyhadia
- paradisekaly@hotmail.com
- 2243022764
- Vlyhadia Beach Kalymnos

No Chipping!

LO SCAVO È REATO!
CHIPPING IS A CRIME!
GRIFFESCHLAGEN IST EIN VERBRECHEN !

AUSTRIALPIN

KINOBI
(KINOBI@KINOBI.IT)

SUPER MARKET STALAS

Myrties, Kalymnos
T: +30 2243 047112
M: +30 6980 688440

KALYMNOS RENT
D. Hatzilaou - I. Mamakas Co.

AVIS rent a car
@lpha rent a bike

Masouri Offices: 0030 22430 47430
0030 22430 47797
Pothia: 0030 22430 28990
Myrties: 0030 22430 47145

www.kalymnosrent.com

KAC
Kalymnos Adventure Center

KAC ACTIVITIES

- CLIMBING
- CAVING
- VIA FERRATA
- HIKING
- HERBAL WALK
- HORSE RIDING
- CATAMARAN SAILING
- KITESURFING
- WINDSURFING
- DIVING
- MASSAGE
- YOGA

Have an Adventure Holiday!
Find us in Massouri, opposite **Fatolitis Climbing Bar**, where climbers meet up.

Climbers' Nest

Welcome to our Shop!

Everything for climbing and more...

The largest selection of **prAna** in Greece!

Some other brands:

- Black Diamond
- SCARPA
- Red Chili
- MAD ROCK
- TENDON
- RÖJK
- sanuk
- SALTIC
- KYMA
- PETZL
- SALEWA

Contact us:

Phone +30 22430 48160
Mobile +30 69849 33327
info@kalymnos-adventure.com
www.kalymnos-adventure.com

IBISCUS Super Market

FIND ANYTHING YOU NEED
Fresh Bread, Fruits - Vegetables, Foreign Press, Magazines, Kalymnian Traditional Products, Unique Greek Variety of Souvenirs

Massouri, Kalymnos, Tel.: +30 22430 48515
ibiscusmarket@hotmail.com

TAVERNA - RESTAURANT
PANOS o Mitilinios

greek specialities & International cuisine

climbers favorite place!...

Massouri - tel.: 2243-0-48822 mob.: 6977 689399

Traditional Taverna
Kalidonis
Fresh sea food

Palionissos Bay

📞 694 894 5936

Come and try our local cuisine! Try our scrumptious goat dipped in red sauce along with a fresh greek salad and locally homemade Kalymnian cheese. Choose fresh fish directly brought to us every morning by the fishing boats in Palionissos! Enjoy your meal sitting indoors or outdoors on our veranda with the best view.

---

restaurant
NOUFARO
Special Vegetarian dishes

Masouri, Kalymnos.
Tel. +30 22430 48110
Mob: +30 6977 594192
www.noufaro-kalymnos.info

European Federation of Promoting Hellenic Tourism 'Better Life' — **Recommended**

Acropolis Hotel Apartments
Kalymnos, Greece

We are located in the heart of the Kalymnos tourist area, **Masouri**. All rooms have two beds, are **fully equipped** and have a balcony with a **sea view** overlooking Telendos Island.

www.acropolishotel.gr, kalymnos@acropolishotel.gr

KOS ⇔ KALYMNOS ⇔ LEROS

TRANSFERS:
To **KOS** airport (MASTIHARI)
From **LEROS** or **KALYMNOS**
- And Vice Versa -

SERVICE TO
ALL CLIMBING AREAS
ON TELENDOS & SIKATI CAVE

EXPRESS LEROS

TELENDOS ★ STAR
REGULAR SERVICE & DAY TRIPS
TO LEROS
BOOKINGS & INFORMATION CALL
CAPTAIN YIANNIS
TEL: (00-30) 6944 - 819073

Zorbas Restaurant

At Masouri Square
Down the Stairs

📞 0030 6956131483
@ www.zorbas-kalymnos.com

f zorbas-restaurant Kalymnos
f Nektarios Lelekis

Restaurant
Το καψούλι
Fish Taverna

Fresh Fish Every Day

Traditional Greek Cuisine

Michail Ellinas
Telendos • Kalymnos - P.C 85 200
Tel : +30 22430 47363 (summer) • 22430 23785 / 6992117250 (winter)

Restaurant Tavern "Miltos"

Traditional Greek Cooking
fresh sea food - fresh meat - mezedes

Massouri square - Kalymnos
T: 22430-47044   M: 697-8795106
@: miltos.masouri@yahoo.gr
:Miltos Taverna   Find us on tripadvisor

Il Posto
OPEN ALL THE YEAR

IL Posto Restaurant-Cafe   ilpostokalymnos@hotmail.com

Restaurant café - Elies square - Kalymnos - Tel. (0030) 2243047001

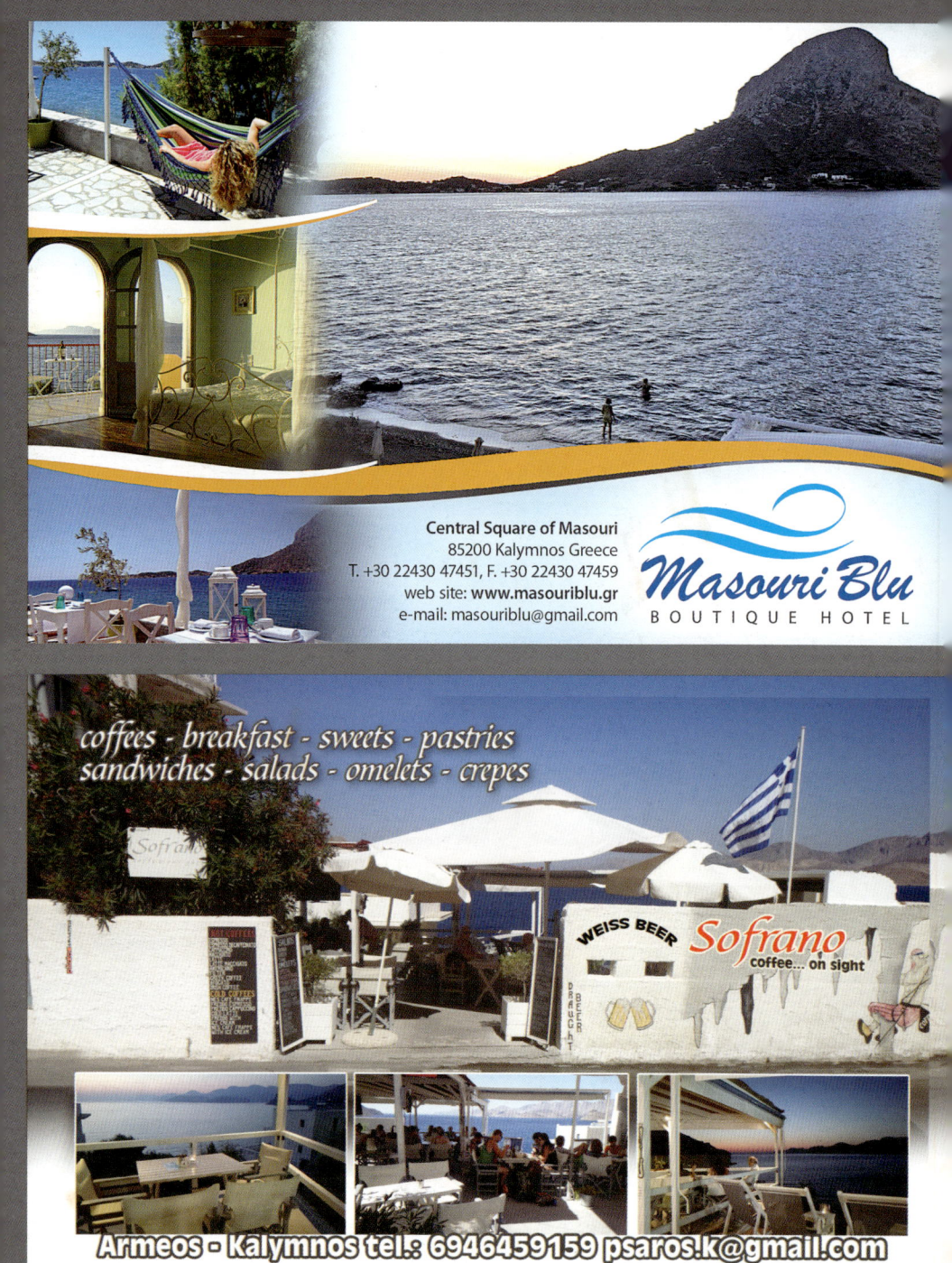

Central Square of Masouri
85200 Kalymnos Greece
T. +30 22430 47451, F. +30 22430 47459
web site: **www.masouriblu.gr**
e-mail: masouriblu@gmail.com

Masouri Blu
BOUTIQUE HOTEL

---

coffees - breakfast - sweets - pastries
sandwiches - salads - omelets - crepes

Sofrano
coffee... on sight

Armeos - Kalymnos tel.: 6946459159 psaros.k@gmail.com

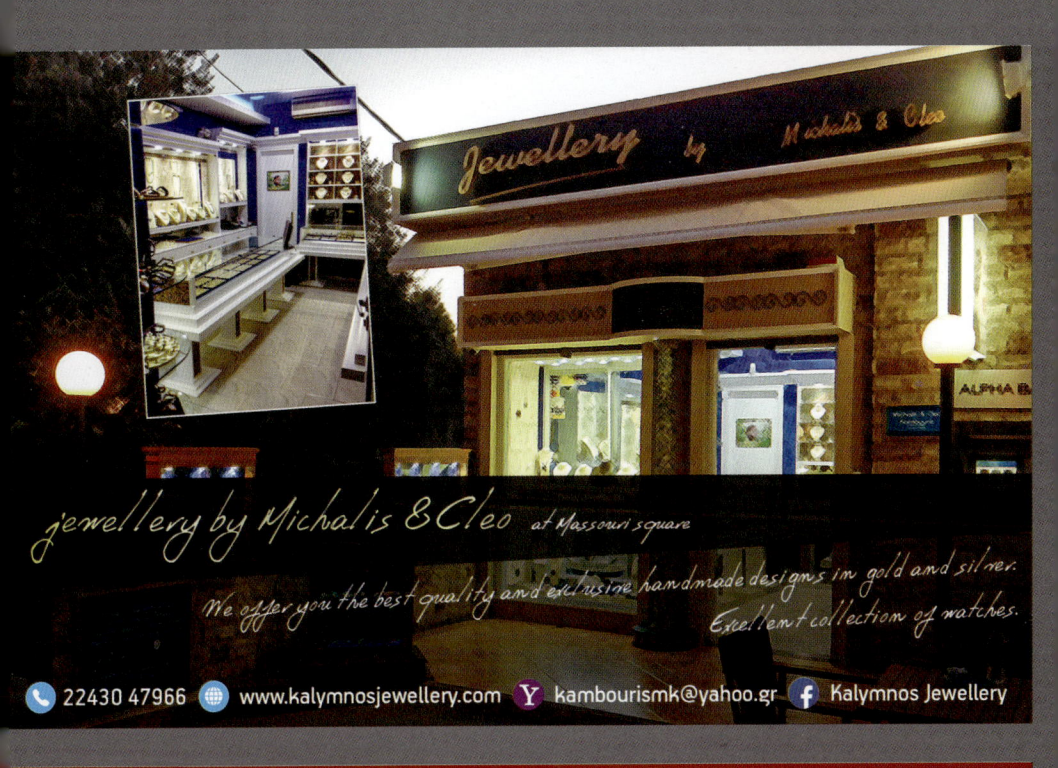

jewellery by Michalis & Cleo at Massouri square

We offer you the best quality and exclusive handmade designs in gold and silver. Excellent collection of watches.

22430 47966 — www.kalymnosjewellery.com — kambourismk@yahoo.gr — Kalymnos Jewellery

climb kalymnos

www.climbkalymnos.com

The official website of the Kalymnos guidebook and your inside source for everything Kalymnos related, including

- An interactive route database
- The latest climbing news
- Loads of general information about Kalymnos
- The Kos-Kalymnos ferry timetable
- A very active Forum

and much more!

SIMON MONTMORY
KALYMNOS CLIMBING GUIDE

**IMPROVE, TRAIN, HAVE FUN
ON THE MOST BEAUTIFUL ROUTES OF KALYMNOS**

- ✓ 5 days climbing course
- ✓ Private coaching
- ✓ Multi-pitchs
- ✓ From 5a to 8a!

Contact Us: +30 69 83 67 41 62
http://www.kalymnosclimbingguide.com

Photo © Elodie Saracco